The Antiques Roadshow
Collectables

The Antiques Roadshow
Collectables

London, New York, Munich, Melbourne, Delhi

Produced for Dorling Kindersley by DK India
Design Manager Arunesh Talapatra
Editorial Manager Glenda Fernandes
Senior Editor Ankush Saikia
Editors Pankhoori Sinha, Alicia Ingty
Designers Ivy Roy, Mitun Banerjee,
   Neha Ahuja
DTP Coordinator Sunil Sharma
DTP Designers Harish Aggarwal, Pushpak Tyagi,
   Dheeraj Arora

Publisher Stephanie Jackson
Art Director Peter Luff
Executive Managing Editor Adèle Hayward
Managing Art Editor Kat Mead
Senior Editor Anne Yelland
Senior Art Editor Helen Spencer
Art Editor Phil Gamble
Editors Martha Evatt, Jo Godfrey Wood, Ellen Hardy,
   Mandy Lebentz, Daniel Mills, M. Astella Saw
Senior Production Editor Jenny Woodcock
Senior Production Controller Mandy Inness

First published in Great Britain in 2008
by Dorling Kindersley Limited, 80 Strand,
London WC2R 0RL

A Penguin Company

2 4 6 8 10 9 7 5 3 1

A CIP catalogue record for this book is available
from the British Library

ISBN 978-1-4053-3288-0

Discover more at **www.dk.com**

Contents

Introduction

Working as a specialist on *The Antiques Roadshow* requires several disciplines: knowledge is obviously extremely important, but so is the ability to communicate that knowledge to the collectors who share our passion.

Pinpointing the reasons for a particular interest has always fascinated me, not just from a personal point of view but from a far wider perspective. The impulse to collect is present in so many of us that I feel there must be an innate motivation that drives us to acquire.

There are few people who haven't stopped to pick up an unusual stone or a shell on a beach. This is collecting at its most pure, a kind of ancient desire to have and to hold—no different in essence from that of our ancestors, who developed a sense of inquiry and the wish to own beautiful and interesting objects. The Greeks and Romans, for example, held markets

for trading art and collectibles, and there have been countless great collectors throughout history— Rudolph II (King of Bohemia), Peter the Great, and William Randolph Hearst, to name just a few. What fired these people to collect in a way that defied all sensible notions of reality? For the early collectors the answer was probably the quest for knowledge; a mixture of alchemy, religion, and power; the search for immortality fueled by great wealth; and perhaps the desire to bequeath a legacy to future generations. These are not essential requirements to start a great collection, however, and monetary value is not always

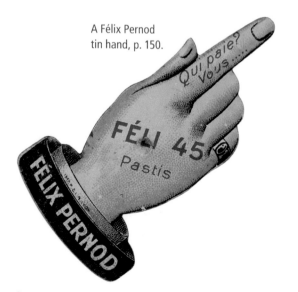

A Félix Pernod tin hand, p. 150.

A Corgi Volkswagen police car, p. 225.

a measure of a collection's importance. This book is an aid to the modern collector and in its own way addresses some of the fundamental desires to collect by providing a springboard of ideas.

Once possessed by the lure of collecting, some people prefer the pursuit—the thrill of the hunt—and find that possession itself can almost be an anticlimax. For me, it's always been about making connections: holding a 20,000-year-old flint arrowhead in the palm of your hand can trigger an emotive experience—it can make the original owner a tangible entity. So what's the best way to "buy into" this kind of emotion?

Anybody who has been involved in the art and collectibles market will be very aware of the major changes that have taken place over the last few years. Economic factors, fashion, and the Internet have all changed what we buy and the way we buy it, and the demise of the local antique shop is a sad epitaph to a business with traditional ideals. However, new markets have opened up, particularly in the world of collectibles, where new areas have gained ground and are traded around the world on Web-based auction sites and specialist online shops. For those who yearn for the thrill of visiting a real auction house, there is still plenty of opportunity, but few modern auctioneers would decline the facility to reach an international market. Viewing sales on the Internet or perhaps bidding live online is a fact of life today, and the traditionalists have had to learn to adapt. In reality, modern collectors need never leave the comfort of their armchairs!

I share a fascination with my *Antiques Roadshow* colleagues that cannot easily be conveyed on paper, but in contributing to this book we all hope to enhance and broaden people's opinions about the nature of collecting. In that respect we make no apologies for the diversity of objects featured in this guide. In an art world dominated by billionaires and tycoons, the frequently asked question, "What's the next big thing?", seems to be of little relevance to the average collector. What is certain is that you should collect what you like and what gives you pleasure, not what other people think you should collect. I hope this guide will help you to tap into our passion and energy. Happy hunting!

A Murano globular vase, p. 105.

Marc Allum
The Antiques Roadshow

How to use this book

This book is divided into nine chapters, each of which features a broad area of collectibles such as Ceramics or Books, Magazines & Ephemera. Within these larger chapters are a series of shorter articles, covering two, four, or six pages, depending on importance, desirability, and interest. Some consider a single subject such as Bisque Dolls or Wristwatches; others deal with a maker or studio,

such as René Lalique or Moorcroft; and some, such as Kitchenalia and Sporting Memorabilia, are more diverse. No matter what the topic, each entry is designed as an easy-to-navigate visual guide to the subject—the key organizing features are highlighted on these pages. More than a simple catalog of items, each article includes expert yet accessible information for beginners and experienced collectors alike.

Introductory text gives a brief discussion of the subject, the people and pieces that are important or noteworthy, why collectors are enthusiastic about it, and what is currently collectible and desirable.

"What's Hot" items are those that are currently desirable and sought after by collectors with the result that some of these pieces may command high prices.

"Look Out For" pieces are desirable, worth searching out to add to your collection, and should not be passed over when you come across them.

"What's Not" are generally less desirable items, because they are either common and easy to find, or simply out of fashion in today's market.

Key facts chart the most important periods in the development of the subject, the most influential people, and milestones in the history of its production.

Informative captions offer a full description of every featured item, and any distinguishing features like makers' marks, together with its size, and an estimate of its value (see box opposite).

"Core Collectibles" are the key items around which those who are particularly interested in a subject build up their collections.

"Ask the Expert" boxes pose some of the most common questions asked about collecting in a certain area with answers provided by experts.

"Top Tips" offer professional hints on how and where to find key pieces, which items you should be wary of, and how to build your collection and keep it in good condition.

"Starter Buys" tend to be less expensive objects that are ideal for new collectors to acquire, and offer a good way into a particular collecting field.

"You may also like" suggestions point you in the right direction for expanding your interest in a related collecting area.

Valuations

The valuations in this book are either actual prices realized at auction or quoted dealer prices. If you are selling, you are likely to be offered less than the suggested valuation, and if you are buying or selling at auction, you should check the auction house's fees and commissions. Always keep in mind that prices vary a great deal depending on condition and desirability, as well as where you are.

$ Less than $100
$$ $100–$500
$$$ $500–$2,000
$$$$ $2,000–$10,000
$$$$$ More than $10,000

The contributors

MARC ALLUM

Marc is a generalist with more than 17 years' experience in the auction business. As a former director of a major London auction house, he has a wide range of interests and has appeared on various shows including *Going For a Song*, *The 20th Century Roadshow*, and *Discovery TV*. His personal favorites include antiquities, South American art, Georgian glassware, and the Grand Tour. His knowledge encompasses collectors' items, 20th-century design, and works of art, an eclectic selection now suited to his work as a freelance consultant, writer, and lecturer. He spends much of his time at Château Coye, his home and lecture venue in southwest France.

BUNNY CAMPIONE

Bunny worked at Sotheby's for 23 years until 1996, first in the furniture department and then in the collectors' department. In 1988, while remaining as a consultant to Sotheby's and then as a senior consultant to Christie's between 1997 and 2002, she started her own company undertaking valuations and buying and selling antiques on behalf of clients. Bunny specializes in automata, birdcages, costume and textiles, corkscrews, dolls, dollhouses, pre-Victorian and miniature furniture, and soft toys. She has written many articles on antiques and frequently gives talks and lectures.

WILL FARMER

Will started collecting at the age of 6, and by the age of 12 had his own stand at a local antique fair. In college he studied silversmithing and jewelry with art and design history, and survived by buying and selling 20th-century design classics. He formed "Odyssey," dealing in 20th-century furniture, then in 1999 took a position as head of fine art and antiques for Weller & Dufty auction house. In 2001 he and his business partner established Fieldings Auctioneers in Stourbridge. He is an avid collector and among his passions are Art Deco ceramics from Clarice Cliff and Poole Pottery together with 20th-century glass and furniture from the UK and Scandinavia.

GRAHAM LAY

Graham joined the provincial firm of auctioneers King & Chasemore in 1975 as a reception porter. He moved to London in 1978 when Sotheby's took over the firm and later became the head of the auction valuations department for their Sussex sale room. In 1988, he joined Bonhams and four years later became a senior board director. He lived in Jersey for six years and ran the company's auction rooms there. In June 2004, he left Bonhams to concentrate on writing and broadcasting. Graham's broad knowledge of antiques encompasses a particular interest in militaria, collectibles, and jewelry.

ANDY MCCONNELL

Andy is a writer and historian specializing in glass. After 25 years as a rock music journalist, video producer, and sometime glass dealer, he returned to writing in 1997 to research and write *The Decanter: An Illustrated History of Glass from 1650*, which was published in 2004. His second book, *20th-Century Glass*, was published in 2006. Andy owns a vast collection of glassware dating from 1650 to the present day and he is as interested in examples that can be bought for a few dollars as those that command thousands. He owns and runs Britain's largest antique and vintage glass shop, Glass Etc., with his wife, Helen, in the historic town of Rye in East Sussex.

SUSAN RUMFITT

In 2002 Susan established her own fine jewelry consultancy based in Harrogate, England. She studied for her postgraduate degree in the decorative arts at Glasgow University in association with Christie's Auctioneers. Following a traineeship in silver and jewelry at Christie's, Susan became an international jewelry specialist at Phillips Auctioneers and headed one of their jewelry departments in London. As well as advising private individuals and auction houses, Susan now regularly lectures on the history of jewelry for the National Association of Decorative and Fine Art Societies (NADFAS) and similar organizations.

DOMINIC WINTER

Dominic has been in the auction business since 1972. After a brief shop-floor apprenticeship with a local firm in Kingston-upon-Thames, Surrey, he moved to Bristol for the opportunity to wield the auctioneer's hammer. He spent nearly 15 years in Bristol and created a thriving book department where previously there was none. Since 1987, he has been running his own auction rooms and is now located at South Cerney, near Cirencester, Gloucestershire, where he specializes in the sale and valuation of old and rare printed books, historical documents, autographs, and related items.

BEN WRIGHT

After working as a front-of-house porter and junior cataloger in the clock and watch department at Christie's, in 1991 Ben was made head of the clock department and later senior director in charge of Christie's clock and watch departments around the world. An experienced auctioneer, he traveled internationally to conduct auctions. In 2006, Ben decided that after 20 years with Christie's, it was time to expand his horizons and set up his own clock business. He joined forces with another experienced clock dealer, Jonathan Carter, and together they formed Carter Wright Ltd., concentrating on buying and selling top-level English clocks all over the world.

1

Ceramics

Decorative & Practical

For thousands of years, men and women have created both useful and decorative items from the clay beneath their feet. Today, ceramics remain among the most popular collectibles, with countless choices for the novice or seasoned connoisseur.

Whatever your taste, there are literally thousands of options when it comes to collecting ceramics. When looking to start a collection, decide on a theme or style, then factor in your budget. Some collectors look to a particular factory, while others are eager to acquire shapes; teapots, for example, have always proved popular and collectors can put together a diverse and exciting display spending from a few dollars to thousands.

Collecting is not an exact science, but there are a few good rules to stick to when creating a display. Fashion is a strong force in this market, and trends in antiques can be as prominent as those in the fashion industry. Early wares from the 17th and 18th centuries are of lasting interest to seasoned collectors and provide a core of items that still retain high market value. In recent years, the more adorned and decorative

A coronation beaker, see Core Collectibles, p. 86.

A Clarice Cliff sugar sifter, see What's Hot, p. 23.

A Doulton "Butterfly Girl," see Core Collectibles, p. 206.

wares from the 19th century, including Staffordshire figures, pot lids, and fairings, have slipped in favor against the rising interest in 20th-century Decorative Arts.

Today's advanced techniques can make restoration extremely successful; however, this does have its pitfalls. Caution and experience should lead you to check your purchases carefully, especially when they are being sold as perfect. Remember that restoration is perfectly acceptable when it is declared and when, more importantly, the price reflects the extent of the damage. Many collectors would rather own a damaged item than never own one at all!

When it comes to care and display of your collection, it's always worth keeping things away from strong direct sunlight and strong heat sources, as these can cause "crazing" in the glaze. When cleaning any piece, avoid abrasive products, chemical cleaners, and excessive rubbing, as all of these can damage surface decoration.

In recent years, an ever-growing number of fakes and forgeries have entered the market, affecting pieces from Clarice Cliff to Staffordshire figures, and at times catching even the most dedicated collectors unawares. Get involved with like-minded collectors and join a society or group that shares your passion. Often these groups will act as a safety net for you, keeping you posted about new fakes on the market. Handling as much of your chosen passion as possible will also help you become more familiar with traits, techniques, and style to allow you to recognize when a piece simply isn't "right."

It is an old adage that collectors never own their pieces: they are merely the custodians of them for generations to come. Whether you have a collection of PenDelfin rabbits or an array of Royal Worcester vases, the key thing is to enjoy your role as their guardian and curator for enthusiasts of the future.

A Poole Pottery plate, see Core Collectibles, p. 52.

A Carltonware ginger jar and cover, see Core Collectibles, p. 58.

Beswick, see Core Collectibles, p. 74.

Wedgwood

Founded on the highest standards in design and manufacture, Wedgwood's immense back catalog of domestic and decorative wares provides a huge resource for collectors in many different fields.

For centuries there have been collectors of Wedgwood pottery, from the early 18th-century admirers of Josiah's "new," highly fashionable Jasper Wares to 21st-century fans of the factories' modern contemporary output. Irrespective of income, Wedgwood provides the modern collector with countless choices, from inexpensive Jasper Ware trinkets to the highly sought-after luster wares of the 1920s.

As with all areas of collecting, fashion has played an enormous role in current market values, with the design-led dynamic pieces of the 20th century rising against the more traditional wares of the 19th century. Rarities from the 18th century, however, have sustained their market appeal with core collectors across the world.

The company has undergone many changes over its history, with a number of key developments in production methods and manufacture. Wedgwood's numerous factories have created a timeline of fashion-led wares that have responded to tastes of the day. The firm developed and excelled in many areas of ceramic production, most famously Jasper Ware.

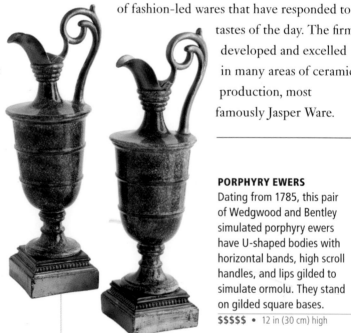

A Pair of Survivors

The Grand Tour was the ultimate vacation experience for the 18th-century young and wealthy, who traveled around Europe taking in the cultural sites. These ewers were produced to look like ancient Greek ewers in the classical style. Immensely expensive, they reflected the patrons' wealth, taste, and fashion sense. The fact that they have survived together increases market appeal.

PORPHYRY EWERS
Dating from 1785, this pair of Wedgwood and Bentley simulated porphyry ewers have U-shaped bodies with horizontal bands, high scroll handles, and lips gilded to simulate ormolu. They stand on gilded square bases.

$$$$$ • 12 in (30 cm) high

KEY FACTS	1759	Mid-19th century	1904	1938	2000s
At the forefront for 250 years	Josiah Wedgwood forms his own independent pottery company at the Ivy House works, Burslem.	After years of decline, the firm undergoes many changes of management and ownership.	John Goodwin is appointed art director, signifying a resurgence in the firm's fortunes.	Foundation stone laid at new Barlaston site; it is soon hailed as the most advanced factory in the Potteries.	Wedgwood remains one of the most important international ceramic manufacturers.

What's Hot

BLACK BASALT VASE
Designed by Keith Murray in the 1930s, this vase has a full signature and impressed marks.
$$$ • 16½ in (42 cm) high

CAMPANA VASE
A 19th-century Wedgwood blue jasper dip campana vase with classical scenes.
$$$ • 16½ in (42 cm) high

Look out for:

Daisy Makeig-Jones's Fairyland luster range, made from 1915 to 1929, is decorated with fantastic landscapes crowded with pixies and elves. Expensive when made, these pieces are now extremely valuable and rare among collectors. Makeig-Jones's more involved and "spooky" examples, featuring ghosts and goblins, are the most popular.

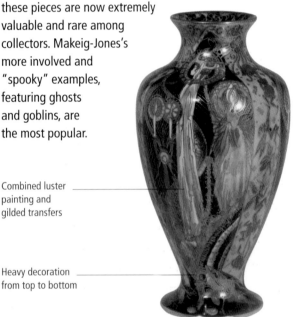

Combined luster painting and gilded transfers

Heavy decoration from top to bottom

"CANDLEMAS" FAIRYLAND VASE
This luster vase designed by Daisy Makeig-Jones is printed and painted in colors and gilt on a black luster ground.
$$$$ • 8½ in (22 cm) high

CANOPIC VASE
Its cover molded as a pharaoh's head, this vase has applied Egyptian motifs.
$$$$ • 9¾ in (24.5 cm) high

DECORATED VASE
This encaustic decorated vase of twin-handled ovoid form dates back to 1790.
$$$$ • 9½ in (24 cm) high

What's Not

Typical of 19th-century everyday domestic tableware, plates such as this are simply decorated with an underglaze blue and white transfer. No longer as popular for decorative purposes, they are both readily found and affordable.

KEITH MURRAY BOWL
A rare simple, earthenware footed bowl with delicate glazed gray body.
$$$ • 12 in (30 cm) in diameter

FAIRYLAND LUSTER BOWL
"Woodland Bridge," by Daisy Makeig-Jones, printed and painted in colors and gilt.
$$$$ • 10½ in (27 cm) in diameter

VINE DINNER PLATE
An 1860 Flo Blue Wedgwood "Pearl Vine" dinner plate decorated with flowers.
$ • 10¼ in (26.5 cm) in diameter

Core Collectibles

THREE-COLOR BOWL
An early-20th-century Jasper Ware bowl decorated in blue, green, and white.
$$$ • 4 in (10 cm) high

"GARDEN IMPLEMENTS"
This rare Wedgwood lemonade jug with four mugs was designed by Eric Ravilious. It is printed in black and pink luster and bears printed factory marks.
$$$ • Jug 8 in (20 cm) high

CLOCK CASE
This Wedgwood Jasper Ware clock case from c. 1895 still has its original movement.
$$$ • 6¾ in (17 cm) high

"BLUE BAMBOO" TEAPOT
Printed in underglaze blue, this is a small, round, compressed pearlware teapot.
$$ • 3½ in (9 cm) high

PEARLWARE TUREENS
Decorated with Greek vases, this pair of early-19th-century Wedgwood pearlware tureens and covers, with matching dishes, bears impressed marks.
$$$ • 8¾ in (22 cm) wide

SAUCER DISH
Wedgwood "Coutts" decorated saucer dish of Langley, Kent, from 1808.
$$$ • 6½ in (16.5 cm) in diameter

Ask the Expert

Q. Why is Jasper Ware so called?
A. The name comes from the ware's stonelike appearance when fired. The material has a similar appearance to natural jasper. Jasper Ware is white and is stained with a metallic oxide coloring agent. The most common shade is pale blue. Dark blue, lilac, sage green, black, and yellow were also used.

Q. Is all Jasper Ware made by Wedgwood?
A. No, once the technique had been developed and perfected by Josiah Wedgwood, many other firms copied the highly fashionable wares. Other makers, such as Adams, Palmer, Wilson Neal, and Hollins, were also manufacturing it. True Wedgwood is well marked and easy to identify.

Applied surface decoration

Q. How is the raised decoration made?
A. The figures and border patterns are separately molded from slip clay, allowed to part-dry, then applied to the body. Check there are no pieces missing or areas of shrinkage.

CYLINDRICAL TEAPOT
An early-19th-century blue Jasper Ware tapering cylindrical teapot and cover.
$$$ • 7½ in (19 cm) long

JASPER CAMPANA VASE
This three-color, 19th-century campana vase is impressed with the "Wedgwood" mark.
$$$ • 7¼ in (18.5 cm) high

WALL PLAQUES
A pair of 19th-century white-on-black plaques, each with raised white figures of classical maidens holding hands and dancing.
$$$ • 18 in (45.5 cm) long

TOP TIPS
- Be aware that the color of Jasper Ware can affect price. Rarer shades, such as pink, black, green, and yellow, command more than the more common blue.
- Ensure that the condition of luster wares is perfect, as damage greatly reduces their value. Also check that the luster isn't rubbed or worn from use.
- When buying Keith Murray wares, color is the key: straw yellow, white, and green are the most commonly found, while blue, bronze, pink, and black command the highest prices.

PAIR OF VASES WITH COVERS
An unusual pair of early-19th-century potpourri vases molded with acanthus leaves.
$$$$ • 7¼ in (18.5 cm) high

WEDGWOOD MEAT DISH
Wedgwood pearlware canted and rectangular meat dish from 1820, printed in underglaze blue with the "Crane" pattern.
$$ • 16¼ in (42 cm) wide

EARTHENWARE BOWL
A Wedgwood earthenware bowl by Norman Wilson, of fluted form, glazed black and white with impressed marks, printed "NW."
$$$ • 11 in (27 cm) in diameter

Starter Buys

COFFEE CAN AND SAUCER
Decorated with swags, vine leaves, and grapes, this is a Jasper Ware can from 1881.
$$ • Approx. 3 in (7.5 cm) high

CHEESE DISH
Wedgwood blue Jasper Ware cheese dish and cover with the knop as an acorn.
$$ • 10¾ in (27.5 cm) in diameter

OVAL PENDANT
A Wedgwood Jasper Ware oval pendant/brooch displaying a classical figure.
$ • 2 in (5 cm) long

CENTERPIECE
Designed by Keith Murray, this earthenware Matt Straw Top Hat has impressed marks.
$$$ • 14 in (35.5 cm) in diameter

You may also like… Doulton, see pp. 44–47

Clarice Cliff

Clarice Cliff has become known as one of the most flamboyant designers of the 20th century, whose work, instantly recognizable with its bold use of color and shape, has become internationally admired and collected.

For more than 30 years, the interest in Clarice Cliff has grown from the awareness of a few shrewd individuals to a worldwide phenomenon, creating a market that has seen dramatic price adjustments over recent years. Today's collectors are specific about what they are looking for, and are eager to seek out rare shapes and patterns.

From the glory years of production between 1928 and 1936, when Cliff was at her most dynamic and experimental, there is a huge range of patterns that tend to fall into three main categories: abstracts, landscapes, and florals, combined with her striking Art Deco forms.

Rare patterns such as "Café" and "May Avenue" as well as the Appliqué ranges can command figures in the tens of thousands and remain the absolute pinnacle of any serious collection. There are, however, many options for a new collector starting at less than $200, with key entry-level patterns such as "Crocus," "Rodanthe," or "Original Bizarre."

A Bold Look for Everyday Use

Jug and bowl sets were an everyday feature of 19th-century homes, but by the 1930s most households had moved over to interior bathrooms. For those still using this traditional method, however, a bold and dramatic Art Deco set was ideal. Clarice has taken this traditional object and catapulted it into the 20th century with its bold form complemented by its rare and striking abstract "Sliced Circle" pattern.

TOLPHIN JUG
Hand-painted with a "Sliced Circle" pattern of radiating lines with circles displaced on either side of them, this very rare Clarice Cliff Tolphin jug and bowl set is dated 1929–30.

$$$$ • Jug 10 in (25.5 cm) high

KEY FACTS	1916	1927	1928–36	1964	1972
Bold, bright, and brave	Cliff takes her first job at A. J. Wilkinson, starting as a junior decorator.	Cliff is given her own studio by the firm's owner, Colley Shorter, and "Bizarre" is born.	The most important pieces are created during the golden days of Clarice Cliff's work.	Shorter, Cliff's husband since 1940, dies. Cliff retires and the firm is sold to Midwinter.	The first Cliff exhibition is held in Brighton. Later this year Cliff passes away suddenly.

What's Hot

WALL CHARGER
A rare "Appliqué Avignon" wall charger, with a radial design inside black borders.
$$$$$ • 18 in (46 cm) in diameter

OCTAGONAL PLAQUE
This rare plaque has the "Appliqué Caravan" pattern and a painted appliqué mark.
$$$$ • 11 in (28 cm) in diameter

Look out for:
Today considered one of Clarice Cliff's most desirable patterns, this vase combines a classic landscape with a bold Art Deco form. Part of the Bon Jour range, the vase has a rare form seldom seen on the market.

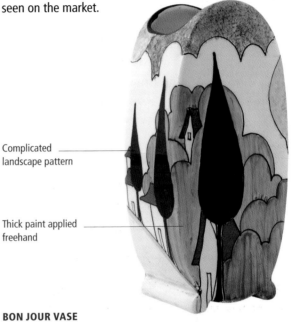

Complicated landscape pattern

Thick paint applied freehand

CIRCUS LAMP BASE
This lamp base was designed by Dame Laura Knight and produced by Clarice Cliff.
$$$$$ • 19 in (48.5 cm) high

SUGAR SIFTER
This sugar sifter in the "Oranges and Lemon" pattern dates from c. 1928.
$$$$ • 5½ in (14 cm) high

BON JOUR VASE
This Bon Jour vase, c. 1933, is decorated with a "May Avenue" pattern in black and shades of blue, green, and red, with the elements outlined in black.
$$$$$ • 4 in (10 cm) high

What's Not

This bowl, in a far safer and more traditional style, lacks the striking bright appeal of the earlier wares. In addition, many were produced, meaning a great number exist on the market.

"362" SHAPE VASE
This rare ovoid vase with a repeating "Football" pattern is from 1929–30.
$$$$$ • 8¼ in (21 cm) high

STAMFORD TEAPOT
A Stamford-shape teapot with an "Orange Roof Cottage" pattern from 1932–33.
$$$$ • 5 in (12.5 cm) high

WATER LILY BOWL
A Clarice Cliff Royal Staffordshire bowl with a printed mark.
$$ • 8¾ in (22 cm) wide

Core Collectibles

OCTAGONAL PLATE
This octagonal plate is hand-painted in the rare "Palermo" pattern, c. 1930.
$$$ • 8½ in (21.5 cm) in diameter

"SOLITUDE" PLATE
A "Solitude" pattern plate from the Bizarre range, with unusual banding combination.
$$$ • 10 in (25 cm) in diameter

ATHENS JUG
This Bizarre Athens jug has an "Orange Roof Cottage" pattern and a printed mark.
$$$ • 7 in (18 cm) high

LOTUS JUG
The ribbed body is painted in enamels in the "Orange Trees and House" pattern.
$$$$ • 11½ in (29 cm) high

DAFFODIL VASE
This is a Clarice Cliff Bizarre 450 Daffodil shape vase in the "Coral Firs" landscape pattern.
$$$$ • 13¼ in (33.5 cm) high

CUP AND SAUCER
Conical cup and saucer in the "Tennis" pattern.
$$$ • Cup 2¾ in (7 cm) high

"AUTUMN" CHARGER
A charger painted in enamels in the "Autumn" pattern.
$$$$ • 13½ in (34 cm) in diameter

Ask the Expert

Q. Can I wash my Clarice vase?
A. Yes, but be sure to wipe the piece over with a damp cloth—not an abrasive sponge—rather than submerge it.

363 VASE
A Fantasque Bizarre shape 363 vase in the "House and Bridge" pattern.
$$$$ • 6¼ in (16 cm) high

Hand-decorated with enamel

Q. My Clarice piece is damaged. Should I get it restored?
A. It depends on how rare the piece is. Restoration can be very successful and worthwhile but also pricey.

Q. How did Clarice decorate her pottery?
A. Her key work (1928–36) was decorated freehand by various workers, who would band, outline, and infill the patterns in oil-based enamel paints that sit on the surface of the glaze. Later pieces were transfer-decorated.

Q. Is it OK to use my Clarice vase for flowers?
A. It's not advisable. Your piece may have faint crazing (where the glaze starts to crackle), and water could make the problem worse.

CYLINDER JAM POT

A drum preserve pot and cover in the "Red Flower" pattern, c. 1930.

$$$ • 3½ in (9 cm) high

HONEY POT

A Clarice Cliff beehive honey pot decorated in the "Pastel Autumn" pattern.

$$ • 4 in (10 cm) high

COOKIE JAR

This Clarice Cliff Fantasque Bizarre Bon Jour cookie jar has a cover and wicker handle in the "Orange Secrets" pattern, a printed mark, and a tiny nick to the rim of the barrel.

$$$ • 6 in (15.5 cm) high

"ALTON" VASE

An "Alton" pattern vase, inspired by a Staffordshire beauty spot, c. 1933–34.

$$$ • 8¼ in (21 cm) high

LYNTON SUGAR SIFTER

Hand-painted in the "Coral Firs" landscape pattern, this sifter dates to c. 1933.

$$$ • 5 in (12.5 cm) high

MEIPING VASE

A Meiping vase with a "Melon" pattern and a printed mark.

$$$$ • 9 in (23 cm) high

"AUTUMN" DOVER JARDINIÈRE

This Clarice Cliff Bizarre cachepot in the "Autumn" pattern has painted trees with sinuous trunks, bushes, a small cottage in a wood, and black printed marks.

$$$ • 6¼ in (16 cm) high

FANTASQUE VASE

This Fantasque Bizarre 265 vase in the "Orange House" pattern has a printed mark.

$$$$ • 6 in (15.5 cm) high

Core Collectibles

JAM POT AND COVER
Dating to 1931–33, this jar
for preserves is painted in
the "Autumn" pattern.
$$$ • 3½ in (9 cm) high

"GIBRALTAR" VASE
A Clarice Cliff Fantasque
Bizarre 195 "Gibraltar"
vase with a printed mark.
$$$$ • 8¾ in (22 cm) high

"RED ROOFS" SUGAR SIFTER
This sugar sifter, a popular,
classic Cliff design, is painted
in a "Red Roofs" pattern.
$$$$ • 5¼ in (13.5 cm) high

CONICAL SUGAR SIFTER
Circa 1932, this landscape-
decorated sifter is in the
"Moonlight" pattern.
$$$ • 5¼ in (13.5 cm) high

STAMFORD TEA SET
A Clarice Cliff Bizarre
Stamford early morning set,
painted in the "Orange Trees
and Houses" pattern, and
with printed marks.
$$$$ • Teapot 5 in (12.5 cm) high

OCTAGONAL CANDLESTICK
This Bizarre candlestick
decorated in the "Lightning"
pattern has a printed mark.
$$$$ • 8 in (20 cm) high

"HOUSE AND BRIDGE" VASE
Circa 1931, this vase is hand-
painted in one of Cliff's most
famous landscapes.
$$$$ • 6 in (15.5 cm) high

"MOONLIGHT" VASE
A Fantasque Bizarre 366
"Moonlight" pattern vase
with some minor paint flakes.
$$$$ • 6 in (15.5 cm) high

"ORIGINAL BIZARRE" VASE
This is a rare Clarice Cliff
"Original Bizarre" 366 vase
with a printed mark.
$$$$ • 6 in (15.5 cm) high

TOP TIPS

- Structure your collection—either by shape, e.g., coffee cans, or pattern, e.g., landscapes—to create a theme.
- Avoid later postwar pieces, which have less appeal in today's market.
- Remember, it's always better to buy a small piece in a fantastic pattern than a large piece in a less desirable design.
- Consider larger pieces such as Lotus jugs, which have recently dropped in price and are good buys for future market increases.

"SECRETS" VASE
An unmarked Clarice Cliff classic 358 vase in the "Secrets" pattern.
$$$ • 8¼ in (21 cm) high

"AUTUMN" BOOKENDS
A pair of Clarice Cliff Fantasque Bizarre 405 bookends in the "Autumn" pattern, bearing printed marks.
$$$$ • 6 in (15.5 cm) high

CROWN JUG
This Clarice Cliff "May Avenue" pattern Bizarre jug bears a printed mark.
$$$$ • 6 in (15.5 cm) wide

CONICAL BOWL
A Fantasque Bizarre conical bowl in the "Broth" pattern, with a printed mark.
$$$$ • 7½ in (19 cm) wide

Starter Buys

FANTASQUE PLATE
This octagonal plate is in the "Blue Chintz" pattern with stylized flowers.
$$$ • 8¾ in (22 cm) wide

GEOMETRIC PLATE
A Clarice Cliff "Original Bizarre" pattern plate with a printed mark.
$$$ • 10½ in (26.5 cm) in diameter

BOUQUET PLAQUE
Decorated with molded, stylized flowers, this roundel has a black printed mark.
$$$ • 8 in (20 cm) in diameter

"MY GARDEN" VASES
A pair of vases modeled as tree stumps and encircled by relief-molded flowers.
$$ • 5 in (12.5 cm) high

PRESERVE JAR AND COVER
Painted in the "Nasturtium" pattern, this cylindrical jar has printed marks.
$$ • 3½ in (9 cm) high

"FARMHOUSE" CANDLESTICK
A "Farmhouse" pattern Fantasque Bizarre candlestick with printed mark.
$$$ • 3¼ in (8 cm) high

You may also like… Poole Pottery, see pp. 48–53

Susie Cooper

Susie Cooper was quite simply one of the most elegant and diverse designers of her day. She produced a catalog of wares that went from Art Deco to Pop with an ease only possible through sheer good design.

Renowned and revered by those around her in the industry, Susie Cooper was a gifted businesswoman who spanned over 60 years of British pottery-making, indelibly leaving her mark on each generation. Her goal was to produce elegant yet functional domestic wares influenced by her love of Modernism and surface pattern.

She predominantly concentrated on the table and tea wares market, together with a small number of vases and fancy wares. During the 1930s, Cooper developed her distinctive style with simple repeat patterns and floral and animal motifs, all decorated by hand. Embracing new techniques, Cooper also introduced aerographed, sgrafitto, and transfer-printed patterns to her wares.

Today, collectors are most interested in the earlier Art Deco earthenwares with top prices being paid for the key Art Deco abstract and animal decorated pieces of the 1930s. However, entry-level pieces can be bought for just a few dollars.

Finished with a Flourish

At the age of 20 in Stoke-on-Trent, Susie Cooper went to work for local potter A. E. Gray, initially as a painter. She was quickly promoted to designer and spent seven years with Gray's, which launched a new "Designed by Susie Cooper" trademark showing a steamship at full speed. After leaving Gray's, she set up her own company. This pottery jug from her Studio range, which was introduced in 1932, displays the elegant freehand painting that Susie became so respected for. Her skill was in the flourish of the final design, which had a flair unique to Cooper.

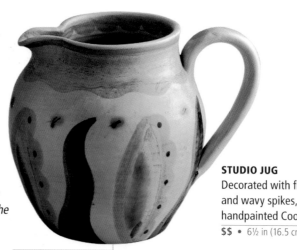

STUDIO JUG
Decorated with flowerheads and wavy spikes, this is a handpainted Cooper jug.
$$ • 6½ in (16.5 cm) high

KEY FACTS	1919	1922	1950s	1966	1980
Cooper's career in ceramics	Aged 17, attends the Burslem School of Art under the tutelage of artist and designer Gordon Forsythe.	Joins A. E. Gray and begins a long career in the pottery industry. She leaves to form her own firm in 1929.	Expands into bone china, designing flamboyant new shapes. Merger with R. H. & S. L. Plant leads to new dinnerware venture.	Cooper is acquired by the Wedgwood group and becomes part of a large parent company with a diverse market.	"Retires" to the Isle of Wight but freelances for Adams pottery clients such as Boots, Tesco, and Tiffany.

What's Hot

ABSTRACT PATTERN JUG
Dated 1928, this jug is painted in the bold, abstract "Moon and Mountain" pattern.
$$$ • 4¾ in (12 cm) high

NURSERY WARE MUG
Printed with a "Skier" pattern, this is a "nursery ware" mug from the 1930s.
$$ • 3¾ in (9.5 cm) high

Look out for:
Cooper's early hand-painted abstracts remain highly sought after due to their strong Art Deco feel. Those produced at Gray's have pattern numbers ranging from 2866 through to 8586. Items showing strong Cubist or Modernist influences are also very popular.

Dramatic color palette

GEOMETRIC JUG
A striking tall jug with a geometric pattern created by Cooper in 1928.
$$$ • 6¾ in (17 cm) high

TABLE CENTER
Made in 1936, this colorful angelfish table piece is highly decorative.
$$$$ • 10¾ in (27.5 cm) high

GEOMETRIC PLATE
This plate, handpainted in an abstract design with strong influences from key European art movements, shows Cooper's geometrics at their very best.
$$$ • 8¾ in (22.5 cm) in diameter

TURKEY PLATE
This rare turkey plate combines lithograph and handpainted techniques.
$$$ • 17¾ in (45 cm) in diameter

GALLEON PLATE
A plate that has been hand-printed and painted with a rare galleon image.
$$$$ • 11 in (28 cm) in diameter

What's Not

Cooper's domestic dinnerware is less desirable because there is lots of it, and large pieces can be awkward to display. More traditional floral patterns are also less sought after.

OVAL PLATTER
This c. 1937 meat plate is from a larger dinner service in a safe traditional design.
$ • 12 in (30 cm) wide

Core Collectibles

MODERNIST JUG
A jug with Modernist bands and panels created by Susie Cooper in 1930.
$$$ • 5 in (12.5 cm) high

CUBIST JUG
Created in 1929, this jug by Susie Cooper has a Cubist geometric design.
$$$ • 4¾ in (12 cm) high

FLORAL COFFEE SET
A Susie Cooper for Gray's stylized floral coffee set with six cups (one shown). The coffee pot was made in 1928 and the set has a very distinctive bright, contemporary design.
$$$ • Coffee pot 8 in (20 cm) high

COFFEE POT
This coffee pot with hand-painted geometric pattern dates from c. 1928.
$$$ • 8 in (20 cm) high

LEMONADE JUG
A Susie Cooper for Gray's lemonade jug decorated with leaves and flowers.
$$$ • 7¼ in (18.5 cm) high

SGRAFFITO JUG
This is a 1930s hand-carved, green glazed Studio jug. Its base has an incised signature.
$$ • 8½ in (22 cm) high

ABSTRACT PLATE
Dated 1932, this Susie Cooper dessert plate with spiral motif is handpainted.
$$ • 8 in (20 cm) in diameter

Ask the Expert

Q. Is Susie Cooper's work always signed or marked?
A. Susie Cooper has had many different marks over the years, including incised, handpainted, and printed. Many are linked with the various factories she was associated with, which aid in dating a piece. The famous leaping deer mark, for example, was introduced around 1932.

Handpainted leaves

"PEAR IN POMPADOUR" PLATE
A handpainted "Pear in Pompadour" plate from 1934.
$$ • *8 in (20 cm) in diameter*

Q. How can I tell if my plate is hand-painted or printed, and which is more valuable?
A. Cooper decorated using both handpainted and transfer-printed techniques. A handpainted piece will have slight differences in the pattern. Handpainted pieces predominantly command higher prices due to the amount of work involved.

Q. Is a Susie Cooper vase from her Studio range worth keeping?
A. From around 1932–38, Susie Cooper designed a range of vases, jugs, and bowls decorated with sgraffito patterns of stylized animal and floral motifs carved into the wet clay. Values have remained low for such stylish work and it is well worth collecting.

"GUARDSMEN" DISH
This sectional child's plate is printed and painted with stylized guardsmen, c. 1933.
$$$ • 8 in (20 cm) in diameter

COWBOY PLATE
A nursery plate printed and painted with a stylized cowboy and horse, c. 1933–34.
$$ • 8 in (20 cm) in diameter

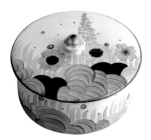

GRAY'S FLORAL BOX
A Susie Cooper for Gray's stylized floral box manufactured in 1929.
$$ • 2½ in (6.5 cm) high

CUP AND SAUCER SET
Dated 1929, this is a striking Gray's cup and saucer in a hand-painted abstract pattern.
$$ • Saucer 5½ in (14 cm) in diameter

"DRESDEN SPRAY" TEA SET
A Susie Cooper Rex shape green "Dresden Spray" tea set. "Dresden Spray" was a popular pattern produced for a long time; this example dates from c. 1938.
$$$ • Teapot 4¾ in (12 cm) high

Starter Buys

MODERNIST TRIO
A classic Modernist design trio from c. 1936–37, with a hand-painted stylized motif.
$$ • Largest 6¾ in (17.5 cm) diameter

"AZALEA" CHINA TRIO
This printed and painted 1950s bone china trio bears gilded highlights.
$ • Plate 6 in (15 cm) in diameter

"DIABLO" SET
This trio is from Susie Cooper's classic postwar years with Wedgwood.
$ • Plate 6½ in (17 cm) in diameter

FLORAL PLATE
Manufactured between 1932 and 1934, this is a green Studio range fruit plate.
$$ • 7¼ in (18.5 cm) in diameter

You may also like… Clarice Cliff, see pp. 22–27

Staffordshire

With subjects as diverse as politics, sports, domestic pets, and wild and exotic animals, Staffordshire figures brought a small slice of the great wide world into the parlors of the Victorian working class.

The manufacture of figures in the Staffordshire region dates back to the early 18th century, when potters from the area, notably John Astbury, began making primitively modeled figures decorated with basic salt and oxide glazes in natural earthy tints. These were unashamedly simple against the sophisticated German and English china wares.

Famous names such as Thomas Whieldon and the Wood family pushed the genre forward with more detailed models and decoration. Today,

examples of these early styles are highly prized. By the 19th century, factories had begun to produce figures from two-piece molds that were left unmodeled and plain at the back and so were known as "flat backs." Often decorated by children, these figures were mass produced and affordable by all.

Although rare pieces fetch large sums, Staffordshire prices generally have fallen in recent years, so figures can be found for as little as $40. Now is a great time to start your collection.

Tea in China

The 18th century saw the rise of tea drinking and with it the creation of associated wares. This example is typical of glazes popularized by Thomas Whieldon. The effect was created using lead glazes, which resulted in this distinctive green hue. The relief-molded decoration is also unusual, reflecting the "new" fashion for items with Asian themes.

TEAPOT WITH CHINESE DECORATION
Dated 1765, this Staffordshire teapot is formed in a pagoda shape and decorated with Chinese scenes. Minor repairs have been made to the spout.
$$$$ • 5¾ in (14.5 cm) high

KEY FACTS	1720s	c. 1750	1837	c. 1850	2006
Potted history of Staffordshire	Staffordshire potteries begin to produce simple pieces using local raw materials.	The works of Astbury, Whieldon, and Wood begin to make a name for Staffordshire ware.	The coronation of Queen Victoria sees a flood of popular royalty-related figures.	The "flat back" method is developed, allowing cheaper, more efficient mass production.	Three Staffordshire creamware figures on a pew, c. 1745, sell for $168,000 at auction at Christie's, New York.

What's Hot

LIONS AND LAMBS
This pair of Staffordshire lions and lambs, by Lloyd of Shelton, is set on cream plinth bases with gold decoration.
$$$$ • 4 in (10 cm) high

NEWFOUNDLAND DOGS
This pair of Staffordshire Newfoundland dogs date back to c. 1850.
$$$$ • 5½ in (14 cm) high

THE SAILOR'S LOT
A pair of Staffordshire figures from c. 1820: "Sailor's Farewell" and "Sailor's Return."
$$$$ • 6¾ in (17 cm) high

TEA CANISTER
A Staffordshire ceramic canister from 1765, decorated in a Classical style.
$$$$ • 6¾ in (17 cm) high

RAILWAY CHILDREN
These figures are classic examples of Staffordshire, paired with rare trains.
$$$$ • 9½ in (24 cm) high

ROMULUS AND REMUS
This Staffordshire group dates to c. 1820 and depicts a scene from Roman mythology.
$$$$ • 8¾ in (22.5 cm) high

Look out for:
Dogs are one of the most common subjects of 19th-century Staffordshire ware, but it is unusual to see them modeled with other figures. The children riding this pair, and the baskets of flowers they hold, make these pieces rare and highly collectible. Look for models of unusual breeds of dogs, which can also attract high prices.

Clothes and collars detailed in gilt

Unusual pairing of dog and child

MATCHING STAFFORDSHIRE SPANIELS
An unusual matching pair of Staffordshire ceramic figures depicting spaniels carrying flower baskets and ridden by children, dating to the late 19th century.
$$$$ • 9¾ in (25 cm) high

What's Not

Figures based on royalty were popular and produced in large numbers, making them cheap and easy to find today. This figure's lack of enamel decoration further reduces its value.

EQUESTRIAN FIGURE
A 19th-century figure of Queen Mary ll.
$$ • 10¼ in (26 cm) high

Core Collectibles

SEATED SPANIELS
A pair of Staffordshire spaniels holding flower baskets, dating from c. 1860.
$$$$ • 8 in (20 cm) high

AESOP'S FABLES PAIR
A rare Staffordshire porcelain pair depicting the fox and the stork from *Aesop's Fables*.
$$$ • 7 in (17.5 cm) high

CAULIFLOWER TEAPOT
This Staffordshire cauliflower teapot, c. 1765, has some restoration work to its handle.
$$$$ • 5¼ in (13.5 cm) high

PORCELAIN HOUND
A mid-19th-century porcelain hound with a gilt chain and handpainted decoration.
$$$ • 4¾ in (12 cm) high

PEARLWARE FIGURINE
This slightly damaged 1820s figurine is decorated in colored enamels.
$$ • 9 in (23 cm) high

PAIR OF DONKEY GROUPS
A 19th-century pair of Staffordshire spill vases, each with a seated figure beside a donkey. Spill vases were usually kept above the fireplace and held rolled-paper tapers, called spills.
$$$ • 9 in (23 cm) high

CIRCUS GROUP
A rare group from c. 1855 depicting circus-style performers on horseback.
$$$$ • 8½ in (21.5 cm) high

Ask the Expert

Q. Why are there so many Staffordshire military figures ?
A. Major 19th-century conflicts such as the Crimean War sparked

MILITARY PAIR
A soldier and sailor pair from the Crimean War, 1850s.
$$$$ • *13¼ in (33.5 cm) high*

Childish freehand painting

demand for military and naval figures, as well as representations of great leaders such as Napoleon and Garibaldi. Figures were often modeled on images in periodicals, but since the same molds were used for a number of different models, they were rarely accurate depictions.

Q. Are named figures more desirable?
A. British and foreign royals, in particular Queen Victoria and Prince Albert; statesmen and politicians, including Sir Robert Peel and Disraeli; and notable public figures of the day (even criminals) are very popular. Expect to pay from $400 up.

SPANIELS WITH BASKETS
A pair of seated spaniels with baskets, c. 1860. Both dogs have gilt collars.

$$$ • 6¼ in (16 cm) high

BULL BAITING
A 19th-century ceramic bull-baiting group, depicting a bull and a terrier.

$$ • 6 in (15 cm) high

FLORAL TEAPOT
A Staffordshire teapot from c. 1770, with floral decoration to handle, spout, and top.

$$$$ • 4¾ in (12 cm) high·

GIRLS ON ZEBRAS
A pair of children riding horses stylistically decorated to look like zebras.

$$$ • 6¾ in (17 cm) high

CREAMWARE LEOPARD
A naïve creamware model of a recumbent leopard with minimal decoration.

$$$ • 3¾ in (9.5 cm) wide

PAIR OF ELEPHANTS
A diminutive pair of Staffordshire elephants, produced around 1860.

$$$ • 2¾ in (7 cm) high

PAIR OF POODLES
This pair of Staffordshire poodles dated c. 1865 is decorated with clay chips.

$$$ • 10¼ in (26 cm) high

Starter Buys

SHEEP AND LAMB
This pearlware model of a sheep bears the inscription "SH" on its back.

$$ • 5½ in (13.5 cm) high

RAM AND EWE SPILL VASES
A pair of spill vases formed as a ram and a ewe, decorated with chips.

$$ • 5 in (13 cm) high

GREYHOUNDS AND GAME
This pair of Victorian greyhounds is modeled carrying dead game.

$$ • 7½ in (19 cm) high

EXOTIC BIRDS
A pair of exotic birds from the late 19th century, with rockwork bases.

$$$ • 9¾ in (24.5 cm) high

GLAZED COTTAGE
From c. 1860, this cottage has a blue glazed roof and granitic decoration.

$$ • 9 in (23 cm) high

KING CHARLES SPANIELS
A 19th-century pair of King Charles spaniels, glazed with gilt highlights.

$$ • 8¾ in (22 cm) high

You may also like… Beswick, see pp. 72–75

Character Jugs

Popular since the mid-18th century, these comic ceramics have become highly collectible. The vast range of characters includes real and fictional characters, rogues and villains, heroes and heroines.

Toby jugs were first produced in Yorkshire and Staffordshire in the mid-18th century, while the Doulton character jug was born in the early 20th century. The charm of these pieces lies in their infectious humor, and the insight they give into stereotypes and caricatures of the time.

Today, early Toby jugs range hugely in price from $200 to $6,000. The Doulton range, however, is more popular with

collectors, with more than 300 patterns providing an immense breadth of choice. Prices for Doulton pieces range from $20 to thousands for the very rarest examples such as the Maori, and they tend to hold their value well.

Toby and character jugs have fallen out of fashion in recent years, but their unique styling and iconic characters continue to attract collectors with a sense of humor.

A Rakish Character

This green-eyed Regency Beau recalls unscrupulous womanizers of historical romance. Designed by David Biggs, the jug ran for only five years, between 1962 and 1967, and was produced in large, small, and miniature models. Unique codes on the bottom of each jug can be used to identify the size and the year of manufacture.

REGENCY BEAU
A Doulton Regency Beau character jug in the small size, pattern number D6562.
$$$ • 4 in (10 cm) high

TOP TIPS

- Remember that a Toby jug models a full figure, while a character jug shows just the head and shoulders.
- Search for models with short production runs or those marked "prototype": these are more valuable and especially collectible.
- Concentrate on Doulton jugs for long-term investment, as these have generally held their price.

KEY FACTS	1760s	1815	1934	1984	2003
The tale of the Toby	Staffordshire potter Ralph Wood develops the first Toby jugs, which feature full-figure caricatures.	Doulton begins its own range of Toby jugs, the first to be factory-produced.	Charles Noke, chief modeler at Doulton, launches the first character jugs.	Schoolboy Toby Gillette is modeled as a Toby jug for the *Jim'll Fix It* TV show.	A 1939 Maori character jug by Doulton, of which only three survive, is auctioned for $36,500.

What's Hot

UGLY DUCHESS
Inspired by Lewis Carroll's *Alice* stories, this is a 1960s Doulton Ugly Duchess jug.

$$ • 4 in (10 cm) high

THE CLOWN
This white-haired Clown is a 1950s Doulton character jug, pattern number D6322.

$$$ • 6¼ in (16 cm) high

Look out for:
Produced only in 1947, Pearly Boy and his counterpart, Pearly Girl, are two of the rarest Doulton character jugs. There are five different versions, with varying colored clothing, all designed by Harry Fenton. These are not to be confused with the 1980s Pearly King and Queen, which are far less collectible.

Blue glaze is rare for this character

PEARLY BOY
A small Pearly Boy character jug produced by Doulton in 1947, with blue decoration.

$$$$ • 3¼ in (8.5 cm) high

Colored buttons add value

Core Collectibles

ROBIN HOOD
The Robin Hood jugs, pattern number D6205, were issued by Doulton from 1947 to 1960.

$ • 6½ in (16 cm) high

GULLIVER
This 1960s Doulton jug portrays Jonathan Swift's fictional traveler to Lilliput.

$$ • 4 in (10 cm) high

CAPTAIN HOOK
Depicting Peter Pan's arch-enemy, this is a 1960s Doulton jug, pattern D6601.

$$ • 4 in (10 cm) high

FALSTAFF
A large Doulton jug of the Shakespearean character, issued from 1950–95.

$ • 6¼ in (16 cm) high

Starter Buys

HENRY VIII
Modeled on Henry VIII, this Doulton character jug, pattern D6642, dates from 1975.

$ • 6½ in (16.5 cm) high

CHARLIE CHAPLIN
This is a 1993 limited-edition jug by Doulton, pattern D6949, with certificate.

$$ • 7 in (18 cm) high

You may also like… Doulton, see pp. 44–47

Moorcroft

The name of Moorcroft is synonymous with quality design and production. Combining tubelined decoration with individual design, the firm has sustained a legacy of highly accomplished fine art wares.

William Moorcroft, born in 1873, first made his mark as an innovative designer and artist after joining the Staffordshire pottery company James Macintyre & Co. in 1897. Here, he produced his celebrated Art Nouveau–inspired Florian Ware and pioneered the use of tubelined slips to create decorative outlines before pieces were painted.

In 1913, Moorcroft set up on his own and, until his death in 1945, produced many important designs, including the "Spanish," "Hazledene," "Moonlit Blue," and "Claremont" patterns. He also perfected the difficult technique of using a rich flambé (red) glaze to give his pottery unusually vivid and deep colors. After William's death, his elder son Walter took over, introducing a variety of new floral patterns such as "Lily," "Hibiscus," and "Magnolia."

The huge range of patterns and variety of both art and domestic wares available allow entry-level collectors to buy into this specific market from as little as $40 to $60 for a small decorated pin dish. At the other end of the scale, early, rare, or important pieces, such as Florian Ware, comfortably command prices in the thousands.

Inspired by Nature

William Moorcroft's interest in botanical studies and organic forms provided the inspiration for his floral patterns. He remained faithful to the fluid, theatrical designs of Art Nouveau even after the popularity from 1925 of the more geometric Art Deco style.

"CORNFLOWER" TEA TRIO
This William Moorcroft "Cornflower" pattern teapot, milk jug, and sugar bowl, c. 1912, has a translucent glaze and brilliant color.

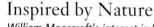

$$$$$ • Teapot 6 in (15 cm) high

KEY FACTS	1897	1913	1928	1940s–80s	1993
Floral pieces from famous potters' hands	William Moorcroft joins James Macintyre & Co. and develops a range of decorative body wares.	Moorcroft leaves Macintyre and opens a new factory with the support of the Liberty family.	After years of success and international medals, Moorcroft is appointed potter to Queen Mary.	William dies in 1945 and is succeeded by Walter. In 1984, the family sells its shares on the open market.	Ownership passes to the Edwards family. Moorcroft thrives under senior designer Rachel Bishop.

What's Hot

"SPANISH" VASE
A trumpet-shaped vase,
c. 1912, decorated in the floral
"Spanish" pattern.
$$$$ • 8½ in (22 cm) high

LOVING CUP
Fitted with three handles, this
c. 1900 cup is decorated in
the "Forget-me-not" pattern.
$$$$ • 8 in (20 cm) high

Look out for:

The secrets of Moorcroft's flambé kiln were closely guarded until his death in 1945. Many of his greatest—and most expensive—patterns were treated to this glorious technique.

Undamaged
tubelining

Flambé glaze
enriches color

"DAWN" GINGER JAR
This jar, with original lid, is in
the "Dawn" pattern, with
contrasting geometric bands.
$$$$ • 8 in (20 cm) high

"POMEGRANATE" CHALICE
With a green celadon glaze
and an everted rim, this vase
dates to 1910–13.
$$$$ • 6 in (15 cm) high

FLAMBÉ LANDSCAPE VASE
From Moorcroft's dedicated flambé kiln, this vase is from
c. 1925. Flambé versions of designs are more valuable;
sometimes the only sign is a pale pink tint to the base.
$$$$ • 7 in (18 cm) high

"MOONLIT BLUE" VASE
This vase is decorated with a
stylized nighttime landscape
over the baluster body.
$$$$ • 12½ in (31.5 cm) high

"CLAREMONT" VASE
A vase with a flared rim,
decorated in the rare
toadstool-motif pattern.
$$$$ • 8¼ in (21 cm) high

What's Not

This piece is in one of the most
popular Moorcroft patterns, but
the then-fashionable color
combination of coral on green
ground is unpopular with
today's collectors.

"HIBISCUS" VASE
This 1960s "Hibiscus"
vase has a flattened
spherical shape.
$$ • 4 in (10 cm) high

Core Collectibles

"LEAF AND BERRY" PLATE
A flambé "Leaf and Berry" patterned plate, this piece has a printed blue signature.
$$$ • 7 in (18 cm) in diameter

"CLAREMONT" PLATE
Initialed in blue, this plate is decorated in the "Claremont" toadstool pattern.
$$$ • 7½ in (19 cm) in diameter

"LEAF AND BERRY" BALUSTER VASE
A richly colored vase with a yellow, red, and blue "Leaf and Berry" pattern on a deep blue background. This piece also bears a printed blue signature.
$$$ • 10 in (25 cm) high

BALUSTER VASE
A hand-decorated vase in the "Pomegranate" pattern with impressed mark and signature.
$$$ • 9¼ in (23.5 cm) high

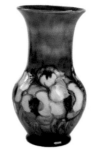

"ANEMONE" VASE
This green, floral patterned vase has a facsimile signature and a flared rim.
$$$ • 10 in (25 cm) high

"PANSY" VASE
Dating back to 1913, this vase is in the rare "Pansy-on-White" pattern.
$$$$ • 11½ in (29.5 cm) high

FLORIAN WARE VASE
This vase is decorated in a version of the popular "Cornflower" pattern.
$$$ • 5 in (12.5 cm) high

Ask the Expert

Q. How do I know whether a vase is by William or Walter?
A. Moorcroft wares carry many identifying marks, including impressed stamps and painted signatures. William would sign or monogram everything; Walter only marked pieces over 5 in (13 cm) in height or width.

Hand-painted

White ground

CORNFLOWER VASE
Painted in the "Revived Cornflower" pattern, this vase has a blue script signature.
$$$$ • 9 in (23 cm) high

Q. Is a Moorcroft vase faulty if it has a very runny, streaked pattern?
A. On occasion, the colored glazes painted between the raised tubelined pattern break free of the line and "bleed" down the body of the pot. This is not really a fault as such, but these pieces do tend to be slightly less valuable.

Q. If a vase is covered in a fine crackled effect, is it part of the decoration?
A. The glaze on your vase has "crazed," which occurs naturally when the glaze has been subject to temperature changes and moisture over the years. This affects some but not all pieces and will only make a small difference to the value of an item.

"TREE BARK THIEF" VASE

A limited edition "Tree Bark Thief" vase, this comes with impressed and painted marks.

$$$ • 14¼ in (36.5 cm) high

MARINE VASE

Designed by Sion Leeper, this vase showcases marine life with turtles and jellyfish.

$$$ • 14½ in (37 cm) high

"ANGEL'S TRUMPET"

Called the "Angel's Trumpet," this is a limited edition vase manufactured in 1998.

$$ • 7½ in (19 cm) high

CHALICE AND COVER

With two gilded handles, this Florian Ware chalice vase with cover is decorated with flowers on a blue and salmon-pink background. It has a printed Macintyre mark.

$$$$ • 8½ in (21 cm) high

"ORCHID" VASE

Made c. 1935, this "Orchid" vase is impressed with "Potter to HM the Queen."

$$ • 5 in (12.5 cm) high

COOKIE JAR

A cookie jar with an electroplated cover, in the "Pomegranate" pattern.

$$$ • 7 in (18 cm) high

GINGER JAR

Both this ginger jar and its cover are decorated with "Fairy Rings" toadstools.

$$$ • 6 in (15 cm) high

TWIN-HANDLED VASE

This Florian Ware vase is tubelined with forget-me-nots, c. 1905.

$$$$ • 5 in (12.5 cm) high

"HIBISCUS" VASE

A baluster vase with a slightly everted rim, this is decorated in the "Hibiscus" pattern.

$$$ • 10 in (25 cm) high

Core Collectibles

FLARED VASE
This wide green vase with a flared rim is decorated with a pattern of large, red-capped, "Claremont" toadstools.
$$$ • 7 in (18 cm) high

"ORCHIDS" JARDINIÈRE
This ovoid jardinière is decorated in the "Orchids" pattern. It has an impressed mark with blue initials.
$$$ • 6¼ in (16 cm) high

SHOULDERED VASE
This salt-glazed shouldered ovoid vase is decorated in the "Anemone" pattern.
$$$ • 9½ in (24 cm) high

"ANEMONE" GINGER JAR
Complete with cover, this jar has an "Anemone" pattern on a dark blue ground.
$$ • 6¼ in (16 cm) high

"PHOENIX" VASE
Signed by Rachel Bishop, this c. 1990 vase has a waisted neck and is extravagantly decorated with blue, green, and orange feathers against a brown-green background.
$$$ • 11½ in (29 cm) high

"HIBISCUS" BOTTLE VASE
A bottle vase, this dark blue piece in the "Hibiscus" pattern has a paper label.
$$$ • 10¼ in (26 cm) high

"RAINFOREST" VASE
Made in the early 1990s, this "Rainforest" baluster vase was designed by Sally Tuffin.
$$$ • 12 in (30 cm) high

"ORCHID" VASE
Dating back to c. 1916, this is a two-handled vase in the "Orchid" pattern.
$$$$ • 12½ in (32 cm) high

"CORNFLOWER" VASE
This vase is decorated in the "Revived Cornflower" pattern, from c. 1925.
$$$$ • 9 in (23 cm) high

FLORIAN WARE PLATE
This is a late Florian Ware plate with a floral pattern. It was manufactured c. 1916.
$$$$ • 8½ in (21.5 cm) in diameter

"FREESIA" BOWL
A flambé "Freesia" bowl with beautiful salmon-pink flowers on a brownish-red background and a painted blue signature.
$$$ • 10¾ in (27 cm) in diameter

TOP TIPS
• Be aware of restoration: if well executed and declared, it shouldn't deter a collector, although it does affect prices.
• Look out for unusual colorways or patterns, particularly ocher and celadon tints of early William Moorcroft designs.
• If collecting modern or contemporary wares, look for the rarer limited editions, especially those signed by the designers.
• Check that a piece has fired well, as the pattern can sometimes "bleed" during the firing process.

"LEAF AND BERRY" VASE
This ovoid vase has a flambé "Leaf and Berry" pattern and printed green signature.
$$$ • 6¼ in (16 cm) high

"ANEMONE" BALUSTER VASE
This baluster vase has impressed marks on it, and is initialed in green. It has been decorated in the "Anemone" pattern.
$$ • 8½ in (22 cm) high

"PANSIES" BOWL
An early William Moorcroft tubelined "Pansies-on-White" bowl with a frill rim. This piece has a printed Macintyre mark.
$$$ • 8 in (20 cm) wide

Starter Buys

"BALLOONS" OVOID VASE
This is a shouldered vase with an inverted rim. It is decorated in the "Balloons" pattern.
$$ • 7 in (18 cm) high

"LEMON" TAPERING VASE
In a tapered shape, this shouldered vase bears the "Lemon" pattern.
$$ • 10 in (25 cm) high

"MAGNOLIA" VASE
A globe and shaft vase, with bold pink magnolias on a dark blue background.
$$ • 6 in (15 cm) high

FLORIAN WARE COMPORT
This comport is decorated all over in a variant of the "Cornflower" pattern.
$$$ • 8 in (20 cm) high

You may also like… Clarice Cliff, see pp. 22–27

Doulton

From the banks of the Thames to the heart of the Potteries, Royal Doulton has created a legacy of excellence in British pottery. Today their wares are among some of the most popular modern collectibles.

In 1871, the firm of Doulton & Co., originally a leading producer of sanitary and industrial ceramics in Lambeth, exhibited about 70 pieces of decorative stoneware at the International Exhibition in Kensington. The display drew great interest, particularly from Queen Victoria, who ordered some to be sent to Windsor Castle. By the late 1800s, the new "Doulton Ware," widely acclaimed by the public, had also become a draw for some of the most important ceramic artists of the day, including

George Tinworth and the Barlow sisters. Before too long, Doulton expanded into the heart of the Potteries in Burslem, quickly establishing itself as one of the leading creators of art-based wares.

The 20th century saw Doulton pushing forth in the decorative markets, with production including figures and a huge range of domestic wares. Collectors today search out both the stoneware pieces of the London site and the immensely popular figures from the Burslem operation.

Pots of Prestige

Recruited by Doulton from Royal Worcester in 1889, senior designer Charles Noke introduced a highly successful range titled "Series Ware" in 1900, which could be applied to standard ceramic forms. The decorations drew inspiration from famous historical, literary, and sporting subjects, including scenes of early motoring, characters from Charles Dickens, and pieces commemorating monarchs from Queen Victoria onward. Pieces with fishing or golfing designs, such as this one, are particularly rare and very popular with collectors, due to their market crossover appeal. The sheer size and condition of this piece, combined with these other factors, make it a hot collectible.

TWO-HANDLED VASE
A large Royal Doulton Series vase of tapering circular form with gilt handles.
$$$$$ • 11 in (28 cm) high

KEY FACTS	1815	1871	1882	1900	2006
Decorating Doulton	The factory opens at Vauxhall Walk in Lambeth, London. It takes the name Doulton in 1853.	Doulton's son Henry launches a studio. With his interest in art, the firm produces decorative wares.	Henry Doulton acquires Pinder, Bourne & Co. in Burslem, Staffordshire, bringing Doulton to the famous Potteries region.	Charles Noke, Doulton's senior designer, introduces the company's Series Ware range.	Royal Doulton is bought by the Waterford Wedgwood group. Many items are now made in Indonesia.

What's Hot

Look out for:

Hannah Barlow (1851–1916) was famed for her hand-carved vases. Horses, cattle, and goats are typical; rarer pieces feature more exotic animals, such as these lions.

STONEWARE VASE
This vase, from c. 1881, was decorated with grazing ponies by Hannah Barlow.
$$$$ • 16½ in (42 cm) high

BALUSTER VASE
A late 19th-century stoneware vase, carved and enameled by Florence Barlow.
$$$ • 14½ in (37 cm) high

Carved borders finished by Barlow

Incised decoration

Salt-glazed stoneware body

OVIFORM VASE
Possibly by Edith Lupton, this is an 1886 Doulton Lambeth shouldered oviform vase, with incised and painted Islamic-inspired stylized foliate decoration, in a subdued palette of blues, greens, and yellow on buff.
$$$$ • 17¾ in (46 cm) high

HANNAH BARLOW VASE
This salt-glazed stoneware vase decorated by Hannah Barlow features a rare frieze of lions.
$$$$ • 12½ in (31.5 cm) high

What's Not

These cauldrons were produced in very large quantities and were rarely decorated by a key designer or artist.

DOULTON SUNG VASE
This Charles Noke vase has a parrot on fruiting branches in flambé glazes.
$$$$ • 8 in (20 cm) high

CHUNG VASE
Designed by Noke, this vase has a complicated Oriental-inspired glaze.
$$$$ • 10¾ in (27 cm) high

CAULDRON VASE
A chine-decorated vase with three short feet and shoulder handles.
$ • 4½ in (11.5 cm) high

Core Collectibles

DOULTON SUNG BOWL
This 1920s Charles Noke bowl is decorated with an exotic plumed bird in flambé glaze.

$$$ • 11 in (28 cm) in diameter

MOON FLASK
A rare 1936 stoneware Toby character moon flask with silver mounts.

$$$$ • 9¾ in (25 cm) high

"PARTNERS IN COLLECTING"
This Collectors Club Exclusive is a Royal Doulton "Partners in Collecting" Bunnykins figure from 1999. Depicting two rabbits in matching dresses, it comes boxed.

$$ • 3 in (7.5 cm) high

OWL JAR
A jar and cover in the form of an owl, painted in shades of brown, blue, and gray.

$$$$ • 8 in (20 cm) high

EDITH LUPTON VASE
Incised with stylized foliate forms of Islamic inspiration, this vase dates to 1888.

$$$ • 12 in (30 cm) high

KOALA BIBELOT
A koala bear sits on the edge of this colorfully painted circular dish.

$$ • 4½ in (11.5 cm) high

FRANK BUTLER BOWL
This bowl by Frank Butler has a compressed, lobed form incised with a foliate design.

$$$ • 8 in (20 cm) wide

"BUTTERFLY GIRL"
A Royal Doulton "Butterfly Girl HN 720" figure decked out in red and black, with printed and painted marks. This color variant is particularly effective and very popular.

$$$$ • 6½ in (16.5 cm) high

"OUT FOR A DUCK"
This 1995 "Out for a Duck" Bunnykins figure is from the Cricketers series.
$$ • 4 in (10 cm) high

"SLEEPYHEAD"
A scarce design by Margaret Davies, this figure was made between 1953 and 1955.
$$$$ • 5 in (12.5 cm) high

TOP TIPS

- Examine the mark on a Royal Doulton piece: if it has been crossed through or drilled to the center, this means the piece is a factory second and should cost less than a perfect example.
- Use the "teeth" test to find out if figures have been restored. A restored piece will feel soft and warm to the teeth, while one in mint condition will feel hard and cold.

Starter Buys

BUNNYKINS FIGURE
A Royal Doulton "Halloween" Bunnykins figure, 1993–97.
$ • 3¼ in (8 cm) high

"JAMES" FIGURE
"James," from Royal Doulton's Snowman collection.
$ • 3¾ in (9.5 cm) high

COOKIE JAR
Decorated with a frieze of horses, this stoneware cookie jar is by Hannah Barlow.
$$$ • 8 in (20 cm) high

BALUSTER VASE
Incised with the number "1042," this flambé baluster vase is decorated with carp.
$$$ • 7 in (18 cm) high

FLAMBÉ VASE
A vase with a pastoral scene, glazed in deep red and black.
$$$ • 6 in (15 cm) high

BLUE IRIS VASE
This vase is handpainted and printed with gilded highlights.
$$ • 6½ in (16.5 cm) high

"HIGHLAND SNOWMAN"
A jaunty Royal Doulton "Highland Snowman" figure with a painted kilt.
$$ • 5¼ in (13.5 cm) high

TWIN-HANDLED VASES
These baluster vases by Hannah Barlow are decorated with an incised frieze of cows.
$$$ • 13¾ in (35 cm) high

FAIENCE WARE VASES
These bright art pottery vases are handpainted with flowers.
$$ • 13½ in (34 cm) high

1930S STONEWARE
This stoneware vase is by artist Vera Huggins.
$$ • 15¼ in (38.5 cm) high

You may also like… Poole Pottery, see pp. 48–53

Poole Pottery

Poole Pottery's key designers across the 20th century have produced some of the most important decorative ceramics of the last 100 years—great news for collectors eyeing the firm's diverse range of wares.

Collectors of Poole Pottery are many and varied, owing to the sheer diversity of the company's output over its long history. Each generation has seen a new design development created in response to the fashions and trends of the day.

Poole Traditional wares provide some of the best Art Deco designs of the period. Prices now range from just a few pounds to a record $26,760 paid in 2001 for a 1926 vase by Anne Hatchard. Though prices have calmed a little in recent years, making it a good time to start collecting, the very strong abstracts are still fiercely fought over.

The Freeform wares of Alfred B. Read, with an elegance of design typical of the 1950s, are still greatly undervalued. Good examples can be bought for as little as $200 and are sure to appreciate.

The market remains strong for postwar pieces from the Delphis range, which have become very popular, as the bright, abstract patterns fit well with contemporary living. Look out, too, for the much rarer Studio wares, which were the early pieces in this hugely popular commercial range.

A Model Partnership

Phoebe Stabler and her husband were highly influential to the Poole factory during the interwar years. In 1912, Phoebe, a recognized figure modeler, set up a studio in Hammersmith, London, with Harold, her art designer and metalworker husband. Her range of sculptured figures would later be developed commercially by Poole in the 1920s, after the partnership of Carter, Stabler, and Adams was formed in 1921. The Stablers went on to help introduce an earthenware range and a series of figures and plaques at Poole, further raising the firm's profile in the British ceramic industry.

"PIPING BOY"
A rare Carter Stabler Adams Poole Pottery stoneware figure, designed by Phoebe Stabler, glazed in shades of blue, ocher, and buff, and bearing an impressed "CSA" mark.
$$$$ • 15 in (38 cm) high

KEY FACTS	1873	1881	1921	1961–66	1980s
Pots of painted pleasure	Jesse Carter buys T. W. Walker's Encaustic & Mosaic Ornamental Brick & Tile Co. in Poole, Dorset.	Carter's son Owen joins the firm. He will be highly influential in the firm's move to domestic wares.	The subsidiary firm of Carter Stabler Adams is established; Poole Pottery enters its Art Deco era.	The Studio range is introduced, and forms the basis of the acclaimed Delphis line, launched in 1966.	Changes in ownership take place, and most production moves to Stoke-on-Trent.

What's Hot

SHOULDERED VASE
A Carter Stabler Adams shouldered vase painted by Mary Brown.
$$$$ • 9½ in (24.5 cm) high

DELPHIS OWL PLATE
Decorated with an owl, this Delphis plate has printed and painted marks.
$$$$ • 10¾ in (27 cm) in diameter

Look out for:

The surge in production during the 1920s and '30s was predominantly thanks to the skills of Truda Carter, whose strong Art Deco designs won many international medals. On this model, the stepped handles reflect the influence of Aztec and ancient Egyptian designs.

Fully handpainted

Abstract floral patterns

DELPHIS PLATE
This Poole Pottery Delphis plate is decorated with a geometric design.
$$$ • 10½ in (26.5 cm) in diameter

TEXTURED VASE
Made in 1968, this early-period textured vase was painted by Angela Wyburgh.
$$$ • 15½ in (39.5 cm) high

RED EARTHENWARE VASE
Dating from 1928–34, this Carter Stabler Adams two-handled Poole Pottery vase was designed by Truda Carter, and is hand-painted in a lesser-known pattern, "995/CS."
$$$$ • 8¾ in (22 cm) high

What's Not

This range of Poole wares, while technically competent, has proved unpopular with modern collectors as items from the series have a typically '70s feel without the flair of the Delphis range. Ionian pieces remain affordable entry-level examples for the junior collector.

ART DECO PLATE
This hand-painted "Sugar for the Birds" pattern plate was designed by Olive Bourne.
$$$ • 10¾ in (27 cm) in diameter

"PIPING FAWN"
A rare relief-modeled roundel designed for Poole Pottery by Phoebe Stabler.
$$$$ • 15¾ in (40 cm) in diameter

STONEWARE BOWL
A small Ionian stoneware bowl with a stylized orchid design from the mid-1970s.
$ • 5¾ in (14.5 cm) in diameter

Core Collectibles

FREEFORM PLATE
This Poole Freeform plate was designed by Alfred Read, c. 1953–54.
$$ • 13 in (33 cm) in diameter

DELPHIS PLATE
This Delphis plate, produced in the 1960s and '70s, shows a geometric design.
$$ • 10½ in (26.5 cm) in diameter

SEAGULL DISH
Designed in three sizes by Sally Tuffin in 1998, this, the largest dish, is the rarest.
$$ • 14 in (35.5 cm) in diameter

TRUDA CARTER VASE
Made between 1928 and 1934, this handpainted red earthenware vase is in pattern "DR."
$$$$ • 8 in (20 cm) high

CAROL CUTLER DISH
A dish by Carol Cutler in shape 57, featuring a bold abstract design in the classic Delphis palette of the 1960s and '70s.
$$$ • 10½ in (26.5 cm) diameter

ART DECO CHARGER
This is a Poole Pottery Art Deco charger with an "SL" pattern from the 1920s and '30s, with painted marks and a firing crack.
$$$ • 15½ in (39 cm) in diameter

Ask the Expert

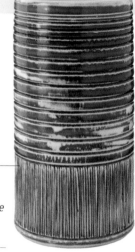

Carved pattern

1966 DELPHIS VASE
This vase, painted by Geraldine O'Meara, bears rare carved decoration in two directions.
$$ • *9 in (23 cm) high*

Q. What do the small painted marks on the base of my vase signify?
A. These are either the decorator's individual marks or, on early pieces, the pattern code.

Q. My Delphis vase has a printed number. Is this how many were made?
A. The number refers to the shape of the vase. Each Poole piece has a different number to identify it in the pattern record books.

Q. Why is some Delphis ware more valuable when it all looks very similar?
A. The more abstract the pattern, the more valuable the piece. Some simpler patterns are not as well executed. Unusual colors such as blue, black, green, and yellow tones can also be more valuable than the more common reds and oranges.

Q. My Delphis vase looks "runny." Is it a second?
A. No, there's nothing wrong with it, but it didn't fire well. The piece got too hot, making the handpainted pattern slip on the body of the vase.

FREEFORM VASE
A Freeform vase from the 1950s, decorated in Alfred Read's "PJB" pattern.

$$ • 7¾ in (19.5 cm) high

CYLINDER VASE
Painted green, gray, and rust, this cylindrical vase has impressed and painted marks.

$$$ • 12 in (30 cm) high

DELPHIS VASE
Painted by Irene Kerton, this 1960s vase is carved. Carving and the purple color are rare.

$$$ • 15½ in (39 cm) high

CARAFE VASE
This Poole Freeform vase in the "YFP" pattern has printed and painted marks.

$$ • 10¼ in (26 cm) high

EARTHENWARE VASE
Handpainted by Gwen Haskins, this is a 1949–50 "Persian Deer" pattern vase.

$$$ • 14¼ in (36 cm) high

1930S STONEWARE VASE
Dating from 1935, this vase has a stylized "Leaping Deer" pattern by Truda Carter.

$$$ • 8¼ in (21 cm) high

1970S ATLANTIS VASE
This shape A51 Atlantis vase by Catherine Connett has impressed and incised marks.

$$$ • 4 in (10 cm) high

CARTER STABLER ADAMS OVOID VASE
Painted in a colorful floral frieze, this 1930s Carter Stabler Adams Poole Pottery shouldered vase has impressed and painted marks.

$$$ • 7 in (18 cm) high

1930S ABSTRACT VASE
This 1930s vase bears a typical abstract pattern from Carter Stabler Adams.

$$$ • 7¼ in (18.5 cm) high

Core Collectibles

1930S VASE
This piece by Carter Stabler Adams has a floral design in blue, orange, and green.
$$$ • 6½ in (16.5 cm) high

ATLANTIS VASE
This 1970s Atlantis range vase with impressed marks was designed by Beatrice Bolton.
$$ • 4 in (10 cm) high

1950S FREEFORM VASE
Marked "Poole England 701," this is a peanut-shaped Freeform "PRB" vase.
$$$ • 12½ in (32 cm) high

FLORAL VASE
A 1930s Poole vase decorated with birds and flowers.
$$ • 6 in (15 cm) high

1930S PAINTED VASE
A Carter Stabler Adams "BX" pattern vase.
$$$ • 10 in (25.5 cm) high

"VIKING" VASE
A 1999 "Viking" vase by Karen Brown, exclusive to the Poole Collectors Club.
$$ • 8½ in (21.5 cm) high

AEGEAN GRAY VASE
Dated 1976–78, this vase by Carol Cutler has an unusual shape, color, and pattern.
$$$ • 9 in (23 cm) high

LIMITED-EDITION PLATE
This late-1990s plate was designed by Tony Morris and painted by Nicola Massarella.
$$$ • 14 in (35.5 cm) in diameter

SOMMERFELT PLATE
A unique 1970s Poole Pottery Aegean charger painted by Ros Sommerfelt.
$$$ • 13 in (33 cm) in diameter

CYLINDRICAL VASE
A 1930s vase painted with gazelles leaping through flowering foliage.
$$$ • 7½ in (18.5 cm) high

AEGEAN CHARGER
A unique 1970s charger by Ros Sommerfelt, a sought-after Aegean-range painter.
$$ • 13 in (33 cm) in diameter

1960S SHIELD DISH
A 1960s shape 91 Delphis shield dish. The bold lines and bright colors are characteristic of items from the Delphis range.
$$ • 12 in (30 cm) long

DELPHIS DISH
This 1967 Delphis dish by Ann Godfrey has a textured, bubbled glaze. Note the simple but effective decorative abstract pattern.
$$ • 8 in (20 cm) in diameter

DELPHIS CHARGER
Painted by Sally Merch, this Poole Pottery Delphis charger from 1968–69 has textured decoration. Abstract designs such as these are a typical Delphis feature.
$$ • 14 in (35.5 cm) in diameter

Starter Buys

DELPHIS PLATE
Dating to 1966, this shape 3 plate was painted by Geraldine O'Meara.
$$ • 8 in (20 cm) in diameter

HAND-POTTED VASE
Made between 1964–70, this shape 83 Delphis vase is by Christine Tate.
$$ • 6 in (15 cm) high

SHIELD DISH
Painted by Carol Cutler, this shape 91 Delphis shield dish dates from 1969–75.
$$ • 12 in (30 cm) long

1930S OGEE SHAPED VASE
A boldly painted vase with a broad band of stylized flowers and leaves on a white ground.
$$ • 4¾ in (12 cm) high

You may also like… British Studio Ceramics, see pp. 78–79

Cornishware

With its distinctive, clean lines, Cornishware has remained quietly fashionable for more than 80 years. Widely collected, this range of domestic wares continues to prove popular in today's market.

Around 1925, T. G. Green & Co., makers of domestic ceramics, introduced a modest range of decorative tablewares and kitchenwares. This was Cornishware, and it would prove one of the firm's most successful products. With its simple lines and no-nonsense approach to kitchen service, it quickly became a must for the modern kitchen.

Over the years, the product has sustained a popularity rarely seen in the domestic interior market. A number of variants were created by the firm, which have their own following; however, the instantly recognizable Cornishware, with its distinctive blue-and-white-banded body, remains the most sought after.

The clean, no-nonsense appeal of these wares means that collectors can create a dramatic display that is also functional. Simple, plain jars can be purchased cheaply and are perfect for stashing your cookies. Get hooked, however, and rare examples could set you back hundreds of dollars.

Time for Tea

There were no limits to the weird and wonderful objects made with the famous blue and white bands. Today, it's the unusual early domestic gadgets that command some of the highest values. Also watch for rare navy blue, black, and orange colorways.

CLOVERLEAF TEAPOT
The Cornishware teapots were introduced in the 1960s. This one has a Cloverleaf stamp on its base.
$ • 5 in (12.5 cm) high

TOP TIPS

- Watch out for common signs of wear, as these affect value.
- Be aware of fakes, especially those printed with rarer names. The lettering often doesn't match the genuine font.
- Be cautious about buying on Internet auction sites: "Cornish Ware" is used to describe similarly styled blue-and-white wares.

KEY FACTS	1864	1880s	c. 1925	1960–61	2007
From Green to Cornish blue	Thomas Goodwin Green founds T. G. Green & Co. in an old pottery works in South Derbyshire.	Green builds a new factory to rival the competing potteries of Stoke-on-Trent.	The firm launches the Cornishware range, which soon becomes the company's most successful line.	Traditional globe teapot designs are replaced by the now-famous straight-sided Cornishware version.	T. G. Green & Co Ltd., now owned by Cloverleaf, goes into administration, ceasing production.

What's Hot

SPICE JAR
A Cornishware ginger spice jar with a lid and a T. G. Green stamp on its base.
$$ • 2½ in (6.5 cm) high

1960S CAFETIÈRE
This Cornishware cafetière was made for the Australian market in the 1960s.
$$ • 7½ in (19 cm) high

Look out for:
Names are everything when it comes to judging the value of a piece, and jars are some of the most desired objects. Clients could request their own unique labels, so look for rarities such as "Borax," "Pimento Seeds," and "Curry."

The famous blue, said to mirror that of the Cornish skies

STORAGE JAR
A rare Cornishware meal storage jar with a lid and a T. G. Green stamp on its base.
$$$ • 7 in (17.5 cm) high

Core Collectibles

SUGAR SIFTER
A Cornishware sugar sifter with a screwtop lid, made from the 1930s to the 1960s.
$$ • 5½ in (14 cm) high

MEASURING JUG
A classic Cornishware measuring jug with a T. G. Green stamp on its base.
$$ • 4¾ in (12 cm) high

Starter Buys

SIMPLE BEAKER
A Cornishware beaker with a T. G. Green stamp on its base.
$ • 4 in (10 cm) high

OLIVE OIL BOTTLE
This bottle was made by the Cornish Collectors Club.
$$ • 7¼ in (18.5 cm) high

ROLLING PIN
A Cornishware rolling pin, one of the more sought-after items in the entire range.
$$ • Barrel 9¾ in (24.5 cm) long

CHEESE DISH
A Cornishware cheese dish with a T. G. Green stamp on the base of the plate.
$$ • 8½ in (21.5 cm) wide

FLOUR JAR
A T. G. Green lidded jar, with the maker's stamp on its base.
$$ • 7 in (17.5 cm) high

RICE JAR
A lidded rice jar with a T. G. Green stamp on its base.
$$ • 4 in (10 cm) high

You may also like… Kitchenalia, see pp. 170–75

Carlton Ware

For over 100 years, the Carlton Ware Pottery in Stoke-on-Trent produced quality ceramics geared to the fashions of the day, creating an incredibly varied legacy of designs, and providing a broad choice for collectors.

Carlton Ware pieces range from the sober Victorian blush ware of the company's youth to the comic "Walking Ware" of the 1970s. Carlton Ware's golden years came between the two world wars, when the firm excelled in the production of high-quality decorative ceramics at the forefront of the Art Deco movement. The fine slipcast forms of this period were decorated with lithographic transfer patterns and detailed hand enameling, and highlighted with expensive oxide and precious-metal glazes. While Carlton Ware of this period is extremely desirable, it is possible to pick up some of the more common pieces without spending a fortune. The novelty ware of the postwar years—such as the pottery's famous Guinness pieces—has a charm of its own, and can be very popular at auction. The market is currently low for the top-end pieces, making this a good time to buy rare examples.

The 1990s saw the firm bankrupted and almost closed. However, in 1997 it was acquired by antiques publisher Francis Joseph, who continued to produce quality wares in the Carlton tradition.

TOMB JAR & COVER
A Carlton Ware tomb jar and cover, in the "Tutankhamun" style (pattern number 2711). Hieroglyphics and Egyptian figures are reproduced in gilt and enamel on a blue glaze background.
$$$$$ • 12½ in (32 cm) high

Egyptian Promise

The discovery of the tomb of King Tutankhamun in 1922 sparked a fascination across Europe with all things Egyptian. At around the same time, Carlton Ware was introducing new techniques, using painted and lithographic patterns applied to a high-glaze base layer. The decorative pieces that resulted mimicked both the intricate hieroglyphics and the vivid gold, ochers, and lapis lazuli of Tutankhamun's treasures. The colors and forms of these pieces remain enduringly popular to this day.

KEY FACTS	1890	1919–34	1960s	1970s	1997
High-fashion ceramics	Partners J. F. Wiltshaw and J. A. Robinson found the Carlton Ware Pottery.	Developments in style and technique make Carlton Ware a household name.	The recession and the death of Cuthbert Wiltshaw see the firm taken over by Arthur Wood & Son.	The "Walking Ware" series is introduced, bringing a resurgence in popularity.	The company goes into liquidation and is acquired by publisher Francis Joseph.

What's Hot

"FLORAL COMETS" VASE
A "Floral Comets" vase, pattern number 3422, with printed and painted marks.
$$$$ • 6 in (15 cm) high

"FLORAL COMETS" JAR
A Carlton Ware ginger jar in the "Floral Comets" pattern, dating to the 1920s.
$$$$ • 5¼ in (13.5 cm) high

Look out for:

The "Red Devil" pattern, number 3765, from the key inter-war period, remains one of the most eagerly sought by collectors. The devil figure has become an emblem for the new firm, popular with collectors of modern Carlton Ware.

Gilt lithograph transfer work

GINGER JAR AND COVER
A large "Chinaland" ginger jar and cover by Carlton Ware, pattern number 3530. The jar is supported by a wooden base. It has some minor wear to the shoulders, but its size and vivid colors maintain its high value.
$$$$ • 12½ in (32 cm) high

"RED DEVIL" BOWL
A 1930s bowl in the "Red Devil" pattern. The value of this piece is enhanced by the preservation of the original paper label.
$$$$ • 9¼ in (23.5 cm) in diameter

What's Not

This postwar dish was made in huge quantities. Its relative abundance, combined with its simple, kitsch decoration, make it a low priority for most collectors.

LEAF DISH
This Carlton Ware dish in a light-blue glaze is leaf-shaped, with a gilt stalk and veining.
$ • 13¾ in (35 cm) long

"PAN" CIRCULAR CHARGER
This circular Handcraft charger is painted in the "Pan" pattern of a seated faun playing panpipes in an exotic floral and foliate landscape.
$$$$ • 15 in (38 cm) in diameter

"FANTASIA" WALL PLAQUE
This Art Deco wall plaque in the "Fantasia" pattern, number 3388, has its original paper label. The back foot rim has been repaired.
$$$$ • 15¾ in (40 cm) in diameter

Core Collectibles

"EGYPTIAN FAN" VASE
Carlton Ware "Egyptian Fan" vase, pattern number 3696.
$$$ • 7½ in (19 cm) high

ART DECO OVOID VASE
A classic late-1920s vase in the "Floral Comets" pattern.
$$$ • 5¼ in (13.5 cm) high

DECO WATER JUG
A jug in the "Tiger Tree" pattern, number 4163.
$$ • 8 in (20 cm) high

GINGER JAR AND COVER
This jar shows pattern number 3449, "Prickly Pansy."
$$$ • 11 in (28 cm) high

"SKETCHING BIRD" VASE
An ovoid vase decorated in the "Sketching Bird" pattern, number 3890.
$$$ • 7½ in (19 cm) high

"BELL FLOWER" VASE
Carlton Ware vase decorated with the "Bell Flower" pattern, number 3738.
$$$ • 4¾ in (12 cm) high

DECORATIVE JUG
This jug is decorated in the "Mandarins Chatting" pattern, number 3654.
$$$ • 7¼ in (18 cm) high

"JAGGED BOUQUET" VASE
This Carlton Ware "Jagged Bouquet" vase, pattern number 3457, is decorated with a matt green underglaze. The pattern combines painted decoration and gilt lithographic transfers.
$$$ • 6 in (15 cm) high

PEDESTAL BOWL
A pedestal bowl in the "Chinese Bird and Cloud" pattern, number 3275.
$$$ • 9¾ in (25 cm) high

"CHEVRON" VASE
A "Chevron" vase, pattern number 3657, in gloss green, black, and silver.
$$$ • 4¼ in (10.5 cm) high

"HOLLYHOCKS" JUG
An ovoid jug decorated with the "Hollyhocks" pattern, number 3972.
$$ • 7½ in (19 cm) high

"SWALLOW AND CLOUD" JAR AND COVER
This ginger jar and its cover are decorated in the "Swallow and Cloud" pattern, number 3073.
$$$ • 8 in (20 cm) high

TOP TIPS
- Be aware that decoration on enameled pieces can be prone to flaking off.
- Guinness ware was widely forged in the 1990s, so check provenance carefully.
- Note that luster wares marked "Royale" were only introduced after 1940, and are not true Art Deco pieces.

"LACE CAP HYDRANGEA" DISH
Decorated in the "Lace Cap Hydrangea" pattern, this twin-handled decorative dish has printed and painted patterns.
$$ • 10 in (25 cm) wide

Starter Buys

VASE AND COVER
A vase and its cover decorated with Rouge Royale coloring and floral motifs. This item retains its original paper label.
$$ • 11 in (28 cm) high

AZTEC-STYLE DISH
This Aztec-style dish shows Carlton's "New Anemone" pattern, number 4219.
$$ • 12 in (30 cm) wide

"CUBIST BUTTERFLY" DISH
This 1930s square dish in the "Cubist Butterfly" pattern has a gloss orange underglaze.
$$ • 11¼ in (28.5 cm) wide

ROUGE ROYALE VASE
This baluster vase, decorated in the "Chinese Tea Garden" pattern, shows Carlton's Rouge Royale coloring.
$$ • 12½ in (32 cm) high

"HOLLYHOCKS" BOWL
A gloss green Art Deco bowl decorated in the "Hollyhocks" pattern, number 3973.
$$ • 10 in (25 cm) in diameter

"SPRINGTIME" DISH
A 1930s Carlton Ware "Springtime" dish with a decoration of crocuses.
$$ • 6¾ in (17 cm) wide

You may also like… Clarice Cliff, see pp. 22–27

Chintzware

Taking their name from a centuries-old Indian fabric, chintzware ceramics are distinctive among collectibles for their bold all-over floral patterns evoking images of garden tea parties of the 1920s and '30s.

In the 1920s, a new interpretation of floral ceramics created a craze that would sweep across the Staffordshire potteries and the world at large. From then until the 1960s, a huge number of chintz patterns were produced by firms such as Royal Winton, James Kent, and Crown Ducal, makers recognized today as leading exponents of the style.

The full range of chintz domestic wares and tablewares, including trays, jugs, and cookie jars, provides the modern-day enthusiast with a wide range of options when collecting. And with so many pieces produced during the heyday of chintz, collectors will often find chintzwares widely available at accessible prices. Watch for rare variants of popular patterns that may have proved less popular when first created, and which are today avidly sought after by collectors. The renewed interest in chintz in recent years has resulted in a number of fakes on the market, however, so buyers should be cautious.

Sweet Summer on a Plate

Chintz derives from a Hindu word meaning "many colored." Following the huge increase in chintzware's popularity, a number of rare color variants were created to extend the life of a favorite pattern. Look for these unusual examples for a higher market value.

"SWEET PEA" PLATE
Marked for Australia on the back, this "Sweet Pea" pattern plate is by Royal Winton. The plates with a blue rim are dated earlier and are more desirable.
$$ • 8¾ in (22.5 cm) wide

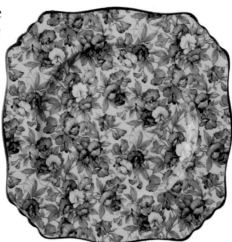

TOP TIPS

- Keep an eye on trends, as patterns tend to go in and out of fashion.
- Check that rare stacking tea sets have not been made up with unrelated pieces. Component pieces should all fit snugly and line up neatly.
- Watch out for signs of wear, such as a loss of color, which affect the value of the pieces.

KEY FACTS	1800s	1920s	1928	1940s	1995
Chintz for all seasons	The fashion for transfer-decorated wares becomes popular across many Staffordshire potteries.	Chintz becomes highly fashionable as a decoration for matching different domestic wares.	The Royal Winton pottery introduces "Marguerite," its first dedicated chintz pattern.	Tastes change after World War II. Quaint chintzware falls out of fashion, and is replaced by plastic.	Royal Winton relaunches its chintzware range with new patterns. Chintz is blooming once again.

What's Hot

COFFEE POT
This Royal Winton "White Crocus" pattern coffee pot dates from the 1940s.
$$$ • 8¼ in (21 cm) high

LAMP BASE
A 1930s Royal Winton "Cotswold" pattern lamp base, with replaced hardware.
$$$ • 13 in (33 cm) high

Look out for:
These small Royal Winton bedside sets were very popular in the 1920s and '30s. Complete original sets are rare because of the number of small pieces included in a set.

Transfer colors match across the set

Core Collectibles

CHEESE DISH
This Royal Winton "Mayfair" pattern cheese dish dates from the 1940s and '50s.
$$ • Tray 6½ in (16.5 cm) wide

SWEETMEAT BASKET
A Royal Winton "Kew" pattern chintz sweetmeat basket from the 1940s.
$$ • 5 in (12.5 cm) wide

BEDSIDE SET
This is a 1940s–50s Royal Winton "Old Cottage Chintz" pattern bedside set or tea-for-one set.
$$$ • Tray 10½ in (26.5 cm) wide

Starter Buys

TOAST RACK
This Grimwades piece is in typically bright colors.
$$ • 6 in (15 cm) long

COOKIE JAR
A mid-1930s Crown Clarence "Briar Rose" cookie jar.
$$ • 6½ in (16.5 cm) high

CRUET SET
The "Cranstone" pattern on this cruet set covers the whole piece, including the sides.
$$ • 6 in (15 cm) long

TENNIS TEA SET
This "Hydrangea" pattern tennis tea set by James Kent is from the 1930s.
$$ • Tray 8¾ in (22 cm) wide

CUP AND SAUCER
A 1930s "Marguerite" pattern cup and saucer.
$ • 3 in (7.5 cm) high

BLOSSOM PLATE
A James Kent "Apple Blossom" plate, 1930s.
$ • 8¾ in (22 cm) in diameter

You may also like… Doulton, see pp. 44–47

SylvaC

From plump rabbits to terriers with toothaches, SylvaC created a range of distinctive household novelties—a small slice of affordable fun. Growing interest has seen prices steadily increase for these novel characters.

Over many years, Shaw & Copestake created a catalog of affordable domestic wares and ornaments produced under the trademark SylvaC. While the factory designed and produced vases, posy troughs, and similar body wares, it is best known today for its huge range of comic animal characters.

Richard Hull, who became a partner in 1903, was responsible for many developments in glaze techniques, along with the modeling of the novelty range. The arrival of his son at the firm in 1935, and the artistic talents of Reginald Thompson and Otakar Steinberger, saw the introduction of some of the most popular models of this era, including the seated rabbit series and "Mac" the terrier.

The sheer volume of SylvaC available makes it a simple area to start collecting: just a few well-spent dollars can create an instant collection. However, the select rarities mean that you can spend into the hundreds developing your collection.

Common Domestic & Rare Wild

The huge menagerie of animals produced by SylvaC over many years covered virtually every type of creature imaginable. While the rabbits have become familiar to collectors, and many breeds of dogs were produced, the more unusual animals have proven harder to find. They were less popular in their day, so fewer were produced, making them difficult to acquire today. When this is combined with an unusual color, such as blue or flambé red, you have a top piece for your collection that will help to develop it into something special, but that is likely to prove expensive. More common tan, orange, and green pieces are more reasonably priced for those starting a collection.

BLUE HIPPO
This piece, stamped "1425," is rare on two counts—its shape and its color.

$$ • 2 in (5 cm) high

KEY FACTS	1894	1902	1903	1938–57	1982
Powers behind the winsome creatures	William Shaw forms the Sheaf Art Pottery Co. in Longton, hand-decorating mass-produced wares.	William Copestake joins Shaw to form Shaw & Copestake, only to leave after just six months.	Richard Hull Sr. joins Shaw as his new business partner, buying out Copestake's share and developing exports.	The firm acquires the Thomas Lawrence (Longton Ltd.) Falcon Pottery and builds a new factory.	The firm goes into voluntary liquidation and all records of styles and production dates are destroyed.

What's Hot

GREEN HARE
This rare green hare is stamped "1300 MADE IN ENGLAND."
$$$ • 9¾ in (25 cm) high

"JOEY DOG"
Dating from the 1930s, this large example is in the rare blue glaze.
$$ • 5¼ in (13.5 cm) high

Look out for:
Produced for more than 40 years, SylvaC's rabbits have remained one of the most popular of all the animal series. Early rabbits had a matt glaze until a gloss finish appeared in the 1970s. Created in a huge range of sizes and variants, they are a key item for any SylvaC collection.

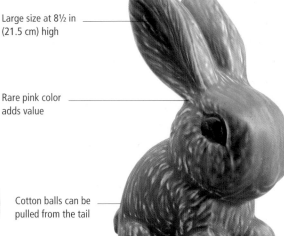

Large size at 8½ in (21.5 cm) high

Rare pink color adds value

Cotton balls can be pulled from the tail

FLAMBÉ FROG
This frog, stamped with its model number, 1399, is in a rare flambé glaze.
$$ • 2 in (5 cm) high

SEATED PIGEON
A rare SylvaC green seated pigeon, stamped with its model number, 1376.
$$ • 3¼ in (8.5 cm) high

PINK RABBIT
This large SylvaC pink rabbit cotton ball holder is stamped "1027 MADE IN ENGLAND." Pink is very rare and one of the most sought-after colors; tan and green are more common.
$$$ • 8½ in (21.5 cm) high

What's Not

Considered kitsch today, this range—a wink to the pebbledash exteriors of many 1970s British houses—is out of fashion with collectors. These planters enjoyed some success when first produced and hence are common on the market.

GREEN ELEPHANT
This is a rare green version of model 770, which was usually glazed in black.
$$$ • 9¾ in (25 cm) wide

CACTUS
This rare two-color SylvaC miniature of a cactus in a beige pot is stamped "738."
$$ • 5 in (12.5 cm) high

SYLVAC JARDINIÈRE
This SylvaC jardinière stamped "3414" is from the Pebble range.
$ • 6¾ in (17 cm) wide

Core Collectibles

CREAM TERRIER
An unusual SylvaC cream terrier stamped "1378"—one of more than 200 dog models.
$ • 5 in (13 cm) high

KOALA BEAR
This rare koala, model 1391, is in one of the factory's most common colors.
$$ • 6 in (15 cm) high

"FLAT CAT"
This SylvaC "Flat Cat," stamped "2722," has clever cutouts to mimic the whites of the character's eyes. It is part of a set of three different-sized figures, c. 1961.
$$ • 5 in (12.5 cm) high

BLUE SEATED DOG
This SylvaC large-headed blue seated dog with shaded decoration is stamped "1117."
$$ • 6¼ in (16 cm) high

"COMICAL DACHSHUND"
A stone-colored SylvaC "Comical Dachshund," stamped "3175."
$$ • 5½ in (14 cm) high

GREEN PUPPY
This puppy was made in a number of different colors. It is stamped "1646."
$ • 5 in (12 cm) wide

Ask the Expert

Q. How did SylvaC come to make their popular rabbits?
A. While traveling through France, Richard Hull came across a stylized figure of a seated rabbit. He recognized the commercial value of this figure and, on his return to England, developed the first bunny for the SylvaC works. The instant appeal of this figure lasted for more than 40 years, during which the firm produced them in a huge range of sizes, from this tiny example through to its much larger brother.

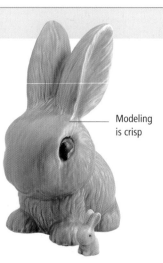

Modeling is crisp

GREEN AND FAWN RABBITS
Stamped "1400," these pieces show the largest and smallest rabbits produced.
$$ • L 9¾ in (25 cm) , R 2 in (5 cm) high

Q. How can I tell if my SylvaC rabbit is genuine?
A. While other companies including Denby Pottery created their own versions, SylvaC are easy to identify from the clear markings to the base. Be wary, however, of fakes that have crept onto the market in recent years. These are identifiable from their poor glazing and lack of clear marks.

LOP-EARED RABBIT
This yellow rabbit, stamped "1302," is one of SylvaC's many rabbit varieties.

$ • 5¾ in (14.5 cm) high

"MR. SYLVAC" ASHTRAY
500 "Mr. SylvaC" ashtrays were produced in 1964. They are stamped "3542."

$$ • 8 in (20 cm) high

FRUIT FACE POT
A SylvaC "Raspberry" face pot—one of a range of jam pots—stamped "4898."

$$ • 3¾ in (9.5 cm) high

"FLAPPER GIRL"
Stamped "880," this "Flapper Girl" has a cellulose-painted finish common to the early SylvaC novelties. As this finish is easily damaged, a pristine-condition figurine is particularly rare.

$$ • 8¾ in (22 cm) high

TARTAR SAUCE FACE POT
This popular household novelty—a tartar sauce face pot—is stamped "4915."

$$ • 3¾ in (9.5 cm) high

"BEE" HONEY POT
This SylvaC "Bee" honey pot with a removable head is stamped "5383."

$$ • 5 in (13 cm) high

SEATED HORSE
Though rabbits and dogs were especially popular, the SylvaC ceramic menagerie included many other animals. This green seated horse is stamped and marked "SylvaC England."

$$ • 6¾ in (17 cm) long

CELLULOSE "BILLIKEN"
Identified by curly ears and a pointy head, this "Billiken" (1222) is a good-luck figure.

$$ • 4¼ in (11 cm) high

Core Collectibles

BREAD SAUCE FACE POT
This face pot stamped "4551" was also produced stamped with "4557."
$$ • 4¼ in (10.5 cm) high

"COMICAL DACHSHUND"
A SylvaC blue "Comical Dachshund," stamped "1332." This figurine successfully captures the amusing aspects of the sausage dog, exaggerating its leanness with a long tail.
$$ • 5 in (12.5 cm) long

"BEETROOT" FACE POT
One of a variety of SylvaC face pots, this "Beetroot" face pot is stamped "4553."
$ • 5¾ in (14.5 cm) high

"MAC DOG"
Stamped "1207," this green "Mac Dog" is the middle size in a series of five.
$$ • 7¾ in (19.5 cm) high

DOG'S HEAD CRUET SET
Part of the Dog's Head range, this SylvaC cruet set, with space for salt, pepper, and sauce, is stamped "1715." The range also included toast racks and jam pots.
$$ • 7¾ in (19.5 cm) wide

"GOOFY"
This stone-colored "Goofy" with perked-up ears is stamped "3182."
$$ • 5½ in (13.5 cm) high

SQUIRREL AND ACORN
The largest in a set of five, this is stamped "1146" and also exists as a cotton ball holder.
$$ • 7¾ in (19.5 cm) high

"FRIGHTENED CAT"
This orange cellulose-painted SylvaC "Frightened Cat" is stamped "1048."
$$ • 6 in (15 cm) high

BOXING CAT
A SylvaC boxing cat on its hind legs, stamped "184," with a fawn glaze.
$$ • 5 in (12.5 cm) high

FAWN SEATED MULE
This fawn-colored and tinted seated smiling mule is stamped "183."
$$ • 5¾ in (14.5 cm) high

POSY HOLDER

This "Lazy Pixie and Watering Can" SylvaC posy holder is stamped "2277."

$ • 3¼ in (8 cm) high

BLUE TERRIER

A SylvaC blue terrier, stamped "1378." This model came in a variety of colors, including fawn, green, cream, and the rare chocolate brown.

$ • 5 in (13 cm) high

1930S LADY

From the 1930s, this SylvaC cellulose-painted lady is stamped "881."

$$ • 9½ in (24 cm) high

Starter Buys

"ONION" FACE POT

Stamped "516," this was the first face pot produced by SylvaC in the 1950s.

$ • 4 in (10 cm) high

"SEALYHAM DOG"

Green in color, this SylvaC "Sealyham Dog" posy holder is stamped "2024."

$ • 7¼ in (18.5 cm) wide

FAWN RABBIT

This fawn rabbit is stamped "MADE IN ENGLAND 1026B" and printed "SYLVAC."

$$ • 6¾ in (17 cm) high

"TOBY" TOOTHACHE DOG

Stamped "3183," this is the smallest of three sizes. The largest size is often faked.

$ • 4¾ in (12 cm) high

MUSHROOM JUG

Stamped "1196," this early version is a dark green, with gnomes forming the handle.

$ • 9 in (23 cm) high

FAWN DOG

A SylvaC fawn dog, stamped "2975." Fawn was a common color for SylvaC novelties.

$ • 7 in (18 cm) wide

You may also like… Beswick, see pp. 72–75

Worcester

Worcester is synonymous with not only a beautiful cathedral city but also some of the finest porcelain ever created. Admired across the world, Royal Worcester wares are some of the most desired pieces in existence.

Porcelain made at Worcester is highly regarded no matter the period in which it was made. Its history features many different factories, owners, and designers, all producing valuable work. For this reason, collectors often form distinct historically based groups, and choosing a period to specialize in is a good starting point for new enthusiasts.

The choices for collectors of Worcester are wide and varied, from early-period pickle dishes to the figurines of Freda Doughty. While 18th-century

wares will always command high prices, they are rare and difficult to acquire. Today, collectors are competing for the highly decorated wares of the late 19th and 20th century. While items from this period are readily available, steadily rising prices make this one of the strongest international markets.

Matching Pairs

Whatever the subject, pairs are instantly more appealing to collectors. As such, it's worth checking that you have a true pair. Make sure that the marks on the base are identical: a pair of this quality should have been created at the factory at the same time and bear matching marks. Furthermore, pairs should complement each other, with the pattern flowing in opposing directions.

PAIR OF TWO-HANDLED URNS
A fine pair of English Royal Worcester covered urns by Frank Southell dating from 1900, each painted with peacocks among foliage and with gilt borders throughout.

$$$$$ • 5 in (12.5 cm) high

KEY FACTS	1751	1789	1862	20th century	2006
Grand designs across the centuries	Physician John Wall forms the first Worcester porcelain factory with a team of 15 men.	King George III awards Worcester with its first Royal Warrant. The firm still produces by Royal appointment.	After a number of changes of management and ownership, the "Royal Worcester" brand is formed.	The company merges with Spode and the original workshop loses workers to overseas competition.	A pair of Royal Worcester vases by George Owen realize $102,000 at auction in New York.

What's Hot

Look out for:

The Stinton family includes some of the most famous artists to have worked at Royal Worcester. John Junior and Harry, in particular, are known for their depictions of cattle and landscapes, and James for his various game-bird scenes.

Unusual intact cover

Characteristic Stinton landscape decoration

Body highlighted with expensive gilding

FLAT BACK JUG
This Royal Worcester flat back jug from 1902 is signed by top artist Charles Baldwin.
$$$$ • 5¼ in (13 cm) high

POTPOURRI VASE
Painted with roses and signed "Sedgley," this covered vase is from 1922.
$$$$ • 9¼ in (23.5 cm) high

WALTER POWELL PLATE
Made in 1909, this plate by Walter Powell is painted with storks drinking from a stream.
$$$$ • 10 in (25.5 cm) in diameter

RETICULATED VASE
This late-19th-century vase by George Owen is decorated with pierced panels.
$$$$ • 4¾ in (12 cm) high

ROYAL WORCESTER OVOID COVERED VASE
Painted in colored enamels by John Stinton and showing Highland cattle in a mountainous landscape, this vase has two leaf scroll handles, a pointed knob, and gilt borders.
$$$$ • 9¾ in (25 cm) high

What's Not

This piece with rolled-leaf handles is decorated in a blush palette, a shade that has fallen out of favor with collectors. Furthermore, it is intended as a jardinière, which is less desirable to display.

HARRY DAVIES VASES
A pair of large vases from 1909 signed "H. Davies," each with a gilt-edged cartouche.
$$$$$ • 11½ in (29 cm) high

CYLINDRICAL-FORM VASE
One of a pair of cylindrical-form vases with pierced rims and four acanthus scroll feet.
$$$ • 8¼ in (21.5 cm) high

LEAF MOLDED VASE
A Royal Worcester vase from 1900 with three leaf handles and three-color decorations.
$$ • 6¼ in (16 cm) wide

Core Collectibles

FLORAL PLATE
This 20th-century plate is painted with flowers in a garden, and signed "Rushton."
$$$ • 10¾ in (27.5 cm) in diameter

LANDSCAPE PLATE
Painted and signed by Frank R. Rushton, this 1935 plate has an acid-etched gilt rim.
$$$ • 10½ in (27 cm) in diameter

HADLEY'S VASE
This Hadley's Worcester baluster vase has a gilt rim and is painted with roses.
$$ • 3¾ in (9.5 cm) high

ROSE JARDINIÈRE
Painted with sprays of roses, this jardinière with a molded scroll border dates to 1912.
$$$ • 6¾ in (17 cm) high

PEDESTAL VASE AND COVER
This large two-handled vase with cover is painted with a wide panel of brilliantly colored birds within a gilt cartouche. The body of the vase is pale blue, with deep-blue scrolls and gilt.
$$$$ • 17 in (43 cm) high

STINTON BOTTLE VASE
Dated 1915, this Harry Stinton bottle vase has a gilt rim and is painted with Highland cattle.
$$$ • 6 in (15 cm) high

LARGE BLUSH VASE
Decorated with colorful flowers on shaded ground, this vase is from 1906.
$$$ • 13½ in (34 cm) high

BLUSH VASES
This pair of Royal Worcester blush vases is painted with birds perched on raised gilt branches. Gilt edging has been used on the base and rims as well.
$$$ • 3¼ in (8.5 cm) wide

PEDESTAL VASE
A small Royal Worcester vase, shape 202, with gilt handles and base, c. 1918.
$$ • 5½ in (14 cm) high

IVORY GROUND JUG
This jug is decorated with painted flowers and gilt on ivory ground, c. 1893.
$$ • 9 in (23 cm) high

TOP TIPS

• Learn the Royal Worcester dating system of letter and dots marked on the base, used between 1867 and 1963, to easily identify the year of production.
• Be aware of concealed repairs. The fineness of the porcelain means shadows implying restorative work will show up when the piece is held up to the light.

Starter Buys

CUP AND SAUCER
A demi-tasse cup and saucer with handpainted roses, dating from 1925.
$$$ • 3¾ in (9.5 cm) in diameter

SQUAT VASE
A Royal Worcester squat vase painted with blackberries by Micky Miller, c. 1953.
$$ • 3 in (7.5 cm) high

OVAL HANDLED DISH
A lobed two-handled dish from 1937 painted in colored enamels by H. H. Price.
$$$ • 12¼ in (31 cm) wide

"PETER PAN" FIGURINE
A Royal Worcester figure of "Peter Pan" modeled by F. G. Doughty, shape no. 3011.
$$ • 8 in (20 cm) high

PERSIAN-INSPIRED VASE
Dating back to 1889, this is a Persian-inspired vase decorated with floral sprays.
$$ • 7¼ in (18.5 cm) high

CABINET PLATE
This plate, painted with fruit by Freeman, has a gilded gadrooned border.
$$$ • 9½ in (24 cm) in diameter

JAMES STINTON PLATE
A James Stinton plate, c. 1911, painted with grouse in a rural landscape.
$$$ • 9¼ in (23.5 cm) in diameter

BALUSTER VASE
This Royal Worcester baluster vase no. 285 is handpainted with blackberries.
$$ • 4¼ in (10.5 cm) high

FLAT BACK JUG
A bulbous-shaped jug with a gilt reeded handle and foliate decoration.
$$ • 5 in (13 cm) high

You may also like… Historical Ceramics, see pp. 88–89

Beswick

Beswick is internationally known for its "storybook" and animal figures—including the famous Beatrix Potter range—whose constant appeal and quality have ensured their success with collectors of all ages.

In 1961 the *Pottery Gazette* recorded, "No potter formed in the last century is more likely to be of future interest to collectors than… the House of Beswick." In today's collector-based market, this prophecy has proved true. Beswick is one of the most eagerly contested ceramics manufacturers of recent years, with its immense range of figures allowing all, whether novice or seasoned collector, to take part.

Formed in 1894, the company's fortunes changed in 1934 with the introduction of the first high-fired bone china figures. Early examples were comic, but the introduction of Arthur Gredington's rearing "Horseman" saw the firm move toward realistic modeling, which proved highly popular. The year 1948 saw the second key development when John Beswick's daughter, Lucy, said she would like her favorite Beatrix Potter characters turned into figures. The figures were an instant success across the world and production ran for many years.

Unusual Colors

Designed by Beswick's legendary designer, Arthur Gredington, this "Walking Racehorse" figure was finally discontinued in 1976. This version is particularly rare, owing to the unusual colorway of the jockey's silks, combined with the palomino finish on the horse. Today these figures remain very popular, not only with Beswick collectors but with many members of the horse-racing fraternity as well.

"WALKING RACEHORSE"
A Beswick figure of a palomino horse and its jockey, in colorway 2. This is a rare color combination; the more commonly seen jockeys have green silks.
$$$ • 6½ in (16.5 cm) high

KEY FACTS	1894	1930s	1948	1952	1969
Telling tales in porcelain	The John Beswick Pottery is founded in Stoke-on-Trent, producing tableware and ornaments.	The pottery first starts producing animal models, some with human expressions and poses.	The first Beatrix Potter range is produced, with 10 figures by chief modeler Arthur Gredington.	A Mickey Mouse figure is the start of several Disney ranges, including the popular Winnie the Pooh.	The Royal Doulton group acquires the Beswick stamp. It ceases all Beswick production in 2002.

What's Hot

BULL CHAMPION
A figure of "Dairy Shorthorn Bull Champion Dwersylt Lord Oxford 74th."

$$$ • 5 in (12.5 cm) high

"CHESHIRE CAT"
The grinning "Cheshire Cat," from Beswick's Alice series, is one of the rarest in the set.

$$ • 3½ in (9 cm) long

Look out for:
Arthur Gredington designed hundreds of animal figures for Beswick, meticulously recreated from hours of drawing. Each figure was issued in a range of colorways.

"ALICE IN WONDERLAND"
An "Alice" figure from the Alice series, which also included the "Mad Hatter."

$$ • 4¾ in (12 cm) high

DULUX DOORSTOP
This piece was an early advertising item often given to Dulux paint suppliers.

$$$ • 12½ in (32 cm) high

Handpainted decoration

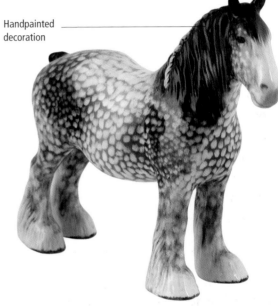

GRAY "SHIRE MARE"
This Beswick horse figure, "Shire Mare," is in gray gloss. Each figure was issued in bay, white, chestnut, palomino, and gray. The gray version is one of the most rare and desirable.

$$$ • 8½ in (21.5 cm) high

"SHIRE MARE"
With light crazing, this "Shire Mare" piebald gloss figure is decorated in a rare colorway.

$$$$ • 8½ in (21.5 cm) high

ABSTRACT BESWICK OWL
An abstract study of an owl by Colin Melbourne with a mottled green effect.

$$ • 5 in (12.5 cm) high

What's Not

This humorous figure sold very well when it was made in the early 1970s, but is less desirable for the modern collector because so many exist today.

"LOCH NESS MONSTER"
Made as a novelty promotional item, this figure doubles as a whiskey flask.

£ • 7.5cm (3in) high

Core Collectibles

FRIESIAN COW AND CALF
A Friesian cow, "Champion Claybury Leegwater," and calf by Arthur Gredington.
$$ • Mother 4½ in (11 cm) high

"GOLDEN EAGLE"
This satin matt "Golden Eagle" figure was modeled by Graham Tongue, 1973–89.
$$ • 9½ in (24 cm) high

"PONY EXPRESS"
A gray gloss Thelwell "Pony Express" figure by Beswick. It was derived from the popular cartoon series, published in *Punch* magazine, illustrating humorous incidents of girls and ponies.
$$ • 4½ in (11 cm) high

"MISS MOPPET"
This gold back stamp "Miss Moppet" figure is from the Beatrix Potter range.
$$ • 3 in (7.5 cm) high

GUINEA PIG
An "Amiable Guinea Pig" figure from the Beatrix Potter series, issued from 1967–83.
$$$ • 4½ in (11 cm) high

"SIMPKIN"
A Beatrix Potter "Simpkin" figure, issued between 1975 and 1983.
$$$ • 4½ in (11 cm) high

BEATRIX POTTER RABBITS
A Beatrix Potter series "Flopsy, Mopsy, and Cottontail" group.
$$ • 2½ in (6.5 cm) high

XAYAL HORSE
A rare Arab Xayal in the mottled Rocking Horse Grey colorway.
$$$ • 6¼ in (16 cm) high

"SIR ISAAC NEWTON"
A 1973 "Sir Isaac Newton" figure from Beswick's Beatrix Potter series.
$$ • 4 in (10 cm) high

NOVELTY CRUET
A Laurel and Hardy cruet set marked "Beswick England" on a stand impressed "375."
$$ • 4 in (10 cm) wide

"BENJAMIN BUNNY"
A gold back stamp "Mr. Benjamin Bunny" figure from the Beatrix Potter series.
$$$ • 4½ in (11 cm) high

"INDIAN ON HORSEBACK"
A gloss "Indian on Horseback" figure introduced in 1955 and retired in 1990. The horse was never issued without its rider.
$$$ • 8½ in (21 cm) high

WALL PLAQUES
Issued in sets, the kingfisher versions of these popular wall ornaments are rare.
$$ • Largest 4¼ in (10.5 cm) long

"SHOVELER"
A Beswick "Shoveler" from the Peter Scott Wildfowl series.
$$ • 3½ in (9 cm) long

SADDLEBACK BOAR
A gloss "Faracre Viscount 3rd" black and white saddleback boar figure.
$$$ • 2¾ in (7 cm) high

BULL FIGURINE
A gloss "Belted Galloway Bull" figure in the black and white colorway.
$$$$ • 7¾ in (19 cm) long

Starter Buys

WALL MASK
A wall mask of a stylish woman with blonde hair and a blue hat.
$$ • 6½ in (16.5 cm) long

BARN OWL FIGURE
This figure with the "split" tail feathers was the first version made by Arthur Gredington.
$$ • 7¼ in (18.5 cm) high

"JEMIMA PUDDLEDUCK"
A popular "Jemima Puddleduck" figure from the Beatrix Potter series.
$$ • 4½ in (11.5 cm) high

GENTLEMAN FOX
A large "Foxy Whiskered Gentleman" figure from the Beatrix Potter series.
$ • 4½ in (11.5 cm) high

You may also like… SylvaC, see pp. 62–67

Troika

In 1963 Leslie Illsley, Benny Sirota, and Jan Thomson established Troika pottery amid much skepticism. But for 20 years it was one of the most successful studio potteries of the late 20th century.

The three founders each had a desire to create a pottery that would be solely concerned with art and design, irrespective of functionality.

While Troika has become best known for its rough, textured wares, their output also featured a range of smooth gloss-glazed wares. The gloss pieces were more difficult to make and produced more seconds than the textured range. They were also more expensive to produce, and the buying market of the late 1960s dictated an increased output of textured wares. Today, the smooth wares are harder to find and often command a higher market value. Particularly rare is the range of abstract and sculptural pieces created for the first Heals exhibition of 1968.

Rather than hand-throwing each piece on a wheel, Illsley and Sirota developed a technique for using molds. Sirota would hand-throw a new piece, and then Illsley, benefiting from his sculptor's background, would make a mold. With great ease it was possible to make a few hundred pots in the new shape. These would then be hand-decorated by Troika's team of decorators.

High Prices for Fragility

Benny Sirota developed a number of decorative wall plaques, including this example now fondly known as the "Calculator" plaque. These were modeled in high relief and decorated by hand with expensive oxide glazes. Today these rare plaques are gems in any collection.

"CALCULATOR" PLAQUE
This oxide-glazed early St. Ives Troika plaque is modeled in high relief with a geometric design.
$$$$ • 10¾ in (27 cm) high

TOP TIP

- Many potters worked at Troika over the years. Look for pieces marked with early St. Ives variants. These include printed and hand painted stamps, often showing a stylized trident in a box. Early pieces are now particularly valuable to collectors.

KEY FACTS	1960 onward	1963	1965	1968	1983
Twenty years of designs for living	Artist colonies form on the South coast, with many small potters working alongside major names.	Troika is formed at the Wheal Dream site, St. Ives, by Benny Sirota, Jan Thomson, and Leslie Illsley.	One of the founding members, Jan Thomson, is bought out of the partnership and leaves Troika pottery.	London department store Heals holds its first dedicated Troika exhibition, to a great deal of acclaim.	Changing fashions and a loss of business from Heals, which stops showing craft pottery, force Troika to close.

What's Hot

WHITE SLAB VASE
This vase with a striking brown motif was designed by Honor Curtis.
$$ • 4½ in (11 cm) high

TROIKA ANVIL VASE
This mid-1970s Troika "Anvil" vase with painter's monogram is by Teo Bernatowitz.
$$$ • 13¾ in (35 cm) high

Look out for:
In the firm's early years, Troika created a number of plaques in small quantities, including the "Calculator," "Love," and "Thames" plaques. These are popular with collectors today.

Relief casting in a mold ———————

Expensive oxide glazes ———————

WALL PLAQUE
Made by Benny Sirota, this abstract Troika wall plaque displays characteristic disks within panels and is decorated in subtle contrasting colors, with painted factory marks, and a monogram.
$$$$ • 15 in (38.5 cm) high

Core Collectibles

BLUE SLAB VASE
This vase was hand-decorated by Louise Jinks.
$$ • 6½ in (16.5 cm) high

CHIMNEY VASE
A pottery vase with textured panels and abstract motifs.
$$ • 6 in (15 cm) high

Starter Buys

AZTEC FLASK
An Anne Lewis flask with a blue Aztec star design.
$$ • 6½ in (16.5 cm) high

DISK-PATTERNED VASE
A Troika vase with typical disks and panels.
$$ • 8 in (20 cm) high

EARLY ST. IVES PLATE
This early plate is decorated with blue and bronze glazes and has an impressed trident mark, found in a range of abstract patterns.
$$ • 7 in (18 cm) high

SMALL WHEEL VASE
This round vase is stylistically decorated with ships in tonal blue glazes, an unusual pattern for Troika, seldom seen on the market.
$$ • 4½ in (11.5 cm) high

You may also like… Clarice Cliff, see pp. 22–27

British Studio Ceramics

With its foundations based on design and quality, the rise of the studio potter grew steadily over the 20th century from individual handcraft workshops to larger firms adopting this now popular style.

The tradition of handcrafted pottery dates back centuries, with the earliest civilizations creating vessels from the clay beneath their feet. The 20th century saw a revival of these skills as a reaction to the standardization of mass-produced ceramics.

"Studio" pottery by definition is generally the work of one individual from start to finish, involved in all aspects from throwing or constructing the vase through to the glazing and firing. In this field there have been many great names that are now seen as the most desired, including Bernard Leach, Lucie Rie, and Hans Coper.

Bernard Leach is seen by many as the founding father of the modern day revival. While studying pottery in Japan he met potter Shoji Hamada, and together they developed a revived and modernized view of traditional Oriental ceramics that they brought back to the UK.

During the postwar years, a number of smaller potteries such as Hornsea adopted ideas to create more manufactured wares with a craft-led theology. This may go against the core views of the studio potter, but represents the commercial end of quality design and manufacture in pottery.

A Flight of Birds
Heavily influenced by ceramics from Korea, Japan, and China, Leach developed a simple yet elegant style working with salt glaze and slipware techniques and firing using a Japanese woodburning kiln.

CIRCULAR PLATTER
This Bernard Leach stoneware platter is painted with a line of flying birds enclosed within a blue striped border.
$$$ • 12½ in (31 cm) in diameter

TOP TIPS

- Condition is key. Damage, not always obvious in handcrafted ceramics, can seriously affect the price.
- Check for a well-made piece. Even the best designers had bad days!
- Learn the basic potters' marks, often the artist's initials in the clay.

KEY FACTS	1920	1938	1946	1958	2003
Potting for Britain	Bernard Leach creates a new studio in St. Ives with Japanese potter Shoji Hamada.	Lucie Rie flees Nazi Austria and moves to London. She starts making ceramic buttons and jewelry.	Lucie Rie employs a young Hans Coper in her studio to help her with firing.	Hans Coper forms his own studio creating dramatic sculptural ceramics.	Grayson Perry wins the controversial Turner Prize with his handcrafted ceramic jars.

What's Hot

STONEWARE BOWL
A brown Shoji Hamada bowl covered in a running temmoku glaze.
$$$ • 6 in (15 cm) wide

SLAB VASE
Designed by Janet Leach, this vase is decorated with brown on a blue and white ground.
$$$ • 11 in (27.5 cm) high

Look out for:
Coper and Rie only exhibited together for a few years before Coper moved to form his own studio. Her work is classically functional with a light and elegant feel and her use of glaze effects makes her work instantly recognizable.

Fine glaze

SALAD POTTERY BOWL
This pale glazed studio bowl by Lucie Rie and Hans Coper has impressed seals to the base.
$$$$ • 6 in (15 cm) high

Core Collectibles

OVAL BUD VASE
This Hornsea Slipware vase bears a zigzag pattern.
$$ • 11½ in (29.5 cm) wide

DAVID LEACH TEAPOT
A David Leach teapot from Lowerdown Pottery, c. 1960.
$$$ • 5¾ in (14.5 cm) high

Starter Buys

POTTERY GOBLET
A c. 1970 Tremar Pottery goblet with raised Celtic decoration.
$ • 5 in (12.7 cm) high

HORNSEA POTTERY VASE
By John Clappison, this has a mold no. "382," c. 1960.
$$ • 11 in (28 cm) high

NARROW-NECKED VASE
A pale ceramic Janet Leach vase from c. 1970.
$$$ • 7¾ in (20 cm) high

YELLOW BIRD DISH
This 1960s Kenneth Clark dish was designed by his wife.
$ • 6¾ in (17 cm) in diameter

CELADON VASE
A David Leach vase with curved fluted decorations.
$$ • 5¼ in (13.5 cm) high

JANET LEACH DISH
This stoneware dish is painted with a temmoku cross motif.
$$ • 6 in (15 cm) wide

You may also like… Cornishware, see pp. 54–55

Fairings

With their simple yet humorous takes on the everyday, fairings have become desirable vignettes of Victorian life. Once inexpensive novelties, today rare and unusual scenes can command high sums.

Fairings emerged around the middle of the 19th century as the fun fair was gaining popularity in England. Fairs gave people an opportunity to meet, relax, and perhaps win one of these small china ornaments that were given away as prizes.

Although fairings commented on everyday English life, they were mostly made in Germany by Conta & Boehme from about 1850 until the outbreak of World War I. Other manufacturers attempted to compete but were outclassed by the German firm's mass-production methods.

Conta & Boehme fairings were made from solid soft paste porcelain and often mounted on a base bearing a caption. They took inspiration from many sources, from family life to politics and animals, with common marriage scenes such as "last in bed to put out the light" depicting a couple climbing into bed with the candle still lit. Rarer views include figures on bicycles or in carriages, or political and professional figures, often accompanied by a humorous phrase. The rarest of these have sold for more than $6,000.

Bicycle Made for Two

This piece has double appeal to both fairing and cycle memorabilia collectors, resulting in a premium value for this fun example. The scene is set intentionally to amuse the Victorian purchaser. All of the decoration is hand-painted, including the title on the base.

BICYCLE FAIRING
"A dangerous encounter" bicycle fairing. Bicycles were introduced in 1865, dating this piece to the late 1860s.

$$$ • 3¼ in (8.5 cm) high

TOP TIPS

- In recent years, many fakes have been created. These are easy to spot, however: the decoration is often gaudy and poorly applied.
- Fake fairings tend to have transfer-printed captions rather than hand-painted script.
- Genuine fairings have firing cracks, often at joints or seams. This is a normal side effect of the manufacture and not to be confused with damage.

KEY FACTS	Mid-19th century	c. 1850	1850 onward	1914	21st century
Giveaway slices of Victorian life	Fairings first appear, mostly in England. They are introduced as prizes at fairs, hence the name.	German firm Conta & Boehme develops an inexpensive method of enamel and gilt decoration.	Uncaptioned fairings, trinket boxes, and match strikers are sold in shops and bazaars as amusing novelties.	World War I brings production of these once-fashionable ornaments to an end.	Fairings are sought after by collectors worldwide, with rare examples commanding premium prices.

What's Hot

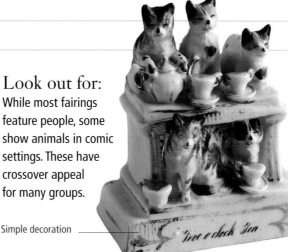

DENTIST'S CHAIR
This Victorian fairing is called "A long pull and a strong pull, the dentist's chair."
$$$ • 5 in (13 cm) long

FRENCH DANCE
A couple dance the "Cancan" in this fairing from the turn of the 20th century.
$$$ • 3¾ in (9.5 cm) high

Look out for:
While most fairings feature people, some show animals in comic settings. These have crossover appeal for many groups.

Simple decoration

CATS' TEATIME
This fairing is entitled "Five o'clock tea." Animals were often posed in human settings, adding to the sense of fun.
$$ • 3½ in (9 cm) high

Core Collectibles

WEDDING NIGHT
A domestic fairing, this one bears the title "Wedding night, undressing by the fire."
$ • 3½ in (9 cm) high

BEDCHAMBER FAIRING
An "Alone at last" bedchamber fairing, similar to the "Wedding night."
$$ • 3¾ in (9.5 cm) high

Starter Buys

TAKING A BEATING
"Taking a beating," an untitled bedchamber fairing.
$ • 3½ in (9 cm) high

FIGURE GROUP
"Two different views," a figure group fairing.
$$$ • 3½ in (9 cm) high

CAT ON THE TABLE
This cat scene fairing is entitled "A spicey bit, a thieving cat upon a table."
$$ • 4½ in (11 cm) high

DRESSING ROOM
The subject of this "Who is coming?" fairing is a dressing room scene.
$ • 3¾ in (9.5 cm) high

WEDDING FAIRING
"Married for money," a bedchamber subject fairing.
$$ • 3½ in (9 cm) high

3 AM FAIRING
A "Three o'clock in the morning" bedchamber fairing.
$$ • 3 in (7.5 cm) high

You may also like… Staffordshire, see pp. 32–35

PenDelfin

For more than 50 years, PenDelfin has created a host of charming figures ranging from rabbits and mice to witches. Collectors today are especially keen on the elusive early examples of these characters.

The first ever PenDelfin piece was created in 1953, when artists Jean Walmsley Heap and Jeannie Todd joined forces to create a number of small gifts for family and friends. Their small workshop overlooked the Pendle "Lancashire Witch Hill" from which the company takes its name. From these simple tokens emerged a successful company with an international appeal.

The initial wall plaque, "The Pendle Witch," was the first of many distinctive character pieces, including further adaptations of witches, pixies, and dragons. The first of

many rabbit figures, "Dungaree Father Rabbit," was introduced in 1955; it was the start of a whole rabbit family. These are the figures for which PenDelfin is most instantly recognized today.

Because early pieces were made in small quantities, their scarcity now drives high market appeal for fans looking to complete their collections.

While collectors are eager to find these early rarities, there are many more figures to collect, including contemporary examples currently produced by the firm.

Father Rabbit Knows Best
This figure was released in 1960 as a remodeled version of "Dungaree Father Rabbit," the first rabbit figure produced by PenDelfin in 1955. The larger ears on the original version caused the model to fall over.

"KIPPER TIE FATHER RABBIT"
A PenDelfin "Kipper Tie Father Rabbit" figure dressed in lilac, with minor wear, from 1960–70.
$$ • 8 in (20 cm) high

TOP TIPS
- Look for unusual colorways or variations of patterns, which can quickly increase the value of a piece.
- Search for children's books illustrated by Jean Walmsley Heap to complement a good collection of PenDelfin figures.
- Avoid chips and scrapes by not grouping figures too closely together, as they are made from a stone-based composite and damage easily.

KEY FACTS	1953	1962	1968	1986	2003
Creating the cute critters	Jean Walmsley Heap and Jeannie Todd make their first PenDelfin figure in Burnley, Lancashire.	The first of many model creations by designer Doreen Noel Roberts is released, called "The Pooch."	Arthur Morley introduces a machine that eliminates air bubbles, making a denser product.	Much of the company is destroyed in a fire. A remembrance model, "Victoria," is created, the only one this year.	PenDelfin celebrate their 50th anniversary by creating and releasing the "Jubilee Theatre" model.

What's Hot

"MOTHER"
A brown "Mother" figure dressed in green, 1961–66.
$$$ • 4¼ in (11 cm) high

"DAISY DUCK"
This rare figure, made c. 1958, is out of production.
$$$ • 4¼ in (11 cm) high

Core Collectibles

"PICNIC BASKET RABBIT"
Dressed in green, this figure looking for its lunch is now out of production.
$ • 5 in (12.5 cm) high

"MEGAN THE HARP"
Wearing a pink dress, this is a PenDelfin "Megan the Harp" rabbit figure.
$$ • 4 in (10 cm) high

Look out for:

Limited edition or large items that were expensive when first made, such as these bookends, retain high market value for modern-day collectors.

Semi-matt glaze

RABBIT BOOKENDS
These bookends, c. 1958–65, were made for a limited time only. Examples still in good condition are especially scarce today.
$$$ • 4½ in (11.5 cm) high

Starter Buys

"NEWSIE"
This "Newsie" figure is a membership piece from 1996.
$ • 4 in (10 cm) high

"LUCY POCKET"
Dressed in green, this figure is now out of production.
$ • 4 in (10 cm) high

"UNCLE SOAMES"
This figure is wearing yellow formal dress. Earlier versions are less colorful.
$$ • 8 in (20 cm) high

"AUNT RUBY"
This limited-edition figure was made for the ruby anniversary of the studio in 1993.
$$ • 8 in (20 cm) high

"CRACKER RABBIT"
A PenDelfin "Cracker Rabbit" figure, c. 2000.
$ • 4½ in (11.5 cm) high

"GENTLEMAN JACK"
This 1999 piece was made for a special PenDelfin event.
$ • 5 in (12.5 cm) high

You may also like… SylvaC, see pp. 62–67

Royal Commemoratives

The majority of royal commemorative ceramics date from the reigns of Queen Victoria and 20th-century monarchs. Relatively few pieces were made prior to Victoria—these form a more expensive, specialist market.

As a nation, the British are perhaps less patriotic than in the past, but despite this there is still great support for the monarchy. Nowhere is this more evident than in the huge market that exists for royal souvenirs, including ceramics.

Many collectors start with commemoratives from the reign of Victoria, which can be acquired quite reasonably. Her reign saw the monarchy, hitherto fairly unpopular with the general public, transformed into a source of national pride.

The 20th century saw an abdication (Edward VIII) and appendicitis (Edward VII) changing coronation plans and dates. The popularity of the monarchy grew with Elizabeth II and a new form of celebrity in Princess Diana, while the rise of designers such as Eric Ravilious added further interest to the market. Plenty of dealers, factory outlets, markets, and auctions source both antique and modern items.

Royal Paragon

Paragon china was introduced in 1903 as the brand name of the Stoke-on-Trent Star China Co. The company was founded by the sons of John Aynsley, the famous ceramics manufacturer. Paragon became very popular and the company changed its name to the Paragon China Co. in 1920. Their reputation for quality preceded them and they enjoyed much royal patronage. Queen Mary regularly purchased items for the royal household and for use as gifts. Paragon was granted a prestigious royal warrant in 1933. Examples such as this Silver Jubilee loving cup remain firm favorites with collectors and can be sourced from specialist dealers, auctioneers, and on the Internet.

COMMEMORATIVE LOVING CUP
The Paragon China Co. produced this bone china loving cup to commemorate the Silver Jubilee of King George V and Queen Mary in 1935.
$$ • 3¼ in (8.5 cm) high

KEY FACTS	1837–1901	1901–10	1910–36	1936	1952 onward
British monarchs since 1837	Queen Victoria reigns. Golden Jubilee (1887) and Diamond Jubilee (1897) mark 50, then 60, years on the throne.	Edward VII becomes king at 59, having been heir apparent for longer than anyone else in British history.	King George V is crowned. He adopts the name of Windsor in 1917 and celebrates his Silver Jubilee in 1935.	Edward VIII reigns for 325 days, abdicating to marry Wallis Simpson. His brother becomes George VI.	Queen Elizabeth II is crowned in 1953. Her Silver Jubilee is in 1977 and Golden Jubilee in 2002.

What's Hot

GEORGE III BUST
This very fine Staffordshire figure, possibly by Enoch Wood, is dated 1790.
$$$$$ • 12½ in (32 cm) high

PRINCE OF WALES BUST
Brown-Westhead, Moore & Co. produced this Parian bust of Prince Edward in 1864.
$$$ • 14¼ in (36 cm) high

Look out for:
There is an extra excitement—and value—in coronation items designed by a famous artist. The design on this mug is by Dame Laura Knight, the first woman ever to be elected to the Royal Academy.

Lion detail on handle

Bold use of primary colors

CORONATION PLATE
The 1837 coronation of Queen Victoria is commemorated on this Staffordshire plate.
$$$ • 7½ in (19 cm) wide

POTTERY BEER MUG
An early-18th-century Vauxhall pottery beer mug with a portrait of Queen Anne.
$$$$ • 8 in (20.5 cm) high

DAME LAURA KNIGHT MUG
Dame Laura Knight designed this earthenware mug in 1936–37 to commemorate the proposed coronation of Edward VIII. It comes with a certificate of authenticity.
$$ • 3 in (8 cm) high

What's Not

Manufacturers eager to exploit important historical events have produced a plethora of poor-quality unlicensed commemorative items.

WILLIAM IV MUG
This royal mug with prints of William IV and Queen Adelaide dates back to 1835.
$$$ • 3 in (8 cm) high

EDWARD VIII MUG
Eric Ravilious designed this Wedgwood earthenware mug in 1936.
$$$ • 4¼ in (11 cm) high

JUBILEE MUG
An earthenware mug made for the Silver Jubilee of Queen Elizabeth II in 1977.
$ • 3¼ in (8.5 cm) high

Core Collectibles

MASON'S JUG
An earthenware jug made by Mason's for the Silver Jubilee of George V in 1935.
$$ • 7¾ in (19.5 cm) high

ENAMEL-ON-TIN BEAKER
The coronation of King George V is commemorated in this continental beaker.
$$ • 3¾ in (9.5 cm) high

ROYAL DOULTON CUP
This earthenware loving cup was made in 1937 for the coronation of George VI.
$$$ • 4 in (10.5 cm) high

KING GEORGE VI VASE
Charlotte Rhead designed this one-handled vase for Crown Ducal in 1937.
$$ • 7¼ in (18.5 cm) high

BONE CHINA LOVING CUP
Royal lions form the handles of this cup, made in 1936 for Edward VIII's coronation.
$$$ • 5¼ in (13.5 cm) high

ELIZABETH II MUG
An earthenware mug made for Queen Elizabeth II's coronation in 1953.
$$ • 4 in (10.5 cm) high

OVAL PRATTWARE PLAQUES
This rare pair of late 18th-century oval Prattware commemorative plaques of George III and Caroline is molded in relief and decorated in manganese, yellow, and green.
$$$$ • 5 in (13 cm) high

Ask the Expert

Q. What are the earliest known royal commemorative ceramics?
A. Early royal ceramics are rare as they were made by hand. They include items such as the "Blue Dash" Delft-style chargers of the Charles II period and can sell for tens of thousands of dollars.

Gold crest

BASALT MUG
A rare Wedgwood basalt mug commemorating the investiture of Charles, Prince of Wales, in 1969, designed by Richard Guyatt, a limited edition of 200.
$$$ • 4 in (10.5 cm) high

Q. Are limited editions worth collecting?
A. Limited editions do not always make an item valuable. Stay with well-known names such as Doulton and Worcester, but do not expect a quick profit.

Q. It seems very difficult to find Victorian coronation items. Why is this?

A. The main reasons are the unpopularity of the monarchy prior to Victoria, the more interesting historical figures of the time, and poorly organized production and transport systems. The "Swansea transfer" mug made for Queen Victoria is perhaps the best known and sells for around $1,200–$2,000 at auction.

COMPORT BY PARAGON
The royal coat of arms decorates this rare comport by Paragon, commemorating the 1937 coronation of George VI.
$$$ • 8½ in (21.5 cm) in diameter

DOULTON & LAMBETH JUG
This earthenware jug was made in 1897 to mark Queen Victoria's Diamond Jubilee.
$$$ • 9¼ in (23.5 cm) high

BUFF STONEWARE JUG
A rare example from 1820, this jug commemorates the coronation of George IV.
$$$ • 9¼ in (23.5 cm) high

GREEN COPELAND JUG
Copeland produced this earthenware jug for Queen Victoria's Diamond Jubilee.
$$ • 6¼ in (16 cm) high

RICHARD GUYATT MUG
Wedgwood produced this earthenware mug for the coronation of Elizabeth II.
$$ • 4 in (10 cm) high

VICTORIA & ALBERT PLATE
Dated 1851, this bone china plate was part of a set sold at the Great Exhibition.
$$ • 8 in (20.5 cm) in diameter

Starter Buys

BURLEIGH LOVING CUP
This 1953 cup marks Queen Elizabeth II's coronation.
$$ • 3¼ in (8.5 cm) high

RYE POTTERY MUG
Elizabeth II's Golden Jubilee in 2002 inspired this mug.
$ • 3 in (7.5 cm) high

THORNTON CROWN TRIO
This set commemorates Queen Elizabeth II's coronation.
$ • 3¾ in (9.5 cm) high

BONE CHINA RIBBON PLATE
Dated 1902, this plate marks Edward VII's coronation.
$$ • 8½ in (21.5 cm) in diameter

You may also like… Doulton, see pp. 44–47

Historical Ceramics

These pieces commemorate key historical figures and events, from generals and politicians to wars and industrial achievements. Collectors are often very specialized, focusing on distinct areas such as the Boer War.

The British have a long history of commemorating people and events with ceramics. Early output was small; everything was handmade, communications were poor, and a largely subsistence population had no spare money to spend on such frivolities.

As the Industrial Revolution gathered pace, this began to change, with improved manufacturing techniques, new materials, and a huge expansion in worldwide distribution from industries such as the potteries. The opening of the first iron bridge at Coalbrooke

Dale in 1779 is the type of historical event favored by collectors, and even the bicentennial pieces may become valuable one day!

Learn how to work the markets. The demand for English Staffordshire figures has decreased enormously in recent years, mainly due to fashion. Buying in a lull is often sensible, and auction prices for some pieces are remarkably reasonable. An attractive Staffordshire figure of John Wesley, circa 1840, may be had for little more than $200 at auction.

Garden Party

Queen Victoria and soldiers of the Australian Army and Militia appear on this superb jardinière, commemorating the federation of the six Australian colonies into the Commonwealth of Australia.

DOULTON JARDINIÈRE
A rare Doulton earthenware jardinière dating to 1901.
$$ • 4¾ in (12 cm) high

TOP TIPS

- Learn to recognize significant figures and become familiar with their history. Look for items relating to heroes such as Nelson or Wellington.
- Explore the possibility of trading pieces acquired on your sorties to improve your own collection.
- Check online price guides based on auction results to familiarize yourself with price ranges.

KEY FACTS	1805	1843	1901	1914–18	1935–45
War and pieces	Nelson is killed at the Battle of Trafalgar, a decisive British victory against Napoleon.	Isambard Kingdom Brunel launches the iron-clad SS *Great Britain*.	The Boer War and the Federation of Australia prompt a range of commemorative ceramics.	The huge death toll of World War I lends poignancy to related memorabilia.	World War II propaganda produces many creative commemorative items.

What's Hot

BOER WAR MUG
Patriotic figures and a gilt rim adorn this Boer War commemorative mug.

$$ • 3¼ in (8.5 cm) high

OLD BILL PLATE
A Royal Winton earthenware plate, c. 1916, commemorating World War I.

$$ • 8½ in (22 cm) wide

Look out for:
Renowned for their "Crown Devon" trademark, Fielding & Co. produced commemorative ceramics and novelty wares. This ashtray, in the shape of a miniature chamber pot, was designed to whip up anti-German sentiment in the wake of the Nazi invasion of Poland in 1939. Hitler's face is printed inside the base.

ASHTRAY
Fielding & Co. produced this humorous ashtray satirizing Adolf Hitler c. 1939.

$$$ • 1¼ in (3.5 cm) high

Image of Hitler inside base

Core Collectibles

FRENCH TRICORN ASHTRAY
Made by Longwy Ceramics, this commemorates the Allied liberation of France in 1944.

$$ • 4¾ in (12 cm) wide

BUST OF PRINCE ALBERT
Prince Albert is the subject of this Parian bust by Robinson & Leadbeater.

$$$ • 7½ in (19 cm) high

Starter Buys

ROYAL DOULTON MUG
The Allies of World War I are the subject of this 1919 mug.

$ • 3 in (8 cm) high

MODEL CENOTAPH
The City of London crest features on this replica.

$ • 6 in (15 cm) high

EARTHENWARE "UGLY MUG"
A caricature of Edward Heath by Willie Rushton, 1974.

$$ • 3½ in (9 cm) diameter

CAVERSWALL MUG
As recently as 1991, the first Gulf War inspired this mug.

$ • 3¾ in (9.5 cm) high

CROWN DUCAL TEAPOT
Patriotic teapots, like this from 1939, rewarded donations of aluminum to the war effort.

$$ • 5¾ in (14.5 cm) high

BLUE AND WHITE JUG
The death of Prime Minister Robert Peel in 1850 gave rise to this commemorative jug.

$$ • 5 in (12.5 cm) high

You may also like… Royal Commemoratives, see pp. 84–87

CHAPTER

2

Glass

Color & Light

Glass is arguably the hottest area in today's antiques and collectibles market. Despite the obvious appeal of its subtle optics, amazing fragility, and brilliant colors, it languished for decades, but now the tide is slowly turning.

Long dismissed as inferior to its bright and beautiful sister, ceramics, the glass scene has been gradually changing in recent years, as the ugly duckling is increasingly recognized as one of the most compelling substances ever created.

The period of glassmaking commanding the greatest interest today is, as in other areas of collecting, the postwar era. Today's collectors are often older than their particular chosen fields, with 40- and 50-year-old people collecting 30- and 40-year-old glass! This is generally

A richly decorated Gallé vase, c. 1900, see What's Hot, p. 101.

"Athena Cattedrale" vase, Murano glassware, see p. 104.

A Varnish and Co. goblet from 1849, see What's Hot, p. 121.

not the case with the traditional favorites in glass: mid-18th-century drinking glasses, 19th-century Bohemian color, and Victorian cameo, which are genuine 100-year-old antiques.

Today's hottest collectible pieces are generally signed, large, in vivid colors, and attributable to the best designers. Pieces requiring demanding craft techniques command premiums, but big, hot, and statuesque are all-important characteristics. Choosing specific patterns and colors, being able to identify reproductions, and tracking down the best deals are the main focuses of glass collecting.

It is most unlikely that collectors will be scooping up today's glassware in 30 years. This is because the previous generation grew up in the midst of one of the most radical periods in design history, unmatched today. The period spanning the late 1950s and early 1970s is now widely recognized as one of many classic moments in design, during which an entirely new aesthetic inspired by dynamic new technologies was created.

Sadly, soaring energy costs, combined with the transfer of manufacturing to East Asia, where labor costs are lower, will combine to ensure that the extraordinary wave of glassmaking that flowered during that period, particularly in Scandinavia, is unlikely to be repeated in Europe.

An Mdina sculpture by Michael Harris, see What's Hot, p. 115.

"Kantarelli" sculpture by Tapio Wirkkala, 1946, see p. 132.

René Lalique

One of history's most gifted glass designer-makers, Lalique possessed a unique sense of design, knowledge of glass molding, and gift for brand marketing that allowed his works to command dazzling prices.

Originally a jeweler, Lalique was over 40 when he first designed glassware. Some of his work was formed by the laborious and skillful *cire perdu* or "lost wax" method, creating unique pieces, but the majority was manually pressed on equipment capable of forming hundreds of identical pieces a day.

Lalique's greatest talent was probably his elevated understanding of glass-molding techniques, enabling production of a wide variety of designs that were sold for premium prices.

By the time of his death in 1945, he ranked among the world's richest and most famous decorative artists.

All Lalique glass is marked with the family name. Pieces made before René's death are marked "R. Lalique," but the "R." is missing from those made posthumously. The value of the glassware varies widely. With opalescent pieces, values rise according to color density. In the case of his iconic Bacchante vase, a colorless example would be worth just 5 percent of a dark amethyst one.

Creature of Grace

"Suzanne," designed around 1925, encapsulates everything for which René Lalique is revered. She is beautifully modeled, has poise, and is sexy, and yet is functional all at once: the cast bronze base disguises the presence of a light.

"SUZANNE" STATUETTE
A Lalique "Suzanne" statuette from 1925, in opalescent glass with a bronze peacock pattern illuminating base, molded "R. Lalique," and engraved "France."
$$$$$ • 11 in (28 cm) high

TOP TIPS

- Do not confuse "Suzanne" with "Thais": the statuettes strike similar poses.
- Look for pieces with original staining, which adds to their value. Colored pieces are the most sought after.
- Always check for damage: grinding, polishing, chips, cracks, or drill holes can greatly affect value.

KEY FACTS	1885	1892	1893	1918	1925
The rise and rise of a master craftsman	After becoming a well-known freelancer, René Lalique establishes his own jewelry studio.	Lalique first starts to work with glass, incorporating it into his jewelry designs.	Lalique wins 500 French francs as second prize for designing a glass goblet, his first glassware.	Lalique opens a large glassworks in Wingen-sur-Moder, in Alsace, France.	Lalique's glass pavilion at the Paris Exposition des Arts Décoratifs proves pivotal in forming Art Deco style.

What's Hot

Look out for:

The "Trois Guêpes" (Three Wasps) scent bottle captures the essence of Lalique's genius. He had clearly made a careful study of wasps and then captured their forms through glass molding, using staining to add depth and realism. A great piece!

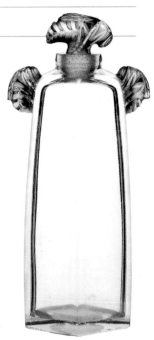

"PERRUCHES" FRUIT BOWL
A 1931 "Perruches" pattern half-hemisphere fruit bowl molded in opalescent glass.
$$$ • 8¾ in (22.5 cm) high

"THAIS" STATUETTE
A "Thais" statuette from 1925 in clear and frosted glass with engraved "R. Lalique" mark.
$$$$ • 8¼ in (20.5 cm) high

SCENT BOTTLE
"Trois Guêpes" bottle designed in 1912 in clear and frosted glass with gray staining, engraved "R. Lalique France No. 498."
$$$ • 5 in (13 cm) high

Core Collectibles

"L'ELEGANCE" BOTTLE
A 1914 Lalique "L'Elegance" perfume bottle for D'Orsay in clear and frosted glass.
$$$ • 3½ in (9 cm) high

"FALCON" ORNAMENT
Molded as a falcon, this is an amethyst-tinted clear and frosted glass hood ornament.
$$$$ • 6¼ in (15.75 cm) high

Starter Buys

SCALLOPED BOWL
A large "Coquille" scalloped bowl from 1924.
$$ • 9½ in (24 cm) in diameter

"CHARDONS" VASE
A 1922 vase with a sepia patina and a design of thistles.
$$$ • 7½ in (19 cm) high

MOLINARD PERFUME BOTTLE
A 1929 "Habanito" perfume bottle for Molinard in clear and frosted glass.
$$$ • 4¾ in (12 cm) high

"MALESHERBES" VASE
Dated 1927, this gourdlike vase is molded in opalescent and frosted glass.
$$$ • 8¾ in (22.5 cm) high

CYLINDRICAL VASE
A Lalique Art Deco tapering cylindrical "Chevreuse" vase from 1930.
$$ • 6½ in (16 cm) high

"LA BELLE SAISON" BOTTLE
A 1925 "La Belle Saison" perfume bottle for Houbigant in clear and frosted glass.
$$$ • 5 in (13 cm) high

You may also like… Émile Gallé, see pp. 100–01

Post-René Lalique

René Lalique's extraordinary design sense was matched by business talents. Most of his glassware required minimal skills to produce, yet his company became so successful that his son, Marc, inherited a fortune.

While neither Marc nor his daughter Marie-Claude matched René's design skills, their business acumen sustained the company's profitability until 1994, when the glassworks left family ownership. Marc's most significant contributions were to abandon color and the laborious color-staining that had added aesthetic depth to his father's pressed designs. He also changed the company's basic glass mix from "demi-crystal" to full lead crystal, enabling molten glass to flow more easily and enhancing its clarity.

Marie-Claude was a graduate of the École Nationale Supérieure des Arts Décoratifs, Paris. For her first piece, she worked from a live dove, fashioning its likeness in plasticine, from which a mold was formed.

Every piece of Lalique glass was applied with the family name and none was ever cheap when new. However, the market in "vintage" Lalique is greatly focused on prewar pieces, to the point where a 1930s René design is valued at at least 10 times more than the same one produced 20 years later.

The Lion Roars

This piece, part of a three-element set of ashtray, cigarette holder (see p. 97), and lighter, is designed like a lion mask. The Lalique glassworks produced a range of ashtrays featuring animal-related subjects.

LION ASHTRAY
This modern ashtray, a sturdy piece with fluid lines, has heavy lion bosses and bears the inscription "Lalique France."

$$ • 5¾ in (14.5 cm) in diameter

TOP TIPS

- Note that, with the passing of time, repeated use of the original molds softens the definition of pieces formed in them.
- Look out for Marc Lalique's best-known designs, including the Cactus Table (price new, $190,000) and the iconic "L'Air du Temps" scent bottle for Nina Ricci.

KEY FACTS	1945	1948	1960s	1977	1992
The family legacy of a master	René Lalique dies. His son Marc, who was born in 1900, takes over the company.	Marc doubles the amount of lead oxide to boost the brightness and clarity of Lalique glass.	Marc's daughter, Marie-Claude (born in 1935), joins the company as a designer.	Marc Lalique dies at age 77. Marie-Claude takes control of the company.	Marie-Claude's diversification from glass is typified by the launch of a Lalique perfume.

What's Hot

Look out for:

The "Dampierre" crystal vase (1948), featuring a frieze of swallows, was one of Marc's first designs after his father's death. In production ever since, new versions are priced around twice as high as this secondhand one.

Frosted relief frieze

FROSTED GLASS BOWL

This large molded and frosted "Luxembourg" bowl bears a deep relief frieze of naked cherubs with laurel garlands. It is signed and has a "Lalique Cristal Paris" sticker.

$$$ • 10¼ in (26 cm) in diameter

URN-SHAPED VASE

Engraved "Lalique France," this crystal vase has a frieze of molded and frosted swallows.

$$$ • 4¾ in (12 cm) high

Core Collectibles

CIGARETTE HOLDER

A modern Lalique cigarette holder with lion bosses, from a set with ashtray and lighter.

$$ • 6 in (15 cm) high

DANCER STATUETTE

A "Danseuse Bras Baissé" statuette from 1975 with engraved marking.

$$$ • 7¼ in (19 cm) high

EAGLE HEAD BOOKEND

Engraved "Lalique France," this "Tête d'Aigle" bookend is made of molded and frosted crystal.

$$$ • 4½ in (11.5 cm) high

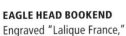

Starter Buys

CRYSTAL LIGHTER

This metal lighter is held in a case of molded and frosted lead crystal glass.

$$ • 4½ in (11 cm) high

HOOD ORNAMENT

This frosted glass ornament is molded as a girl with an arched back and flowing hair.

$$$ • 5 in (12.5 cm) high

FROSTED DEER

This 1929 "Daim" is a prewar design produced after the war. It has engraved marks on a rectangular base.

$$ • 3¼ in (8 cm) high

You may also like… Lalique-Inspired Glass, see pp. 98–99

Lalique-Inspired Glass

The worldwide sensation created by René Lalique's designs inspired many copyists. Some, particularly those like Marius Ernest Sabino who signed their work, are widely collected and command significant prices.

In the century preceding Lalique, pressed glass had largely been a means of supplying the working classes with lookalike cut glass. The same shapes were decorated with pressed equivalents of the grooves and lenses found on expensive crystal pieces. Lalique treated pressing entirely differently, creating radically new themes and shapes.

The best-known Lalique copyist was Sabino, who had a lighting studio in Paris but was soon inspired to switch to glass production. His designs always bear his name, are commonly opalescent, and are sometimes virtual copies of Lalique pieces. Lesser French producers of Lalique-esque pressed glass include Verlys, Edmund Etling, André Hunebelle, Pierre D'Avesn, and Genet & Michon, several of whom used the same mold-maker, Etienne Franckhauser. The maker of the most stylish Czech pressed glass was also a mold-maker: Heinrich Hoffmann. His work can often be distinguished by a butterfly "signature."

Boldness and Originality

German and Czech pressed glass designer–makers, particularly Walther & Söhne of Radeberg, expanded Lalique's themes to create pieces like this, demonstrating an originality and boldness generally absent from French, British, and American equivalents.

CHILD & TORTOISE
Bowl insert, probably Czech, 1930s. Inserts of sufficient quality still retain value without bowls.
$$ • 7 in (18 cm) high

TOP TIPS

- Be aware that while mass manufacturing enabled the Lalique "look" to become both affordable and popular, some mass-produced pieces lack the detail and sophistication of original Lalique.
- Look for high-quality, stylish scent bottles, in various colors and styles, which continue to be highly collectible. The popularity of commercial perfume since WWI has created a ready market.

KEY FACTS	c. 1920	1920	1925	1935	1945
Emulating Lalique's style all over Europe	The Verlys company and Edmund Etling start producing their wares in Paris.	Sicilian artist Marius Ernest Sabino founds his own lighting company in Paris.	Lalique and Sabino first produce opalescent glass, based on cobalt oxide, deepest in thick sections of glass.	British glassmaker Jobling registers opalescent Lalique copy, Opalique.	Walther & Söhne is nationalized and becomes V.E.B. Saschenglas, still in business today.

What's Hot

FROSTED VASE
A Czech or German pressed vase, 1930s, in frosted and blue-tinted opalescent glass.
$$ • 6½ in (16 cm) high

SABINO VASE
Molded with exotic birds, this 1930s opalescent glass vase is by Sabino.
$$$ • 9½ in (24 cm) high

Look out for:
The Viard family ranked among France's greatest artistic perfume bottle designers. They commissioned glassmakers such as Baccarat to produce the bottles before applying stains and other finishes at their own premises.

Stained colors

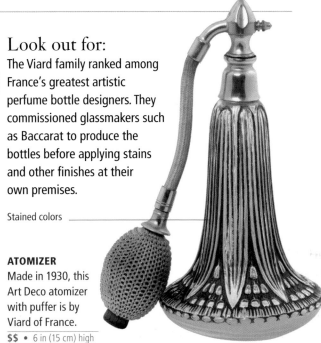

ATOMIZER
Made in 1930, this Art Deco atomizer with puffer is by Viard of France.
$$ • 6 in (15 cm) high

Core Collectibles

POWDER BOX
This 1935 Verlys amber glass powder box has a molded chrysanthemum cover.
$$ • 5 in (12.5 cm) in diameter

VERLYS VASE
A Verlys frosted glass vase from 1940, with a molded pattern of leaves and flowers.
$$ • 7½ in (19 cm) high

Starter Buys

LEAPING FISH BOWL
Sky-blue pressed-glass bowl with removable insert. The smooth "satin" finish was created by immersing it in acid. Probably Czech, c. 1935.
$ • Insert 6 in (15 cm) high

CATTEAU BOWL
This 1920s footed bowl, designed by Charles Catteau, has a cloudlike pattern.
$$ • 10½ in (27 cm) in diameter

FEEDING BIRD
A Sabino frosted glass figure of a feeding bird with molded marks.
$$ • 6½ in (17 cm) wide

KOI CARP VASE
Lightweight globular vase mold-blown in deep relief with a series of interlocking koi carp in a manner reminiscent of the Dutch illusionist artist M. C. Escher. Probably Czech, c. 1930.
$$ • 7½ x 7 in (19 x 18 cm)

You may also like… Postwar Czech Pressed Glass, see pp. 138–39

Émile Gallé

Art Nouveau glass is epitomized by the work of its greatest creative genius, Émile Gallé. While Gallé produced richly inlaid furniture and ceramics as well, it is for his glass that his name will remain immortal.

In a life dedicated to expanding the boundaries of glassmaking, Gallé's work spans his early commercial "transparent period," during which glass was marked by clear, lightly tinted vessels decorated with colorful enamels, and leads to his later use of acids on multilayered cameo blanks.

By the end of the 19th century, Gallé's production was increasingly split in two, with his more daring, experimental, and expensive "studio" work contrasting with his more commercial "factory" output. Expert knowledge is generally required today to discern the difference between his factory and studio pieces.

Gallé died in 1904, though his designs continued to be produced until 1935. Posthumous pieces are marked with a star beside his signature.

There are few surprise finds among Gallé glasswares today; most pieces are easily recognized, signed, and expensive, with prices starting at a few hundred dollars.

Homage to Nature

This extraordinary vase, which seemingly could have been grown in the ground rather than made in a glassworks, positively screams Art Nouveau. The lifelike clematis leaves rising up the neck are typical of Gallé's acute powers of observation.

FLORAL CAMEO VASE
Made c. 1900, this Gallé cameo glass vase has a scalloped rim above a body of vegetable form. It is adorned with purple flowers. As with all Gallé glass, it is signed.
$$$$$ • 8 in (20 cm) high

TOP TIPS

- Be alert to the presence on the market of brand-new Gallé-style reproductions made in Romania.
- All glassware depends on light to attain its maximum effect, but this is perhaps more true with Gallé pieces than any others: being formed so thickly, they require careful lighting to bring out the subtlety of their beauty.
- Remain realistic when faced with bargains: reproductions greatly outnumber genuine period pieces.

KEY FACTS	1846	1873	1889	1901	1935
The rise of a master glassworker	Émile Gallé, son of a furniture-maker, is born in Nancy, in the Lorraine region of northeastern France.	Gallé establishes his own glass studio in his home town in the years following the Franco-Prussian war.	His display of carved cameo and *pâte de verre* at the Paris Exhibition wins him the Grand Prix.	Gallé forms the design forum École de Nancy with fellow artists Victor Prouvé and Louis Majorelle.	Thirty-one years after Gallé's death from leukemia in 1904, production of Gallé glass ceases.

What's Hot

ORANGE GALLÉ VASE
Dating to c. 1900, this is a typical Gallé vase decorated with flowers and leaves.
$$$$$ • 12½ in (31.5 cm) high

FLOOR VASE
This floor vase is acid-carved with flowers, leaves, and stems in green and amethyst.
$$$$ • 17¼ in (44 cm) high

Look out for:

One way to discern genuine Gallé cameo vases from some fakes is to run your fingers over their interior surface. Genuine pieces are regular and smooth, whereas with some fakes, their inner surface will feature indentations that mirror the external profile of the design.

Amethyst overlay

OVOID TINTED VASE
This compressed ovoid vase was designed around 1900. Its eye-catching decoration is achieved with an amethyst-tinted overlay, which forms a trailing floral vine around the body.
$$$ • 3 in (7.5 cm) high

Core Collectibles

ENAMELED GLASS VASE
An enameled and acid-etched glass vase, this piece is signed "Gallé/deposé" in enamels.
$$$$ • 7 in (18 cm) high

FLOWERED VASE
This tall green cameo glass vase, c. 1902–03, is decorated with a pattern of purple flowers. Its "Gallé" mark is on the foot.
$$$$ • 20 in (51 cm)

Starter Buys

OVOID GALLÉ VASE
A rich yellow vase with a dark floral pattern, from c. 1900.
$$$ • 9½ in (24 cm) wide

ENAMELED DECANTER
A decanter with enameled and silver deposit decoration.
$$$ • 5¼ in (13.5 cm) high

TWO-HANDLED VASES
These enameled glass vases with rope twist handles, decorated with colorful insects and flowering plants, date to c. 1895.
$$$ • 4½ in (11.5 cm) high

CABINET VASE
An acid-cameo gourd vase featuring dark purple cherries.
$$$ • 4 in (10 cm) high

SMALL BLOSSOM VASE
This vase is inspired by flora from Gallé's native Lorraine.
$$$ • 3¾ in (9.5 cm) high

You may also like… French Art Glass, see pp. 102–03

French Art Glass

French glassworks enjoyed great success during the early 20th century, and the popularity of their products endures today. Pieces are fiercely fought over at auction, their elegant forms commanding sky-high prices.

After the death of Émile Gallé in 1904, the output of the members of the École de Nancy continued to confirm the town as the center of French Art Nouveau and art glass manufacture, and to encourage a particular identity in local glassware. While including the classic features of sensual, sinuous, and naturalistic flora and fauna that are common to Art Nouveau, Nancy art glass also carried a strong Gothic influence and hints of Japanese and Moorish design.

The optimism of Art Nouveau was considered inappropriate in the wake of World War I; French postwar art glass—notably by its leading makers, Daum, Schneider, and Lalique—is mostly characterized by a shift toward more industrial techniques involving acids and molds.

Most French art glass that survives today is easy to identify and collect—most pieces are signed—but the greatest challenge may be reaching deep enough into your bank account.

Cameo Performance

The value of Gallé-style acid-cameo glass depends on a combination of factors: its particular color scheme, its designer, its subject matter, and the quality of craftsmanship. This vase, designed by Edmond Rigot for Villeroy & Boch (better known for its ceramics than its glassware) is more pleasing than outstanding, and so of medium rather than top value.

LANDSCAPE VASE
Designed in the style of Émile Gallé by Edmond Rigot in around 1930, this acid-etched cameo glass vase bears a reddish landscape decoration of hills, trees, rocks, and a stream on a sky-blue ground.

$$$ • 12 in (30 cm) high

TOP TIPS

- Look for pieces by the biggest names in French art glass—they will command the greatest values.
- Beware damaged items: while experts can remove some stains and chips, it's better to invest in an undamaged piece if you can.
- Search out French art glass table lamps with their original shades: they are particularly avidly collected and can fetch dizzying prices.

KEY FACTS	1875	1914	1921	1926	1945
Gallé's heirs and successors	Jean Daum founds Daum Frères in Nancy, France. His sons Auguste and Antonin Daum manage it.	Former Sèvres ceramicist Gabriel Argy-Rousseau exhibits *pâte de verre* for the first time.	Louis Majorelle begins blowing glass into wrought-iron frames, a key part of the Art Nouveau architecture.	Charles Schneider wins the French *Légion d'Honneur* after his display at the 1925 Paris Exposition.	Under Michel Daum, colorless crystal definitively replaces colored production at the Daum glassworks.

What's Hot

MAURICE MARINOT VASE
Marinot glass is very rare and extremely valuable.
$$$$$ • 6¾ in (17 cm) high

"SCARABÉES" VASE
An Argy-Rousseau *pâte de verre* vase with scarab beetles.
$$$$$ • 5¾ in (14.5 cm) high

Look out for:

This huge vase, which appears to be growing out of the ground, epitomizes its genre—the fact that it was once owned by actor Michael Caine enhances its already high value.

Intricate floral stem

FLOOR VASE
This toweringly slender floor vase, decorated with delicate stems of flowers, is a hallmark Daum design from the Art Nouveau period.
$$$ • 23½ in (59.5 cm) high

Core Collectibles

SCHNEIDER VASE
A 1920s Schneider glass vase, this has a tapering ovoid form and an applied amethyst foot.
$$$ • 13 in (33 cm) high

FOOTED CAMEO VASE
This Daum vase is etched with a flowering iris design and painted in enamels.
$$$ • 8¼ in (21 cm) high

Starter Buys

CAMEO POPPY VASE
An acid-cameo poppy vase signed "De Vez," by Parisian glassmaker E. S. Monot.
$$$ • 6 in (15 cm) high

TREES IN SNOW
This Legras & Cie vase, c. 1900, is enameled with leafless trees in a winter landscape.
$$$ • 13¾ in (35 cm) high

MULLER CAMEO VASE
This hemispherical Muller Frères acid-cameo vase is overlaid in amethyst and blue.
$$$$ • 7 in (18 cm) high

DAUM ENAMELED BOWL
A semi-hemispherical bowl with floral enameling and a gilded signature.
$$$ • 6¼ in (16 cm) high

SWAN ENAMELED VASE
A vase decorated with swans in polychrome enamels, signed "Legras," c. 1903.
$$ • 10¾ in (27 cm) high

IRIS DECORATED VASE
Green shading and painted irises on iridescent glass mark this enameled vase, c. 1900.
$$ • 8 in (20 cm) high

You may also like… Émile Gallé, see pp. 100–01

Designer Murano

Murano glassware, characteristically flamboyant in style, has been produced since the 13th century. Today, designer Murano pieces still hold the power to wow—and command prices worthy of their heritage.

Antique Venetian glass remains actively sought after—a goblet dating to around 1450 recently sold for $270,000 at auction—but the most active market today is in 20th-century examples, split between two extremes. The high end comprises rare, attributable designer pieces that can command tens of thousands, while the low end is composed of so-called "tourist-quality" pieces that can be bought for single-digit prices. The irony of this division is that the same craftsmen working in the same glassworks often produce both high- and low-end pieces.

The differences that divide exceptional from ordinary Murano glass are complex and can be difficult to discern, particularly as very little of it bears signatures. However, crucial factors include the identity of the designer, whether the piece appeared at prestigious exhibitions, if and how it is signed, and the difficulty of manufacture, as well as the usual size and color criteria. Collectors will find that irrefutable attributions to designers such as Dino Martens, Flavio Poli, and Fulvio Bianconi can multiply values by a factor of 10.

Window Dressing
In this 1967 series inspired by the Athena Cathedral, Ercole Barovier used preformed square or diamond-shaped canes to represent ecclesiastical windows.

"ATHENA CATTEDRALE" VASE
A rare Barovier & Toso "Athena Cattedrale" vase designed by Ercole Barovier and made of clear glass with a blue and green murrine pattern, 1967.
$$$$ • 13 in (33 cm) high

TOP TIPS
- Be sure to research colors and forms so you can buy with confidence in a market where copies abound.
- Avoid novelty forms such as clowns and fish, which have been widely reproduced and are now mostly manufactured in China.
- Look out for chips, scratches, and imperfections such as interior bubbles. These can decrease pieces' values.

KEY FACTS	1920	1921	1930s	1996	2000s
Fusing tradition and modernity in glassware	Ercole Barovier assumes control of the centuries-old family firm, later to become Barovier & Toso.	Giacomo Cappellin and Paolo Venini found their own glassworks, Venini, on Murano.	Designers including Venini, Barovier, and Carlo Scarpa perfect new glassworking techniques.	The Barovier family enters the *Guinness Book of World Records* as the oldest glassmaking family.	The rising dominance of studio glassmaking revives the popularity of limited-edition Murano glass.

What's Hot

Look out for:

This decanter was originally designed in 1946 for Venini by Gio Ponti, one of the giants of 20th-century design. Four decades after its debut, the decanter was reissued as a design classic. A new reproduction is, of course, worth considerably less than an original.

Incalmo technique used

SALVIATI VASE
A 1960 vase made using the *incalmo* technique to join two pieces of identical diameter.

$$$ • 10 in (25.5 cm) high

"FASCE VERTICALI" CARAFE
An acid-stamped Venini carafe composed of alternating canes of different hues.

$$$ • 10 in (25.5 cm) high

Core Collectibles

VENINI DECANTER
A Venini decanter shaped as a woman, with a yellow bust fused onto the turquoise body by the *incalmo* technique. The base has the engraved signature, "Venini Italia 83."

$$$ • 14¼ in (36 cm) high

VENINI VASE
This c. 1980 glass vase is elongated and globular, with colorful vertical canes.

$$$ • 15½ in (39.5 cm) high

BOTTLE VASE
A Venini brown bottle vase dating from 1966–70, designed by Tony Zuccheri.

$$ • 9 in (23 cm) high

Starter Buys

"SCOTSASI" VASE
A Venini vase of flattened ovoid form with "Scotsasi" tartan pattern.

$$$ • 8¾ in (22 cm) high

"SOMMERSO" VASE
A Seguso Vetri d'Arte *sommerso* vase designed by Flavio Polio, 1960.

$$$ • 7 in (18 cm) high

GLOBULAR VASE
This teal blue and ruby glass vase with a short collared neck dates to the 1970s.

$$ • 7 in (17.5 cm) high

AVEM "TUTTI FRUTTI" DISH
"Tutti Frutti" glass, dating from the 1950s, is made of a kaleidoscope of mixed canes.

$$ • 12¾ in (32.5 cm) wide

You may also like… Murano Tourist Glass, see pp. 106–07

Murano Tourist Glass

"Tourist-quality" Murano glass from the 1950s and '60s is often based on key works by the major designers of the era, allowing something of the color and style of the originals to be obtained for a modest price.

The heyday of Murano "tourist" glass spanned the mid-1950s, when Europe began to recover from the material privations of war, and reached into the late 1960s, when popular taste turned toward Scandinavian design for homewares and furniture.

This glassware, generically known as "tourist," was most often made by noted glass craftsmen working in the island's leading glassworks, such as Barovier & Toso and Seguso. Virtually none of it was signed, however, and foil and paper stickers were applied instead.

Murano tourist glass appeared in all shapes, colors, and sizes, though archetypes certainly exist. The most common color was ruby, often contrasted with colorless glass containing gold leaf highlights. A vast collection of naturalistic and bizarre animal, fish, and human figures were produced by dozens of Murano studios. The most popular type today are vases formed by the *sommerso* method of casing, in which one color is "submerged" beneath another. In more complex examples, pieces may contain as many as five successive colors.

Layers of Value

The number of layers of color in this typical example of basic Murano "sommerso" glass provides a good indication of its quality. Two-tone examples such as this one are worth less than those with four or five layers of color.

YELLOW "SOMMERSO" VASE
This *sommerso* cased vase from the 1960s has diamond-shaped facet-cut sides, which add optical interest to it when viewed.
$ • 6½ in (16 cm) high

TOP TIPS

- Look for fluid, curving forms or free-form shapes with unusual rims.
- Large, impressive, sculptural pieces formed using the *sommerso* technique have retained higher values than more idiosyncratic and gaudy pieces.
- Among novelty and souvenir items, keep an eye out for fine detail and sophistication of design, as well as degrees of craftsmanship.

KEY FACTS	1850	1922	1930s–1940s	1950s	1960s–1980s
Revival, renaissance, and renown	Venetian glassmaking, which saw a downturn in its fortunes in the previous century, enjoys a revival.	The first art glass objects are exhibited publicly at the Venice Biennale exhibition.	The *Stile Novocento* ("New Century") period is one of experimentation, seeing a move away from functionalism.	The *Forme Nuove* ("New Form") era is the most dynamic decade in Murano's glassmaking history.	Murano sees an influx of foreign designers coming from as far afield as Finland and the United States.

What's Hot

Look out for:

This appealing *sommerso* vase is made in the manner of Flavio Poli, designer at Vetri d'Arte Seguso from the early 1940s. A definitive attribution to Poli would multiply its value by at least a factor of 10.

More colors indicate a higher quality

CASED LAMP BASE
An amber and green cased lamp base with a strong, elegant line.
$ • 11 in (28 cm) high

OPAQUE GLASS VASE
This high-quality Murano vase with an hourglass form has red vertical inclusions.
$$ • 12 in (30.5 cm) high

"SOMMERSO" VASE
An ovoid balanced on a narrow base, this vase has four layers: blue, green-to-amber, red, and colorless.
$$ • 6 in (16 cm) high

Core Collectibles

"SOMMERSO" VASE
A heart-shaped *sommerso* vase with the remains of the original foil label, 1950s.
$$ • 4½ in (11.5 cm) high

GLASS SCOTTIE DOG
With black glass and gold inclusions, this Venetian dog has an original label, 1950s.
$ • 9 in (23 cm) long

Starter Buys

GLASS DOVE
A late 20th-century Murano figure of a dove in green glass with gold foil inclusions encased in clear glass.
$ • 3¾ in (9.5 cm) high

MURANO GLASS DUCK
This triple-color *sommerso* duck is applied with a green and gold foil "Made in Murano" sticker linked to the Seguso workshop.
$ • 6 in (16 cm) high

TRIFORM GLASS ASHTRAY
This 1950s Murano ashtray has mottled blue coloring.
$ • 4 in (10 cm) wide

BUBBLE BOWL
A vibrant ruby ribbed bubble bowl, c. 1965.
$ • 5½ in (14 cm) in diameter

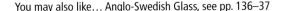

You may also like… Anglo-Swedish Glass, see pp. 136–37

Whitefriars

A glassworks with a centuries-old history, Whitefriars is once again hot, hot, hot! Collector interest has grown massively since the late 1990s, and values have risen correspondingly.

Whitefriars, founded in 1680, was Britain's oldest glassworks when it moved to the London suburb of Wealdstone in 1923, its final closure following two generations later in 1980. Whitefriars glass has since become the subject of intense collector interest.

The greatest demand for Whitefriars glass is two-pronged: for the designs produced on both sides of 1900 by Harry Powell, and for those dating from the 1960s and '70s by Geoffrey Baxter.

Powell designed in several decorative styles, including historical revival, Arts and Crafts, and Art Nouveau. Many of his pieces enjoy a timeless elegance and were produced by the works for several decades in a palette of soft pastels.

Baxter was recruited from the Royal College of Art in 1954. He largely borrowed from the Scandinavian repertoire during the 1950s and '60s, and it was not until 1966 that he began to establish his own identity. In that year, he designed many of his most idiosyncratic pieces, including the "Banjo," "Drunken Bricklayer," and "Bark" vases.

Values of larger Whitefriars pieces continue to rise and fall in the manner of stock market shares today, depending on their specific color.

Meadow Green "Banjo"

Geoffrey Baxter's large "Banjo" vase is one of Britain's most familiar decorative objects. Prices fluctuate, and are color-dependant, with Meadow Green and amethyst being the most sought after.

"BANJO" VASE
A "Banjo" vase designed in 1966, produced between 1967 and '73.
$$$$ • 12½ in (32 cm) high

TOP TIPS

- Check current prices through Internet auction sites, as Whitefriars values are volatile.
- When looking for Harry Powell pieces, note that some of his designs from the 1880s were produced until World War II.
- Beware fake "Drunken Bricklayer" vases: the 8-in (20-cm) is banned from reputable Internet sites.

KEY FACTS	1680	1834	1878	1954	1980
The growth of a historic glassworks	The Whitefriars glassworks is founded on the site of a former Carmelite monastery.	Wine merchant James Powell buys the glassworks to provide his sons with employment.	After studying chemistry at Oxford, Harry Powell joins the works. He stays until his retirement in 1919.	Geoffrey Baxter is hired; he remains at the works as principal designer until 1978.	After three centuries, Whitefriars closes its doors and the site is sold for development.

What's Hot

BAXTER VASE
This 1974 vase is one of Geoffrey Baxter's last designs before his retirement in 1978.
$ • 7½ in (18.5 cm) high

TEARDROP LAMP BASE
A glass teardrop lamp base, produced by Whitefriars in around 1957.
$$ • 11½ in (29 cm) high

Look out for:
Geoffrey Baxter's idiosyncratic vases—including "Cello," "TV," and "Nuts & Bolts"— dating from 1967 are all highly collectible.

Bark effect

PEWTER "BARK" VASE
Geoffrey Baxter's small "Bark" vase in pewter was introduced in 1967.
$ • 6 in (15 cm) high

MEDIUM "BARK" VASE
This bark-textured vase in eggplant was designed by Geoffrey Baxter in 1967.
$ • 9 in (23 cm) high

Core Collectibles

"STREAKY" VASE
The precise designer of this 1936 vase remains unknown.
$$ • 9 in (23 cm) high

WILLIAM WILSON VASE
This vase, c. 1935, is cut with a Modernist pattern.
$$ • 8 in (20 cm) high

Starter Buys

"TOTEM POLE" VASE
The pattern on this 1966 vase was created by nailing a thick wire inside the mold.
$$ • 10¼ in (26 cm) high

"CIRRUS" VASE
A rare "Cirrus" asymmetric vase designed by Geoffrey Baxter and made in 1979.
$$ • 9½ in (24 cm) high

WEALDSTONE VASE
This 1933 Whitefriars/Powell Sea Green vase was designed by Barnaby Powell.
$ • 6 in (15 cm) high

"COFFIN" VASE
Geoffrey Baxter's textured "Coffin" vase in Sage was designed in 1969.
$ • 6 in (15 cm) high

You may also like… Mdina, see pp. 116–17

Carnival Glass

Working-class, iridescent pressed glass, now known as Carnival glass, was a cheap and popular alternative in the early 20th century to the expensive, craft-made glassware of Webb, Loetz, and Tiffany.

In contrast to the complex, highly skilled creations of luxury iridescent glass, Carnival was made by simply spraying pieces of pressed glass with a chemical "dope." And while three Tiffany vases cost as much as a new car, barrels of Carnival could be bought for less than the price of a headlight.

Carnival originated in five US glassworks around the Mississippi Basin. The manufacturing techniques have been widely copied, making this a complex and exhilarating area for collectors, with nearly 2,000 patterns now recorded in almost 60 different colors.

Most Carnival glass remains relatively cheap, especially for common orange (Marigold), blue, and amethyst pieces. The record price for a piece of Carnival, $95,000, was paid for a Northwood "Peacock at the Fountain" punch set in aqua-opal. However, the vast majority of pieces change hands for less than $100.

Iridescent Marvels

This wavy-rimmed bowl by the Northwood Glass Co. is a fine example. It is a good color—amethyst—and shows a particularly attractive iridescence.

AMETHYST "GOOD LUCK" BOWL
A glass bowl in Northwood's "Good Luck" pattern, c. 1908–18. This design is found on both plates and bowls, with pie-crust or ruffled rims.
$$ • 8½ in (22 cm) in diameter

TOP TIPS

- Look for pieces by the early producers: Fenton, Northwood, Imperial, Dugan (later renamed Diamond), and Millersburg.
- Search out trademarks that distinguish original designs from contemporary fakes and reproductions.
- Choose green, amethyst, and smoke colors: they are the most highly sought-after pieces.

KEY FACTS	1907	1908	1909	1925	1970
Affordable glassware from the Mississippi	Fenton Art Glass introduces the first pressed "Iridescent Glass Ware," with 150 patterns at its height.	Harry Northwood Co. introduces Marigold, the classic orange Carnival glass color.	The Imperial Glass Co. launches two new Carnival colors: Rubigold and Peacock.	Northwood, by now the leading producer of Carnival glass, closes as public interest wanes.	Fenton revives its production of Carnival glass, continuing to the present day.

What's Hot

DIAMOND GLASS PITCHER AND BEAKERS
A set including an amethyst glass pitcher and six beakers,
produced by the Diamond Glass Co. in the 1930s.
$$$ • Pitcher 8¾ in (22 cm) high

Look out for:

The swung vase is an American
specialty. The basic molded shape
was swung back and forth while
the glass was still soft, to stretch
it by centrifugal force.

Distinctive fluted "swung" shape

"RIPPLE" SWUNG VASE
A "Ripple" pattern vase
by Imperial in iridescent
amethyst glass, c. 1911–25.
$ • 10½ in (26.5 cm) high

Core Collectibles

**"GOLDEN HARVEST"
DECANTER**
A rare 1920s decanter,
possibly by Diamond Glass Co.
$$ • 12 in (30.5 cm) high

"SINGING BIRDS" BEAKER
A "Singing Birds" pattern
beaker by Northwood,
dating to c. 1908–18.
$$ • 4 in (10 cm) high

Starter Buys

STORK AND RUSHES CUP
A Diamond punch cup from
the Stork and Rushes range.
$ • 2½ in (7 cm) high

IMPERIAL PUNCH CUP
This "Diamond Rings" glass
punch cup is by Imperial.
$ • 2½ in (6.5 cm) high

"GOOD LUCK" BOWL
This is a rare green-glass
variety of the "Good Luck"
pattern bowl by Northwood.
$$ • 8¼ in (21 cm) in diameter

NORTHWOOD MILK JUG
A Northwood milk jug in the
"Grape and Cable" pattern,
introduced in 1910.
$$ • 3 in (7.5 cm) high

"WISHBONE" BOWL
A "Wishbone" pattern bowl in
Marigold color and shape,
made by Northwood.
$$ • 7½ in (19 cm) in diameter

DUGAN COMPOTE
This "Question Marks"
pattern piece by Dugan/
Diamond dates to 1910–20.
$$ • 6½ in (16.5 cm) wide

You may also like… Depression Glass, see pp. 112–13

Depression Glass

Depression glass is a generic term widely used to categorize mass-produced, low-grade American utility glassware made using machinery and techniques developed during the Great Depression.

Depression glass was produced by 19 American works, led by the Indiana, Hocking, Federal, US, Jeannette, MacBeth-Evans, and Hazel-Atlas glass companies, which produced a combined total of 92 patterns. The first, "Avocado," was introduced in 1923, while the most enduring, Westmoreland's "English Hobnail," spanned the years 1928–83.

The glass is divided into several subcategories, including Depression Glass, which was retailed straight from the mold, and Depression-Era Glass, which has a finer finish.

Individual patterns were formed in a variety of colors and qualities, from rough to hand-finished, and most depended on busy designs to disguise their poor quality. The products were cheap—generally sold at nickel-and-dime stores, and even given away at fairs and to movie-goers.

The subject of numerous well-illustrated books and guides, Depression glass is widely available, and is now very popular among collectors—almost exclusively in the United States—for its bright colors and sociohistorical significance.

Dining-Table Elegance
These classic Chintz candlesticks were produced by the Fostoria Glass Co. from the 1940s until 1976. This pair are in one of at least three patterns in the Chintz range, the others being set with varying angles of curve.

CHINTZ CANDLESTICKS
A pair of clear glass candlesticks dating from the 1940s.
$ • 5¼ in (12 cm) high

TOP TIPS
- Compare patterns carefully with industry records to reduce the risk of buying recent reproductions.
- Avoid pieces that are heavily scratched, or permanently clouded by automatic dishwashing.
- Look for complete sets, which are generally more valuable than single pieces.

KEY FACTS	1923	1925	1929	1950	1983
Glass for the masses in the 20th century	The first Depression glass pattern, "Avocado," is introduced by the Indiana Glass Co.	Invention of a machine for the production of a colored crackle effect in glassware.	The first complete ranges of machine-made glass table settings are produced.	The Fostoria glass company's business peaks this year, making over 8 million pieces of glass.	Production of Westmoreland's English Hobnail range ceases after almost 60 years.

What's Hot

MISS AMERICA GLASS
Pieces from Hocking's pink Miss America range are highly sought after.
$$ • 5¾ in (15 cm) high

"COLONY" PITCHER
A clear glass pitcher in the "Colony" pattern, produced by the Fostoria glassworks.
$$ • 8¼ in (21 cm) high

Look out for:

The most complex pieces generally command the highest prices. This "Candlewick" pattern candy box, with its vulnerable interior dividers, lid, ball protrusions, and double tier finial is among the more expensive pieces in the range.

Intact lid is unusual ⎯⎯⎯⎯

Interior dividers ⎯⎯⎯⎯

"CANDLEWICK" CANDY BOX
A clear glass candy box, complete with intact lid and ball finial, made by the Imperial Glass Company.
$$ • 7½ in (19 cm) in diameter

Core Collectibles

BLUE "CAPRICE" CREAMER AND SUGAR BOWL
A blue creamer and sugar bowl set in the "Caprice" pattern, produced by the Cambridge Glass Company between the 1930s and 1950s.
$ • 3 in (8 cm) high

Starter Buys

IRIS GLASS PITCHER
This clear glass pitcher was made by Jeannette Glass Co.
$ • 9 in (23 cm) high

MODERNTONE SET
A Moderntone cup and saucer by Hazel Atlas Glass Co.
$ • Saucer 5½ in (14 cm) in diameter

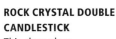

ROCK CRYSTAL DOUBLE CANDLESTICK
This clear glass candlestick was produced by the McKee Glass Co.
$ • 5½ in (14 cm) high

HERMITAGE TUMBLER
A yellow Hermitage tumbler produced by Fostoria.
$ • 4 in (10 cm) high

MOONDROPS TUMBLER
This deep-red tumbler is by the New Martinsville Glass Co.
$ • 4¾ in (12 cm) high

You may also like… Carnival Glass, see pp. 110–11

Michael Harris

Michael Harris was Britain's first successful studio glassmaker. He established three glassworks still in operation today, all located on islands: at Mdina on Malta, on Gozo, and on the Isle of Wight.

After nine years as a tutor at the Royal College of Art, Harris grew tired of its lack of practical facilities. His frustration culminated in 1968, as he watched and worked alongside American studio glassmaker Sam Herman, whose hands-on creative drive proved a revelation. Inspired by Herman's use of color and form, within months, Harris had quit the RCA, assembled 10 tons of equipment, and moved to Malta to establish his own studio. He returned to Britain four years later.

An almost entirely self-taught technical glassmaker, Harris learned on the job, with his designs and general approach becoming increasingly sophisticated and complex. His 1979 Azurene range, in which silver and gold leaf were fused onto glass—a collaboration with a Royal College student—won Isle of Wight Glass a Design Council Award. Today, his sons Tim and Jonathan each run their own works, making high-quality pieces: Tim working on the Isle of Wight, and Jonathan at Ironbridge, Shropshire.

Rich Textures

Michael Harris was probably the first European to appreciate the commercial possibilities of studio glass-making. He first experimented with bark-textured glass in 1964, when working as a consultant at the Rogaška Slatina glassworks in Yugoslavia. He later claimed that Geoffrey Baxter at Whitefriars had "borrowed" the idea (see pp. 108–09).

MDINA DARK GLASS
Rich blues and greens are characteristic of the glass Harris produced in Mdina. This bark-effect finish was widely imitated.

$$ • Largest 11½ in (30 cm) high

TOP TIPS

- Look for signed pieces. Harris preferred not to sign his work, as he considered his pieces to be joint rather than individual creations. The presence of Michael Harris's signature will increase the value of a piece by a factor of five.
- Be careful what you buy: the Mdina factory continued to make pieces designed by Harris until the late 1980s.

KEY FACTS	1933	1950–51	1956–68	1968	1972
From London to Malta and back again	Michael Harris is born in the rural town of Belper in the county of Derbyshire, England.	His interest in glassmaking grows during his foundation year at the Stourbridge Art College.	He becomes a student, then a technical support worker, and finally a tutor at the Royal College of Art, London.	Harris quits the RCA to found Maltese Glass Industries (later Mdina Glass) at Ta'Qali airfield, Malta.	Harris sells his share in Mdina and returns to the UK to found Isle of Wight Studio Glass.

What's Hot

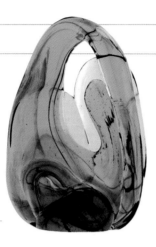

KNOT SCULPTURE
This Mdina glass "knot" type sculpture, showing characteristic free expression of color and form, dated c. 1970, is signed "Michael Harris Mdina Glass."

$$$ • 13 in (33 cm) high

Core Collectibles

SIGNED PAPERWEIGHT
Signed "Michael Harris Isle of Wight," this paperweight has pink and white swirls, with an applied bar.

$$ • 2¼ in (6 cm) high

TORTOISESHELL CHARGER
Harris developed the Tortoiseshell range at Mdina c. 1970, but modified it for the Isle of Wight works.

$$ • 18 in (45 cm) in diameter

PINK AZURENE GLASS VASE
An Isle of Wight vase from the Azurene range with 22kt gold and sterling silver leaf decoration, 1978–84.

$$ • 3¼ in (8 cm) high

ISLE OF WIGHT VASE
From the 1970s, this "Pink and Blue Swirls" Isle of Wight glass vase has a flame logo pontil.

$$ • 3½ in (9 cm) high

Look out for:
Harris's bottle vases, designed in 1970, transform familiar functional shapes into decorative objects. Similarly, the American glassmaker Dale Chihuly made an extensive series of glass "baskets" in the early 1980s.

Exaggerated bottle form

MDINA BOTTLES
Everyday bottle shapes are exaggerated to create decorative objects.

$$ • 14¾ in (37.5 cm) high

Starter Buys

"SHAMROCK" VASE
This "Shamrock" colored glass vase is from 1978.

$ • 13¼ in (13.5 cm) high

TEXTURED MDINA GLASS
An unsigned cylindrical vase from the early 1970s.

$ • 8 in (20 cm) high

BLACK AZURENE VASE
A black Azurene series vase designed in 1978, the first of the Azurene series, still in production.

$ • 2½ in (6.5 cm) high

You may also like… Kaj Franck, see pp. 134–35

Mdina

Founded in 1968, Mdina Glass still thrives on Malta today. Though pieces from the glassworks' early days are the most desirable, all Mdina glass has enjoyed increasing values over recent years.

Mdina glassware can be divided into three categories: pieces made during Michael Harris's regime, work dating from the 20 years or so after his departure in 1972, and modern designs from the mid-1990s onward. Such was the enduring commercial appeal of Harris's designs, most especially his Mediterranean color schemes, that they and their derivatives continued to be produced at Mdina into the early 1990s.

Collector values conform to and are dictated by these categories. Pieces directly associated with Harris are by far the most sought after: his engraved signature on a Mdina piece increases its value by up to 500 percent. Conversely, items from Mdina's recent production have yet to establish a collector base outside Malta.

Collectors today are likely to find glassware made between 1972 and the mid-1990s to be the most accessible, and should look for unsigned pieces made during the Harris era and those made later but still retaining Harris's themes. The bases of many of these feature the distinctive looping engraved Mdina signature that was introduced after 1972.

A Colorful Craft

Compelling color schemes and a handmade quality are the main attractions of Mdina glass. This vase works on both scores: the darker glass is wound around the inner core using basic craft skills, and the volcanic colors achieve a hot harmony.

RED STREAK VASE

An Mdina glass vase from the early 1980s with red streak decoration and random blue trails.

$ • 7½ in (19 cm) high

TOP TIPS

- Look for larger pieces that were less commonly produced—much of Mdina's output has consisted of smaller pieces aimed toward the tourist market.
- Try to find characteristic Harris shapes such as the sought-after Fish vase.
- Note that pieces signed "Michael Harris Mdina Glass Malta" are by far the most valuable.

KEY FACTS	1968	1972	1976	1985	2000 onward
Glassmaking in the Mediterranean	Michael Harris and Eric Dobson found Mdina Glass on Malta.	The Harris family sells its share in the Mdina glassworks to Dobson and leaves Malta.	Mdina hires more skilled glassworkers to meet an increase in demand.	Joseph Said, Harris's first local apprentice, becomes the owner of Mdina Glass.	Production expands, and more designer and limited-edition pieces are introduced.

What's Hot

ONION-SHAPED VASE
A mid-'80s opaque-ocher onion-shaped bottle vase with a central multicolored band.
$ • 6 in (15.5 cm) high

FACETED VASE
A brown and blue clear cased vase with two large polished faces, signed "Mdina 1978."
$ • 7 in (17.5 cm) high

Look out for:
It did not take long for Michael Harris to capture the colors and atmosphere of the Mediterranean in his glass after arriving on Malta in 1968. This particular colorway suggests the vision that a snorkel diver would see after diving into a Maltese reef on a sunny summer day.

Typical chunky, thick glass

Blue-green colorway

Yellow streaks made by adding silver chloride

HARRIS VASE
This 1970s Mdina vase is in classic Mediterranean Harris colors.
$ • 5¼ in (13.5 cm) high

Core Collectibles

HARRIS-ESQUE VASE
This blue-green vase is based on a Harris design, and was produced in the early 1980s.
$ • 5 in (13 cm) high

"LOLLIPOP" VASE
This ovoid vase features a typical yellow, green, and blue core within a clear overcasing.
$$ • 8¾ in (22 cm) high

STREAKY CYLINDRICAL VASE
An early 1980s Mdina vase decorated with red streaks and random blue trails.
$ • 6 in (15 cm) high

"TIGER" PATTERN VASE
This mid-1970s landscape-inspired vase was designed by Eric Dobson.
$$ • 7 in (18 cm) high

Starter Buys

GLASS PAPERWEIGHT
This spherical paperweight in blue-green glass bears a Mdina factory mark.
$ • 5 in (13 cm) high

PERFUME BOTTLE
This spherical bottle from the 1980s is signed on the base and has a glass stopper.
$ • 5 in (13 cm) high

You may also like… Michael Harris, see pp. 114–15

Nazeing

Besides its many industrial commissions, glass factory Nazeing Glass Works produced a range of original art glass for a limited period. This output is readily available to collectors today.

Generally undertaking customers' commissions rather than producing its own designs, Nazeing has made an astonishing variety of industrial, architectural, pharmaceutical, promotional, and domestic glassware through a similarly impressive variety of methods.

Collectors are particularly interested, however, in the extended series of decorative glassware introduced from the mid-1930s. Characterized by light and darker streaking tones, mottled and swirling effects, and random bubbles of varying

sizes, the glass was retailed through fashionable London stores such as Harrods and Heal's. Production of this art glass was halted during World War II, but resumed after the war and continued into the 1950s.

Nazeing's output also included a prolific series of pressed-glass ashtrays formed in a range of colors and shapes, and applied with promotional logos intended for the pub trade. These ashtrays are currently out of fashion and can be picked up for relatively small sums. They do, however, hold future potential for forward-thinking collectors.

Cloud-Spotter's Guide

In 1935, Nazeing introduced its own range of decorative art glass. Drawing on a palette of pale blue, pink, orange, purple, and this green, the majority of pieces in this Cloud range are distinguished by marbled, mottled, and swirling effects, as in this lightweight vase.

GREEN CLOUD VASE
Dating from the 1930s, this Nazeing glass vase is in May Green.
$$ • 10 in (25 cm) high

TOP TIPS

- Look for the mottled and swirling pastel-colored art glass produced during the 1930s and '50s.
- Learn about the characteristics of the style, to help identify pieces. The Nazeing palette of the 1930s is dominated by pale blues, greens, purple, and pink, with light and darker streaking tones and random bubbles, large and small.

KEY FACTS	1928	1930s	c. 1935	1939–45	1960s onward
Diversity and design over the years	Kemptons glassworks in Vauxhall, London, relocates 15 miles (24 km) northeast to Nazeing.	The glassworks produces a range of Venetian-style wire-cage lamps.	Nazeing introduces its new range of colored art glass with bubbled, mottled, and swirling color effects.	During the war, the glassworks makes black vitrite glass and technical lightbulbs and tubes.	Nazeing continues its tradition of commissions with a diverse range of products including stemware and lights.

What's Hot

GLASS BOWL
This Nazeing glass bowl in swirled mulberry was made in the 1930s.
$ • 8 in (20.5 cm) diameter

MOTTLED GREEN BOWL
This specific color and pattern is now attributed to Stevens & Williams.
$ • 4¾ in (12 cm) high

Look out for:
A mottled texture, as seen in this bubbled glass, is typical of Nazeing decorative glasswares.

Clear glass decorated with colored powdered enamels

BUBBLED BLUE VASE
A 1930s bubbled vase, in which the color "lies" in the bubbles.
$ • 8¼ in (21 cm) high

Core Collectibles

SWIRLED VASE
This vase from the Cloud range has opaque, mottled, and swirled coloring.
$ • 7½ in (18.5 cm) high

MOTTLED LAMP BASE
This spherical pink mottled glass lamp base was made in the 1930s.
$ • 6¼ in (16 cm) high

Starter Buys

GLASS SALT
A 1950s Nazeing salt in deep pink.
$ • 5¼ in (13 cm) in diameter

YELLOW VASE
This yellow Nazeing glass vase, c. 1950, has a clear foot.
$ • 4¾ in (12 cm) high

1950S BOWL
Made in the 1950s, this pale blue glass bowl with a wide rim bears the characteristic mottling and swirling of Nazeing art glass of the period.
$ • 9½ in (24 cm) in diameter

MARBLED WHITE JUG
This is a marbled, opaque white Nazeing jug with a clear glass handle, 1930s.
$ • 6½ in (16.5 cm) high

PRESSED TRICORN BOWL
The mold for this bowl was bought by Nazeing from Sowerby glassworks in 1972.
$ • 6½ in (16.5 cm) in diameter

You may also like… Mdina, see pp. 116–17

Drinking Glasses

Interest in collecting drinking glasses has been growing apace since the late 1960s. Today, collector potential is gathering momentum in the wide variety of 18th-, 19th-, and 20th-century pieces available.

The 1968 disposal in two auctions of a large collection of 18th-century drinking glasses amassed by an American, Walter F. Smith, is generally regarded as marking the dawn of wide interest in this subject. The prices the auctions generated became regarded as the benchmark figures by which similar pieces were traded.

While there continues to be a clear demand today for drinking glasses from the 18th century, 19th-century glasses tend to be ignored despite their tremendous potential appeal. The best pieces,

particularly colorful Bohemian glasses, can sell for thousands of dollars, but average-to-good pieces offer remarkable value, with examples often available for pennies.

Meanwhile, very few collectors have yet set their targets on 20th-century glass, so enthusiasts should start collecting early. The main attraction of this group is its wide spectrum of colors, textures, and forms, and—thanks to an improving body of literature devoted to the subject—the ability to link given examples with their designers and makers.

Bright Lights, Big Ideas

Ronald Stennett-Willson designed his influential Harlequin tumblers in the late 1950s for the GEC lightbulb glassworks at Lemington, near Newcastle, after the production of bulbs was switched to another plant. The glowing colors of this set, each one a different shade, are highly evocative of the popular styles and fashions of the late 1950s.

HARLEQUIN TUMBLERS
A GEC Lemington glassworks set of six Harlequin tumblers in blue, amber, amethyst, red, green, and gray, designed by Stennett-Willson in 1959. Their ingenious shape means that they are virtually impossible to tip over.

$ • 3½ in (9 cm) high

KEY FACTS	1830s	1936	1950s	1967	1968
Making beautiful glasses	The first European pressed glass is produced. It is also used commercially for making windows.	Orrefors Glasbruk invents the Ariel method of trapping bubbles in glass.	GEC Lemington glassworks expands its production from lightbulbs and tubes into drinking ware.	Dartington glassworks is founded in south Devon, with the aim of sparking economic regeneration.	The Walter F. Smith glass collection goes under the hammer at Sotheby's.

What's Hot

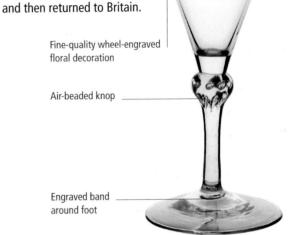

Look out for:

It is now known that the group of finely engraved mid-18th-century wine glasses widely known as "Newcastles" were, in fact, made and decorated in Holland. Previous generations believed that they were made in Newcastle, exported to Holland to be engraved, and then returned to Britain.

Fine-quality wheel-engraved floral decoration

Air-beaded knop

Engraved band around foot

BEILBY WINE GLASS

A Beilby wine glass from 1765, with a plain conical foot, its bowl enameled with fruiting vine decoration, and its stem with a double series opaque twist.

$$$$ • 6 in (15 cm) high

18TH-CENTURY WINE GLASS

Dating to 1750, this wine glass has a trumpet bowl on a drawn multiple-spiral, air-twist stem, its bowl engraved with the Jacobite rose, two buds, an oak leaf, and a star.

$$$$ • 6 in (15 cm) high

"NEWCASTLE" WINE GLASS

A so-called "Newcastle" wine glass from 1750, with the trumpet bowl finely engraved around the rim. The glass has a plain stem with an air-beaded knop and a plain conical foot.

$$$$ • 6¾ in (17.5 cm) high

VARNISH & CO. GOBLET

This 1849 Varnish & Co. golden goblet is decorated with a delicate tracery of foliage, flowers, and birds on the bowl and base.

$$ • 9 in (23 cm) high

CHAMPAGNE GLASS

A green T. G. Jackson champagne glass designed for J. Powell's Whitefriars in 1870. This has a wide bowl and a darker stem and base.

$ • 4¾ in (12 cm) high

What's Not

The value of cranberry glass has roughly halved over the past decade, because of the difficulty in differentiating genuine Victorian pieces from reproductions being handmade in China today.

CRANBERRY GLASS

This is lovely to look at but is otherwise unexceptional.

$ • 5 in (12.5 cm) high

Core Collectibles

LATE 18TH-CENTURY GOBLET
This glass goblet from 1790 has a round, diamond-cut bowl on a plain square foot.
$$ • 6 in (15 cm) high

BONNET GLASS
Dating to 1740, this mold-decorated glass has an ogee bowl.
$$ • 3 in (7.5 cm) high

EARLY CUT WINE GLASS
A rare early glass, 1735–40, with an eight-sided slice-cut stem and a petal-cut bowl.
$$ • 6¼ in (16 cm) high

TRUMPET WINE GLASS
A drawn trumpet wine glass with a tear in the stem and a folded foot, c. 1750.
$$ • 6 in (15.5 cm) high

SET OF WINE GLASSES
Two of a set of six flute-cut wine glasses dating to 1830–40. These fine examples have conical fluted bowls and bladed knop stems.
$$ • 5 in (13 cm) high

DWARF ALE GLASS
This bowl of this dwarf ale glass has a flamiform edge or "fringe," 1730.
$$$ • 4¼ in (11 cm) high

CRANBERRY GLASS TUMBLERS
Cranberry is such a strong color that most cranberry glassware is composed of around 90 percent colorless glass.
$$ • 4 in (10 cm) high

Ask the Expert

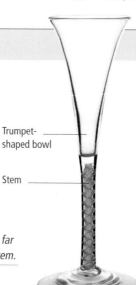

Q. Why were 18th-century drinking glasses frequently so small?
A. At the dining table, they were used exclusively for down-the-hatch toasting, so the capacity of their bowls needed to be restricted.

Trumpet-shaped bowl

Stem

GLASS FLUTE
The value of this glass would be far greater with a colored twisted stem.
$$$ • 7½ in (19 cm) high

Q. What is a rummer?
A. A British lead-glass goblet with a generous bowl, usually of half-pint capacity. Generally dating from between 1790 and 1830, these glasses were either left plain or had cut or engraved decoration. The name is probably derived from the Dutch or German *roemer* or *römer*.

Q. Are there any special tips for starting to collect glassware?
A. Do your research before you start and then choose a style, pattern, and color that appeals to you. Note that certain styles are more popular in certain countries: colorful Depression glass, for instance, is highly collectible in the US, but much less so elsewhere.

EARLY WINE GLASS
A drawn trumpet wine glass, c. 1740, with a ball knop containing a tear.
$$$ • 6¼ in (16 cm) high

GLASS RUMMER
Dating to 1800, this rummer has a lemon-squeezer base and a bucket bowl finely engraved with a stagecoach theme. The reverse shows a view of a church spire, with the initials "MBH" finely engraved.
$$$$ • 6¼ in (16 cm) high

BALUSTROID WINE GLASS
This 1720 glass has a bell bowl with a shoulder knop, and central and base ball knops.
$$$ • 6¾ in (17 cm) high

TRUMPET WINE GLASS
A drawn trumpet wine glass from 1745 with multi-spiral air twists and a plain foot.
$$ • 7 in (17 cm) high

DECEPTIVE GLASS
A deceptive bowl gin glass with a stylish ball knop stem, dated 1840.
$ • 4 in (10 cm) high

ANGLO-VENETIAN GLASS
A copy of a late 17th-century wine glass, probably made between 1890 and 1920.
$ • 5½ in (14 cm) high

"COLONIAL BLOCK" GOBLET
A green pressed Depression-era goblet made by Hazel Atlas Glass Co. in the 1930s.
$ • 5¾ in (15 cm) high

BELL-BOWLED GOBLET
A c. 1910 Art Nouveau glass with applied green tendrils, designed by Harry Powell.
$ • 5¾ in (14.5 cm) high

TAVERN RUMMER
A bucket-shaped tavern rummer from 1870 with a gadget mark.
$ • 5½ in (14 cm) high

Core Collectibles

GLASS TANKARD
This cranberry tankard is engraved "To Madame Fontana as souvenir from Mr Voisin, 1840."
$ • 5½ in (14 cm) high

CRANBERRY CHAMPAGNE GLASS
The cranberry overcasing of this champagne coupe is cut through to reveal the colorless glass beneath, creating a dramatic optical effect.
$ • 5 in (12.5 cm) high

AMETHYST WINE GLASS
It is often tricky dating colored Georgian glass accurately, but this one dates to c. 1790–1820.
$ • 4¾ in (12 cm) high

VICTORIAN GOBLET
A Victorian marriage goblet made by John Ford of Edinburgh, c. 1865.
$$ • 9½ in (24 cm) high

WINE GLASS SET
A set of light-green wine glasses from 1840 with flute-cut bowls and knopped stems.
$ • 5 in (13 cm) high

ENGRAVED GOBLET
A goblet from 1820 engraved with a stagecoach theme, its reverse depicting a hamlet.
$$ • 8¼ in (21 cm) high

RUBY-CASED GLASS
This delicate wine glass, c. 1870, has a petal-cut bowl and a hollow stem. Mrs. Beeton included colored wine glasses in her illustration of a perfect table setting, published in 1861.
$ • 5 in (13 cm) high

ISLE OF WIGHT GOBLET
A fine Timothy Harris goblet with an abstract glass knop on the stem, from the 1990s.
$$ • 5½ in (14 cm) high

LOBMEYR WINE GLASSES
The bases of these goblets are enameled with the distinctive portcullis logo of the Viennese luxury glass retailer J. L. Lobmeyr.
$$$ • 4½ in (11.5 cm) high

CONICAL-BOWL WINE GLASS
A green wine glass with a conical bowl and a knopped stem, c. 1810.
$$$ • 5 in (13 cm) high

HOCK GLASS
Predominantly orange, this two-color hock glass is a Stevens & Williams piece.
$$ • 8 in (20 cm) high

ETCHED WINE GLASS
This green wine glass, machine-acid-etched in gilt, has a plain stem.
$ • 5 in (13 cm) high

PURPLE HOCK GLASS
This is a purple Stevens & Williams two-color German white wine glass.
$$ • 8 in (20 cm) high

RED GOBLET
A Sandwich goblet in eye-catching red, with embossed decorations.
$ • 5½ in (14 cm) high

Starter Buys

AMBER GLASS
A mid-19th-century delicately colored amber-tinted glass with a slice-cut bowl and a waisted stem, c. 1840.
$ • 5 in (13 cm) high

18TH-CENTURY WINE GLASS
A typical bottom-rung mid-18th-century wine glass, dated c. 1750, with a plain stem and folded foot.
$$ • 7½ in (19 cm) high

You may also like… Whitefriars, see pp. 108–09

Swedish Postwar Glass

With its micropopulation of just six million and a history virtually devoid of noteworthy glass, it is an extraordinary fact that Sweden emerged as the most important glassmaking nation of the 20th century.

Glassmaking at Kosta (founded in 1742 with royal patronage) has been going on for centuries, but it was not until Albert Ahlin of the then-obscure Orrefors Glasbruk recruited Knut Bergquist as master blower, Gustav Abels as cutter, and Simon Gate and Edward Hald as designers in 1914–17 that Swedish glass began to possess a unique identity. Orrefors' supremacy was ensured by its succession of designers, including Sven Palmqvist, Nils Landberg, Edvin Öhrström, Ingeborg Lundin, and Gunnar Cyren in the postwar period, and at least a dozen more notable designers over the decades.

Erik Höglund, arguably Sweden's greatest postwar glass designer, was recruited by the Boda glassworks in 1953. He created a broad range of offbeat, rustic, humorous pieces for Boda between 1953 and 1973, and inspired a further generation of talent to follow, including Bergt Edenfalk (Skruf), Lars Hellsten (Skruf & Orrefors), and Wiktor Berndt (Flygsfors).

The best Swedish glass usually bears an engraved signature beneath its base, but many "production signatures" were applied with stickers that have since been removed, and it can be difficult for collectors and experts to attribute them to specific designers.

Pool of Blue and Green

Designed by John Orwar Lake, chief designer at Sweden's Ekenäs Glasbruk between 1953 and 1976, this shallow dish is formed in Lake's most successful color scheme: blue over green.

EKENÄS BOWL
A characteristically strongly colored design, signed "Ekenäs Sweden J. O. Lake L.1456/17."
$ • 8¼ in (21 cm) wide

TOP TIPS

- Look out for engraved signatures on the bases of pieces for the best-quality glass. Pieces without stickers are difficult to attribute.
- Note that sludgy colors generally signify older, less valuable pieces. The bright colors of more recent production are more sought after.
- Avoid chips on cut edges or the rim as these significantly reduce value.

KEY FACTS	1742	1913	1925	1970	1980
The world reputation of Swedish glass	Kosta glassworks is founded in Småland, the future glassmaking capital of Sweden.	Papermaker Johan Ekman buys Orrefors, and appoints Albert Ahlin its manager.	The Paris "Art Deco" Exhibition first brings the Orrefors company to the world's attention.	By now, 4,000 glassmakers are employed in the southern Småland region.	Swedish glass employment halves in a decade as limited editions replace table-glass manufacture.

What's Hot

KOSTA GLASS VASE
A "Ventana" vase with cut facets, designed in 1957 by Mona Morales-Schildt.
$$ • 9 in (23 cm) high

HÖGLUND GLASS VASE
This textured glass vase was designed by Erik Höglund for Boda, c. 1960.
$$ • 8½ in (21.5 cm) high

Look out for:

Erik Höglund had just graduated as a sculptor when he was recruited in 1953 by the ailing Boda glassworks as chief designer. He soon emerged as the most significant glass designer of his generation.

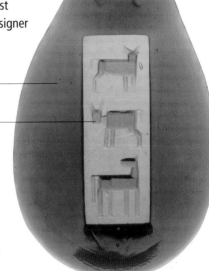

Freeform shape ⎯⎯⎯⎯

Pressed primitive animal designs ⎯⎯⎯⎯

Core Collectibles

BODA SUNCATCHER
This suncatcher, signed "H866/F," was designed by Erik Höglund, c. 1960.
$$ • 11¾ in (30 cm) wide

PAUL KEDELV VASE
This still-blown vase, c. 1965, was designed for Reijmyre by Paul Kedelv.
$ • 8¼ in (21 cm) high

"JAGGED EDGE" VASE
A blue and green vase with interior bubbles, designed by Göran Wärff for Kosta.
$$ • 9½ in (24 cm) high

Starter Buys

ORREFORS GLASS CHARGER
A large, freeform "Expo" blown-glass charger, designed by Sven Palmqvist for Orrefors, c. 1955.
$$ • 20½ in (52 cm) diameter

FREEFORM VASE
A c. 1955 Gunnel Nylund vase, signed "Stromgergshyttan G. Nylund" on the base.
$ • 4¼ in (11 cm) high

BODA VASE
This green carafe vase with celestial motifs is signed by the designer Bertil Vallien.
$$ • 5¾ in (14.5 cm) high

You may also like… Michael Harris, see pp. 114–15

Danish Glass

Denmark ranks behind Sweden and Finland in 20th-century Nordic glassmaking. This says more about the quality of Swedish and Finnish glassware than the paucity of Danish equivalents.

Like Sweden and Finland, Denmark had produced no glassware of international consequence before around 1920. The previous products of its glassworks were poor generic copies of mostly British stemware and French Art Nouveau cameo.

Everything changed when Jacob Bang joined the Danish royal glassworks at Holmegaard in 1927, bringing an original aesthetic that combined utility and sophistication. Some of his 1930s exhibition pieces, derivatives of which entered standard production, are among the finest of their age.

Bang left Holmegaard to join its rival Kastrup and was replaced by Per Lütken in 1942. Over a 56-year career at Holmegaard, Lütken's output captured its times probably better than any other, from his early 1950s organic aqua-blue tinted "Heart" and "Beak" vases through the boldly color-cased "Carnaby" in 1968, to his sculptural suncatchers in 1975.

Lütken was joined in 1968 by Bang's son Michael. Trained in ceramics and glass, Michael designed lighting and utility ranges, some in vividly twin-color-cased opaque glass.

Tall and Stately Glass

Universally attributed to Otto Brauer, Holmegaard's Gulvæse (floor vase), from 1962, was in fact the culmination of a design that began to evolve with Per Lütken around 1955 and was continued by Jacob Bang at Kastrup around 1960.

OTTO BRAUER VASES
Designed for Holmegaard in 1962, this is a selection of Otto Brauer floor vases.

$$$ • Largest 17 in (45 cm) high

TOP TIPS

- Look for typical Danish glass designs from after 1950, which were inspired by organic themes such as landscapes, ice, frost, and bark.
- Note that the top designers moved freely between the main glass manufacturers, exchanging ideas and inspiration.
- Large, colorful pieces are still manufactured at Holmegaard and are therefore priced competitively.

KEY FACTS	1825	1927–42	1942–98	1965	1985
Glassmaking in the Danish style	Royal glassworks Holmegaard is founded at Fensmark, 60 miles (100 km) southwest of Copenhagen.	Architect Jacob Bang (1899–1965) becomes Holmegaard's chief designer.	Per Lütken replaces Jacob Bang at Holmegaard, continuing and developing his work.	Holmegaard amalgamates with Kastrup, Hellerup & Odense.	Holmegaard is bought by Royal Copenhagen, owner of Venini and Orrefors/Kosta/Boda.

What's Hot

Look out for:

Per Lütken was one of the most influential postwar glass designers. Many of his pieces, particularly those from the 1950s, like his classic "Heart" vase, below, are organic in shape, appearing to have been harvested rather than manufactured.

Smooth contours

Organic shape

MICHAEL BANG ELEPHANT
A 1969 Bang Holmegaard suncatcher, from the Noah's Ark series.
$ • 5 in (13 cm) diameter

TRI-FORM VASE
This purple tri-form section vase was designed by Lütken for Holmegaard in 1955.
$$ • 10¼ in (26 cm) high

"HEART" VASE
This small heart-shaped vase was designed by Lütken for Holmegaard in 1952. This particular piece was made in 1959 and is signed and dated.
$$ • 2 in (5 cm) high

Core Collectibles

ICE BUCKET
Designed for Holmegaard by Jacob Bang in 1937, this is signed "Holmegaard 8715."
$ • 6 in (15 cm) high

PER LÜTKEN VASE
This Holmegaard "Maygreen" vase was designed by Per Lütken in 1963.
$ • 11½ in (29 cm) high

Starter Buys

HOLMEGAARD VASE
This Holmegaard vase, designed by Per Lütken in 1953 and made in 1961, is signed on the base.
$ • 4 in (10 cm) high

ATLANTIS SERIES BOWL
This white glass bowl, with blue freeform streaks, was designed by Michael Bang.
$ • 3 in (7.5 cm) high

PER LÜTKEN SUNCATCHER
A suncatcher/sculpture from Lütken's Four Seasons series, designed in 1975.
$$$ • 16½ in (42 cm) diameter

SMOKY GLASS BOWL
A Holmegaard smoky glass bowl, with an asymmetric flaring form and rim, this piece was designed by Per Lütken in the 1950s. Its base is engraved "Holmegaard PL."
$ • 9½ in (24 cm) diameter

You may also like… Kaj Franck, see pp. 134–35

Lindstrand at Kosta

The quality of Vicke Lindstrand's work at Orrefors (1928–40) is universally acknowledged, and the best examples command high prices. However, his designs for Kosta (1951–74) remain largely unstudied.

Victor Emanuel Lindstrand was born in Göteborg, Sweden, in 1904, and demonstrated an early talent for drawing. He was working as a commercial artist when, aged 24, he was recruited by Orrefors in 1928. By the mid-1930s he was probably the firm's most important designer, applying sinuous, figurative decoration to strikingly bold forms.

Wartime shortages of materials and customers forced Lindstrand's departure from Orrefors in 1940. He designed ceramics until 1951, when he was reunited with glass at Kosta, where he remained for 23 years. The vast majority of his glassware, barring basic utility pieces, was signed beneath the base, both at Orrefors and Kosta.

Lindstrand's Kosta period saw him explore across the ranges of free-formed to mold-blown, and functionalism to abstract. He used several different decorative techniques: engraving, cutting, optic, and internal, and applied both sober and whimsical approaches to design.

Seasons Passing

This internally decorated "Winter" vase was designed by Lindstrand for Kosta, c. 1962. His similarly formed "Spring," "Summer," and "Autumn" appeared in 1953, but "Winter" proved particularly difficult to create. Given the production number 1801, it was never cataloged and remains extremely rare.

"WINTER" VASE
This vase, signed "Kosta LH 1801," has an ethereal quality evoked by its color and form.
$$$$ • 10½ in (27 cm) high

TOP TIPS

- Look for engraved Lindstrand glassware: this is currently unfashionable, and all but the finest pieces are relatively cheap.
- Consider size. "Dark Magic" vases were produced in two sizes: roughly 5 in (12.5 cm) and 8 in (20 cm). Larger sizes can command up to four times as much as smaller ones.
- Note that some Lindstrand designs enjoyed prolonged production, with early examples the most valuable.

KEY FACTS	1904	1928	1940–51	1951–74	1978–83
A glorious career at two great factories	Lindstrand is born in Göteborg, Sweden. He shows an artistic flair at a young age and goes on to study illustration.	After a meeting at an industry exhibition, Lindstrand is invited to join Orrefors' design team by Simon Gate.	Designs a variety of ceramics, particularly figures and vases, for Upsala-Ekeby and the Karlskrona factory.	Lindstrand is appointed chief designer at the Kosta Glasbruk glassworks, later to become Kosta Boda.	Lindstrand designs at Studio Glashyttan, Åhus, founded by former Kosta glassblower Arthur Zirnsack.

What's Hot

Look out for:

Lindstrand's designs for Kosta bridged the divide between daring and demanding, and plain and simple. In this vase, fine amethyst and white canes were first incorporated into colorless crystal, and the whole was then stretched into an hourglass shape.

Graceful stripes

"SAFARI" VASE
Lindstrand's visit to Kenya in the early 1950s influenced later pieces such as this one.
$$$$ • 12½ in (32 cm) high

ENGRAVED CLEAR VASE
This tapering glass vase is engraved with a decoration of birds and foliage.
$$$$ • 12½ in (32 cm) high

CASED HOURGLASS VASE
A tall, waisted, and cased vase with internal, vertical alternating amethyst and white glass canes, signed "Kosta LH 1257."
$$ • 12¼ in (31 cm) high

Core Collectibles

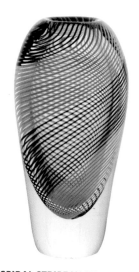

SPIRAL STRIPE VASE
An internally decorated vase designed by Lindstrand for Kosta in 1960.
$$ • 6¼ in (16 cm) high

GRADUATED COLOR VASE
This vase has an air bubble trapped in its base. It is signed "Kosta LH 1859."
$$ • 9 in (23 cm) high

Starter Buys

TRI-FORM GLASS DISH
This 1960 tri-form clear-cased Kosta dish has a decoration of swirling canes.
$$ • 6¼ in (16 cm) wide

"DARK MAGIC" VASES
Two Lindstrand "Dark Magic" vases made for Kosta, with bases signed "Kosta LH 1605."
$$$ • 5 in (13 cm) high

HEAVY GLASS BOWL
A blue-gray bowl designed as a table decoration by Lindstrand in 1970.
$ • 13 in (33 cm) in diameter

"MOONSHINE" BOWL
A small ovoid "Moonshine" bowl signed "Kosta LH 1316/90."
$ • 3 in (7.5 cm) high

You may also like… Swedish Postwar Glass, see pp. 126–27

Wirkkala & Sarpaneva

Some glassworks were fortunate to employ one great designer during the 20th century. Iittala of Finland was one of very few to employ at least two of them: Tapio Wirkkala and Timo Sarpaneva.

Wirkkala joined Iittala, at age 31, in 1946. After working in wood, plastics, metal, ceramics, and architecture, he became a glassman. His reputation was established in 1951, when he won the Grand Prix at the Milan Triennale for his "Kantarelli" and "Foal's Foot" engraved objects. A huge, bearded, pipe-smoking bear of a man, Wirkkala spent half the year in Lapland. Surrounded by its alternately verdant and ice-blasted expanses, he became absorbed in its traditions, people, wildlife, silence, and textures. The natural patterns created by low temperatures and searing winds feature in many of his designs.

Sarpaneva was only 22 when united with Wirkkala at Iittala in 1950. His contribution to the glass world was at least comparable to that of Wirkkala. Remarkably, he too won the Milan Triennale in 1953, for his "Lancetti" art object.

Delicate Organic Shapes

One of the most important pieces of postwar glass design, this sculptural vase won the Grand Prix at the Milan Triennale design competition in 1951. Examples of these sculptures are housed in most of the world's leading decorative arts museums, and are highly prized by collectors.

"KANTARELLI" SCULPTURE
This engraved "Kantarelli," an homage to the trumpet-shaped chanterelle mushroom, was designed by Wirkkala for Iittala in 1946.
$$ • 8 in (20.6 cm) high

TOP TIPS

- Learn to distinguish between Wirkkala's work, which displays an intuitive natural force, and Sarpaneva's, which usually shows a more graphic, less organic approach.
- Look out for the distinctive Sarpaneva-designed Iittala logo (a white "i" in a red circle), usually on the glass as a cellophane sticker.

KEY FACTS	1881	1950	1951 & 1953	1956	1985 & 2006
Northern stars	The Iittala glass factory is founded in Finland by Petrus Magnus Abrahamsson, a Swede.	Wirkkala and Sarpaneva meet at Iittala. Sarpaneva, 22, is overshadowed for many years.	First Wirkkala then Sarpaneva win the Milan Triennale Grand Prix for their innovative glass designs.	Sarpaneva designs the famous "i" logo for Iittala, winning the Lunning prize for design.	Wirkkala dies in 1985 and Sarpaneva passes away in 2006, leaving behind them a rich design legacy.

What's Hot

"AURINKOPALLO"
A mold-blown "sunball" sculpture designed by Timo Sarpaneva in 1960.
$$$ • 6½ in (16.5 cm) in diameter

WIRKKALA VASE
Originally designed as a colorless piece, this features clear glass over smoke blue.
$$ • 6½ in (16.5 cm) high

Look out for:
The Finlandia series, inspired by charred wood, became one of the most influential designs in postwar glass. The glass was blown into wooden molds that intentionally burned out through use.

Burned wood effect

Core Collectibles

"PINUS" VASE
Signed "TW" on its base, this "Pinus" vase was designed by Wirkkala for Iittala. Inspired by nature, the piece resembles ice formations on tree bark.
$ • 8¾ in (22.5 cm) high

FINLANDIA VASE
A smoke-gray Finlandia vase designed by Timo Sarpaneva in 1964, with an engraved signature: "TIMO SARPANEVA 3351."
$$ • 6½ in (17.4 cm) high

Starter Buys

IITTALA CANDLESTICKS
Candlesticks with an irregular, textured, barklike pattern, from Sarpaneva's bestselling Festivo series, 1967.
$ • Largest 8½ in (21.5 cm) high

"KANTO" VASE
This mold-blown crystal glass "tree stump" vase is signed "3241 Tapio Wirkkala."
$ • 4½ in (11.5 cm) high

"COG" VASE
An architectural mold-blown vase designed by Wirkkala and signed "Tapio Wirkkala 3552."
$$ • 6½ in (16.5 cm) high

KLINKA WHISKEY TUMBLER
One of a set of clear textured whiskey glasses designed by Sarpaneva for Iittala.
$$ • 3½ in (8.5 cm) high

ULTIMA THULE TANKARDS
Two still-mold blown tankards, part of Wirkkala's bestselling range.
$ • 4¾ in (12 cm) high

You may also like… Drinking Glasses, see pp. 120–25

Kaj Franck

One of Finland's greatest and most versatile designers, Kaj Franck was known as "the conscience of Finnish design" in his work as director of design at Arabia ceramics and Nuutajärvi glassworks.

Franck designed a vast array of everyday and studio pieces in ceramics as well as glass, many of which defined a decorative vocabulary that still dominates today, most notably at Ikea. He was widely exhibited, and won the Lunning Prize in 1955 and the Milan Triennale two years later, yet he has never received wider credit, largely because his work was often unsigned. As he put it: "I want to make utensils that are so self-evident that they pass unnoticed."

When Franck went to work at Arabia in 1945 he was put in a position to directly influence the style of the Finnish home. He did this with his "smash the services" campaign, in which he introduced mix-and-match tableware, which was highly functional as well as good-looking, to replace old-fashioned china. At Nuutajärvi he produced a wide variety of functional glassware sets plus some decorative pieces such as his award-winning "Woodcock." He was fascinated by color and experimented widely with it, believing that Finnish colors were "subtle, elegant... intimately related to nature."

Unique Goblets
The Pokaali series of goblets was designed in 1972 at the peak of Franck's powers. Each example was unique, and hand-formed in three pieces: the bowl, foot, and a disk between the two, all in different color combinations. They were produced until 1977, but although they bear engraved signatures, they are never specifically dated.

GOBLET VASE
This deep amethyst Pokaali (goblet) vase was designed by Kaj Franck in 1972.
$$$ • 8½ in (21.5 cm) high

TOP TIPS
- Choose signed pieces. Though Finnish glassworks did not routinely sign their output, the more expensive pieces often were signed.
- Know (and pronounce!) your names: Nuutajärvi, Iittala, and Riihimäki, all situated north of Helsinki, were Finland's leading postwar glassworks.

KEY FACTS	1793	1932	1973	1983	1992
Creating timeless Finnish forms	Nuutajärvi glassworks is founded in Finland. It is the oldest Finnish glassworks still functioning today.	Kaj Franck graduates as an interior architect from the Central School of Applied Art in Finland.	Franck is appointed professor at the Finnish Institute of Applied Arts, a position he holds until 1978.	The Royal College of Art in London awards Franck an honorary doctorate in recognition of his design work.	Design Forum Finland establishes the Kaj Franck prize, awarded annually to an artist working in his spirit.

What's Hot

NOTSJÖ OBJET D'ART
A modern classic, this signed sculptural object was designed by Franck in 1962.
$$ • 3½ in (8.5 cm) wide

CYLINDRICAL VASE
This sculptural vase was produced in three sizes from 1960–66.
$$ • 4½ in (11 cm) high

Look out for:
This design was produced in relatively large numbers between 1957 and 1969. Its disk-shaped knop and "hourglass" silhouette were formed using the mold-blown technique. The use of soft contours and muted colors is typical of Franck's sculptural approach.

Disk-shaped knop

Core Collectibles

RUSTICA TUMBLERS
The Rustica range of tumblers and tankards, designed in 1963, rank among Franck's functional designs.
$ • 10 in (26 cm) high

EGG SCULPTURE
Designed by Franck in 1951, this finely balanced, futuristic sculpture is typical of his understated ethos.
$$$ • 7 in (17.5 cm) high

NOTSJÖ "HOURGLASS" VASE
This Nuutajärvi Notsjö piece, designed in 1956, was produced until 1969 in a variety of colors.
$$ • 7 in (17.5 cm) high

Starter Buys

MOLDED NOTSJÖ VASE
A mold-contoured vase designed by Franck in 1958.
$$ • 5 in (12.5 cm) high

SIGNED VASE
A Kaj Franck vase signed "KF Nuutajärvi Notsjö 64."
$$ • 10½ in (26 cm) high

KAJAKKI ART OBJECT
A freeform and polished piece designed by Kaj Franck in 1951, with the engraved signature "K Franck N-N-51."
$$$ • 14½ in (37 cm) diameter

SMOKED GRAY SALT DISH
A triangular section pressed-glass dish designed in 1956.
$ • 2 in (5 cm) wide

You may also like… Lindstrand at Kosta, see pp. 130–31

Anglo-Swedish Glass

"Anglo-Swedish glass" describes the output of three British glassworks founded in the 1960s by designers with first-hand experience of Swedish glassmaking: Caithness, King's Lynn/Wedgwood, and Dartington.

Each of these factories was founded to alleviate unemployment in rural areas, and until the mid-1970s all three works had several hundred employees. Until recently, collectors had ignored the output of these glassworks, but this has changed, with certain designs now fetching large sums.

Though Caithness is best known for its paperweights, all three works produced extensive ranges of table glass. All broke away from cut decoration, which had been the defining characteristic of British glass for three centuries. Instead, Anglo-Swedish glass relied on the simple, understated lines and cool colors that had long been associated with their Nordic equivalents.

While small, common pieces will never create strong collector demand, recent exhibitions have caused an increase in prices commanded by the best designs in the largest sizes and boldest colors.

Classical and Modern Combined

O'Broin (Caithness), Stennett-Willson (Wedgwood), and Thrower (Dartington) "borrowed" from Scandinavian glass design. It is easy to find precedents for their colors and shapes in Swedish and Finnish glass. These Greek Key vases recall Timo Sarpaneva's "Crocus" vase, originally designed for Iittala.

GREEK KEY VASES
Designed by Frank Thrower for Dartington in 1968, these vases have textured bodies, mold-blown rims, and flaring necks.

\$\$ • 3½ in (9 cm) high

TOP TIPS

- Note that Dartington pieces were usually only marked with stickers, but pieces by Wedgwood can have both stickers and etched marks.
- Look for the colors of Caithness glass. These have evocative names such as Heather and Peat, which were inspired by the Scottish landscape in which the designers worked.

KEY FACTS	1961	1967	1969	1987	1992
Scandinavian lines in England	Caithness Glass is founded at Wick, near John o' Groat's in Scotland.	The King's Lynn and Dartington glassworks are both founded in England in this year.	Wedgwood buys King's Lynn and changes the name of the company to Wedgwood Glass.	Frank Thrower dies. He had designed 500 of Dartington's pieces in his lifetime.	Wedgwood is bought by Waterford, and King's Lynn glassworks closes.

What's Hot

WEDGWOOD VASE
A Studio vase with a swirling red and white body designed by Ronald Stennett-Willson.
$$$ • 5 in (13 cm) high

SET OF CANDLE HOLDERS
Stennett-Willson designed these Brancaster candle holders in 1967.
$ • 8 in (20 cm) high

Look out for:
Ronald Stennett-Willson spent his early working life importing Orrefors and Pukeberg glass from Sweden. It was in his Studio range that his work came closest to the excellence of top Swedish glass.

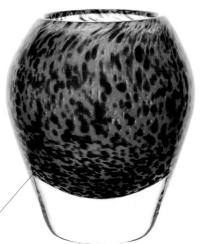

Three-dimensional internal colors

STENNETT-WILLSON STUDIO VASE
This unique vase with a random swirling design belongs to Stennett-Willson's Studio range, designed for Wedgwood.
$$$ • 4½ in (11 cm) high

Core Collectibles

CANISBAY DECANTER
A Caithness Canisbay range decanter designed by Domhnall O'Broin in 1967.
$ • 11¼ in (28.5 cm) high

"SATURN'S RINGS" DECANTER
A Wedgwood orange decanter with a clear stopper designed by Ronald Stennett-Willson.
$ • 12 in (30 cm) high

GLASS CANDLE HOLDERS
Two candle holders designed by one of Dartington's Swedish glassblowers, 1969.
$ • 7½ in (18.5 cm) high

Starter Buys

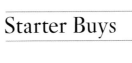

CAITHNESS LAMP BASE
A wide green Caithness Glass lamp base with its original factory label.
$ • 7¼ in (18.5 cm) high

O'BROIN LAMP BASE
A 1967 purple Caithness Glass lamp base designed by Domhnall O'Broin.
$ • 10 in (25.5 cm) high

CANDLE HOLDER
A Dartington clear glass candle holder designed by Frank Thrower, 1982.
$ • 7 in (18 cm) high

CAITHNESS CASED VASE
This heavy cased blue vase was designed around 1965 for Caithness Glass.
$ • 4½ in (11.5 cm) high

You may also like… Postwar Czech Pressed Glass, see pp. 138–39

Postwar Czech Pressed Glass

Czechoslovakia was the most unlikely star of world glassmaking in the postwar era. Behind the Iron Curtain, where it remained until the Velvet Revolution of 1989, the craft flowered and flourished.

Czech glass developed postwar both commercially and artistically. Its cheap, pressed products sold in vast numbers across Europe, while its more artistic output won the Grand Prix at the Brussels Expo of 1958 and provided the crucial stimulus that inspired the fledgling American studio glass movement.

The Czech glass industry, which dates back to at least the 12th century, had long been dominated by ethnic Germans. After their expulsion in 1945, nationalization from 1948 involved the grouping of separate glassworks into larger conglomerates, with only Moser retaining relative independence due to its international reputation. Success encouraged gradual liberalization and artistic freedom.

Since 1989, economic liberalization, increasing environmental standards, rising wages, and soaring energy prices have cost the Czech glass industry dearly. Many works have since ceased to exist and the remaining few are, like many of their European and American counterparts, struggling to survive.

Amber Splendor

A decade ago, pieces like this would have been ignored by collectors despite low prices. However, it is now widely recognized as the "Hobnail" vase, designed around 1964 by Rudolf Jurnikl for the Rudolfova glassworks of Sklo Union at Teplice, and its value has multiplied.

SKLO UNION VASE
With a hobnail-like circular pattern, this small amber glass vase by Rudolf Jurnikl dates from 1970–72.

$$ • 5 in (12.5 cm) high

TOP TIPS

- Don't expect signatures: only rare, finest-quality Czech studio pieces are signed.
- Examples of Czech postwar pressed glass outnumber studio pieces by hundreds to one.
- Pay attention to color: postwar pieces were made in colorless, amber, amethyst, green, and blue only.

KEY FACTS	1948	1967–68	1970	1982	1989
Glass in a time of political turmoil	The Communists take power. They control most artistic expression, but overlook glassmaking.	Czech glass is exhibited abroad, at Montreal, for the first time since 1945. Russia invades, halting liberalization.	Glass is produced specifically for one of the largest and most popular World Expos, in Osaka, Japan.	American glassmaker Dale Chihuly invites Czech glass artists to his studio, confirming their influence.	The Velvet Revolution restores democracy, but glassmaking suffers with the loss of Soviet markets.

What's Hot

CLEAR GLASS VASE
This well-attributed Sklo Union glass vase with conical spikes dates from 1970–72.

$ • 10 in (25.5 cm) high

JURNIKL VASE
A tall pressed vase composed of a series of "cogs," designed by Rudolf Jurnikl in 1973.

$$ • 7½ in (19 cm) high

Look out for:

The permission granted to Czech glass artists to exhibit at the Osaka World Expo in 1970 is evidence of their importance to the Soviet Czech economy. With annual exports in millions, most of the leading figures were permitted to show designs in the Czech Pavilion.

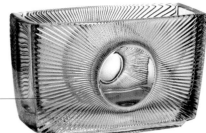

Radial-lined pattern

JURNIKL "OSAKA"
A pressed "Osaka" pattern jardinière designed by Rudolf Jurnikl in 1969 for inclusion in the display of Czech glass exhibited at the World Expo at Osaka in 1970.

$$ • 4 x 7 in (10 x 18.5 cm)

Core Collectibles

MATURA SERVING DISH
A smoked oval pressed serving dish by Adolf Matura for Rudolfova Hut, 1965.

$ • 11 in (28 cm) diameter

ADOLF MATURA VASE
Monolithic amber vase attributed to Adolf Matura, for Rudolfova Hut, late 1960s.

$$ • 7 in (18.5 cm) high

VLADISLAV URBAN VASE
This 1960s heavy geometric press-molded vase was designed by Vladislav Urban.

$$ • 8 in (20 cm) high

FRANTIŠEK PĚCENY VASE
Pressed "candlewax" vase designed in the 1960s for Hermanova Hut, c. 1974.

$ • 9 in (23 cm) high

Starter Buys

RUDOLF JURNIKL VASE
Glass vase with two raised, hobnail-like, circular patterns.

$$ • 8¾ in (22.5 cm) high

FRANTIŠEK VIZNER VASE
A Sklo Union glass vase with geometric pattern, 1965.

$ • 9¾ in (25 cm) high

VLADISLAV URBAN ASHTRAY
An ashtray designed by Vladislav Urban for Rosice.

$ • 8 in (20 cm) long

VÁCLAV HANUŠ ASHTRAY
A 1960s lobed ashtray attributed to Václav Hanuš.

$ • 2 x 6 in (5 x 15 cm)

You may also like… Danish Glass, see pp. 128–29

Paperweights

These charming collectibles hold an artisanal history dating back to the Italian millefiori glass paperweights of the 1840s. With their cool, smooth exteriors, they are popular with collectors around the world.

The classic period of paperweight production is generally agreed to lie around 1845–60, with European production first centered on the great French glass houses of Clichy, Baccarat, and St-Louis, where many migrant workers from Italian glassworks were employed. Factories in Bohemia and Britain quickly followed suit, and American production commenced a little later, as European glassmakers moved to the United States. Many of the fine-quality paperweights from this midcentury period are prized by collectors today, and prices for exceptional examples can reach thousands of dollars.

The revival of the craft in the 20th century has led to greatly increased interest, not just in antique paperweights, but also in high-quality contemporary weights as well as limited-edition pieces. For collectors, the best sources for all of these are auctions and specialist dealers on the Internet.

A Fine Specimen

Paul Ysart's skill and virtuosity with paperweights elevated his production from a 19th-century glassmaker's sideline to an art form in its own right. His virtuosity with lamp-work, latticino, and filigree millefiori canes has made his work collectible the world over.

BUTTERFLY PAPERWEIGHT
A blue butterfly encircled by purple and pink canes is the centerpiece of this 1970s Paul Ysart paperweight.

$$ • 2¾ in (7 cm) diameter

TOP TIPS

- Familiarize yourself with patterns and production techniques so you can begin to date and identify unsigned weights.
- Don't turn up your nose at contemporary designs. Paperweights by John Deacons, Steven Lundberg, William Manson, Paul Ysart, and the 20th-century master Charles Kaziun are highly sought after.

KEY FACTS	1845	1904	1940	1995	21st century
Weights of the world	The earliest officially recorded glass paperweights with a date cane are exhibited.	Paul (Pablo) Ysart is born in Spain. His family moves to France, then Britain, while he is still young.	American designer Charles Kaziun starts producing paperweights, keeping his designs simple and stylish.	A Baccarat weight depicting a horse sells for $40,250 at a Sotheby's auction in New York.	There are approximately 20,000 paperweight collectors in the world who hold regular conventions.

What's Hot

Look out for:

The French company Baccarat was founded by royal charter in 1764. It began producing paperweights in the 19th century, and its delicate designs with bold, primary colors have been popular across the world ever since. Prime examples can sell for thousands of dollars.

ST-LOUIS PAPERWEIGHT
The St-Louis works in France produced this blue clematis on a pink jasper ground.
$$$$ • 2½ in (6.5 cm) in diameter

GLASS INK BOTTLE
This late 19th-century millefiori paperweight doubles as an ink bottle and stopper.
$$$ • 6 in (15 cm) high

Blue torsade —————

BACCARAT PAPERWEIGHT
The millefiori tuft at the center of this piece is surrounded by a torsade of white gauze entwined with cobalt threads.
$$$ • 3¼ in (8 cm) diameter

Core Collectibles

FACETED SULFIDE WEIGHT
The large star-cut base of this paperweight bears the profile of a military man.
$$ • 3 in (7.5 cm) diameter

MANTEL ORNAMENTS
This pair of unusual American ornamental paperweights dates to the 19th century.
$$$ • 8 in (20 cm) high

Starter Buys

BACCARAT DEER WEIGHT
Striking silhouettes decorate this 20th-century weight.
$$$ • 3 in (7.5 cm) diameter

LALIQUE "NAIADE"
This paperweight is decorated with an intaglio mermaid.
$$ • 3¾ in (9.5 cm) high

PAUL YSART PAPERWEIGHT
A mid-20th-century Paul Ysart paperweight with 13 canes on a green background.
$$$ • 3 in (7.5 cm) diameter

CLICHY PAPERWEIGHT
Dated c. 1850, this rare weight has millefiori canes underneath a Clichy rose.
$$$ • 2¾ in (7 cm) diameter

ISLE OF WIGHT WEIGHT
A "Night Scape" glass weight in blue and brown tones.
$ • 3 in (7.5 cm) diameter

REMNANTS PAPERWEIGHT
Leftover glass remnants form this colorful paperweight.
$$ • 1 in (3 cm) diameter

You may also like… Drinking Glasses, see pp. 120–25

CHAPTER

Household
Accessories

Collecting the House & Home

This chapter is about necessity and excess, functionality and embellishment. Humans have through the ages developed an amazing ability to reinvent everyday objects of life, providing a wealth of collectible products.

The earliest household items were little more than tools. Unless you were wealthy, ornamentation was scant and objects were purely practical; spoons, plates, cooking vessels, and candlesticks were of basic manufacture, relatively plain form, and specifically constructed for the job in hand. As successive generations became more affluent,

the forms and materials of these items evolved to reflect social status. The priorities of form and function gradually altered, allowing purely decorative objects to enter the home.

The Victorian era demonstrates this perhaps better than any other epoch in history. However, it also saw the advent of production-line manufacturing

Box of Lever Sunlight soap, see Core Collectibles, p. 150.

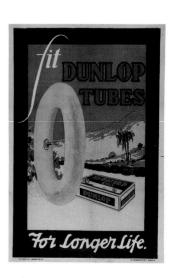

Printed Dunlop poster, see What's Hot, p. 147.

for the masses, which revolutionized the household with the invention of labor-saving devices, mechanized glass production, and commercial packaging. No longer were the luxury imports of the British Empire reserved for the wealthy: tea, for example, became affordable for all, the laws of supply and demand altered, and suppliers reacted with affordable versions of what had been an upper-class preserve. A huge expansion in the manufacturing base was required to supply an increasingly affluent society with the household accessories it needed.

Despite current trends toward more minimalist interiors, there is no shortage of collectors for this continually evolving detritus of life. Many household products are taken for granted and, strangely enough, the 20th century saw a marked move toward simplicity of design and functionality, a full-circle return to basic principles. Stores such as Ikea have revolutionized the way we buy. We now expect design, functionality, and value to run hand in hand, and we also expect a broad range of choice. Can this kind of mass-market "designer" consumerism produce the antiques of tomorrow? The obvious answer is no: how can items produced in such vast quantities ever become collectible? Maybe our acceptance of built-in obsolescence is the answer. Disposable objects are already destined to become rare or collectible because we throw most of them away: the skill is choosing what might be worth saving. In hindsight we can now see what the advent of throwaway culture in the 1960s has meant to collectors of postwar material: items that seemed mundane at the time have become attractive or socially valuable because so few of them now survive. Variations in collecting habits can be cultural or regional, and this is truly an area in which, as the old adage says, "one man's junk is another man's treasure."

Tunbridge ware box, see Core Collectibles, p. 155.

Bottle set, c. 1840, in amethyst, blue, and green, see p. 162.

Silver Wraith Rolls-Royce desk piece, see p. 180.

Packaging & Advertising

Most of the collectibles in this market were designed to be thrown away, so survivors are rare. Despite this—or perhaps because of it—the best pieces provide a fascinating insight into the social history of their era.

Collecting in this field can be achieved on a small budget, but it's important to pick just one area, such as perfume bottles or cookie tins, in which to concentrate your efforts: while social historian Robert Opie's obsessive collections form the basis for the Museum of Brands, Packaging and Advertising in London, collecting on such a scale is a lifetime's work that few of us are likely to emulate.

Original advertising and packaging artwork is a good growth market, and it's surprising how much appears either at auction or on the Internet.

Historic advertising giants such as Coca-Cola continue to attract high prices for rare pieces, while kitsch 1950s items are also popular, especially in the US, where the often-saucy iconography of the period has been heavily reproduced in recent years.

Happily for the amateur collector, quite a large variety of relatively recent original labels, posters, and other assorted memorabilia dating from the last 50 years or so are available for small amounts of money.

A Royal Find
During the late 19th and early 20th centuries, British cookie companies such as Huntley & Palmers, MacFarlane Lang, and McVitie & Price competed to produce the most fanciful, most memorable cookie tins. Tins came in all kinds of novelty shapes— mailboxes, windmills, baskets, and books— and those with movable parts proved especially popular. In this example, the royal connection makes this ornate Jacobs cookie tin even more desirable.

ROYAL COACH COOKIE TIN
Made in the shape of the royal coach, this A. W. & R. Jacobs & Co. cookie tin is dated 1936.
$$$ • 9 in (23 cm) long

KEY FACTS	1841	1930s	1940s	1950s–60s	2000 onward
Wrapping it up	The first advertising agent is Volney Palmer in Philadelphia. His firm is the forerunner of the advertising agency.	As plastics start to appear, gummed labeling wanes, to be replaced by heat-activated adhesives.	Packaging design is dictated by war rations. Tin boxes are replaced by cardboard; paper labels shrink in size.	Television and radio spark a sophisticated change in advertising, known as the "creative revolution."	New, biodegradable materials become popular as excess packaging is considered wasteful.

What's Hot

DUNLOP POSTER
The exotic illustration on this poster reflects the global ambitions of Dunlop Tire Co.

$$$ • 30 in (76 cm) high

DISPLAY STAND
Lithographed tin was used for many packaging materials, like this 1920s shop display.

$$$ • 15¼ in (38.5 cm) long

Look out for:
More than just advertisements, many tin signs evoke a bygone age when street hardware was more homey and more permanent. They are a direct contrast to these days of modern advertising, where large billboards are temporary media paid for by the week.

Lithographed image

Mounting holes should be rust-free

PLAYER'S ADVERTISING SIGN
An embossed tin sign for Player's, the tobacco and cigarette manufacturer, bearing the Navy Cut logo, c. 1910.

$$$ • 15¼ in (38.5 cm) diameter

CARR'S COOKIE TIN
This 1920s Carr's cookie tin is shaped as a London tram, with excellent detailing, bright colors, and moving wheels.

$$$$ • 8½ in (21.5 cm) wide

LOCKSMITH'S TRADE SIGN
Metal signs like this were hung outside tradesmen's shops to advertise their products or services.

$$$ • 39 in (99 cm) wide

What's Not

Collecting packaging is a specialized field and many of the objects hoarded by such enthusiasts have little apparent value to the average person.

COCA-COLA STANDEE
A rare advertising card from the 1930s, featuring the movie star Lupe Velez.

$$$ • 20½ in (52 cm) high

COCA-COLA CALENDAR
The 1946 "Sprite Boy" calendar is very rare, and this copy is in near-mint condition.

$$$ • 21 in (53 cm) high

CUE HAIR DRESSING GLOSS
This bottle of Cue hair dressing gloss from the 1950s is by Colgate.

$ • 5¼ in (13.5 cm) high

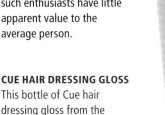

Core Collectibles

SCOTSMAN FIGURE
Grant's Standfast Scotch produced this 1930s figure.
$$$ • 10¼ in (26 cm) high

SMASH ROBOT
The "Smash Martians" were a 1970s advertising sensation.
$ • 7 in (18 cm) high

WINDOW ADVERTISEMENT
A rare store advertisement for a man's truss, dated c. 1930.
$$ • 35½ in (90 cm) high

JAPLAC CARD SIGN
This colorful advertising card promotes Japlac lacquer paint.
$ • 14 in (36 cm) high

GUINNESS BUTTONS
Each of the six buttons in this set has a domed glass top with a reverse-cut and painted Guinness character decoration.
$$ • Box 9 in (23 cm) wide

FRY'S CHOCOLATE RULER
Fry's Chocolate advertising featuring children is especially highly sought after. This tin fold-up promotional ruler is from c. 1905.
$$ • 12 in (30.5 cm) long

Ask the Expert

Red "lantern flame"

Q. Why did the Victorians make glass soda bottles that wouldn't stand up?
A. One distinctive type, the Hamilton, was a torpedo-shaped mineral-water bottle with a pointed bottom and corked stopper, made to be stored sideways so its cork wouldn't dry out and let the gas escape. It was so named for its inventor, William Hamilton.

Q. How should I care for my antique cookie tin?
A. Condition is key, and mint examples command premium prices. Do not immerse your tin in water to clean it, as this can cause rusting. Keep

the tin out of direct sunlight as well, to prevent the artwork from fading.

COOKIE TIN
This Huntley & Palmers cookie tin is in the form of an Arts and Crafts lantern.
$$ • 9½ in (24 cm) high

Q. What are the oldest brands still being sold in the UK?
A. Lyle's golden syrup and Marmite, both 19th-century brands, spring to mind. Note that the oldest brands, such as these, often retain their original packaging styles.

SCOTCH WHISKEY FIGURE
This figure was produced in the 1950s.

$$ • 8½ in (22 cm) high

GUINNESS ADVERTISING FIGURE
Guinness advertising has always been distinctive, like this 1950s rubber toucan decorated with a classic catchphrase.

$$ • 6¾ in (17 cm) high

MICHELIN MAN ASHTRAY
An Art Deco Bakelite ashtray from the 1930s.

$$ • 5 in (12.5 cm) high

COCA-COLA MIRROR
A promotional "Juanita" celluloid pocket mirror.

$$ • 2¾ in (7 cm) long

ELECTROLUX ASHTRAY
Made by Sculptural Promotions Inc. of New York, this 1950s ceramic ashtray advertises Electrolux vacuum cleaners.

$ • 6½ in (16.5 cm) wide

PINUP CALENDAR
A 1958 calendar used to promote *Ballyhoo* magazine.

$$ • 11 in (28 cm) high

HORLICKS PIN
Horlicks issued this pin and a matching mirror in the US.

$ • 1 in (3 cm) wide

SEXTON'S COCOA TIN
Printed branding identifies this late 19th-century tin.

$$ • 9½ in (24 cm) high

PEPSI-COLA SIX-PACK
This 1950s miniature six-pack has a full set of glass bottles.

$ • 2½ in (6.5 cm) wide

HAIRNET CARD SIGN
A card sign used to promote Marquise hairnets.

$ • 12½ in (32 cm) high

Core Collectibles

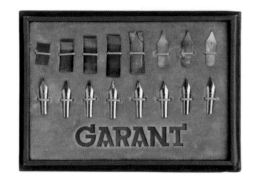

HEINZ TRADE CARD
A color lithographed and embossed advertising trade card for Heinz, c. 1900.

$ • 5 in (12.5 cm) high

FOUNTAIN PEN DISPLAY
The 16 stages of fountain pen nib manufacture are shown in this 1930s display. They include rolling, cutting, die-stamping, shaping, burnishing, splitting, polishing, and plating.

$$ • 6¾ in (17 cm) wide

SUNDIAL TIN
This sundial-shaped tin, for Crawford's cookies, dates from 1926.

$$ • 9½ in (24 cm) high

TALCUM POWDER TIN
With an exotic design, this tin from 1910 contained Bouquet Rose Imperatrice talcum.

$$ • 4½ in (11.5 cm) high

GENERAL ELECTRIC TAPE MEASURE
The reverse of this celluloid and metal tape measure advertising General Electric refrigerators is printed with the address of an electrical appliance shop in Oklahoma.

$$ • Tape measure 1½ in (3.5 cm) in diameter

CIGARETTE STANDEE
The cloak on this card figure folds out to reveal a scantily clad woman.

$$ • 11¾ in (30 cm) high

SUNLIGHT SOAP
Copious text on this box of Lever Sunlight Soap from 1935 touts the product's qualities.

$ • 6 in (15.5 cm) wide

PERNOD TIN HAND
Félix Pernod released this advertising novelty c. 1910. The tin hand was placed flat on the table and spun; whomever the finger pointed at had to buy the next round of drinks.

$ • 2¾ in (7 cm) high

VALENTINO COOKIE TIN
The artwork on this 1920s American Rudolph Valentino cookie tin is by Henry Clive.

$ • 7½ in (19 cm) diameter

CORONATION PERISCOPE
Hovis produced this periscope for seeing over crowds at the coronation of Elizabeth II.

$ • 12½ in (32 cm) long

BOOT POLISH WHISTLES
Two 1920s English tin whistles for Nugget boot polish. Whistles were one of the many novelty items offered as free tokens by advertisers.

$ • 1½ in (4 cm) high

Starter Buys

CHARLES AND DIANA TIN
The wedding of Charles and Diana in 1981 was used on many promotional items.

$ • 5 in (13 cm) diameter

HOMEPRIDE SHAKER
Homepride Flour's "Fred" character forms this herb shaker by Spillers.

$ • 4¼ in (11 cm) high

HANGING SCALE
A Kasco Feeds brass-front hanging scale with painted black highlights.

$ • 12 in (30.5 cm) long

GINGER BEER BOTTLE
This North & Co. home-brewed ginger beer bottle dates from the 1920s.

$ • 7½ in (19 cm) high

SOAP POSTER
Advertisements like this, for Gibbs soap, were strung for hanging on the wall.

$ • 14 in (35.5 cm) wide

ROWNTREE CORONATION TIN
A 1902 tin commemorating the coronation of Edward VII and Queen Alexandra.

$ • 5 in (12.5 cm) wide

WOODBINE ASHTRAY
This Woodbine Virginia Cigarettes advertising ashtray is from 1960.

$ • 4½ in (11.5 cm) wide

BAR ASHTRAY
A naked woman by a roaring fire appears on this 1950s ashtray promoting a bar.

$ • 4¼ in (10.5 cm) wide

You may also like… Cigarette Cards, see pp. 216–17

Treen & Boxes

One of the most natural and versatile materials on earth, wood has been the basis for many products for thousands of years. Its beauty in the hands of a craftsman gives rise to countless collectible treen objects.

Treen is a huge subject for collectors, many of whom specialize in a particular area such as Tunbridge ware or Mauchline ware.

Among treen objects—these charming household items of turned or carved wood, often with decoratively inlaid woodwork—small is often beautiful, and naïve period carvings are always in demand. These can take the form of snuffboxes, pipe tampers, chalices, watch holders, and so on. Dated or commemorative pieces carry a premium, with items from the 17th and 18th centuries particularly in

demand, while patination and wear can add character and value. Note, too, that American collectors gather many items under the term "folk art," a label that carries a costlier price tag.

Auctions can be good hunting grounds for treen objects, particularly those sold in mixed lots that cannot be displayed well on the Internet. Elsewhere, many treen specialists sell in the retail market, and decorative 19th-century boxes remain good, cheap starting points for the novice collector.

Elegance and Functionality

The intricate pictorial wooden tessera pictures commonly found on Tunbridge ware boxes, panels, caddies, and bookends remain a firm favorite with serious collectors. This 19th-century desk stand combines functionality with decoration and, despite the lack of pictorial motifs, encompasses many elements to interest collectors.

TUNBRIDGE WARE ROSEWOOD DESK STAND
The numerous parts of this desk set include a candle sconce, a pair of cylindrical seal boxes, an inkwell stand, two stamp boxes, an ivory match stand, and a metal match strike.
$$$ • 6½ in (16.5 cm)

KEY FACTS	c. 1820	c. 1825	c. 1830	1851	1965
Carving and craftsmanship	Carvers in the Swiss town of Brienz start creating the figures that become famous as Black Forest ware.	William and Andrew Smith begin making snuffboxes and other wooden souvenirs in Mauchline, Scotland.	James Burrows of Tunbridge Wells introduces and develops the tessellated mosaic technique.	Edmund Nye and other makers exhibit Tunbridge ware at the Great Exhibition, to wide acclaim.	Birmingham Museum and Art Gallery purchases scholar Edward Pinto's 7,000-piece treen collection.

What's Hot

Look out for:
Black Forest treen has its roots not in the Bavarian region of the same name, as one might expect, but rather in the Swiss town of Brienz. Since the early 1800s, the region has been associated with the wooden handicrafts and accomplished carved replicas of the town's surrounding flora and fauna, now sought after by enthusiastic collectors.

HUMMING TOP
This 19th-century Tunbridge stickware top has a turned ebony handle.
$$$ • 4 in (10 cm)

PIPE TAMPER
Dating from c. 1740, this boxwood pipe tamper has minor restoration to the leg.
$$$ • 4 in (10 cm) long

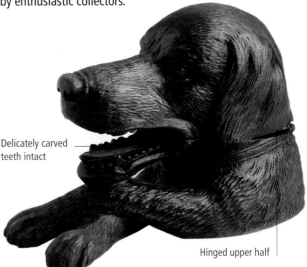

Delicately carved teeth intact

Hinged upper half

THERMOMETER STAND
A Tunbridge ware Cleopatra's needle thermometer stand made from ebony and ivory.
$$$ • 8¾ in (22 cm) high

WINE TABLE
This rare Tunbridge ware rosewood table is on an octagonal stem.
$$$$ • Top 20 in (51 cm) square

DOG NUTCRACKER
Carved in the form of a dog, possibly a retriever, this fine treen nutcracker dating to c. 1870 is in the Black Forest style.
$$$ • 4 in (10 cm) high

What's Not

Victorian truncheons are surprisingly cheap and are an interesting illustration of an item that should really be worth a little more. Despite their decorative gilded and painted "VR" ciphers, most sell for less than $100.

SPECTACLE CASE
A Scottish Mauchline ware penwork and brushwork case in sycamore, c. 1820–30.
$$$ • 4¾ in (12 cm) wide

SNUFF MULL
This 19th-century Mauchline ware burr maple snuff mull has a hinged sycamore lid.
$$$ • 5½ in (14 cm) long

VICTORIAN TRUNCHEON
This Victorian truncheon, dated 1848, is painted with a crowned Garter motto containing the initials "PP."
$ • 17½ in (44.5 cm) long

Core Collectibles

NUTMEG GRATER
A Tunbridge ware whitewood nutmeg grater with a colored print of Brighton Pavilion.

$$$ • 2¾ in (7 cm) in diameter

OCTAGONAL GAMES BOX
This Tunbridge ware ebony-ground box has a central tessera mosaic flower spray.

$$$ • 10¾ in (27 cm) wide

ROSEWOOD TANGRAM PUZZLE BOX
The top of this Tunbridge ware box has a lozenge panel centered on an eight-point star with green checkered cross-banding. Inside, one of the seven puzzle pieces is missing.

$$ • 2 in (5 cm) wide

BOOK MARKERS
A pair of 19th-century mahogany book markers, each carved in the shape of a book with gilded "pages."

$$$ • 10½ in (26.5 cm) long

ROSEWOOD STAMP BOX
This 19th-century box depicting the head of Queen Victoria is thought to contain some 1,000 pieces of inlay.

$$ • 1½ in (4 cm) long

TARTAN WARE WHISTLE
This whistle, with an ebonized turned finial and mouthpiece, has a Prince Charlie tartan on its tapered body.

$$ • 2½ in (6.5 cm) long

ROSEWOOD WORK BOX
A view of Eridge Castle graces this Tunbridge ware box containing stickware cotton reels and other accessories.

$$$$ • 11¼ in (28.5 cm) long

Ask the Expert

Q. What exactly is Tunbridge ware?
A. The term refers, in general, to a process of wood mosaic developed and practiced at Tonbridge and Tunbridge Wells in Kent, England. Woodworking in the area blossomed as Tunbridge Wells developed into a fashionable spa from the 17th century onward, with visiting tourists creating a market for local souvenirs. The elaborate tessellated mosaic technique is characteristic of Tunbridge ware, and superb scenes and portraits in this technique can command high prices among collectors.

BAYHAM ABBEY BOX
This Tunbridge ware rosewood box has a cushion lid and view of Bayham Abbey ruins, waisted sides with a floral mosaic band, and a blue silk interior.
$$$ • 10½ in (27 cm) long

Elaborate mosaic inlay work

THERMOMETER STAND
An octagonal rosewood thermometer stand and compass with an ivory scale.
$$$ • 5 in (12.5 cm) high

PERFUME BOX
This Tunbridge ware box has a domed lid inlaid with a butterfly and holds two cut-glass bottles. The box and its hinged cover are decorated with bands of intricate mosaic flowers.
$$$ • 4½ in (11.5 cm) wide

CLEOPATRA'S NEEDLE THERMOMETER STAND
This Tartan ware piece has an ivory gauge.
$$ • 6¼ in (16 cm) high

YARN-BALL HOLDER
A wooden yarn-ball holder decorated with a view of Margate Sands.
$$ • 4 in (10 cm) in diameter

BOOK SLIDE
This Tunbridge ware rosewood book slide, with a view of Tonbridge Castle on one end and of Penshurst Place at the other, has ends with tessera mosaic banding.
$$ • 13 in (33 cm) wide

WATCH CASE
Dating from c. 1850, this is a Victorian Mauchline ware watch case.
$$ • 2¾ in (7 cm) high

MATCH HOLDER
A Scottish McBeth Tartan ware match holder for the wall, c. 1870.
$$$ • 4½ in (11.5 cm) high

TUNBRIDGE WARE PIN TRAY
This Tunbridge ware satinwood pin tray showcases a gaugework view of a small cottage on a satin birch ground. A single tessera mosaic band runs along the tray's sloping walls.
$$ • 6¾ in (17 cm) wide

THREAD REEL BOX
A Tunbridge ware coromandel thread reel box with a tessera bouquet on the lid.
$$$ • 6½ in (16.5 cm) long

Core Collectibles

STATIONERY BOX
This Tunbridge ware box hides a running wild rose mosaic band on the inside.
$$$ • 9 in (23 cm) wide

SHOE SNUFFBOX
A 19th-century Masonic snuffbox whose decorations include the moon and sun.
$$ • 4½ in (11 cm) long

CHAMBERSTICK
Decorated with the tartan of the McPherson clan, this Tartan ware chamberstick has painted gold detailing on the stem, sconce, and disk-shaped handle.
$$ • 3½ in (9 cm) in diameter

WATCH BARREL
This Mauchline ware larch and sycamore watch barrel is dated c. 1880.
$$ • 3¼ in (8.5 cm) high

MONEY BOX
A Mauchline ware piece with an engraved cylindrical body featuring St. James's Park.
$$ • 3¾ in (9.5 cm) high

TUNBRIDGE WARE ROSEWOOD BOX
This rosewood box has a cushion-shaped lid with a tessera mosaic view of Hever Castle within flower banding and waisted sides of ebony ground tessera mosaic flower banding.
$$$ • 10¾ in (27 cm) wide

APPLE CORER
Made of fruit wood, this very rare apple corer has a handle that depicts a woman, c. 1780.
$$$ • 6½ in (16.5 cm) long

TEA CADDY SPOON
A 19th-century Tunbridge ware rosewood spoon with a tessera mosaic turned bowl.
$$$ • 4 in (10 cm) long

MAGNIFYING GLASS
This 19th-century magnifying glass has a tessera-framed lens and a stickware handle.
$$$ • 6 in (15.5 cm) long

GLOVE STRETCHERS
This pair of Tartan ware glove stretchers with Prince Charlie tartan is dated c. 1870.
$$ • 5¾ in (14.5 cm) long

SOVEREIGN BALL
A Tunbridge ware ebony sovereign ball with eight-point-star roundels.
$$$ • 2 in (5 cm) in diameter

BIRDSEYE MAPLE TEA CADDY
This 19th-century Tunbridge ware piece has a tessera view of Eridge Castle on its dome top and a broad band of tessera roses on its sides.
$$$$ • 10¼ in (26 cm) long

Starter Buys

SPINNING DIE
A Tartan ware spinning die with numbered sides on a Fraser tartan ground.
$$$ • 2 in (5 cm) high

NUTCRACKER
This carved wooden nutcracker is designed in the shape of a man's head.
$$ • 7 in (18 cm) high

BOOK SLIDE
Both folding ends of this Tunbridge ware book slide have perspective cube panels.
$$ • 15½ in (39 cm) wide

EGG TIMER
A Tartan ware piece with an all-over decoration in the McGregor tartan.
$$ • 3 in (7.5 cm) high

BOTTLE STOPPER
A Tunbridge stickware stopper in contrasting shades of light and dark wood.
$$ • 2¼ in (5.5 cm) high

STICKWARE VESTA CASE
Modeled as a capstan, this Tunbridge ware vesta match case has a mosaic top.
$$ • 2 in (5 cm) high

BOOK-SHAPED BOX
A 19th-century Tunbridge ware novelty mahogany box with three spine drawers.
$ • 3¾ in (9.5 cm) long

WALNUT BEZIQUE BOX
The lid has tessera mosaic lettering spelling "Besique" within geometric bands.
$$ • 7 in (18 cm) long

You may also like… Writing Tools, see pp. 180–83

Stainless Steel

Invented in 1913, stainless steel is a versatile medium that lends itself to simple, unassuming, and functional kitchenware. This design ethic has become increasingly attractive to collectors.

Once popular in the 1950s, '60s, and '70s, stainless steel tableware, though enjoying a slight revival today, is still an underrated area where good designers can be found at reasonable prices.

A key name in stainless steel design and production is Robert Welch, whose work is collected in public institutions worldwide, including the Museum of Modern Art in New York. While his midcentury designs have recently been reinvented

or relaunched for sale in UK stores such as Habitat and Heals, originals of Welch's design output from the 1950s and 1960s are still found fairly cheaply at antique fairs and auctions.

Stainless steel wares by the celebrated Danish architect and designer Arne Jacobsen are worth looking for as well, particularly his streamlined, minimalist cutlery for A. Michelsen and his iconic 1967 "Cylinda" line for Stetson.

A Niche Market for an Underrated Material

Some objects need the right environment to shine, and this "Alveston" tea set, designed by Robert Welch, is a case in point. The type of collector who appreciates the style and design ethic behind such a set generally works to a different set of rules. This is simplicity, practicality, and innovation, all achieved with a basic material and still largely underrated.

"ALVESTON" TEA SET
This c. 1962 tea set was made for Wiggin's Old Hall brand.
$$ • 7½ in (19 cm) high

TOP TIPS

- Look for rare examples in mint condition, saved from the scratches, dings, and dents of daily use.
- Research key shapes and ranges, upon which the value of a piece depends.
- Try to buy pieces—cutlery, tea sets, or otherwise—in their original boxes.
- Invest in 1950s and '60s designs that would have been considered innovative and avant garde at the time.

KEY FACTS	1955	1964	1965	1968	1984
Excitements in the kitchen	Robert Welch is appointed design consultant at J. & J. Wiggin, Birmingham tableware makers.	Arne Jacobsen begins work on St. Catherine's College in Oxford, designing buildings, gardens, and flatware.	Welch's Scandinavian-influenced "Alveston" range wins the prestigious Design Council award.	Arne Jacobsen's futuristic right- and left-handed spoons are used in the film *2001: A Space Odyssey*.	J. & J. Wiggin closes down, ending the production of their Old Hall brand and work with Robert Welch.

What's Hot

COFFEE POURER SET
Part of the "Alveston" range, this 1960s coffee pourer set with wooden handles was designed by Robert Welch.

$$ • 9¾ in (25 cm) high

TRIPLE CANDLESTICKS
A pair of Old Hall stainless steel triple candlesticks with wooden feet, designed by Robert Welch.

$$ • 9 in (23 cm) high

Look out for:
Among Robert Welch's many designs, his "Campden" (1957) and "Alveston" (1964) ranges are perhaps the best known. His 1958 "Oriana" range, no less acclaimed, was originally designed for the P&O cruise liner of the same name, before being produced and sold commercially.

Pagoda curves

"ORIANA" TOAST RACK
This Old Hall "Oriana" toast rack by Robert Welch, with its pagoda-esque lines and extreme simplicity, won a design award in 1958 and was exhibited at the XII Milan Triennale.

$ • 7¼ in (18.5 cm) long

Core Collectibles

DESSERT SET
This c. 1970 "Sable" set by Gerald Benney for Viners has bark-textured handles.

$ • 5 in (13 cm) long

OLD HALL TOAST RACK
With rectangular section bars and a riveted base, this 1961 toast rack is by Robert Welch.

$ • 6½ in (16.5 cm) long

FIVE-PIECE CRUET SET
A five-piece cruet set designed by Robert Welch under the Old Hall brand owned by J. & J. Wiggin. It dates from c. 1965.

$ • 7¾ in (20 cm) wide

Starter Buys

SELECTION OF TOAST RACKS
This selection of toast racks by Robert Welch is for Old Hall.

$ • Larger rack 9½ in (24 cm) long

"CONNAUGHT" TEAPOT
A 1960s Old Hall ¾-pint "Connaught" teapot.

$ • 3¼ in (8.5 cm) high

FISH KNIVES AND FORKS
This set of three pairs of forks and fish knives in the original boxes was designed by Gerald Benney for Viners in the 1960s.

$ • 8¼ in (20.8 cm) long

You may also like… Whitefriars, see pp. 108–09

Pot Lids

During the 19th century, a great number of exotic ointments, foodstuffs, and preparations were sold in simple ceramic jars. Highly decorated lids enticed consumers then, and continue to attract modern-day collectors.

While a number of manufacturers entered the field of pot lid production, F. & R. Pratt of Fenton is regarded as the main exponent of the trade, having created around 550 different examples.

Other main manufacturers were T. J. & J. Mayer, Brown Westhead & Moore, and Ridgway, who, while not as prolific as Pratt, produced items of an equally high standard. Many manufacturers recognized the commercial possibilities of producing decorative covers and bases for products such as grease,

cosmetics, gentleman's relish, and other foodstuffs. The plain bases were thrown away or got broken.

Predominantly, three sizes of lids were produced: 3 in (7.5 cm), 4 in (10 cm), and 5 in (13 cm) in diameter, with minor variations in form. The decoration was applied with layers of transfers locating to a registration point on the outer borders. A good example should display well-registered colors, each exactly on top of the other, and the colors should be strong and even with no ghosting or fading.

Bear's Grease for Hair

During the 19th century there was a fashion for using bear's grease, an early form of perfumed hair ointment, which had been thought to improve hair health from the 17th century onward. Today these quirky lids are considered the most desirable by many collectors.

"BEAR IN A RAVINE"
This Staffordshire "Bear in a Ravine" lid, while restored at the rim, is rare.
$$$$ • 2½ in (6.5 cm) diameter

TOP TIPS

- Look out for the ornately gilt-decorated range Pratt produced for the Great Exhibition of 1851.
- Note that a pot lid with its original base is more valuable than a lid alone. The value increases further if the base is also decorated with marbled pattern or trade names.
- Check that the decoration is under the glaze and printed. A number of rare designs have been faked by the application of transfers glued to a plain lid and over-varnished.

KEY FACTS	1756	1835	1850s onward	1920s–30s	c. 2000
Tightening the lid on history	Sadler & Green of Liverpool invents a new process of decorating ceramics using a copper plate.	George Baxter develops his oil color process of printing, using up to 20 plates at a time.	The development of commercial markets creates a fashion for decorated jars selling everyday products.	Pot lids become popular with wealthy Midlands collectors and condition standards are set.	The record auction price of $5,400 is paid for a lid with a scene of an Eastern lady and her attendant.

What's Hot

"BEARS ON ROCK"
The rare bear scene on this lid is highlighted with a gilded border at the rim.
$$$ • 3¼ in (8.5 cm) diameter

NEW YORK EXHIBITION
Portraying a scene from the New York Exhibition of 1853, this is a rare early lid.
$$$ • 5 in (13 cm) diameter

Look out for:
The value of this standard object is related to the rarity of the subject matter. This particular image of a Gothic archway is seldom seen. Lids were often kept to display on the wall.

Layers of transfer printing

GOTHIC ARCHWAY
This particular image of a Gothic archway is just one example from a series of Historic Buildings and Scenes, which proved very popular when first made.
$$ • 3 in (7.5 cm) diameter

Core Collectibles

HOUSES OF PARLIAMENT
A Staffordshire pot lid with an image of the new Houses of Parliament in Westminster.
$$ • 5 in (13 cm) diameter

BUCKINGHAM PALACE
This Staffordshire lid is decorated with a popular view of Buckingham Palace.
$$ • 5 in (13 cm) diameter

"THE SPANISH LADY"
This pot lid has a gilded border and comes with a matching base.
$$$ • 4 in (10 cm) diameter

ADMINISTRATION BUILDING
This lid bears an image of the Administration Building at the Chicago World's Fair of 1893.
$$ • 4¼ in (10.5 cm) diameter

Starter Buys

"LANDING THE CATCH"
Dating from the 19th century, this is a Pratt ware lid.
$ • 4¼ in (10.5 cm) diameter

"DEERHOUND"
The famous image on this lid is from a work by Landseer.
$$ • 3 in (7.5 cm) diameter

"FISHER-BOY"
This scene is taken from a work by J. G. Naish.
$$ • 3 in (7.5 cm) diameter

"COUNTRY QUARTERS"
This lid was produced by the Pratt works.
$$ • 4¾ in (12 cm) diameter

You may also like… Staffordshire, see pp. 32–35

Wine & Drink Accessories

In the 18th century, many gadgets were invented to enhance the pleasure of a tipple. Wine was enjoyed by the wealthy, and gin and beer by the masses, as depicted by Hogarth in his famous engravings.

There is a great sense of ritual associated with using an antique corkscrew, pouring claret into an 18th-century decanter, and using a silver wine funnel to serve it.

Many collectors are prompted to acquire beautifully made glass, silver, and plate in order to perpetuate a sense of history—and perhaps to be reminded of the elegance and the

debauchery associated with drinking alcohol in times gone by. Despite this draw, some accessories are not fashionable at the moment. Decanters, for example, are little used these days, so they are good buys, particularly when purchased in mixed lots.

Corkscrew prices are buoyant, with the best patent and antique novelty examples selling well. Despite falls in the silver market, wine-related items command good prices, though Sheffield plate is undervalued and worth exploring.

SPIRIT BOTTLE SET
This set of three spirit bottles, in amethyst, blue, and green, has silver-plated cork mounts and is housed in a silver-plated trefoil stand. The set dates from around 1840.
$$ • 15½ in (39 cm) high

Spirits of the Past
You don't have to use a decanter set like this fine and colorful Victorian set to appreciate the frivolity, banter, serious discussion, and political arguments and intrigue that are likely to have surrounded it in another epoch. If only objects could tell their tale, this item would have much to say. Period pieces such as this decanter stand are generally well made and constitute good value in comparison to a modern handmade equivalent. They also look good, provide a stylish addition to the dining room, and hold their value well, as fewer sets tend to survive intact for so many years! For an interested collector, auctions are generally the best source for period glassware and other drinking accessories.

KEY FACTS	1795	1837	19th century	1920s	1930s
Raising a glass over the years	Reverend Samuel Henshall takes out the first corkscrew patent in Middlesex, England.	Queen Victoria is crowned. Her era brings back low-key spirit drinking—from the right bottles.	Britain only imports wine, so it is the expensive drink of the privileged, with accessories to match.	During Prohibition in the US, many barware makers invent clever ways of disguising drinking accessories.	Art Deco cocktail shakers and barware become popular as martinis flourish during this glamorous era.

What's Hot

SILVER GILT WINE LABELS
A pair of George III silver gilt wine labels, of canted oblong outline, c. 1790.

$$$ • 1¾ in (4.5 cm) wide

COCKTAIL SHAKER
Shaped like a bowling pin, this shaker has a hardwood neck and stopper, c. 1935.

$$$$ • 15½ in (39.5 cm) high

Look out for:
Novelty corkscrews are firm favorites with collectors and the slightly saucy nature of this 19th-century German example has made it a perennial bestseller. These are sometimes known as the "Gay Nineties" corkscrews. The miniature version is the most difficult to find.

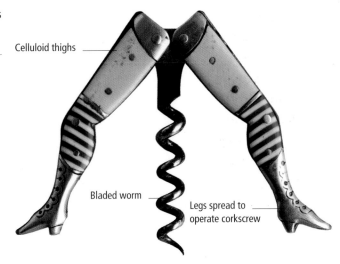

Celluloid thighs

Bladed worm

Legs spread to operate corkscrew

"RED-PORT" LABEL
This Staffordshire enamel "red-port" label, decorated with flowers, is from c. 1780.

$$$ • 2½ in (6 cm) wide

WHISKEY DISPENSER
A Regency Scottish dispenser with carved wood and a detachable whiskey cask.

$$$ • 26 in (65 cm) high

LADIES' LEGS CORKSCREW
This German celluloid-covered ladies' legs corkscrew has green-striped half-length stockings. The corkscrews come in different sizes with a variety of colored full or half stockings, c. 1880–90.

$$$ • 2½ in (6.5 cm) long

What's Not

Bottle openers are common tourist souvenir items. Mostly diecast and plated, these mementos have little collectible value.

MERMAID CORKSCREW
A German celluloid mermaid corkscrew, with metallic painted scales, c. 1900.

$$$ • 4¼ in (10.5 cm) long

DECANTER WAGON
This Sheffield Plate decanter wagon is raised on spoked wheels, c. 1830.

$$$$ • 19 in (48.5 cm) long

SOUVENIR BOTTLE OPENER
A modern diecast Greek souvenir bottle opener, with a classical head on one side.

$ • 3 in (7.5 cm) long

Core Collectibles

SILVER TASTEVIN
A French silver tastevin, used by winemakers to judge the taste of a wine, c. 1870.
$$ • 3 in (7.5 cm) in diameter

SILVER WINE COASTER
An antique George IV coaster marked by Rebecca Emes & Edward Barnard in 1824–25.
$$ • 7 in (19 cm) in diameter

POCKET CORKSCREW
A Dutch silver pocket corkscrew with a decorative raised design, c. 1850.
$$$ • 3½ in (9 cm) high

GEORGE III WINE LABEL
This label has an openwork surmount of foliate festoons and an oval cartouche, c. 1785.
$$ • 1¾ in (4.5 cm) wide

CLARET JUG
This early acid-etched jug by Richardsons of Stourbridge was made in around 1860.
$$$ • 12 in (30.5 cm) high

SPIRIT DECANTER
A Spirit decanter tantalus with nickel-mounted carved oak case from the 1900s.
$$$ • 14½ in (37 cm) wide

WINE FUNNEL
This silver wine funnel was made in London by Emes and Barnard in 1816.
$$$$ • 6 in (16 cm) high

SILVER WINE COOLER
A campana-shaped Victorian wine cooler on a square fluted base with a floral stem.
$$$ • 12¼ in (31 cm) high

Ask the Expert

Q. Is there any way of telling how old a decanter is?
A. Styles vary, but a "triple-ring" decanter (made with three glass rings around the neck) generally dates from the late 18th or early 19th centuries. However, styles are often revived and these were popular again in the Edwardian period.

Q. Are "bright-cut" decanter labels more collectible than other kinds?
A. Bright-cut is a form of engraving on silver (and sometimes plate), often in the form of small, short cuts. The engraving tool is polished and this causes the cut to reflect light. Bright-cut labels are popular because they are so decorative.

Filigree decoration

RICHARDSON DECANTERS
A pair of translucent yellow glass decanters.
$$$ • 14¼ in (36.5 cm) high

Q. I have an old decanter marked "cork" on the base. It looks roughly molded but the stopper is cut. Can you help?
A. Your decanter sounds like a "blow-molded" example, which is blown into a wooden mold with the hand-cut stopper fashioned separately. Marked examples are rare and worth several hundred dollars each.

TOP TIPS

- Take advantage of changes in fashion to acquire underappreciated pieces such as antique handmade glass decanters.
- Look for the unusual in an item: a good coat of arms, initials, or a crest can add character to a piece of silver or glass.
- Consider interesting 17th- and 18th-century examples with applied seals, particularly if they have a "wreck" provenance, or if the seal is traceable.
- Watch out for fake corkscrews, especially on the Internet, where fakes include rare pieces as well as other costly examples.

VICTORIAN LABEL
This label has a border of foliate shells and gadrooning, Birmingham, 1840.

$$ • 1¾ in (4.5 cm) wide

GLASS SECTION FLASKS
These two continental glass rectangular section flasks from the 18th century are painted with flowers and leaves.

$$$ • 8 in (20 cm) and 7 in (17 cm)

TRIPLE-RING DECANTER
A triple-ring glass decanter with a bull's-eye stopper, dating from c. 1800.

$$ • 11 in (27 cm) high

TAPERING DECANTER
This decanter has a slice-cut neck and shoulders with a cut bull's-eye stopper, c. 1800.

$$ • 10½ in (26 cm) high

DOUBLE-ACTION CORKSCREW
A bone and brass Thomason-type corkscrew, by Wilmot & Roberts, c. 1810.

$$ • 7 in (17.5 cm) long

BAR CORKSCREW
"The Original Eclipse" bar corkscrew, by Gaskill & Chambers from the 1920s.

$$$ • 16 in (40.5 cm) wide

Starter Buys

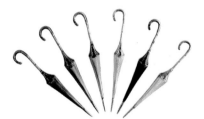

"ZIG-ZAG" CORKSCREW
A chrome-plated hinged lattice corkscrew with original box and instructions, c. 1920.

$$ • 6 in (15.5 cm) long

1930S BARMAN'S TOOL
This French combination tool has a bottle opener, ice pick, can opener, and corkscrew.

$ • 6¾ in (17 cm) long

ENAMEL COCKTAIL STICKS
Six umbrella-shaped cocktail sticks made from silver and enamel, dating from 1909.

$$ • 2¾ in (7 cm) long

GLASS DECANTERS
This decanter and stopper pair has split-cut sides and three steps to the shoulders, c. 1835.

$$ • 11 in (29.5 cm) high

You may also like… Fob & Pocket Watches, see pp. 374–75

Plastic Wares

Many people think of plastic as a cheap product, but it has a fascinating history encompassing many scientific advances and myriad applications. There are many plastic objects that have become collectible.

Collecting plastic for the lure of the material is not the most common reason for its acquisition. Typically, people are attracted by brand names such as Bakelite and Catalin but may decide to specialize in particular pieces such as radios or celluloid toys.

The variety of objects manufactured with plastic often means that "plastic" is collected by default. However, there are always those who take collecting to extremes, and today even vintage Tupperware seems to have a niche market!

Classic designs in modern milestone materials attract the more affluent collectors, and the golden age of plastics in the first half of the 20th century provides ample choice for enthusiasts of this adaptable material. Shiny surfaces and fluid curves all found their way into decorative or functional household objects such as ashtrays, cigarette boxes, dressing table accessories, and thermos flasks. Examples of these items can all be readily found today at collectors' fairs and flea markets, and increasingly are becoming available on the Internet.

Tortoiseshell Grand

Celluloid is widely regarded as the first thermoplastic. The trade name was registered in 1870, though the material had existed under various other names since 1856—a fact that led to many legal disputes regarding patents. Its constituent parts of nitrocellulose, camphor, and other ingredients made it volatile to work with. Not only is it highly flammable but it also degrades. This little jewelry box is typical of celluloid objects made to imitate tortoiseshell. They are often divorced from dressing table sets and as such have minimal value to collectors. Examples can be found at antique fairs and secondhand stores.

PIANO JEWELRY BOX
This tortoiseshell celluloid jewelry box from the 1920s is designed in the form of a grand piano.
$ • 5 in (13 cm) wide

KEY FACTS	1862	1907	1927	1931	1953
The development of plastics	Alexander Parkes unveils Parkesine, the first synthetic plastic. It will later became known as celluloid.	Bakelite, the "material of a thousand uses," is invented in 1909 by New York chemist Leo H. Baekeland.	After the expiry of Bakelite's patent, the Catalin corporation starts making it under the name Catalin.	DuPont discovers the polyacrylic Lucite, also developed by Rohm & Haas as Plexiglas, or Perspex in the UK.	Daniel Fox, a chemist at General Electric, discovers an acrylic-like and highly durable plastic, Lexan.

What's Hot

BROWN DESK STAND
A rare Bakelite "Eloware" desk stand and double inkwell by Birkby's, c. 1936.
$$ • 9 in (23 cm) wide

CARVACRAFT INK STAND
An amber Carvacraft ink stand of cast phenolic resin by Dickinson, c. 1948.
$$ • 10¾ in (27 cm) wide

"PLASTALITE" DESK LAMP
This 1930s Art Deco "Plastalite" desk lamp was designed by Wells Coates for E. K. Cole Ltd., a plastics firm best known for its transistor radios. Coates designed many products for the company.
$$$ • 14½ in (37 cm) high

Look out for:
Manufactured by Roanoid Ltd. from 1930 to 1939, the "tennis ball" Bakelite ashtray, as it is popularly known, is heralded as a design classic and was originally made for Dunlop as a promotional item. It was lead-weighted and proved very useful as an ashtray on ocean liners.

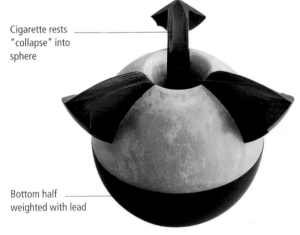

Cigarette rests "collapse" into sphere

Bottom half weighted with lead

DUNLOP ASHTRAY
A promotional ashtray by Roanoid Ltd., with three black cigarette rests that fold inward into the ball over the ashtray to complete the sphere, c. 1930.
$$ • 5 in (12 cm) diameter

What's Not

Victorian and Edwardian celluloid simulated tortoiseshell items are very common and are sometimes confused with real tortoiseshell, which is also malleable when heated. The same identification problems occur with "ivorine" or ivory lookalike plastics from the same period, particularly items such as knife handles.

FINGERNAIL BUFFER
A 1930s–1940s early plastic Art Deco fingernail buffer, with revolving center.
$$ • 4 in (10.5 cm) high

ACRYLIC INK STAND
This ink stand from the 1940s is made of a rare green acrylic and black Bakelite.
$$ • 6½ in (16.5 cm) diameter

DRESSING TABLE ITEMS
English celluloid simulated tortoiseshell items from the 1920s.
$ • 11¾ in (30 cm) long

Core Collectibles

KODAK FOLDING CAMERA
This brown mottled Bakelite camera was designed by E. K. Cole in 1927.
$ • 7 in (18 cm) high

VELOS DESK SET
A mottled brown Bakelite desk set from the 1930s made by Velos for Marconi.
$ • 11¾ in (30 cm) wide

CIGARETTE BOX
A brown Bakelite cigarette box for Teofani cigarettes from the 1920s.
$ • 6¼ in (15.5 cm) wide

ART DECO FRAME
This 1930s brown Bakelite frame has a stepped base and arched and stepped sides.
$ • 6¼ in (16 cm) high

MARBLED BEAKERS
These two marbled Bandalasta beakers are from the 1930s.
$ • 5 in (12.5 cm) high

MARBLED MUFFIN DISH
A LingaLonga Ware muffin dish, in orange marbled urea-formaldehyde, from the 1930s.
$ • 6 in (15 cm) diameter

GREEN CHANDELIER
This rare pale green urea-formaldehyde chandelier is from the 1930s.
$$ • 21 in (53 cm) diameter

BAKELITE ASHTRAY
A 1930s green mottled Bakelite ashtray with its original box.
$ • 3 in (7.5 cm) diameter

Ask the Expert

Q. Is it possible to tell whether a Bakelite item is genuine or reproduction?
A. There are a few clues: real Bakelite will not warp or melt. Neither will it have any seams because of the way it was cut. Over the years it oxidizes and develops a patina, so the exterior should be slightly discolored.

Aged patina

TABLE LIGHTER
A mottled Bakelite 1930s "D. L. I. Flintless" table lighter by Dorset Light Industries.
$ • 4¼ in (11 cm) high

Q. What's the best way to clean Bakelite?
A. Car polish such as Turtle Wax makes Bakelite shine beautifully. It's slightly abrasive and removes the dull finish on old pieces.

Q. Are there any brand names in particular that are worth looking for?
A. LingaLonga and Beetleware produced ranges of wares in bright neon colors, often with a marbled effect. These were considered the height of fashion at the time and are now very collectible. Another company, Carvacraft, was known for its attractive desk sets carved from large slabs of Catalin. The sets were available in creamy white, yellow, and bright green.

CATALIN CRUET SET
An orange Catalin cruet set from the 1930s. Catalin was often dyed bright colors.
$ • 2¼ in (6 cm) high

BIRD CIGARETTE DISPENSER
Made of brown Bakelite and cream urea-formaldehyde, this bird cigarette dispenser dates from the 1930s.
$ • 7½ in (19 cm) high

TEA CUP AND TRAY
This tea cup and cookie tray from the 1930s is made of marbled Bandalasta.
$ • Cup 3 in (8 cm) diameter

ANIMAL NAPKIN RINGS
These four novelty animal-shaped napkin rings from the 1930s are made of different colored cast-phenolic, which is the generic term for Bakelite or Catalin.
$ • Squirrel 2¾ in (7 cm) high

THERMOS ICE BUCKETS
Two modernistic 1930s urea-formaldehyde and Bakelite thermos ice buckets.
$ • 8½ in (22 cm) wide

STAMP SPONGE HOLDER
A 1940s green Carvacraft stamp sponge holder; green is the rarest color.
$$ • 3 in (8 cm) wide

LEMON SQUEEZER
This blue marbled urea-formaldehyde lemon squeezer dates from the 1930s.
$ • 5¼ in (13.5 cm) diameter

Starter Buys

RUSSIAN PEN HOLDER
An acrylic Russian pen holder dating from the 1950s–1960s.
$ • 4½ in (11.5 cm) wide

BAKELITE FLASHLIGHT
This maroon mottled Bakelite flashlight is from the 1940s.
$ • 4¾ in (12 cm) high

CRUET SET
A 1940s multicolored urea-formaldehyde cruet set.
$ • Pepper pot 2 in (5 cm) high

ART DECO BUTTONS
Five French celluloid Art Deco buttons from the 1930s.
$ • 1 in (2.5 cm) diameter

You may also like… Treen & Boxes, see pp. 152–57

Kitchenalia

Kitchenalia collectors have an avid interest in items of household history, looking to acquire not just objects from the kitchen, but also items from the dairy, laundry, brewhouse, or any other area of domestic toil.

The evolution of mechanical aids, from a clockwork spit-turner to a classic Kenwood Chef, all have a place in the collecting market. Perhaps it is the nostalgic memory of a grandmother's sponge cake or rabbit-shaped gelatin molds that spur collectors on to acquire these nostalgic items.

The market now is not as buoyant as it was during the 1990s, perhaps because of the trend for clean, modern kitchens. However, the recent trend for retro style and a more eclectic look has sparked new interest. Early functional pieces of kitchenalia dating from the early 19th century, such as hand-carved butter stamps or bread plates, are very popular, as are large, elaborate copper and ceramic gelatin molds, and pieces from the Arts and Crafts period of 1880–1910.

But discerning buyers these days favor quality over quantity, with the result that items in poor condition are far less desirable.

Pats of Butter

This butter-working table, intended as a labor-saving device, is typical of charming kitchenalia items that encapsulate notions of healthy home-produced food, country living, and farmers' wives with strong arms—and that are totally alien to our modern environment. These tables were used to wash, drain, and salt the butter to preserve it. The rolling mechanism was worked back and forth across the butter to smooth it; then, with the table tilted at one end, the buttermilk drained away easily. Larger commercial variations were available, often with cast-iron frames and hand-cranked wheel mechanisms. Values of such items remain relatively low, perhaps due to size and the difficulties of display.

BUTTER TABLE
This early 20th-century sycamore butter-working table has a mechanism that is worked back and forth to smooth the butter.
$$ • 27 in (69 cm) long

KEY FACTS	1800–50	1861	1870–1900	1950	1955
Milestones in kitchen utensils	Benjamin Thomson designs his "Rumford" stove; expensive copper utensils are used in large kitchens.	English cookery writer Mrs. Beeton's *The Book of Household Management* is published.	Kitchen gadgets such as pastry cutters, gelatin and pie molds, and cookie tins are now mass-produced.	Kenneth Maynard Wood introduces the Kenwood Chef at the Ideal Homes Exhibition in London.	The Alessi design factory starts working with external designers, producing potential collectibles.

What's Hot

COPPER GELATIN MOLD
A copper gelatin mold, crafted in the mid- to late 19th century.
$$ • 6¼ in (16 cm) wide

SYCAMORE DAIRY BOWL
This functional early-20th-century bowl is made from sycamore wood.
$$ • 13¾ in (35 cm) diameter

PINE & TIN CANDLE MOLD
Dating from the early 19th century, this candle mold retains its original surface.
$$$ • 13 in (33 cm) wide

Look out for:

Mocha ware is difficult to classify as it comprises different kinds of pottery. Made in the 18th and 19th centuries as humble home or tavern ware, it came with varied finishes and designs. Its sheer diversity now fascinates collectors worldwide, and early items are particularly of interest.

1-quart measure   1-pint measure

PAIR OF ALE MEASURES
A pair of Mocha ware ale cups made in the 19th century. This type of Mocha ware is sometimes called "banded creamware" or "Leedsware" by modern collectors.
$$$ • Largest 6 in (15 cm) high

What's Not

Fashions come and go. Current trends are for clean lines and chic designer kitchens. Cheaply made, mass-produced items with little decorative or historic merit do not hold much appeal for collectors, so aluminum or utilitarian pieces are unlikely to sell. Instead, focus on finding pieces that are unusual or from an interesting period.

BRONZE POSNET
This mid-18th-century American bronze posnet is inscribed with its maker's name, "Washbrough."
$$$ • 15¾ in (40 cm) long

ALUMINUM GELATIN MOLD
Manufactured between 1920 and 1930, this is a standard kitchen gelatin mold made of aluminum.
$ • 5 in (13 cm) wide

Core Collectibles

WEDGWOOD GELATIN MOLD
A gelatin mold with pineapple motif—a recognized symbol of hospitality.
$$ • 6¼ in (15.5 cm) wide

COPPER MEASURING JUGS
This is a set of three measuring jugs made of copper, with Imperial ½-gill, 1-gill, and 1½-gill capacities. The 1-gill measure (0.142 liters, or about 5 fl oz) is a rare piece.
$$ • Largest 4¼ in (11 cm) high

ADVERTISING COOKIE JAR
Made in Ohio in the 1950s, this cookie jar features the Borden mascot, Elsie the Cow.
$ • 12 in (30.5 cm) high

COPPER GELATIN MOLD
This copper gelatin mold dates from the mid- to late 19th century.
$$ • 6¾ in (17 cm) wide

CERAMIC GELATIN MOLD
An octagonal gelatin mold molded with a basket-of-flowers motif.
$$$ • 6 in (15 cm) wide

BLANCMANGE MOLD
This ceramic blancmange mold dates from 1916. An early example of advertising for Brown & Polson's corn starch, the mold is decorated with a recipe for corn starch blancmange.
$$$ • 6¾ in (17 cm) wide

SALTER SCALE
A Salter scale from the 19th century. In 1884, the Salter trademark, showing a Staffordshire knot pierced by an arrow, was registered and used on all the company's balances.
$$ • 13½ in (34 cm) high

SANTA CHOCOLATE MOLD
This metal chocolate mold, featuring a bearded Santa Claus with sack of toys, is in very good condition.

$ • 9½ in (24 cm) high

BUNNY CHOCOLATE MOLD
A classic piece and a favorite with children, this metal seated Easter bunny mold is in excellent condition.

$ • 10 in (25.5 cm) high

HEN CHOCOLATE MOLD
Featuring a hen sitting on a nest, this chocolate mold, made of metal, is in good condition.

$$ • 11 in (28 cm) high

FLOUR DREDGER
Made from tin, this flour dredger dates back to around 1900.

$$$ • 5¼ in (13.5 cm) high

ENTRÉE MOLDS
This set of entrée molds from the 19th century was made in London.

$$ • Crown 2¾ in (7 cm) wide

COPPER ALE MULLER
A 19th-century ale muller—a special warming device used to mull ale or wine.

$$ • 10 in (25.5 cm) long

Ask the Expert

Q. Are tabletop mincers worth buying?
A. Not really: they can be bought for just a few dollars simply because the cast-metal type of mincers that clamp onto a table are very common.

Q. Why are copper and brass cheap at auction?
A. First, it depends what the object is. If it's a copper kettle designed by the influential Arts and Crafts movement's Dr. Christopher Dresser, for example, it will command a higher price. But there is less demand these days for everyday copper or brass items, probably because these bulky antique pieces don't really "fit" in modern kitchens. Also, copper and brass quickly become tarnished as a result of oxidization—and most of us just don't have the time to keep cleaning it!

"Goose neck" spout slows water flow

COPPER KETTLE
This 19th-century copper kettle is engraved with the phrase "Good Luck."
$$$ • *11 in (28 cm) high*

Core Collectibles

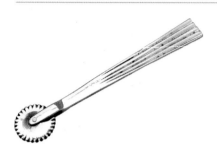

PASTRY CRIMPER AND CUTTER
A 19th-century brass tool used to trim and shape pastry.
$$ • 5½ in (14 cm) long

WOODEN PANTRY BOX
Dating from the mid- to late 1800s, this box has a swing handle and a metal trim.
$ • 9 in (23 cm) diameter

WOODEN MILK PAIL
A late-19th- or early-20th-century milk pail with an associated 1-pint measure.
$ • 23 in (58 cm) high

ICE CREAM DISPENSER
This brass ice cream wafer dispenser dates from the 1920s.
$$ • 4 in (10 cm) wide

VEGETABLE CUTTER
This Gilpin cast-steel vegetable cutter dates to the 19th century.
$$ • 6½ in (16.5 cm) wide

BUTTER CHURN
A 6-pint Blow butter churn with a registration year of 1948.
$$ • 13 in (33 cm) high

BRASS HOT WATER CAN
This Victorian brass hot water can would have been used for numerous chores, such as filling a bedwarmer.
$ • 11½ in (29 cm) high

EAGLE BUTTER STAMP
Molded with a stylized eagle, this butter stamp is a rare piece, dating to the 19th century.
$$ • 4 in (10 cm) diameter

FOOT WARMER
A pierced-tin foot warmer in a wooden frame, decorated with multiple heart motifs. It dates to c. 1820.
$$ • 11¾ in (30 cm) wide

WALNUT PESTLE
This is a 19th-century walnut pestle with attractive graining and patina.
$$ • 8¾ in (22.5 cm) high

19TH-CENTURY BUTTER SCOOP
A butter scoop from Wales, made in the late 19th or early 20th century.
$ • 9 in (23 cm) long

HOT WATER BOTTLE
Dating from the 1920s, this is a Gladstone-bag-shaped hot water bottle.
$$ • 9 in (23 cm) wide

DOUBLE BUTTER STAMP
A very rare 19th-century double butter stamp depicting the wheatsheaf, a symbol of wealth.
$$ • 4¾ in (12 cm) wide

TOP TIPS
• Look for unusual gelatin or chocolate molds—besides being quite sought after, they are also fun to use.
• Snap up copper and brass items going cheap at auctions.
• Watch out for late-19th-century copper kettles designed by Dr. Christopher Dresser; stark, stylized handles were his trademark.
• Think about quirky contemporary pieces from Italian company Alessi, which could well be collectibles of the future.

Starter Buys

COPPER EGGCUP
Dated 1951, this is a Festival of Britain copper eggcup with an applied enamel logo.
$ • 1½ in (3.8 cm) high

CREAM CAN
A vintage can used for storing cream, probably before pasteurization.
$ • 11½ in (29 cm) high

SALT-GLAZED GELATIN MOLD
This stoneware mold was salt-glazed to achieve the shiny brown finish.
$ • 7½ in (19 cm) wide

SYCAMORE BUTTER PATS
This pair of sycamore children's butter pats date from the early 20th century.
$ • 5¾ in (14.5 cm) long

JAPANESE CRUET SET
A ceramic pixie and mushroom cruet set made in Japan, dating from c. 1930.
$ • 5½ in (14 cm) wide

BEETLEWARE GELATIN MOLDS
A set of three pink mottled Beetleware gelatin molds from the 1930s.
$ • 2¾ in (7 cm) diameter

You may also like… Plastic Wares, see pp. 166–69

Sewing Tools

This is an immensely diverse area: the 18th and 19th centuries saw an explosion in the manufacture of sewing consumables, and the variety in just one category can often satisfy a lifetime's curiosity.

The lure of an old sewing box is hard to describe. Many are handed down from generation to generation and often become depositories for small collectible items such as Tartan ware or Mauchline ware.

In this diverse area, a little specialization is a sensible thing, and collectors often concentrate on specific objects such as thimbles or needle cases. Even within such categories, there can be thousands of different designs based on countless different materials. While a single novelty needle case can

be worth hundreds of dollars, this field gives ample opportunity for a chance purchase and is a good area for all budgets.

Look to the Internet or estate sales to start or add to your collection: at the latter, auctioneers often feature mixed lots, some even selling 19th-century sewing boxes complete with their contents. Beware, however, of the many fakes on the market, particularly silver items such as novelty needle cases, which can slip easily through auctions and shop cabinets.

A Box of Tricks
A box to hold useful accessories was a must for an 18th-century traveler, and this is a beautifully made lacquer-and-gold example. With separate compartments to hold scissors and other items, it even includes a miniature of the box's probable owner, perhaps a member of the French aristocracy.

FRENCH NÉCESSAIRE DE VOYAGE
A fine 18th-century piece with gold borders and small animals amid floral scrolls. A diamond-set thumbpress opens the box.
$$$ • 6½ in (16.5 cm) high

KEY FACTS	18th century	c. 1850	1851	1889	1920s
Threads through time	Pincushions become more elaborate, incorporating new materials and taking new shapes.	A machine is made to punch regular dimples in the surface of silver thimbles. Previously, this was done by hand.	A number of special collectible thimbles are made to commemorate the Great Exhibition in Hyde Park, London.	The first electric sewing machines are developed and produced by Singer Sewing Co.	Silversmiths Adie & Lovekin Ltd. cease manufacturing, increasing the value of their sewing tools.

What's Hot

Look out for:

Silver novelty pincushions are amongst the most collectible of sewing tools and accessories. The Birmingham-based company of Adie & Lovekin Ltd., who were in business from the late 1800s to the 1920s, specialized in miniature silver items ranging from bookmarks and button hooks to an array of pincushions, including this one.

NEEDLE CASE
With a fine mosaic-like pattern, this straw work case is from the mid-19th century.
$$ • 4½ in (11.2 cm) long

TINY MARVEL
This Spanish walnut piece, a tiny frivolity, nonetheless includes various useful things.
$$ • 1¾ in (4.3 cm) high

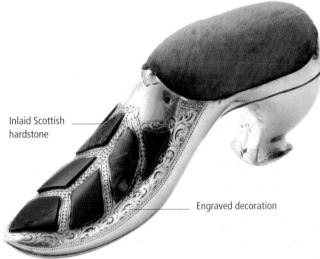

Inlaid Scottish hardstone

Engraved decoration

SEWING COMPANION
A scarce novelty Tunbridge ware whitewood piece in the form of the Brighton Pavilion.
$$$ • 7¾ in (19.7 cm) high

SEWING KIT
This early-19th-century tortoiseshell kit has ivory bands and a red plush interior.
$$$ • 4 in (10 cm) high

NOVELTY PINCUSHION
Shaped like a shoe, this late-Victorian novelty pincushion, made for the Scottish market, is set with seven shaped panels of varicolored hard stones between engraved borders, c. 1891.
$$$ • 5¼ in (13.25 cm) long

What's Not

Grandmothers' sewing boxes can harbor an amazing selection of items: for example, it's surprising how many packets of 19th-century needles survive, unopened! The industrial manufacture of needles means there are plenty around, however, so they are not particularly valuable.

SILVER SCISSORS CASE
The rounded oval top of this 18th-century case has a simple acanthus engraving.
$$$ • 4 in (10 cm) long

SILVER NEEDLE CASE
Engraved with foliate and line decorations, this is marked "SP" for Samuel Pemberton.
$$$ • 3½ in (9 cm) long

NEEDLE PACKET
This color-printed and embossed card needle packet holder has an inset mirror.
$ • 2¼ in (6 cm) wide

Core Collectibles

SEWING COMPENDIUM
An egg-shaped Mauchline ware sewing compendium.

$$ • 2 in (5.3 cm) high

MOTHER-OF-PEARL CASE
This 1830s French needle case has acanthus leaf ends.

$$ • 3¼ in (8 cm) long

IVORY PIN CASE
The cover of this French piece, with silk and fabric interior, is carved with a foliate design.

$$ • 2½ in (6.4 cm) long

STERLING THIMBLE
This Irish-themed thimble, by James Fenton, is covered with a band of clovers and a harp.

$ • 1 in (2.5 cm) high

SEWING KIT
Covered in leather, this 19th-century sewing kit has an embroidered pincushion.

$$$ • Case 7¾ in (19.5 cm) long

MEASURING TAPE
An early-20th-century novelty measuring tape in the form of a chess table.

$$ • 2¼ in (6 cm) high

WOODEN NEEDLE CASE
This c. 1820 amboyna wood needle case is lined with ebony and ivory bands.

$$ • 3 in (7.8 cm) long

SOUVENIR NEEDLE CASE
Hand-carved, this unusual fruitwood needle case is carved "Mer de Glace."

$$ • 4 in (10 cm) long

IVORY NEEDLE CASE
This vegetable ivory needle case from c. 1860 has acorn-shaped ends.

$$ • 3 in (7.3 cm) long

TATTING SHUTTLE
Used for making handmade lace, this Tartan ware tatting shuttle has a "McBeth" label.

$$ • 2¾ in (7 cm) long

Ask the Expert

Q. How can you spot if an item is genuine?
A. The desirability of small silver objects such as novelty pincushions has led to fakes coming on the market in recent years. A careful eye can often discern the sham objects. First, as the fakes are generally cast from an original, the assay, date, and makers' marks often lack the crispness of a

EDWARDIAN PINCUSHION
This charming novelty pin-cushion is in the form of a hatching chick, c. 1909.
$$ • 1¼ in (3 cm) high

Stuffed and loaded

stamped mark. Second, the fake items are often formed from two halves and joined in a different manner than the originals. Finally, the velvet pincushion is nearly always bleached to suggest age. Pulling the velvet slightly will reveal this along the edge.

GLASS NEEDLE CASE
This reverse-painted needle case and packet holder is from the mid- to late 19th century.
$$ • 2½ in (6.2 cm) wide

NOVELTY PINCUSHION
In the form of a lady's shoe, this late-Victorian pincushion is loaded and stuffed, 1891.
$$ • 2½ in (6.4 cm) high

NEEDLE PACKET CASE
A pressed brass needle packet case in the form of an artist's easel and painting by W. Avery & Son, Redditch, c. 1897.
$$$ • 4½ in (11.5 cm) high

THIMBLE AND NEEDLE CASE
This mid-19th-century French kingswood and fruitwood thimble and needle case has gilt bands and contains an ivory and gold thimble.
$$$ • 3 in (8 cm) high

Starter Buys

THREAD WINDER
An early-19th-century carved mother-of-pearl thread winder.
$ • 1½ in (3.8 cm) wide

NEEDLE PACKET HOLDER
A chromolithographed needle holder with a pull-out drawer.
$$ • 2 in (5.2 cm) high

PINCUSHION CLAMP
A 19th-century Tunbridge ware rosewood clamp.
$$ • Cushion 2¼ in (6 cm) long

CARD NEEDLE CASE
A "synoptical needle case" patented in November 1867.
$$ • 3¾ in (9.5 cm) high

SHELL-COVERED PIN CASE
An abalone shell and red silk souvenir pin case, c. 1890.
$$ • 2¼ in (5.5 cm) high

SEWING CLAMP
A Regency rosewood sewing clamp with a pincushion.
$$ • 8¼ in (21 cm) high

You may also like… Treen & Boxes, see pp. 152–57

Writing Tools

Sadly, we write less and less, but the action of forming letters with a fountain pen is something many still hold dear. From the humblest quill to a Dunhill-Namiki, the variety of writing implements is infinite.

The mid-1980s saw a boom in vintage pen prices, and unrivaled records were set at auctions. Although many of us rely on a ballpoint for everyday use, status and style still exude from marques such as Mont Blanc, Tiffany, Cartier, Asprey, Dunhill, and Mappin & Webb—names that are synonymous with the most collectible, albeit the highest-priced, accessories.

From a collector's viewpoint, the most desirable pens are those from the 1880s to the 1930s, the so-called "golden age" of the fountain pen. Pens from this era came in a vast range of handsome styles and materials, as dozens of manufacturers competed to outdo each other in technical innovation and creative design.

Post–World War II pens tend to be mass-produced, and are more limited in style and material than those from the classic era. Although of excellent quality, they lack the handmade individuality of their earlier counterparts, so have rather less cachet among collectors and are more easily affordable.

Spirit of the Age

Some of the iconic images of our time have found their way into desk ornaments and writing paraphernalia. This superb personalized desk piece is constructed from a Rolls-Royce Spirit of Ecstasy hood ornament and makes an elegant addition to any writing table. The earliest version of the figure, The Whisper, was produced by Charles Sykes for cars belonging to his friend Lord Montagu, and was modeled on Montagu's mistress, Eleanor Thornton. The ornament was so popular with Rolls-Royce that in 1911 Sykes was commissioned to adapt it for use on all Rolls-Royce cars, and the Spirit of Ecstasy was created. This kneeling version was produced between 1934 and 1959, with a lower profile designed to avoid obstructing the driver's view.

SILVER WRAITH AWARD
Chrome-plated desk piece featuring a Rolls-Royce Spirit of Ecstasy ornament. The kneeling figure dates this piece to the 1930s–1950s.
$$$ • 3¾ in (9.5 cm) high

KEY FACTS	1787	1800s	1884	1912	1943
Making the perfect pen	A quill pen is used to write and sign the Constitution of the United States of America.	Quill pens start to be replaced with steel dip pens, which soon begin to be mass-produced.	Lewis Waterman's patent sets the standard for the first reliable fountain pen.	Walter A. Sheaffer invents the lever-filler for fountain pens, which is a runaway success.	The first commercial ballpoint pens become available, following the Biro brothers' patent.

What's Hot

ROCK CRYSTAL DESK SEAL
A gold-mounted oblong
French desk seal, c. 1900.
$$$ • 2½ in (8.2 cm) high

LIMITED-EDITION PARKER
This "Spanish Treasure Fleet
1715" pen is made of silver.
$$$ • 6 in (15 cm) long

Look out for:

The highly priced Namiki pens, created by craftsmen using
maki-e, the ancient Japanese art of lacquering, are the
ultimate goal for pen collectors. Namiki was the original
name of the Pilot Pen Company founded by Ryosuke
Namiki in Japan in 1916. After the Dunhill
company secured exclusive marketing rights
in 1925, Dunhill-Namiki was born.

Top lacquer layer _____

SILVER LETTER OPENER
This tool is in the shape of
an 1845 infantry sword.
$$$ • Blade 9¼ in (23.5 cm) long

TIFFANY & CO. INKWELL
Made of cut glass and silver,
this inkwell dates to c. 1890.
$$$$ • 5½ in (14.5 cm) high

Gold flowers in _____
raised inlay work

1930S JAPANESE PILOT PEN
A Dunhill-Namiki *maki-e* balance with *kacho-e* by Kohkyo, this
pen has a rare Pilot Falcon (extra fine) 14K nib.
$$$$ • 6 in (15 cm) long

What's Not

The more common pens are of small value. Although a classic
writing implement, the standard Parker 51 is merely a good
"workhorse" and will remain at the low end at around $40.

CUT GLASS INKWELL
This inkwell has a silver
watch set into its cap, 1917.
$$$ • 3½ in (9 cm) high

INKWELL WITH CALENDAR
A Mappin & Webb cut glass
and silver inkwell.
$$$ • 3½ in (9 cm) wide

PARKER 51
A 1950s Parker 51 Custom, this pen has a black plastic
aerometric filler, with medium nib, and is in mint condition.
$ • 6¼ in (16 cm) long

Core Collectibles

DINKIE NO.526

A 1920s Conway Stewart Dinkie no. 526, this pen has a mottled hard rubber lever filler.

$$ • 4¾ in (12 cm) long

BLACKBIRD BB 2-46 PEN

This blue and gold-bronze marbled celluloid pen is from Mabie Todd & Co., c. 1934.

$$$ • 5½ in (14 cm) long

PARKER VACUMATIC

This oversized pen with a gold Parker arrow nib is set in emerald pearl laminated celluloid.

$$ • 5½ in (14 cm) long

SWAN LEVERLESS 275-60 PEN

A black celluloid twist-filling leverless pen made c. 1934 by Mabie Todd & Co.

$$$ • 6 in (15 cm) long

SILVER DESK SEAL

A late-19th-century desk seal with mother-of-pearl handle.

$$ • 3¾ in (9.5 cm) high

ROSEWOOD WRITING SLOPE

Mosaic banding adorns this Tunbridge ware writing slope, with an inkwell inside.

$$$ • 12 in (30 cm) long

TREEN DESK STAND

A 19th-century Tunbridge ware desk stand housing a glass ink bottle.

$$ • 5 in (12 cm) long

GOTHIC BRASS WRITING BOX

Made of Coromandel ebony wood, this writing box has a hinged lid and pen tray.

$$ • 12 in (30.5 cm) long

ROSEWOOD WRITING BOX

This rosewood brass-bound writing box dates back to the 19th century.

$$ • 18 in (46 cm) long

Ask the Expert

Q. Could you date an old glass ink bottle with a jagged neck?
A. These bottles are known as "shear tops" or "penny inks" and date from the late 19th century. They have jagged tops where they were taken out of the mold but not smoothly finished.

Q. Is it possible to restore vintage pens to "writing" condition?
A. For many people, this is the whole point. What better way to sign a letter than with a vintage fountain pen? A specialist can restore most pens, and an Internet search will give you a wide choice.

Hard rubber exterior   Gold-filled trim

WATERMAN 52V
A Canadian Waterman's 52V, this pen has a blue and yellow rippled hard rubber lever filler and a hallmarked 9kt gold cap band, c. 1928.

$$ • 5 in (13 cm) long

VASE-SHAPED DESK SEAL
A modern silver desk seal with a gilt interior, c. 1916.
$$$ • 3½ in (9 cm) high

FOUNTAIN PEN DESK SET
This Wahl-Eversharp 1920s pen set has an oval onyx base decorated with a spelter dog.
$$ • 6 in (15 cm) wide

1960S GUCCI PENCIL
A 1960s double-ended pencil, marked "925," "GUCCI," and "MADE IN ITALY."
$$ • 5½ in (14 cm) long

SHEAFFER NOSTALGIA PEN
Overlaid with vermeil filigree, this 1970s cartridge pen has a fine 14K nib.
$$$ • 5½ in (14 cm) long

SILVER DESK SEAL
A mounted silver 19th-century Dutch desk seal.
$$ • 3½ in (9 cm) high

VEST POCKET PEN
Made in the 1930s, this Dunhill-Namiki vest pocket pen has a black luccanite lever filler.
$$$ • 5 in (13 cm) long

MONTBLANC K2
This rare Danish pen, dated 1937–46, has a coral red button filler with a fine 14C 2 nib.
$$ • 5 in (13 cm) long

Starter Buys

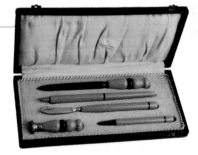

GOLF CLUB PENCIL
An unusual propelling pencil designed in the shape of a golf club.
$$ • 3½ in (9 cm) long

GOLD-PLATED PENCIL
Hanging on a sprung chain, this 1950s Aristocrat pencil has an engraved pin.
$ • 4 in (10 cm) long

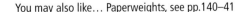

ACRYLIC WRITING SET
This 1930s writing set comprises a pen and matching accessories in peach and violet acrylic, all presented in their original box.
$$ • 6½ in (16.5 cm) long

TUNBRIDGE WARE PAPER KNIFE
Patterned flower bands decorate the rosewood handle and blade of this paper knife.
$$ • 12 in (30.5 cm) long

CYGNET STYLO
This late 1930s Mabie Todd & Co. stylo has a burgundy and black marbled lever filler.
$$ • 5 in (13 cm) long

You may also like… Paperweights, see pp.140–41

24 April, 1954

PICTURE POST

MARILYN MONROE— IN A NEW ROLE

HULTON'S NATIONAL WEEKLY

VOL 63 • NO 4

CHAPTER

Books, Magazines & Ephemera

The Power of the Printed Word & Image

Printed matter is a vast and ever-expanding collecting area, covering everything from books and magazines to cigarette cards and album covers. With thousands of possible themes, there's something to tempt the hidden collector in everyone.

Collecting in this area can be complex, but also very fulfiling. The price of a book is determined by a myriad of different factors—which edition it is from, which printing, the condition and style of the binding, whether the book has an author's signature, whether it contains illustrations—and a wise collector must know about all of them to ensure that he or she is paying a fair price. Printed matter is also prone to many different kinds of damage, from damp, to torn pages, lost or battered dust jackets, dirt and dust, faded coloring, and simple disintegration from long years of use.

Album cover signed by the members of the Rolling Stones, see Core Collectibles, p. 195.

Cigarette card, see What's Hot, p. 217.

Spider-man cover, No.10, March 1964, see What's Hot, p. 213.

Given all these complications, going it alone and learning by your mistakes can be a costly venture. If you are looking for a get-rich-quick scheme or an easy subject to become expert in, then printed matter may not be the area for you. An important collection can only be gathered by devoting years to learning the minutiae of a subject and spotting rarities that relate specifically to it.

Thankfully, whatever your chosen area of interest, you will find that you are not alone. The popularity of printed-matter collecting ensures that a community of like-minded enthusiasts will always be available to share information with you, and help you develop your own expertise. The Internet has turned thousands of people into collector–dealers, eagerly offering duplicate or unwanted items to an international audience to fund the search for coveted pieces. Moreover, there are still plenty of traditional auction rooms and specialist dealers offering some of the best treasures. Prices at auction can often be half the retail price, but the real benefit of dealing with a specialist is the lifetime of hard-won knowledge and experience that they are willing to share with the true collector.

Prices for the rarest pieces can reach astonishing heights, and competition at the top end of the market is intense, but such is the variety of material on offer that hidden treasures can still be found by those patient enough to seek them out. In fact, it's the hidden treasures that make this such an exciting collecting area—finding a rare edition in perfect condition brings enormous satisfaction, and the thrill of the chase enhances the pleasure of owning these fascinating pieces.

Harry Potter and the Philosopher's Stone,
see What's Hot, p. 197.

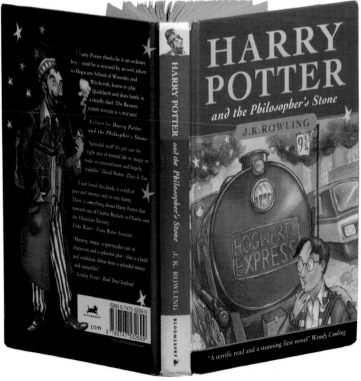

A gelatin silver print publicity photo of a circus performer, see Starter Buys, p. 191.

Postcards

Picture postcard collecting is still a very affordable area, with the vast majority of cards unlikely to cost more than a few dollars each, even if hunted out at a specialty postcard fair.

Since the first British postcard was mailed on October 1, 1870, hundreds of millions have been bought, kept, or sent. From 1902, when the Post Office allowed the message to be written on the same side as the address, until the end of World War I, postcard sending and collecting was at its zenith. The spread of telephone systems accounts for the decline back then just as much as emails have had an impact on letter-writing in recent years.

Most postcard collectors are interested in one theme only and there is much to choose from: transportation, topography, military, comic, historical events, indigenous peoples, novelty postcards, advertising cards, real photo postcards, embroidered cards. In most areas you can still find good cards for less than $10. One irresistible area to collect is local topography, to build a pictorial archive of how your town or county used to be.

Team Spirit

Choose a subject that interests you, such as sports team lineups, for example. These are of great interest and tell a story about the fashions and social mores of the times that goes way beyond the sport itself. But do also consider offbeat themes that can be collected for tiny amounts and built into an archive of institutional importance.

EVERTON F.C. CARD
This postcard of the Everton Football Club, published by Carbonora, includes noted centerforward "Dixie" Dean.
$$ • 5½ in (14 cm) wide

TOP TIPS

- Look for real photo cards, as they are often more rare and interesting in all subject areas.
- Be aware that postcards that have been through the mail are self-authenticating.
- Don't ignore dull Edwardian postcard albums; they can often be hiding places for a few well-preserved gems.
- It's possible to collect even seemingly boring subjects, such as gas stations—no subject is too trivial!

KEY FACTS	1870	1894	1907	1930s	1973
Images through time	The first British postcard is issued by the Post Office, a plain buff card with printed halfpenny stamp.	British publishers are allowed to produce and distribute postcards to send via the Royal Mail.	"Divided back" postcards are introduced, with a vertical line separating message and address.	The infamous British "Saucy" seaside postcards reach the peak of their popularity.	The Royal Mail starts to issue "PHQ" cards, with designs of commemorative GPO stamps.

What's Hot

HOVIS SHOP POSTCARD
This location postcard of the Hovis shop in West Ham, London, is from c. 1910–15.
$$ • 5¼ in (13.5 cm) high

JACK JOHNSON CARD
A signed black-and-white photographic postcard of the champion boxer, c. 1914.
$$$ • 5½ in (14 cm) high

Look out for:
Commemorative postcards that are produced to celebrate special occasions are highly collectible.

Stylish real-photo postcard

ESSO PAVILION CARD
A souvenir of the Art Deco Esso pavilion at the Empire Exhibition, Glasgow, c. 1938.
$ • 5½ in (14 cm) high

Core Collectibles

OMNIBUS POSTCARD
A fine Edwardian-period transport card of the Kilburn and Marble Arch omnibus.
$ • 5½ in (14 cm) wide

"GRAND STAND" POSTCARD
A postcard of the women of the "Grand Stand" at the Dymock Flower Show, 1910.
$ • 5½ in (14 cm) wide

Starter Buys

"FACES IN THE MOUNTAINS"
This Swiss cartoon postcard dates from c. 1900.
$ • 5½ in (14 cm) wide

COLONEL RYAN D.S.O. CARD
A patriotic 1915 card of planes leaving Ludgershall.
$ • 5½ in (14 cm) wide

POST OFFICE POSTCARD
A rare, dated postcard of the West Tytherley Post Office in Salisbury, Wiltshire.
$ • 5½ in (14 cm) wide

HALTON TRAMWAY CARD
This postcard, depicting the opening of the tramway route at Halton, is dated April 1915.
$ • 5½ in (14 cm) wide

WINSTON CHURCHILL CARD
A 1939 postcard in aid of the *Daily Sketch* War Relief Fund.
$ • 5¼ in (13.5 cm) high

"GOOD OLD SUMMERTIME"
This 1900s seaside postcard shows boaters ogling a lady.
$ • 5¼ in (13.5 cm) high

You may also like… Autographs, see pp. 192–95

Vintage Photography

Collecting photographs has been popular for 30 years, and while a shortage of fresh 19th-century material grows, the Internet has increased the chances of private buying and selling of small-value photos.

Frenchman Louis-Jacques-Mandé Daguerre and Englishman William Henry Fox Talbot separately perfected ways of making permanent images that still exist today. For most collectors, Fox Talbot's image of a window at Lacock Abbey in 1835 is the date it all began. Fox Talbot's system of producing a negative from which positives could be made was revolutionary. There are dozens of photographic processes, but most 19th-century photographs were made using an albumen process that gave the photographs a sepia tone.

Wealthy collectors pay gigantic sums for the "right" perfect-condition images by Francis Frith or Julia Margaret Cameron. From the end of the 19th century, the albumen print was superseded by the gelatin silver print and Eastman's roll-film process, which survived until the digital era.

Choose a theme, check out real and Internet catalogs, go to photography fairs and dealers, and get buying. Whether it's photographs featuring Edwardian toys or seaside snapshots, it's out there and waiting to find you.

Unique Images

Daguerreotypes were unique images—which led to the art's decline in the 1850s. Their quality, however, still fascinates some collectors. Often tarnished or solarized, family portraits are still reasonable to buy. Fine examples are hard to come by, and unusual subjects, like this one, are very rare.

AMERICAN HOUSE
This single-gable Midwestern house from c. 1855 is an unusual subject.

$$$ • Case 3¼ x 4¼ in (8 x 11 cm)

TOP TIPS

- Care for your photographs. Bright light and other atmospherics will slowly damage most images.
- Carbon prints, platinum prints, and Woodburytypes are more resilient than most processes to atmospheric and age deterioration.
- Choose an interesting theme that nobody else is collecting and trust your instinct. It could build into an important archive.

KEY FACTS	1835	1850	1880	1888	1890s
Capturing small pieces of history	William Henry Fox Talbot produces the first photographic image on paper that still survives today.	The albumen print process is perfected and sets the standard for over 40 years.	The first newspaper photograph is published in the *New York Daily Graphic* on March 4.	George Eastman markets the first Kodak, opening up mass-market photography.	Color photography first becomes a practical possibility.

What's Hot

Look out for:
These three women are from the Micmac tribe. Portraits in fine condition of indigenous people are highly sought after and command very high prices.

ENGLAND RUGBY XV
Taken prior to the match vs. Scotland, March 5, 1877.
$$ • 7½ x 10½ in (19 x 25.5 cm)

MICK JAGGER "FUR HOOD"
Iconic '60s portrait of the Rolling Stone by David Bailey.
$$$$ • 19½ x 19½ in (50 x 50 cm)

NATIVE AMERICANS
A superb condition albumen print, c. 1859.
$$$$ • 7½ x 5½ in (18.5 x 14.5 cm)

Typical pose of the time

Core Collectibles

EGYPTIAN VIEW
This 1880 photograph is from an album of 100, collected by Kossuth and Mary Robinson.
$$$ • 8 x 10 in (20 x 25 cm)

VICTORIAN FAMILY ALBUM
This photo album is enhanced by skilled pen-and-ink and watercolor decorations.
$$ • 12 x 12 in (30 x 30 cm)

BHAVNAGAR VIEWS
An excellent, clear image from the days of the Raj from an album by the Indian photography studio of Bourne and Shepherd, c. 1900.
$$$ • 8¼ in (21 cm) high

Starter Buys

JAPANESE ALBUMEN PRINT
Hand-colored prints of people and views are quite affordable.
$ • 8¼ x 10½ in (21 x 27 cm)

CIRCUS PERFORMER
A gelatin silver print publicity photograph, c. 1960s.
$ • 10 x 5 in (25 x 20 cm)

AMBROTYPE BROOCH
Brooches and lockets bearing images are still inexpensive.
$ • 3 x 3 in (7.5 x 7.5 cm)

CARTE DE VISITE
The subject of this carte is the historian Thomas Carlyle.
$ • 4 x 2½ in (10 x 6 cm)

You may also like… Magazines, see pp. 214–15

Autographs

Perhaps no other collecting area is so endangered by the Internet as the autograph market. Nonetheless, enthusiasts across the world continue to vie for coveted authentic signatures in a minefield of forgeries.

Authentic signatures can give us a profound sense of personal connection with great figures and key events, past and present—a sense eagerly sought by enthusiasts of history and modern celebrity alike.

Working out what you should pay, however, is a complex matter. Value is always subjective, but key factors in determining price include the age of the signer when they died, how famous they remained after death, and how important the item is to their legacy. Where letters are concerned, content is key: any note from,

say, Charles Darwin is exciting, but prices—and collectors' heart rates—really go up if the note includes some mention of his theory of evolution.

In this area more than most, research pays off. Reference lists of facsimile autographs can be useful in distinguishing authentic signatures from forgeries, but nothing beats the experience of viewing good collections of genuine autographs. Collectors who fail to take precautions like these run a severe risk of throwing their money away on something literally worthless.

Hidden Treasure

The task of plowing through visitors' books filled with hundreds of names can be rewarded with an uplifting surprise. This 1900 Winston Churchill signature could easily have been missed among all the others. What also adds to its attraction is that its context makes it self-authenticating. A good talking piece.

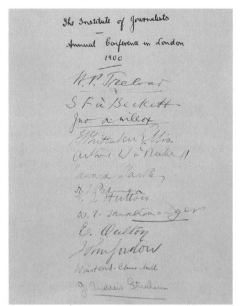

WINSTON CHURCHILL'S SIGNATURE
Second from the bottom is the immensely collectible autograph of one of the greatest Britons, Sir Winston Spencer Churchill, making this otherwise minor item expensive.
$$$ • 6½ in (16.5 cm) high

KEY FACTS	1804	1900	1935	1995	2007
Signing on—and off—the dotted line	President Thomas Jefferson begins using the autopen (a robot machine), still used by celebrities today.	Winston Churchill wins his first political seat at Oldham, making this a key year for his signature.	The ballpoint pen is introduced by Ladislas Biro, but takes 10 years to take commercial hold	eBay launches, and the number of famous autographs available increases dramatically.	Singaporean singer JJ Lin sets a new world autographing record, signing 3,052 CDs in two and a half hours.

What's Hot

PRINCESS DIANA
A signed black-and-white photo of the Princess and her sons, with Diana's monogram at the head, c. 1995.
$$$$ • 8½ x 9½ in (22 x 24 cm)

PRESIDENT KENNEDY
A great rarity, this photograph comes with the signatures and squiggles of all four members of JFK's young family, 1962.
$$$$$ • 9½ in (24 cm) wide

Look out for:

Dickens's signature is collectible in any state and though not uncommon, interesting specimens are keenly fought for. Often in blue ink and in a legible neat hand, the signature itself is often with a difficult-to-forge paraph or flourish, a series of lines underneath the name. This letter is all nicely laid out on one page, making it perfect for framing.

Handwritten rather than typed script

Typical flourish difficult to forge

CHARLES DICKENS'S CORRESPONDENCE
In this handwritten and signed one-page letter, dated September 12, 1868, Dickens declines an invitation as he must see his son off to Australia, an interesting personal touch.
$$$ • 7 in (18 cm) high

JIMI HENDRIX EXPERIENCE
Signatures of Jimi Hendrix, Noel Redding, and Mitch Mitchell: the Jimi Hendrix Experience.
$$$ • 4¼ in (11 cm) wide

QUEEN ELIZABETH I
Torn from the head of a document, c. 1570, this fine specimen reads "Elizabeth R."
$$$$ • 8½ in (21.8 cm) wide

C. S. LEWIS
A handwritten and signed letter from Lewis, explaining his creative thinking.
$$$$ • 7½ in (20 cm) high

KING EDWARD VIII
This rare document is a 1936 royal pardon signed "Edward RI."
$$$ • 11 in (28 cm) high

What's Not

Autopen, secretarial, forgery, or original? Many flat-signed celebrity autographs are produced, so it's better to pay more for a personalized autograph with provenance you can trust.

SIGNED BECKHAM PHOTO
An autopen David Beckham signature from the England vs Greece 2002 World Cup match.
$ • 10 in (25.5 cm) high

Core Collectibles

SIGNED PUBLICITY PHOTO
A signed photograph of Eric Morecambe and Ernie Wise.

$$ • 11½ in (29 cm) high

SIGNED BRUNEL CHECK
A personal check for £5 from Isambard Kingdom Brunel.

$$$ • 15½ in (39.5 cm) high

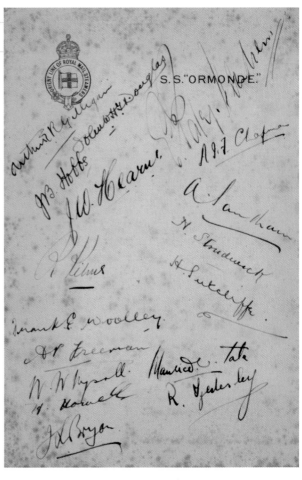

ENGLAND IN AUSTRALIA 1924–25 TEAM SHEET
Complete sports-team sheets are always popular, and an early date pushes up their value. This autograph team sheet of all 17 England cricket players is on SS *Ormonde* headed paper.

$$$ • 7 x 5 in (18 x 12.5 cm) high

ROYAL CHRISTMAS CARD
Elizabeth II and Prince Philip signed this card in 1953.

$$$ • 9¾ in (25 cm) high

BELA LUGOSI PHOTOGRAPH
Lugosi is depicted as Dracula, perhaps his most famous role.

$$$ • 5 in (13 cm) high

MARGARET THATCHER
The then prime minister signed this photo in 1982.

$$ • 9¾ in (25 cm) high

SARAH BERNHARDT
This signed carbon print photograph is from 1917.

$$ • 11½ x 10¼ in (29 x 26 cm)

CHARLES DARWIN
A one-page autograph letter, signed and dated March 1880.

$$$$ • 7 in (18 cm) high

DUKE OF WELLINGTON
Wellesley's signature is typically illegible on this 1840 letter.

$$ • 7 in (18 cm) high

"IT'S ONLY ROCK 'N' ROLL" ALBUM COVER
Signed by Mick Jagger, Keith Richards, Mick Taylor, Charlie Watts, and Bill Wyman.
$$ • 9¾ x 9¾ in (25 x 25 cm)

PRINCESS MARGARET
The young "Marscaret" drew this picture for her grandfather, George V, c. 1935.
$$$ • 5 x 8¼ in (13 x 21 cm)

PUBLICITY STILL FROM "THE GRADUATE"
Black-and-white publicity stills, like this one signed by stars Dustin Hoffman and Anne Bancroft, are popular autograph material.
$$ • 7¾ x 9¾ in (20 x 25 cm)

DANTE GABRIEL ROSSETTI
Signed checks such as this one, dated February 10, 1879, are almost self-authenticating and less likely to be forgeries.
$$ • 6½ in (17 cm) wide

LOUIS ARMSTRONG
Dedicated by Armstrong to a fellow trumpeter, c. 1932.
$$$ • 9¾ in (25 cm) high

LAUREL AND HARDY
A signed large silver print photo of the comedy duo.
$$$ • 9¾ x 12¾ in (25 x 32.5 cm)

WILLIAM GILBERT GRACE
Legendary Grace's signature is one of the most collectible cricketing autographs.
$$$ • 5½ in (14 cm) high

Starter Buys

ROGER MOORE
Moore's 12-year stint as James Bond made his autograph popular around the world.
$ • 6 in (15 cm) high

BRIGITTE BARDOT
This publicity photo is "flat-signed," bearing just the name of the actress with no personal dedication.
$ • 7¾ x 9¾ in (20 x 25 cm)

STANLEY MATTHEWS
The soccer hero endorses Crookes Halibut Oil for fitness and health in this 1948 signed letter.
$$ • 7¾ in (20 cm) high

You may also like… Magazines, see pp. 214–15

Children's Books

Collecting children's books and annuals need not be an expensive pursuit. Vivid colors and beloved characters allow even reprints and copies in poor condition to retain value and charm.

Many of us are devoted to the stories we read as we grew up, and there is always a new generation of collectors prepared to fight to reacquire the lost books of their childhood. First-generation readers of J. R. R. Tolkien and C. S. Lewis have long been pushing up prices for key editions, and fans of J. K. Rowling and Philip Pullman are just beginning to enter the collecting market.

Children's publishing really developed in the 18th century, with cheap volumes and woodcut illustrations. The survival rate of these books is low, however, and the great swath of Victorian children's books is a better starting point.

Modern titles can also be highly collectible. Children's annuals are rarely in demand, early *Rupert* and *Beano* being prized exceptions, but early editions of the *Famous Five* and *Secret Seven* series and the *Biggles* books remain high on collectors' wish lists.

The Original Pottermania

Such is Beatrix Potter's standing that early editions of her work in almost any condition are highly collectible, although many thousands were originally printed. First editions will usually have the date at the foot of the title page, which this copy does not. However, it transcends this major flaw by being in particularly fine condition and retaining the very rare and fragile printed glassine dust wrapper.

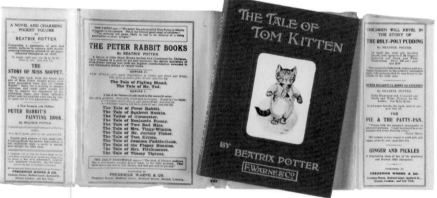

"THE TALE OF TOM KITTEN"
This edition of the famous story was published by Frederick Warne c. 1915. It has the original green boards of the first edition and is in the original printed glassine dust wrapper, making it highly desirable.
$$$$ • 6½ in (16.5 cm) high

KEY FACTS	1865	1901	1906	1942	1997
Tall stories for small people	Lewis Carroll's *Alice's Adventures in Wonderland* is first published.	Beatrix Potter issues the first private edition of *Peter Rabbit* in a run of 250 copies.	J. M. Barrie's classic story *Peter Pan* is published, with its famous illustrations by Arthur Rackham.	The first of Enid Blyton's *Famous Five* series is published: *Five on a Treasure Island*.	J. K. Rowling's first Harry Potter book is published, turning children's publishing on its head.

What's Hot

Look out for:

This first printing of *Harry Potter* is a true collector's item, with only around 300 copies extant. A first edition can be identified from the copyright page, which shows the year of publication as 1997, and has the numbers from 10 to 1 inclusive printed on the copyright page. The lowest number in the number string is the number of the printing.

A. A. MILNE
Milne's first book of poems, here in its 1924 first edition, in its original dust wrapper.

$$$$ • 7½ in (19 cm) high

"THE WIND IN THE WILLOWS"
Published in 1908, this copy has its original gilt-decorated cloth binding.

$$$$ • 8 in (20 cm) high

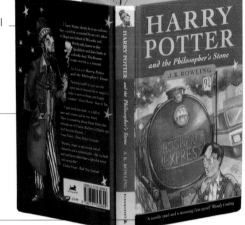

Laminated pictorial boards without dust wrapper

Boards in good condition

Quote by Wendy Cooling and no mention of the Smarties award

"LITTLE BLACK SAMBO"
The 1899 first edition of this little book, massively popular in its day, is now very rare.

$$$$ • 4¼ in (11 cm) high

PETER RABBIT DRAWING
A Beatrix Potter watercolor of Mr. McGregor and Peter Rabbit, signed, 1927.

$$$$$ • 6¾ in (17 cm) high

FIRST-PRINTING HARRY POTTER
The first printing of the original edition of Harry's first outing ran to just 300 copies, released by Bloomsbury in 1997. A copy like this one, in mint condition, is a genuine rarity.

$$$$$ • 8 in (20 cm) high

What's Not

Enid Blyton was so prolific that prices tend to be low for many of her books. Concentrate on sets of the popular series, such as *Famous Five*. Only fine copies of first editions in dust wrappers from 1950 and earlier are likely to attract three-figure sums.

DR. SEUSS
Copies like this one of the 1957 first edition of the book are very rare.

$$$$ • 9½ in (24 cm) high

INFANT'S CABINET
A set of hand-colored engraved cards in original wooden box, 1801.

$$$$ • Cards 2¾ x 2 in (7 x 5 cm)

"TALES ABOUT TOYS"
The first edition was published by Brockhampton Press in 1950. This copy is badly worn.

$ • 8 in (20 cm) high

Core Collectibles

"BUNTER'S LAST FLING"
Cassell published this first edition of Frank Richards' novel in 1965.

$$ • 8 in (20 cm) high

"JARDIN DES PLANTES"
A fantastical botanical garden appears in this foldaway "peep show" from the 1830s. The eyepiece gives views into a layered panorama of hand-colored engravings.

$$$ • 5½ in (14 cm) high

FAIRY TALES
Stories by Hans Christian Andersen, illustrated by Kay Nielsen, in a 1924 edition.

$$$ • 11 in (29 cm) high

JUST WILLIAM STORIES
The 1965 first edition by Richmal Crompton was published by George Newnes.

$$ • 8 in (20 cm) high

"DUCK AND THE DIESEL ENGINE"
Published by Edmund West, London, in 1958, this is a first edition from Reverend W. Awdry's Railway Series, whose most popular character was Thomas the Tank Engine.

$ • 5 in (13 cm) high

"LANGUAGE OF FLOWERS"
One of Kate Greenaway's hugely successful books, dating from 1884.

$$ • 6 in (15 cm) high

Ask the Experts

Q. Do inscriptions, names, and doodles affect the value of children's books?
A. Most collectors will be untroubled by a neat name or inscription in the front of a book, but scribbles, creases, and fingermarks will decrease the value of a book.

Q. Are politically incorrect books likely to be poor investments?
A. Do remember that these are historical items, reflecting the culture of the time of their publication. As such, the value of a well-written, well-illustrated book, such as *Little Black Sambo*, will stand the test of time.

Publication details

Q. How can I spot a first-edition Beatrix Potter?
A. The publication date should appear at the foot of the title page, underneath the publisher's imprint.

"SQUIRREL NUTKIN"
A first edition of one of Beatrix Potter's most popular titles.

$$$ • 5½ in (14 cm) high

BIGGLES FIRST EDITION
A first edition of Captain Johns' 77th Biggles title, published in 1963.

$$ • 7½ in (19 cm) high

"THE STORY OF A FIERCE BAD RABBIT"
Beatrix Potter's much-loved story was written for Louie—the young daughter of her publisher, Harold Warne—who wanted a tale about a really naughty rabbit. This copy comes from the second issue of the first edition, published in 1906.

$$$ • 4 in (10 cm) high

"PINOCCHIO"
This rare 1940 Walt Disney picture book features illustrations from the film.

$$ • 9 in (23 cm) high

"THE SECRET SEVEN"
The first outing for Blyton's child detectives, illustrated by George Brook, was published by Brockhampton Press in 1949.

$$ • 7¾ in (19 cm) high

"FLOWER FAIRIES OF THE SUMMER"
A 1940s copy of one of Cicely Mary Barker's famous picture books, clean and with dust-wrapper, but with a slightly damaged spine.

$$ • 5½ in (14 cm) high

"TOM THUMB"
Woodcuts illustrate this chapbook from c. 1800, in its original wrappers.

$$ • 5 in (12.5 cm) high

"ALICE, WHERE ART THOU?"
This first-edition Guinness Booklet, 1952, with color pictures and original pictorial wrappers, is one of a series of Christmas annuals.

$$ • 9 in (23 cm) high

"THE PEEK-A-BOOS IN WINTER"
Published by Oxford University Press in 1912, this edition is bound in accordion style, with printed board covers and color plates inside.

$$ • 8¾ in (22 cm) high

Core Collectibles

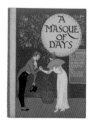

"NURSERY RHYMES"
Louis Wain illustrated this 1905 title from the "Father Tuck's Nursery" series.

$$ • 9½ in (24 cm) high

"A MASQUE OF DAYS"
Charles Lamb's writings are here illustrated in color by Walter Crane.

$$ • 9½ in (24 cm) high

"FUN LAND"
Louis Wain's rare set of illustrations, from the series "Father Tuck's Panorama," were first published by Raphael Tuck and Sons in 1910.

$$$ • 9½ in (25 cm) high

"THE TRAVELS OF LITTLE TOM TRANSIT"
This paper doll book from 1811 has eight cut-out hand-colored figures loosely inserted, showing Tom Transit in various costumes. The set is almost never found complete.

$$$ • 5 in (12.5 cm) high

"THE GOLLIWOGG'S DESERT ISLAND"
Although naïve in terms of political correctness, these stories by Florence and Bertha Upton have wonderful illustrations. This is a 1906 first edition, bound in original cloth-backed boards.

$$ • 9 in (23 cm) wide

"THE BALD TWIT LION"
Spike Milligan's popular children's book, beautifully illustrated by Carol Barker, was first published in 1968.

$$ • 12 in (30 cm) high

"THE FAIRY BOOK"
Thirty-two color plates are included in this first edition, illustrated by Warwick Goble and published in 1913.

$$ • 8 in (20 cm) high

"THE 'TROCIOUS TWINS AT THE SEA"
B. and N. Parker's 1926 story contains numerous full-page illustrations, and is bound in the original color picture boards. Less-familiar authors such as these can still find value if the condition is tip-top and the book has strong visual appeal.

$$ • 12½ in (32 cm) wide

TALES BY EDGAR ALLAN POE
This 1923 edition was
published by Harrap.
$$ • 9½ in (24 cm) high

"RUBAIYAT"
A well-preserved 1909 copy
of Fitzgerald's translation.
$$ • 9½ in (24 cm) high

DODIE SMITH'S DALMATIANS
This first edition was
published in 1956.
$$$ • 8 in (20 cm) high

Starter Buys

"TOOTSIE WOOTSIE KIDDIES"
An eight-section panorama-
style accordion by Chloe
Preston, c. 1915.
$ • 9½ in (24 cm) high

A G. A. HENTY ADVENTURE
The original cloth binding
adds value to this first edition,
published by Blackie in 1902.
$$ • 7½ in (19 cm) high

"THE BLUE BIRD"
Maurice Maeterlinck's 1911
book has 25 color plates,
still bright in this copy.
$$ • 9 in (23 cm) high

NODDY BOOKS
A set of 1950s first editions of
numbers 1–15 of Enid Blyton's
series is still easy to come by.
$ Each • Each 7 in (17 cm) high

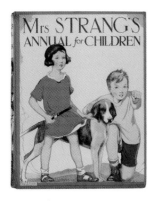

"ANNUAL FOR CHILDREN"
Published in the 1920s, this
annual is bound in the original
pictorial boards with dust
wrapper. Attractive children's
annuals like this are plentiful,
but very difficult to find in
pristine condition.
$ • 9½ in (24 cm) high

NOVELS OF CAPTAIN FREDERICK SADLEIR BRERETON
A regular officer in the British Army, Brereton wrote a series
of adventure stories for boys in the early 20th century.
$ • 7½ in (19 cm) high

You may also like… Modern First Editions, see pp. 202–07

Modern First Editions

The complex trading world of modern first editions is full of smoke and mirrors. Value is dependent on various factors, including the size of the initial printing and the condition of other editions.

For most collectors, the start date for modern first editions is around 1900, with a few honorable earlier exceptions such as *Treasure Island* or *The Jungle Book*. There has been an increasing number of printed price guides and "top 100" book lists, and this, coupled with Internet listings of booksellers' stock and prices, has led many to believe that all modern first editions have value. Condition and demand are critical, and prices change with the times: you'd be hard-pressed now to give away first editions of once-collected authors like John Galsworthy. The other factor to distort the market is people chasing new, quick investments. Auction prices are the only reliable indications of which authors are in or out, allowing level-headed comparisons to be drawn.

In the end, it is best to collect what you like and buy the best copies you can find. The more modern the book, the fussier you must be about its condition.

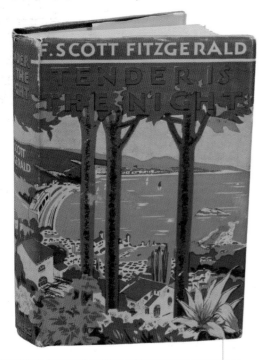

Exuding Style and Glamour
When it comes to setting price records for prized first editions, American collectors are world champions. F. Scott Fitzgerald is a collector's dream ticket, with a great literary reputation, small output, and guaranteed investment longevity.

"TENDER IS THE NIGHT"
An exceptionally fine copy from the first edition, published by Scribner's in 1934, signed by the author. The dust wrapper is in near-fine condition, and the inside front flap bears reviews by T. S. Eliot, H. L. Mencken, and Paul Rosenfeld.
$$$$$ • 8 in (20 cm) high

KEY FACTS	1897	1930	1945	1965	1998
Spinning contemporary yarns	Bram Stoker's *Dracula* is published. This is regarded as the cutoff point for "modern" first editions.	F. Scott Fitzgerald's wife is diagnosed with schizophrenia. *Tender Is the Night* describes their marriage.	Wartime economic restrictions are slowly lifted, paper quality improves, and print runs increase in size.	Margaret Drabble's novel *The Millstone* is the first to be typeset on computer.	A first edition of *The Hound of the Baskervilles* in a rare dust wrapper sells for $120,000 at Sotheby's.

What's Hot

"LOLITA"
Nabokov's controversial novel in two volumes, published by Olympia Press, Paris, 1955.

$$$$$ • 6½ in (17 cm) high

"THE CATCHER IN THE RYE"
The first edition, published Boston, 1951, has the author's photo on the back panel.

$$$ • 7½ in (19 cm) high

Look out for:
Ian Fleming is perhaps the highest-profile postwar author, whose early first editions became intensely collectible, and command ever-rising prices. The most minute imperfections in a dust wrapper will affect the price far more than with prewar collectible modern first editions.

Watch out for nicks to the dust wrapper edges

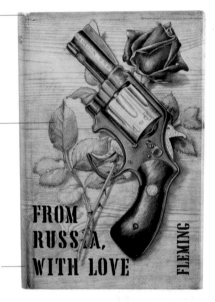

Stylish Richard Chopping design

Beware of faded or sunned spines

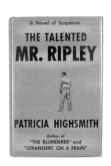

"DRACULA"
A copy of the very first bound issue, from 1897, in original yellow cloth.

$$$$ • 7½ in (19 cm) high

"THE TALENTED MR. RIPLEY"
A neat copy of the first edition, published Coward-McCann, New York, 1955.

$$$$ • 7½ in (19 cm) high

"FROM RUSSIA WITH LOVE"
This copy of Fleming's fifth Bond novel, first published in 1957 by Jonathan Cape, has its cover and binding in fine condition.

$$$ • 7½ in (19 cm) high

What's Not

Check copyright pages to find out which edition and which printing of a book your copy comes from. The lowest number in the number string (here "3 5 7 9 8 6 4") indicates the printing. For many titles, later printings even of first editions are significantly less valuable.

"LORD OF THE FLIES"
A scuffed copy of the 1954 edition, published by Faber & Faber, London.

$$$ • 7½ in (19 cm) high

"DUNE"
The first in the series, 1965, published by Chilton Books, Philadelphia and New York.

$$$$ • 7½ in (19 cm) high

COMMON EDITION
The copyright page from a third printing of the fifth edition of Tolkien's The Hobbit.

$ • 7 in (17.5 cm) high

HarperCollins*Publishers*
77–85 Fulham Palace Road,
Hammersmith, London W6 8JB

This new edition published by HarperCollins*Publishers* 1997
3 5 7 9 8 6 4

First published in Great Britain by
George Allen & Unwin 1937
Second edition 1951
Third edition 1966
Fourth edition 1978

First published by HarperCollins*Publishers* 1991
Fifth edition (reset) 1995

Copyright © George Allen & Unwin (Publishers) Ltd
1937, 1951, 1966, 1978, 1995, 1997

Core Collectibles

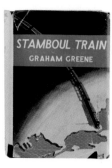

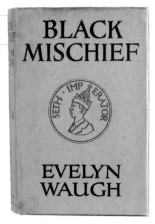

"THE RACHEL PAPERS"
A first edition, published by Jonathan Cape in 1973, of one of Martin Amis's first books.
$$$ • 7½ in (19 cm) high

"THE ITALIAN GIRL"
A copy of the original 1964 edition published by Chatto & Windus, London.
$$ • 7½ in (19 cm) high

"STAMBOUL TRAIN"
Published by Heinemann in 1932, this copy has a distressed dust wrapper.
$$$$ • 7½ in (19 cm) high

"BLACK MISCHIEF"
This copy is from the 1932 edition published by Chapman & Hall, London.
$$$ • 9 in (21 cm) high

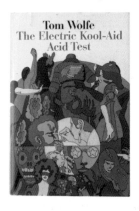

HYSTERICAL REALISM
Tom Wolfe's seminal work of hysterical realism was first published by Farrar, Straus & Giroux in 1968. The bright cover and neat binding on this copy add to its value.
$$$ • 7½ in (19 cm) high

"MASTER & COMMANDER"
A copy from the 1978 first edition of the first novel in O'Brian's long-running series featuring Jack Aubrey and Stephen Maturin. This is one of the rarest of the series.
$$$$ • 8 in (20 cm) high

Ask the Expert

Q. Are American first editions worth more than UK first editions?
A. The general rule is that collectors want the first edition in the author's country of origin, regardless of rarity or precedence. There are expensive exceptions like Mark Twain, but a general rule is to avoid overseas first editions.

Q. How much does the dust wrapper contribute the value of a book?
A. It's impossible to give a rule, but most collectors are only interested in buying first editions in dust wrappers, and most copies of postwar first editions without wrappers are valued as reading copies only. If the price has not been clipped, this adds to value.

Dust wrapper in good condition

Atmospheric artwork by Robin Macartney

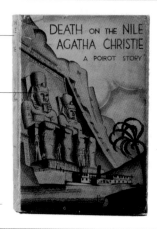

"DEATH ON THE NILE"
The Agatha Christie classic, published by Collins Crime Club, London, in 1937.
$$ • 7½ in (19 cm) high

"A POCKET FULL OF RYE"
Although not a first edition, the dramatic cover art makes this version very collectible.
$$ • 7½ in (19 cm) high

"THE SHINING"
A first edition, published by Doubleday & Company, Garden City, New York, 1977.
$$$ • 8 in (20 cm) high

"A MOVEABLE FEAST"
This first American edition was published by Charles Scribner's Sons in 1964.
$$$ • 7½ in (19 cm) high

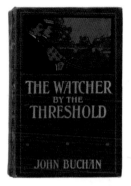

FIRST EDITION JOHN BUCHAN
This collection of stories, first published by Blackwood in 1902, is in its original binding.
$$ • 7 in (18 cm) high

"SHARPE'S SWORD"
The value of this 1983 Collins edition is enhanced by the dust jacket in good condition.
$$$ • 8 in (20 cm) high

"FIVE LITTLE PIGS"
This edition was published by Collins Crime Club in 1942. The dust jacket is intact.
$$ • 8 in (20 cm) high

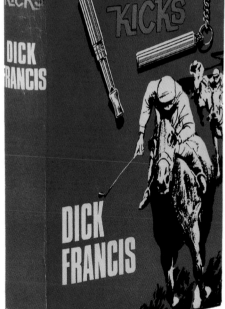

"LORD JIM"
The 1900 first edition, published by Blackwood, in its original binding.
$$$ • 7 in (18 cm) high

"FOR KICKS"
Published by Michael Joseph, 1965, this copy of the first edition preserves its original cloth binding and an intact dust jacket. The author's third novel, it is also the third most expensive.
$$$ • 7½ in (19 cm) high

"THE CHRYSALIDS"
A fine copy of the Michael Joseph first edition, 1955, in original binding and wrapper.
$$ • 7½ in (19 cm) high

Core Collectibles

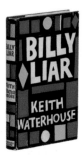

"BILLY LIAR"
This copy from the original 1959 Michael Joseph edition has a worn dust wrapper.

$$ • 7½ in (19 cm) high

"BRAVE NEW WORLD"
Published in 1932 by Chatto & Windus, London, with original dust wrapper.

$$$$ • 7½ in (19 cm) high

"LAST SEEN WEARING"
Colin Dexter's second Morse novel was published by Macmillan in 1976. Fans often aim to collect complete sets of detective series, keeping prices high while the author is in vogue.

$$$ • 8½ in (22 cm) high

SHERLOCK HOLMES NOVEL
First published in book form in 1902, this copy is from the very first issue.

$$$ • 7 in (18 cm) high

"QUIET DAYS IN CLICHY"
This copy, published by Olympia Press, Paris, 1956, has its original wrapper.

$$$ • 8 in (20 cm) high

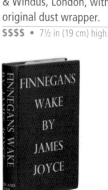

"FINNEGANS WAKE"
Joyce's last novel, published by Faber in 1939, in its original cloth binding.

$$$$ • 8½ in (22 cm) high

"THE CASTLE"
This 1930 edition published by Secker & Warburg was Kafka's first appearance in English.

$$$$ • 7½ in (19 cm) high

"FROST AT CHRISTMAS"
The first novel in the Jack Frost series, first published in the UK by Constable in 1989.

$$ • 8½ in (22 cm) high

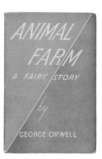

"ANIMAL FARM"
A short print run and fragile binding make this Secker edition, May 1945, very rare.

$$$$ • 7 in (18 cm) high

"THE DA VINCI CODE"
Early editions like this have "scotoma" misspelled as "skitoma" on p. 243.
$$ • 8½ in (22 cm) high

"THE MAURITIUS COMMAND"
More common than the first in the series, this fourth Aubrey novel, 1977, is still popular.
$$ • 8 in (20 cm) high

"OUT OF AFRICA"
A copy of the original Putnam edition from 1937, with faded dust jacket and cloth binding.
$$ • 7½ in (19 cm) high

TOP TIPS

- Don't forget that first means first; later editions rarely count.
- Remember that the majority of the value lies in the condition of the dust wrapper; correct ordering of pages and neat binding are a given.
- Consult author or subject bibliographies to help you distinguish first editions and printings from later ones. It could save you a fortune.

Starter Buys

"LOST IN A GOOD BOOK"
First published in the UK by Hodder & Stoughton in 2002.
$ • 8½ in (22 cm) high

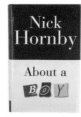

"ABOUT A BOY"
Published by Gollancz in 1999, this is signed by the author.
$ • 8½ in (22 cm) high

"SPIES"
Spies won the Whitbread Award for best novel in 2002, the year it was published by Faber & Faber. This copy is signed by the author.
$ • 8¼ in (21 cm) high

"THE AMAZING MAURICE"
This 2001 title was published by Doubleday.
$ • 8½ in (22 cm) high

"THE LEMON TABLE"
An original edition, published by Jonathan Cape in 2004.
$ • 8½ in (22 cm) high

"BLACK AJAX"
Although not part of the collectible Flashman series, this first edition, published by Harper Collins, 1997, is signed by the author.
$ • 8½ in (22 cm) high

You may also like… Magazines, see pp. 214–15

Nonfiction Books

Every possible subject of human interest has its own body of literature and historical records to explore, and nonfiction books offer infinite possibilities for collectors at all budget levels.

People often become book collectors without realizing it, as they acquire out-of-print specialty books as reference tools to another hobby, be it art collecting, cooking, or vintage car restoration.

Traditional areas to collect include great travel books (usually organized by explorer or country), works on natural history, early printings of classics, fine books on architecture, and groundbreaking works on science, medicine, philosophy, or economics. Though not always limited to a particular topic, superior bindings are the basis of many a collection as well.

Changing tastes and a decline in classical education and the understanding of Latin may account for a reduced demand for medieval volumes, and a less desirable incunable (a book printed before 1501) can be had for only a few hundred dollars.

What surely must come up again in price in the long term are the best copies of the great color-plate travel books of the early to mid-19th century. These luxurious, lavishly hand-colored aquatint books are perfect for the visually attuned collector-investor.

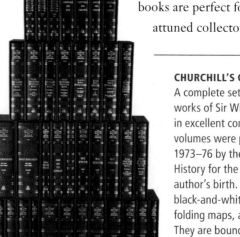

Commemorating Churchill

Sir Winston Churchill's prolific writings won him the Nobel Prize for Literature, to cap his many other achievements on the world stage. This immaculate 1970s edition of his collected works is one of only 20 sets bound in red leather, and is complete with all 38 volumes. Most sets include only 34 volumes, omitting the collected essays, and many are bound in a cream vellum that tends to blemish. Imposing and impressive, this is a library centerpiece.

CHURCHILL'S COLLECTED WORKS
A complete set of the collected works of Sir Winston Churchill, in excellent condition. The 38 volumes were published in 1973–76 by the Library of Imperial History for the centennial of the author's birth. The books include black-and-white illustrations, folding maps, and facsimile letters. They are bound in red leather with gilt finish and matching slipcases.

$$$$$ • Each book 10 in (25.5 cm) high

KEY FACTS	1455	1611	1901	2000	2008
Speaking volumes	Gutenberg's Bible is the first European book to be printed in movable metal type.	The King James Bible is published, setting the standard for large-scale book production.	The first Nobel Prize for Literature is awarded (to Sully Prudhomme), inadvertently creating a collectors' niche market.	John James Audubon's *Birds of America* sells for $8.8 million at auction in New York.	A set of 40 volumes of John Gould's acclaimed bird illustrations sells for $2.5 million at Christie's in London.

What's Hot

WRITINGS ON GOLF
A rare 71-page collection published by the *Montrose Standard* newspaper in 1891.
$$$$$ • 6¾ in (17 cm) high

CHAGALL CATALOGS
Marc Chagall's *Catalogues raisonnés*, volumes I–IV, with original lithographs.
$$$$ • 12½ in (32 cm) high

Look out for:

The first King James Bible was printed in 1611 in a tall folio size with blackletter (Gothic) script. All early editions are expensive and most copies will be worn from use over the centuries. Note that a perfectly preserved Old Testament title page is a great rarity and increases the price considerably.

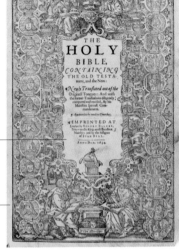

No ownership inscriptions

Larger book size indicates a more luxurious edition

"THE GOLFER'S HANDBOOK"
Written by Robert Forgan, this is an extremely rare first edition published in 1881.
$$$$$ • 7 in (18 cm) high

FOREST PORTRAITS
A J. G. Strutt etching from *Sylva Britannica*, published by Henry A. G. Bohn in 1826.
$$$ • 15 in (38 cm) high

KING JAMES BIBLE
Dated 1634, this rare fourth edition of the King James Bible was printed by Robert Barker of London. This Bible is recognized—even among secular observers—as a major work of literature.
$$$$ • 14 in (36 cm) high

19TH-CENTURY ATLAS
The *New and Elegant Imperial Sheet Atlas* was published by Laurie and Whittle in several editions. This copy dates to 1809.
$$$$$ • 21 in (53.5 cm) high

What's Not

Religion was the dominant theme of early printed books, and collectors tend to lose interest in titles from the 18th century and later, even turning down Victorian bibles and famous theology texts.

"THE ANALOGY OF RELIGION"
A copy of Joseph Butler's 18th-century text, a classic of British theology.
$ • 7 in (18 cm) high

Core Collectibles

BOOK OF STAGE MAGIC
This 1920s edition by Will Goldston comes with a brass clasp, padlock, and key.

$$ • 12 in (30 cm) high

"PARROTS IN CAPTIVITY"
A rare three-volume set of first editions published in the 1880s, with original binding.

$$$$ • 12 in (30 cm) high

"LADIES' OLD-FASHIONED SHOES"
Published by David Douglas in the 1880s, this work by Thomas Watson Greig features black-and-white illustrations and striking color lithographs of mostly 17th-century shoes.

$$$ • 15 in (38 cm) wide

MILITARY TREATISE
A Critical Inquiry into Antient Armour by Meyrick, 1842, with hand-colored prints.

$$$ • 14½ in (37 cm) high

HALLE'S "CHRONICLE"
The key historical text by Edward Halle from 1548, with 19th-century russia binding.

$$$$$ • 12 in (30 cm) high

WISDEN'S "ALMANACK"
Edited by the venerated sports journalist Sydney Pardon, this volume is an early edition.

$$$ • 6¾ in (17 cm) high

"MERCURIUS RUSTICUS"
A 1685 reprint of a political newsbook published during the English Civil War.

$$ • 7½ in (19 cm) high

Ask the Expert

Q. Is it important to have a first edition?
A. Yes and no—although the cult of the first will always win out with most books, later editions can be equally collectible, depending on the editor and the corrections made.

Q. As color-plate books are broken up for their prints, does external condition matter?
A. It can. A set of *Morris's British Birds*, for example, is generally valued at $2 per colored plate by the print market, but this superior set (pictured, right) in unusually early dust wrappers attracts a premium price among ornithology book collectors.

"MORRIS'S BRITISH BIRDS"
Printed in the 1860s, with rare original dust wrappers.
$$$ • 10 in (25 cm) high

Rare dust jackets

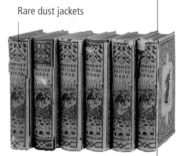

"JOURNAL OF A ROUTE ACROSS INDIA"
Lieutenant Colonel George Fitzclarence's text includes eight fine hand-colored aquatints in this 1819 first edition published by John Murray.
$$$ • 12½ in (32 cm) high

"NEW BRITISH ATLAS"
An atlas of Britain by Isaac Slater, 1847, with colored engraved maps.
$$$ • 14 in (35.5 cm) high

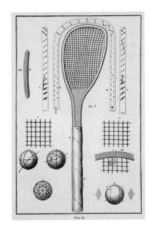

CAMDEN'S "BRITANNIA"
A first edition of Gibson's translation, printed in 1695, with 19th-century binding.
$$$$ • 16 in (40.5 cm) high

"A GAY DOG"
Printed in 1905, this copy has its original binding of linen-backed boards.
$$ • 11 in (28 cm) high

"THE ANNALS OF TENNIS"
This picture is from the first edition of the work by Julian Marshall, published in 1878 by the Field Office. It is bound in the original blind-stamped cloth and is illustrated with fine black-and-white wood engravings. This is a good copy of the definitive work on the popular sport of real (or royal) tennis.
$$$ • 12 in (30 cm) high

Starter Buys

FRENCH ALMANACK, 1840
Bound in gilt and silvered metal, this unused almanac comes with a lead pencil.
$$ • 4 in (10 cm) wide

YANGTZE VALLEY JOURNAL
This is a first edition of Isabella Bird's account of her travels in China, 1899.
$$ • 8½ in (22 cm) high

"TELEVISION"
Alfred Dinsdale's 1926 text was the first book ever written about TV.
$$$ • 10½ in (26.5 cm) high

ELLEN TERRY SHAKESPEARE
A complete set of 40 miniature volumes with original 1904 bindings and a revolving case.
$$$ • Bookcase 6 in (15 cm) high

You may also like… Modern First Editions, see pp. 202–07

Comics

Comics and their related annuals make up a market largely split in two for the English-speaking world: American comics and British comics. What you collect will be largely determined by your own childhood memories.

Collecting is an indulgence, but perhaps collecting comics is an area that wears its heart on its sleeve more than most. It's a hobby that can start early by accident and then get out of hand. The good news for beginners is that there are mountains of second-hand comics costing next to nothing, but for the majority, who choose to collect original issues of, say, *X-Men* or *Spider-Man*, there is bad news. To get the rarest early issues in mint condition will likely cost you a lot more than all the other issues put together.

The cardinal collecting rule of condition is essential, and "mint" really should mean brand new. As investments, the only big number swings will be with super-rare comics like *Superman* number ones. The second rule is to stick to a theme. Finally, just let your inner child play, and enjoy.

Super Spidey Stories!
This is not the most expensive comic you can find, but it clearly demonstrates some key points. That the condition is excellent and the cover visually striking is a given. It is also a Marvel Comics production and an early number in this series. The bonus is the introduction of new characters The Enforcers by creators Stan Lee and Steve Ditko.

"THE AMAZING SPIDER-MAN"
Spider-Man meets the Big Man and the Enforcers in this 1964 issue.
$$$ • 10¼ x 6½ in (26 x 16 cm)

TOP TIPS

- Beware of reprints masquerading as originals if paying serious money.
- Top-end prices for ultra rarities depend on small numbers of wealthy players who can come and go from the market, so be wary of using these prices as benchmarks for high-level investment policies.
- Look to the Internet for a wealth of detailed information for collectors.

KEY FACTS	1884	1929	1937	1965	1985
Top comic creations	Ally Sloper's *Half Holiday* is launched, the first comic strip magazine to feature a recurring character.	The adventuring Tintin first appears in a supplement to the Belgian newspaper *Le Vingtième Siècle*.	Children's entertainment *The Dandy Comic* first appears and is followed the next year by *The Beano* magazine.	US college students rank Spider-Man and The Hulk as two of their favorite revolutionary icons.	A story from the fifth issue of *Weird Science* is expanded to become a feature film directed by Joel Silver.

What's Hot

"MAD" NO. 15
One of the most popular humour and satire magazines of the 1950s and '60s.
$$ • 10¼ x 6½ in (26 x 16 cm)

"BATMAN" NO. 6
Published by DC Comics, this Aug./Sept. 1941 issue is in fine to near-mint condition.
$$$ • 10¼ x 6½ in (26 x 16 cm)

Look out for:
An example of a highly collectible comic, with a bright cover, in excellent condition.

Visually striking cover ——————

"WEIRD SCIENCE" NO. 19
This issue of the sci-fi comic features a Ray Bradbury tale.
$$ • 9¾ in (25 cm) high

Core Collectibles

"DR. STRANGE"
This comic has original Steve Ditko pen and ink artwork.
$$$ • 10¼ x 6½ in (26 x 16 cm)

"X-MEN" NO. 98
An April 1976 issue featuring cover art by Dave Cockrum.
$ • 10¼ x 6½ in (26 x 16 cm)

"WONDER WOMAN" NO. 97
A 1958 issue including a book-length story in three parts.
$ • 10¼ x 6½ in (26 x 16 cm)

"THE DANDY"
From April 1945, this is a rare wartime copy of the *Dandy*.
$ • 11¾ in (29 cm) high

Starter Buys

"HOTSPUR BOOK FOR BOYS"
This 1940 comics annual was published by DC Thomson.
$ • 8½ in (22 cm) high

"EAGLE" NO. 31
From 1950, an early issue of the popular British weekly comic.
$ • 14 in (35 cm) high

"THE BEANO"
The 1 August 1970 issue of the long-running comic.
$ • 11¾ in (29 cm) high

"WYATT EARP" NO. 4
A May 1956 issue starring Atlas Comics' cowboy hero.
$$ • 10¼ x 6½ in (26 x 16 cm)

You may also like… *Star Wars*, see pp. 324–27

Magazines

Whether collected for their cover art or the articles and stories within, magazines—these highly illustrated records of the days of our lives—attract fans looking for a snapshot of a different time.

General-interest magazines date back to the 18th century, but in this collectibles market it is not simply age that commands the highest prices. Rather, the value of an item often lies in its cover. The satirical mid-19th-century magazine *Punch* may be a respected title, but the cover comics often fail to please in the current market. Issues of *Vogue* from any decade, however, are likely to tickle someone's fancy and their covers are worthy pieces of wall art in their own right.

First issues are popular choices, especially those featuring iconic images of celebrities splashed on the front. The 1953 first issue of *Playboy*, for example, featuring a jubilant Marilyn Monroe on its cover, is a collector's dream, and a copy in good condition can cost more than a thousand dollars.

Magazines across most subjects, however, should cost less than $20 each—usually far less—and you can often pick up a large pile at auction for next to nothing.

Frills, Fluffs, and Finery

This French fashion production is typical of the high standards of lifestyle periodicals for the urban, well-bred leisure class of the Jazz Age. Here, the intact set of fine, hand-colored prints by celebrated designer George Barbier is a special prize.

"FALBALAS & FANFRELUCHES"
This is the 1926 volume with twelve glorious George Barbier hand-colored pochoir Art Deco prints.
$$$$ • 10 in (25 cm) high

TOP TIPS

- Edit your collection by choosing works by a specific writer, illustrator, or photographer, or create a coherent collection by picking covers with a common pictorial theme.
- If storage space is an issue, confine yourself to first and last issues in good condition.
- Look for colorful advertising inserts in older black-and-white magazines, as these are collectibles in their own right.

KEY FACTS	1891	1892	1920s	1930s	1953
All the news that's fit to print	*The Strand* magazine is founded and helps promote the popularity of the famous sleuth Sherlock Holmes.	*Vogue* is founded in the US by Arthur Baldwin Turnure. It is later bought by Condé Nast in 1909.	Fashion magazines become a forum for innovative Art Deco designs in the wake of World War I.	The foundation of magazines *Picture Post* and *Life* begins the golden age of photojournalism.	Hugh Hefner publishes the first issue of *Playboy*, with actress Marilyn Monroe on the cover.

What's Hot

"VOGUE"
A simple posterlike cover speaks for this 1929 "Spring Millinery" issue of *Vogue*.
$$ • 12¾ in (32 cm) high

"PICTURE POST"
This issue of *Picture Post*, dated April 24, 1954, stars a stunning Marilyn Monroe.
$$ • 13 in (33 cm) high

Look out for:
Magazines are collected primarily as visual mementoes, and striking cover images of collectible cult personalities—particularly if they are suitable for framing—will command premium prices.

Striking close-up photograph ———

"LIFE" MAGAZINE
This cover, dated December 19, 1969, is a rare edition featuring cult leader and pop-culture icon Charles Manson.
$$ • 14 in (35.5 cm) high

Core Collectibles

"L'ILLUSTRATION"
In a characteristically Art Deco style, this beautiful Guy Sabran cover is from 1931.
$ • 12 in (30 cm) high

"PHOTOPLAY"
A young Elvis Presley graces this November 1962 issue of *Photoplay* magazine.
$ • 11½ in (29 cm) high

Starter Buys

"POPULAR FLYING"
This first issue featured stories by Captain W. E. Johns.
$ • 10 in (25 cm) high

1960S "VOGUE"
A bright and graphically witty cover from April 1964.
$ • 11½ in (29 cm) high

"PLAYBOY"
This May 1998 edition of *Playboy* picks up the colors of Geri Halliwell's Union Jack.
$ • 11 in (27.5 cm) high

"ASTOUNDING"
A July 1940 edition of this sci-fi title, with a vivid cover depicting life in the future.
$ • 9¼ in (23.5 cm) high

"SMASH HITS"
This edition of *Smash Hits* from 1979 features The Police.
$ • 11¼ in (28.5 cm) high

"SHOWTIME"
A November 1964 issue with Sean Connery as James Bond.
$ • 11 in (27.5 cm) high

You may also like… Movie Posters, see pp. 316–21

Cigarette Cards

"Cartophily" is the technical name for cigarette-card collecting. These cards were mostly given away with cigarettes, but the area is broadened to include similar cards given away by, for example, tea manufacturers.

Cigarette cards started life as blank cards used as stiffeners for cigarette packets in the mid-19th century. They evolved into advertising cards bearing product details and by around 1890 pictures as well as advertising was introduced. Initially these had blank backs, but later they included details about the cards and then the concept of "sets" was introduced. Other trades, including tea manufacturers and confectioners, mimicked this marketing ploy and the numbers of sets and subjects proliferated.

Most collectors want to display favorite sets on the wall and use double-sided glass frames so that text on the backs can be read and condition clearly seen in the event of resale. However, cigarette-card collecting has stagnated and prices do not appear to be increasing. There are now hundreds of sets that have little commercial worth, so if you buy odd sets on flowers or sculpture, be prepared to buy for pleasure not profit. The higher-end price market is often associated with sports.

Marketing Tricks

Cigarette cards are marketing tricks and, with so many produced, quality was variable. Taddy & Co. are a rarer brand, but had high standards and many of their sets are desirable. This is a complete set of 20 prints of real people and events.

"VICTORIA CROSS HEROES"
This Taddy & Co. "Victoria Cross Heroes" (second series) is dated 1901. An individual card costs around $100, while a full set of 20 cards costs about $2,400.

Set $$$$ • 2¾ in (7 cm) high

TOP TIPS

- Use the price guides to find out how much you need to pay.
- The smaller the value of a set, the harder it is to sell.
- Cards stuck into albums are nearly always worthless.
- Study the quality of printing as well as the physical condition.
- Completeness and perfect condition, back and front, are all-important in card-collecting; the older the cards, the better.

KEY FACTS	1875	1900s	1940s	1995	2000
Card-collecting milestones	The Allen and Ginter tobacco company issues the first cigarette cards.	This period was the height of cigarette card popularity, with companies around the world taking part.	Cigarette cards fall out of fashion during the war years and only isolated companies try to use them.	Edward Wharton-Tigar bequeaths his record-breaking collection of two million cards to the British Museum.	Doral starts producing cards, featuring the 50 states, the first major manufacturer to do so since the 1940s.

What's Hot

Look out for:

Beautiful women as a pictorial theme stand up well in most collecting areas, especially when you consider that most collectors tend to be men. Issued in 1905 under the Loadstone cigarette brand, individual cards from this rare set of 12 "Beauties," in fine condition, have a nice period feel and a catalog price of around $100.

No tears or finger marks along edge

GALLAHER'S CIGARETTES
Gallaher Ltd.; "Votaries of the Weed" from 1916. Individual card $10, full set of 50 $600.
Set $$$ • 2¾ in (7 cm) high

F. & J. SMITH'S
"Prominent Rugby Players," 1924. Individual card costs $20, full set of 25 is $525.
Set $$$ • 2¾ in (7 cm) high

LOADSTONE CIGARETTES
Franklyn Davey & Co. Beauties ("Cerf"), 1905. Individual card $100, full set of 12 $1,350.
Set $$$ • 2¾ in (7 cm) high

Core Collectibles

FORTY FAMOUS CRICKETERS
"Famous Cricketers 1923," issued by R. & J. Hill Ltd.
Set $$ • 2¾ in (7 cm) high

POLAR EXPLORATION CARDS
This 1915 25-card series was issued by John Player & Sons.
Set $$ • 2¾ in (7 cm) wide

Starter Buys

HOLIDAYS IN BRITAIN CARDS
"Holidays in Britain," a 1937 48-card series.
Set $ • 2¾ in (7 cm) high

CELEBRITIES OF SPORT
Fifty 1939 cigarette cards issued by R. & J. Hill Ltd.
Set $$ • 2¾ in (7 cm) high

AUSTRALIAN CRICKETERS
Thirty-six series "Australian Test Cricketers 1928–29."
Set $$ • 2¾ in (7 cm) high

AEROPLANES CARDS
"Aeroplanes," a 1939 series of cards, by Gallaher Ltd.
Set $ • 2¾ in (7 cm) wide

CIVIL AEROPLANES CARDS
Fifty "Aeroplanes (Civil)" cigarette cards series, 1935.
Set $ • 2¾ in (7 cm) wide

You may also like… Magazines, see pp. 214–15

Toys, Dolls & Teddy Bears

Toys Galore: Recapturing Lost Childhood

Nostalgic childhood memories form an important factor in fueling this ever buoyant and continually evolving area of the market, one where the advent of "tie-in" merchandising has revolutionized our perception of what is collectible.

Since the second half of the 19th century, the spectrum of children's playthings has expanded beyond all recognition, so that today there is a huge range of remote-controlled airplanes and robots, talking dolls, PEZ dispensers, Barbie dolls, and all the traditional Dinky and Corgi, Britain's, Hornby, and Märklin toys, to name but a few. Children today are truly spoiled for choice.

For a toy to appreciate in value, the following three criteria are important: condition, rarity, and

Dinky *Thunderbirds* Rolls-Royce, see What's Hot, p. 223.

French games compendium, see Core Collectibles, p. 264.

quality. Toys made with extraordinary craftsmanship have usually stood the test of time, and French and German porcelain dolls from the 1800s are an example of dolls that may be worth a great deal of money today. Metal pedal cars from the turn of the century are also valuable if they haven't been left to rust. Children's china tea sets and miniature cast-iron stoves from the early 1900s are also very popular.

When buying tinplate and metal trains, trucks, boats, planes, and lead soldiers, condition is paramount and chipped paint and dents reduce value. This applies even more with early wooden dolls, Noah's arks, and skittles. Twentieth-century soft toys and teddy bears should show no sign of moth damage, hand-sewn repairs, or fading of color.

Ironically, the most collectible toy is one which has been played with very little, or preferably not at all.

If it has been put away and kept in its original box, this is even better. If you give an expensive battery-operated robot to a ten-year-old or a soft cuddly animal to a one-year-old, don't expect these playthings to hold their value!

Buying a modern toy today will only be profitable if it is one of a limited edition of less than 5,000, and then it could take 10 to 20 years before it proves a good investment. If you think a toy might be valuable, keep it in its box out of direct sunlight, extreme heat, or moisture, and store it in a dry place; years later you may find that the toy you had almost forgotten has become that valuable treasure.

Jumeau portrait head doll, see What's Hot, p. 243.

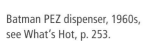

Batman PEZ dispenser, 1960s, see What's Hot, p. 253.

Blonde Steiff bear, 1920s, see What's Hot, p. 255.

Dinky Toys

Undoubtedly the most famous UK children's toy-car brand, Dinky was started by Meccano in 1934 and quickly became popular. Nostalgia for the brand is driving up prices across all Dinky ranges.

Huge quantities of Dinky vehicles have been manufactured over the last 70 years, but the nostalgia still remains for collecting—indeed, it's this sense of nostalgia that generally drives adults to recapture their childhood, perhaps collecting the toys that were too expensive, or were broken and thrown away when they were young.

Rarity and condition are the usual criteria for collectors chasing anything from the earliest lead Dinkys to rare racing car box sets, special South

African editions, or television-show-related models from the 1970s. In March 2008, a rare 1930s W. E. Boyce delivery truck sold at auction for close to $40,000, the highest price ever paid for a Dinky toy.

With this kind of potential, it's not surprising that there are plenty of fake models and reproduction boxes on the market. However, given the sheer variety and abundance of vehicles around, it is possible to start a collection relatively cheaply and work your way up the ladder.

Ready, Set, Go!

The No. 149 Dinky sports cars gift set was a schoolboy's dream, and finding this scarce ensemble in good condition is particularly difficult. Issued between 1958 and 1961, the five cars featured are the M. G. Midget, Austin Healey, Sunbeam Alpine, Aston Martin, and Triumph TR2, all in competition finish.

SPORTS CARS GIFT SET
This complete collection comes in its original box—a factor that can double the value of a model.
$$$$ • Each car 6½ in (16.5 cm) long

TOP TIPS

- Buy the best you can afford. Vehicles in poor condition or with missing parts are rarely worth hoarding.
- Know the difference between "good" and "mint" condition—the latter is difficult to achieve.
- Visit swap meets and toy fairs to get a feel for general value and to gain advice from other collectors.

KEY FACTS	1934	1954	1960s	1994	2008
A big history for a Dinky Toy	Meccano Ltd. of Liverpool introduces Meccano Dinky Toys, a new line of modeled miniatures.	Dinky Toys start to be sold in individual boxes with their own catalog numbers.	Tri-ang takes over Meccano. Dinky Toys continues and new "Speedwheels" range is launched.	A 1937 Bentalls delivery van sells for $19,000 at Christie's in London.	A box set of six Dinky Type 1 delivery trucks, each bearing a different brand, sells for $60,000 at auction in the UK.

What's Hot

CAPTAIN SCARLET CAR
A Dinky 103 Spectrum patrol car, as used by Captain Scarlet in the television series.
$ • 5½ in (13 cm) long

SUPERTOYS GUY VAN
This 1950s all-metal box van, like all the Supertoys guy vans, has opening rear doors.
$$ • 6¼ in (16 cm) long

Look out for:
Frank Hornby was already famous for his Meccano sets, first marketed in 1900. This was followed by Hornby trains in 1918, Modelled Miniatures in 1933, and then Meccano Dinky Toys in 1934.

Drop-down radiator with spring-loaded missile

Original box

DINKY "THUNDERBIRDS" FAB1 ROLLS-ROYCE
Lady Penelope's model 100 from Gerry Anderson's *Thunderbirds* series, with the detailed diecast body finished in bright pink.
$$$ • 6¼ in (16 cm) long

Core Collectibles

AUSTIN NESTLÉ'S VAN
This model 471 Austin Nestlé's van is in the original box, in slightly worn condition.
$$ • 4 in (10 cm) long

JAGUAR COUPE
A model 157 Dinky Jaguar XK 120 coupe in gray and yellow, boxed.
$$ • 4 in (10 cm) long

FODEN FLAT TRUCK
A green model 905 Foden flat truck with chains, c. 1955–58. The model came in a maroon and a red-and-gray finish as well.
$$ • 6¾ in (17 cm) long

Starter Buys

POLICE VAN
A model 255 Mersey Tunnel police van with its box.
$ • 2¾ in (6.9 cm) long

SHADO 2 MOBILE
A Dinky model 353 Shado 2 Mobile in its original box.
$$ • 6 in (15.2 cm) long

STATION WAGON
This Dinky 344 Station Wagon comes with the original box.
$ • 4 in (10 cm) long

OBSERVATION COACH
A gray model 280 observation coach with red flashes.
$ • 4½ in (11.4 cm) long

You may also like… Tinplate Toys, see pp. 236–37

Corgi Vehicles

Corgi began as part of the Mettoy company in 1956. The original factory was based in Swansea, Wales, and the distinctive red and white silhouette of the Welsh corgi remains the company's logo to this day.

Corgi challenged Dinky head to head, and was extremely successful. Its products and marketing had a contemporary feel that made Dinky's postwar products seem tired and old-fashioned. Corgi models boasted transparent plastic windows, spring suspension, opening hoods and trunks, and even diamond-jeweled headlights.

Corgi was adept at securing licensing deals and its television and film tie-in vehicles are still firm favorites among collectors. Classic pieces like the Batmobile and James Bond's Aston Martin sold by the millions, and examples in excellent condition can still fetch hundreds of dollars at auction.

Condition and rarity remain the key factors for pieces at the top end of the market. Unlike the simpler Dinky models, there seem to be far fewer fake Corgis on the market, although reproduction boxes are rife. However, long production runs and manufacturing idiosyncrasies can make all the difference to the value of a vehicle.

"Truly Scrumptious"

Corgi's "Chitty Chitty Bang Bang" was released in 1968 to accompany the film. This toy, which includes four models of the film's characters, has a lever-operated retractable wing mechanism. The box floor has a cloud effect.

"CHITTY CHITTY BANG BANG" FILM TIE-IN

This Corgi model, no. 266, is in mint condition, complete with four figures and in its original box.

$$$ • 5 in (13 cm) long

TOP TIPS

- Remember that condition is of paramount importance. Pieces worn from play are less valuable.
- Pick boxed pieces, which command premium prices.
- Be clear on what "mint" means. A piece classified as such must not only be in perfect condition, but must also have all its original packaging and box inclusions as originally sold.

KEY FACTS	1956	1957	1960s	1960	1995
The story of Corgi Toys	Corgi Toys are first manufactured by Mettoy Playcraft Ltd. in Wales.	A new range of larger commercial vehicles, called Corgi Majors, is introduced.	Corgi begins producing film and TV tie-ins, such as the Batmobile and James Bond cars.	The Aston Martin DB4 with a hinged hood is released. It is the first model with open-and-close features.	A management buyout ends Mattel ownership and sees the birth of Corgi Classics Ltd.

What's Hot

LOTUS RACING TEAM
This boxed Corgi racing team gift set no. 37 contains three race cars, a breakdown van, and other accessories.
$$$ • Each car 3¾ in (9.5 cm) long

MONKEEMOBILE
A tie-in with the *Monkees* TV series. All four figures are included with this boxed 1965 Corgi model no. 267.
$$$ • Car 6 in (15 cm) long

Look out for:
Produced in 1966 and released in time for Christmas, Corgi's Batmobile is one of the best-selling model cars in history. The model features Batman and Robin figures, a flaming exhaust, a "chain-cutter" that extends from the front, and rocket launchers. Examples in mint condition should include a badge, a leaflet of operating instructions, and a paper packet of plastic rockets.

Cog operates rocket launchers

Core Collectibles

"THE SAINT" VOLVO
A toy Volvo P.1800, based on the car in the TV series.
$$ • 3½ in (9 cm) long

VOLKSWAGEN POLICE CAR
This model, no. 492, is of a European police car.
$$ • 3¾ in (9.5 cm) long

BATMOBILE
This first issue of Corgi model 267, the wildly popular Batmobile with Batman and Robin, is in its original box.
$$$ • 6 in (15 cm) long

MONTE CARLO MINI COOPER
A 1965 model autographed by Timo Mäkinen and Paul Easter.
$$ • 2¾ in (7 cm) long

JAMES BOND ASTON MARTIN
This gadget-packed 1965 toy car includes an ejector seat.
$$$ • 3½ in (9 cm) long

Starter Buys

BUICK RIVIERA
A Buick Riviera, model no. 245, with spoked wire wheels.
$$ • 3½ in (9 cm) long

CARRIMORE TRANSPORTER
A 1957 Carrimore car transporter, model no. 1101.
$$ • 9¾ in (25 cm) long

You may also like… Dinky Toys, see pp. 222–23

Diecast & Steel Toys

The diecast market is dominated by Dinky and Corgi toys, but many other producers over the years have created model vehicles to delight generations of children, examples of which are often highly collectible.

The earliest diecast models were produced by traditional metal toymakers diversifying from tinplate and pressed metal into diecasting. Later ranges were produced by companies specializing in the diecast method.

Part of the charm of collecting in this area is the enduring simplicity of diecast models. The same basic techniques were used to produce a 1930s Dinky and a 1980s Lledo. The best diecast companies managed to maintain their specialized production process despite operating in a world where children demanded ever-more sophisticated models and toys. Tonka is a prime example of a company whose basic, durable toy vehicles have captivated children across the decades.

Postwar Japanese producers have arguably provided collectors with some of the best tinplate vehicles ever produced. The very finest pieces by companies such as Yonezawa and Bandai can sell for thousands of dollars. Lower-end pieces remain affordable, however, and despite the challenge presented by cheap reproductions imported from China, this remains a wide and varied market with plenty to offer collectors at all levels.

Spot-On Detail

Models in Tri-ang's Spot-On series were designed with unprecedented accuracy. This rare Austin Prime Mover comes with an articulated trailer, complete with a crate containing a turquoise MGA.

AUSTIN PRIME MOVER
A Tri-ang Spot-On Austin Prime Mover, model no. 106 A/OC, with original packaging.
$$$ • 7¾ in (20 cm) long

TOP TIPS

- Watch out for "worm" rusting under the paint layer.
- Beware of corroded battery compartments on models with working electrics.
- Don't dismiss corroded models. Many can be disassembled, and corroded components replaced.

KEY FACTS	1934	1947	1950s	1968	1983
Enthralling generations of children	The Dinky toy company first starts to produce diecast miniature models.	Lesney begins making diecast toys, including the famous Matchbox 1-75 series.	Mettoy launches the Corgi brand, and Tri-ang launches the larger-scale Spot-On series.	Mattel introduces Hot Wheels; it becomes one of the world's top-selling series.	Based in Enfield, England, Lledo introduces the Days Gone range.

What's Hot

DOUBLE-DECKER BUS
This rare early Tri-ang Minic 2nd Series bus no. 60M carries Ovaltine and Bovril advertising on its burgundy upper decks.
$$ • 7 in (18 cm) long

TOOTSIE CAR
A Tootsie Toy car produced in Chicago in the 1930s. Made of diecast steel with solid metal axles, this model has rubber tires, now looking quite worn.
$$$ • 4 in (10 cm) long

Look out for:

The American market is particularly strong for large-scale, pressed-steel American cars. Most prized are the 1950s and '60s pieces produced by Japanese manufacturers such as Asahi, Bandai, Yonezawa, and Line Mar Toys.

Fragile aerial

LINCOLN MARK II CONTINENTAL
A rare find, this boxed example of a Lincoln Mark II Continental with its dramatic styling is by Line Mar Toys, Japan.
$$$$ • 11¼ in (28.5 cm) long

Core Collectibles

BEDFORD MOVING VAN
A rare Matchbox series MB17 moving van with silver trim and metal wheels. There is minor rusting on the axles.
$$ • 23 in (58.5 cm) long

ROADSTER SPORT CAR
This boxed Hubley diecast MG open-top sports car in red has silver-embossed seating, trim, and grille.
$ • 8¾ in (22 cm) long

ZEPHYR AND CAMPER
A Kingsbury Zephyr and matching camper, in painted pressed steel. This is in good condition with some wear.
$$$ • 23 in (58.5 cm) long

FORD SEMI TRUCK
This very rare Tonka private-label Dobson Movers truck, in brown and white pressed steel, is in very good condition.
$$$ • 23½ in (59.5 cm) long

Starter Buys

SERVICE TRUCK
This rare Rover truck is part of Tri-ang's Mini Hi-Way series.
$ • 6 in (15 cm) long

FORD ZODIAC
A 100 SL gray Spot-On Ford with battery-powered lights.
$$ • 4 in (10 cm) long

TEKKEN MORRIS OXFORD
This model (no. 179) has slight age wear to its bumpers.
$$ • 3½ in (8.9 cm) long

FALCK ZONEN TRANSIT
A Tekno Falck Zonen Taunus transit (no. 415), slightly worn.
$$ • 3¼ in (8.2 cm) long

You may also like… Corgi Vehicles, see pp. 224–25

Automata & Clockwork Toys

The Greek word *automaton*, adopted in the 17th century, means "spontaneous motion." It was widely used in the 19th century to describe the elaborate clockwork figures made by craftsmen for wealthy adults.

Clockwork figures that simulated the actions of living beings, often manufactured by family companies, were the height of fashionable entertainment in the grand salons of wealthy merchants and the aristocracy, mainly in 19th-century France. These figures became increasingly elaborate in their costumes and actions and included bears, monkeys, magicians, ballerinas, trapeze artists, singing bird cages, and performing acrobats, many with Swiss-made musical movements.

The clockwork and musical movements were usually concealed within the figure or base, the only signs being a key and sometimes a stop/start button.

From the early 20th century, not only France, but also Britain, the US, Germany, Russia, Switzerland, China, and Japan all manufactured cheaper, more functional clockwork toys that are now affordable to everyone. The Japanese clockwork toys were so well made and strong that even the pre–World War II figures still run smoothly.

A Lean, Green Machine

This green Tri-ang Minic clockwork single-decker London bus is from the second Series 53M. It is special mainly because it has retained its original box, which increases value, and because of the advertising on its body—it reads "Bisto" on the back. As a general rule, clockwork toy vehicles—not just buses but trucks, planes, and cars as well—with advertising on them are considered more collectible than plain versions.

TRI-ANG MINIC SINGLE-DECKER BUS
This Green Line bus says "London Transport" on the side, and carries an advertisement for Bisto on the back. The detailed decoration includes a numberplate that reads "LB2 174."
$$ • 6½ in (16.5 cm) long

KEY FACTS	1700	1850s	1860	1880–1910	1930–60
Clockwork toy production	French craftsmen begin to make expensive clockwork toys from materials such as silver.	Alexandre Théroude of Paris designs many clockwork figures propelled on three-wheeled platforms.	The golden age of automata dawns. Paris-based Lambert, Martin, Vichy, and Phalibois thrive.	Charles Rossignol and the Roullet and Decamps company in Paris are prolific automata makers.	Peak production period for clockwork toys; producers include Bing, Louis Marx, G&J Lines, and Nomura.

What's Hot

ROULLET & DECAMPS TIGER
Made of papier mâché covered with cow hide, this tiger dates back to 1910.
$$$$ • 21 in (53 cm) long

GERMAN-MADE CHAPLIN
Made by Schuco, this c. 1920 figure is felt and tinplate and has an original wind-up key.
$$$ • 6½ in (16.5 cm) high

Look out for:
Popular subjects, such as Popeye, and toys by recognized makers, like Louis Marx, are widely collected, particularly if they are in good condition.

Black shirt made of tin

WOODEN LIBERTY SEAPLANE
Made of painted wood and lithographed tin, this is a large and rare toy.
$$$$ • 21 in (53 cm) wide

Parrot cages move

DISNEY CLOCKWORK TRAIN
This train has a built-in key. The words "Casey Jr., Disneyland Express" appear on the three carriages, as well as illustrations of Disney characters such as Mickey and Minnie Mouse.
$$$ • 12 in (30.5 cm) long

POPEYE TINPLATE TOY
Made of lithographed tin, this is a mint-condition Marx Toys Popeye, dressed in a black shirt and blue trousers, and carrying a pair of parrot cages. This early version has red-trimmed pockets. It has a clockwork mechanism, and its box, with a replaced end flap, reads "Walking Popeye."
$$$ • 8 in (20 cm) high

What's Not

The kind of toy that was never very expensive to buy, and that will not rise in value, is something like this Bo Peep. Its plastic will discolor over time and little cracks will appear, making the toy look shabby.

GUSTAVE VICHY BUST
This typical c. 1900 papier mâché bust has moving eyelids and tongue.
$$$$$ • 21¾ in (55 cm) high

MARX MERRY MUSIC MAKER
Made of lithographed tin c. 1935, this clockwork toy features a mouse band.
$$$ • 9 in (23 cm) high

LITTLE BO PEEP
A postwar English plastic clockwork Bo Peep and sheep.
$$ • 8 in (20 cm) high

Core Collectibles

CLOCKWORK ROBOT
A clockwork robot by Japan's Takara from c. 1977, with box and wind-up key included.

$$ • 8¼ in (21 cm) high

JAPANESE KOBI TOY
Made of carved fruitwood and operated by hand, this is from c. 1920.

$$ • 4 in (10 cm) high

TINPLATE RODEO JOE
One of the last all-tin American crazy cars, this lithographed tin clockwork toy of a Unique Art Rodeo Joe is in excellent condition, with just a minor bend in the hat brim at the back.

$$ • 7½ in (19 cm) long

TINPLATE BUBBLE CAR
A Japanese Isetta clockwork bubble car in shades of green.

$$ • 7½ in (19 cm) long

WIND-UP BIGO-FIX CLOWN
Made of fabric and felt, this Schuco clown comes with an original wind-up key and box.

$$ • 6¼ in (16 cm) high

FERDINAND STRAUSS BUS
Apart from some wear on the wheels, this tin clockwork bus is in excellent condition.

$$ • 10 in (25.5 cm) long

WIND-UP DRUMMER BOY
This felt lithographed tinplate wind-up Schuco drummer boy comes with an original key.

$$ • 5 in (13 cm) high

Ask the Experts

Q. Where is the best place to store clockwork toys?
A. Ideally, they should be kept free of dust, at room temperature, and away from moisture and extreme heat.

Entertaining movement

Sturdily made

TROMBONE PLAYER
A Japanese tinplate clockwork clown playing a trombone.
$$ • 9¼ in (23.5 cm) high

Q. Will a post-WWII Japanese toy, like the clown shown here, go up in value, and, if so, why?
A. These Japanese toys are relatively cheap, and will hold their value. They are very well made with expertly painted faces, sturdy mechanisms, and entertaining movements.

Q. Is it better to look for a clockwork toy or an automaton that has a stop/start button or knob?
A. The only advantage in having a stop/start knob is if the toy tends to play or move for a very long time, rather like a music box. Clockwork toys with smaller keys usually do not offer a stop/start facility.

POPEYE THE CHAMP TIN
This lithographed clockwork tin toy has celluloid figures, good action, and strong imagery. The box is missing two side flaps and one set of decorated end flaps.

$$ • Box 7½ in (19 cm) high

CHARLESTON TRIO TIN TOY
A Louis Marx boxed example of a color lithographed tin toy that is clockwork activated.

$$$ • 9¼ in (23.5 cm) high

GREYHOUND BUS
This scarce Japanese Hadson tinplate Greyhound bus is friction-driven.

$$$ • 13 in (33 cm) long

ALABAMA JIGGER
A Ferdinand Strauss lithographed clockwork figure that moves and dances.

$$ • 10½ in (26.5 cm) high

MINIC SEARCHLIGHT LORRY
Tri-ang Minic searchlight truck in glossy dark green with red chassis and plated wings.

$$ • 5 in (13 cm) long

Starter Buys

CLOCKWORK TIPPING LORRY
This Tri-ang Minic truck has some minor wear and comes in its original box.

$$ • 5 in (13 cm) high

POLICE MOTORCYCLE
A clockwork Marx policeman motorcycle in lithographed tin with an on-and-off switch.

$$ • 8½ in (21.5 cm) long

TRANSPORT EXPRESS VAN
A Minic tinplate clockwork model of a Transport Express service box van.

$$ • 5½ in (14 cm) long

CLOCKWORK RACER
A clockwork Marx racer in lithographed tin with a checkerboard grille pattern.

$$ • 13½ in (34.5 cm) long

You may also like… Tinplate Toys, see pp. 236–37

Trains & Steam Toys

The clatter of tinplate has an obvious attraction, and there is interest at all levels for the huge variety of trains and steam toys available. Wonderful prewar 0-gauge trains, in particular, continue to entice collectors.

This is an area of the market that has seen investment buying as well as collecting. In this field fueled by nostalgia, the best brands, such as Lionel, Ives, and American Flyer, Britain's Hornby and Bassett-Lowke, and Germany's Bing and Märklin, continue to appreciate, with condition and rarity strongly influencing an item's value.

Buying at auction can be attractive. Mixed lots are often featured, taken from estate clearances and sold by the box lot. In such sales, look for prize pieces mixed in with a selection of lower-value items. Meanwhile, some postwar toys still constitute good value as well. Mamod and Stuart, the British makers of live steam models, have been gathering ground in recent years and vintage pieces are worth looking at: they are still in production and have a good historical heritage. Elsewhere, companies such as Tucher & Walther specialize in limited-edition steam-powered toys, which may well prove to be tomorrow's collectibles.

Peak Time for German Trains

During the Edwardian period, German manufacturers Bing and Marklin dominated the toy-train market, producing some beautiful, realistic models that are today among the most prized products of their age. Bing's range of model steam engines was also one of the most diverse. The company perfected what became known as the "Nuremberg style" of manufacturing toys on steel sheets. Lithographed designs were stamped out of the metal and assembled using tabs and slots. Bing was forced out of the export market at its peak during World War I and eventually went out of business in 1933. The Bing family, who were Jewish, fled to England as Adolf Hitler rose to power in Germany.

BING LNER SALOON COACH
An 0-gauge Bing LNER coach in lithoprint teak woodgrain effect with red and cream lining. Its white roof, which has been refinished, opens to reveal interior tables and chairs.
$$ • 6½ in (16.5 cm) long

KEY FACTS	1840s	1900 onward	1910	1920	2007
Miniature railroad milestones	The first "carpet railways" include working cast-iron models of 19th-century steam engines.	Model electric railways are constructed for the first time in the US, but with dangerously high voltage.	The first toy train society, The Model Railway Club, is founded. Today it has a library of 5,000 books and other printed matter.	Frank Hornby brings clockwork toy trains to the Meccano company in England; electric trains follow in 1926.	A record Hornby sale: $12,000 for a Southern Railways Folkestone Flyer electric passenger train set.

What's Hot

STEAM FIRE PUMPER
A Weeden live steam fire pumper, this has a cylinder engine and a brass boiler mounted on a painted cast-iron frame.

$$$$ • 12 in (30 cm) long

SIR MADOR DE LA PORTE TRAIN
This is a coal-fired live steam model from the mid-20th century. Furnished in green livery, it has an opening smoke-box door.

$$$$ • 73 in (185 cm) long

WRENN LONDON & NORTH EASTERN RAILWAY LOCOMOTIVE
In mint condition, this Wrenn Woodcock locomotive is furnished in gray livery. Its box and paperwork are still intact.

$$$ • 12 in (30 cm) long

Look out for:
Made in 1937, this Princess Elizabeth cab no. 6201 was perhaps Hornby's finest product ever. In its time, this locomotive was every schoolboy's dream. Valued at around $4,000, it is still a catch for any Hornby collector.

Presentation box with printed label

Precise detailing

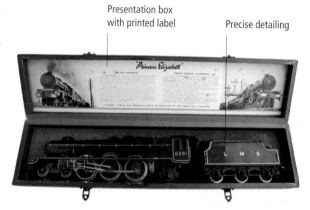

PRINCESS ELIZABETH ELECTRIC LOCOMOTIVE AND TENDER
Hornby's celebrated replica of the Princess Elizabeth locomotive is powered by electricity. The original train hit the headlines in 1936 for traveling from London to Glasgow in record time.

$$$$ • 24 in (61 cm) long, including tender

What's Not

Toy-train collectors are sometimes regarded as being almost obsessive. This means that train-related products find customers at varying levels. Mass-produced items are often collected, but may give smaller returns.

TANK LOCOMOTIVE
An 0-gauge Leeds electric-powered tank locomotive with green Southern livery.

$$ • 5½ in (14 cm) long

MÄRKLIN HO-GAUGE TRAIN
This Märklin RET 800 overhead electric locomotive has its original box, c. 1956.

$$ • 6 in (15 cm) long

VALE OF YORK ELECTRIC LOCOMOTIVE
A Lima 00-gauge Vale of York electric locomotive with its original box. Lima was a popular, inexpensive Italian brand produced from the 1950s until 2004.

$ • Box 14 in (35 cm) long

Core Collectibles

CLOCKWORK TURNTABLE
This is a rare turntable that dates from the 1920s and operates by clockwork.
$ • 16½ in (42 cm) wide

HORNBY SALOON COACH
Complete with its intact, original box, this saloon, a first-class coach by Hornby, is furnished in maroon with a gray roof.
$$ • 13½ in (34.3 cm) long

STUART STEAM ENGINE
This single-cylinder vertical steam engine has a cast-iron box bed. True-to-life detailing includes a spoked flywheel, crankshaft, and piston rod.
$$$ • 13½ in (34.3 cm) high

HORNBY CATALOGUE
A Hornby Dublo catalog listing the popular 00-gauge range of electric models.
$ • 8 in (20 cm) wide

LEEDS TANK LOCOMOTIVE
Made by Leeds Model Co, this 0-6-2 locomotive has side tanks. The underside of the cab roof has a Leeds label on it.
$$ • 6 in (16 cm) long

MAMOD STEAM MODEL
A live steam model with a train car, an open wagon, and a track, made by Mamod, a British toy manufacturer founded in 1937.
$$ • 8 in (20.3 cm) long

Ask the Expert

Q. Is it possible to get spare parts for Hornby 0-gauge locomotives?
A. There are several companies producing spares such as mazac- (alloy-) cast lamps, wheels, and decals. Specialist restorers often break damaged models for spare parts. The Internet is a good place to start looking for spares.

Q. What is the smallest gauge for a model train?
A. 6.5 mm is the smallest gauge for commercially produced models.

Q. What does it mean when a train is described as "scratchbuilt"?
A. It means that the train has been made by an individual modeler rather than by a toy company.

Realistic weathered finish

Every detail faithfully reproduced

0-GAUGE TANK LOCOMOTIVE
This scratchbuilt locomotive has a metal chassis and a wooden body.
$$ • *10 in (24 cm) long*

LIVE STEAM LOCOMOTIVE
This spirit-fired locomotive, a Bowman model, features twin oscillating cylinders.
$$ • 7¾ in (19.7 cm) long

NORD LOCOMOTIVE AND TENDER
A French Hornby 4-4-2 Nord locomotive (no. 31240) and double-bogie tender (no. 31801) finished in dark brown with gold lining.
$$$ • 17 in (42.5 cm) long

HORNBY CORRIDOR COACH
Made in 1938, this 0-gauge model in maroon LMS livery has Mansell wheels.
$$ • 8 in (20 cm) long

BRIGHTON BELLE PULLMAN CAR
This rare Leeds Model Co. 0-gauge Southern Railways Brighton Belle Pullman car has brown and cream livery with full lining.
$$ • 11 in (28 cm) long

WRENN FREIGHT
In mint condition, this 00-gauge freight train in maroon London, Midland and Scottish Railway livery has its box and paperwork intact.
$$$ • 11 in (28 cm) long

HORNBY GOODS PLATFORM
An 0-gauge goods platform complete with a litho-detailed building and a model crane.
$$ • 16¾ in (42.5 cm) long

HORNBY WINDSOR STATION
This set comes with labeled side ramps and doors that open to waiting rooms.
$$ • 17 in (43 cm) long

Starter Buys

HORNBY PULLMAN COACH
This electric 00-gauge Pullman coach dates to c. 1962.
$ • 9 in (22 cm) long

BLACK FIVE LOCOMOTIVE
Complete with tender, this is a Hornby 00-gauge locomotive.
$ • Box 13 in (33 cm) long

MALLARD LOCOMOTIVE
A Hornby class A4 locomotive with its original box intact.
$ • Box 13 in (33 cm) long

MAMOD ROAD ROLLER
This live steam model SR1A road roller has its original box.
$$ • Box 11¼ in (28 cm) long

You may also like… Die-cast & Steel Toys, see pp. 226–27

Tinplate Toys

Tinplate toys were among the first mass-produced children's products. The best examples evoke a golden age of imaginative playtime, with loving attention to detail and ingenious mechanical features.

Tinplated steel replaced wood as the favored material for toy producers in the mid-19th century. It is easily cut and pressed into shape, and finished products are durable and hold decoration well, making them ideal as toys.

Collectors in this area are well placed to appreciate the evolution of toys. Tinplate pieces range from simple clockwork to friction-powered mechanical toys and battery-operated electronics.

It is fascinating to observe how toymakers have responded over the years to changes in technology and the demands of their market.

Classic German pieces from the late 19th century are very collectible, as are more complex toys from postwar Japan—most of which were aimed at the American market and inspired, it is said, by magazines left by GIs after World War II. The best pieces can sell for hundreds of dollars, but there are still plenty of entry-level bargains to be found.

TOP TIPS

- While some damage is to be expected on older items, avoid pieces with damage to lithographed designs, as this is impossible to repair.
- Check for "worm" rust underneath paint or lithography.
- Search for popular tinplate lunchboxes.

Talking Teddy

A Japanese piece imported to the United States by distributors Cragstan, this is a rare example of a battery-operated tinplate toy. When the larger telephone is dialed, the bear's own telephone lights up and he lifts the receiver and speaks.

TEDDY THE MANAGER TOY
This Japanese-made toy incorporates a battery-operated mechanism and light and sound effects.
$$$ • 8 in (20 cm) high

KEY FACTS	1850s	1893	1919	1950s	1970s
From clockwork to batteries	George W. Brown & Co. is the first large-scale manufacturer of clockwork toys.	William Britain invents hollow casting method, for producing cheap, lightweight models.	Louis Marx & Co. founded in New York; goes on to be the world's largest toymaker.	The first battery-operated designs appear. Japan becomes the world's leading producer.	Plastic largely replaces tinplate as the most common material for toys and models.

What's Hot

ROWBOAT PENNY TOY
A rare embossed rowboat with lithographed detail, produced by Meir, Germany.
$$$ • 3½ in (9 cm) long

CHILDREN'S PAIL
This 1930s lithographed children's pail is decorated with Disney characters.
$$ • 8 in (20 cm) high

Look out for:
JEP was a French company formed in 1929 from the merger of Les Jouets de Paris and Sif. Their complex, detailed model cars from the 1930s rivaled anything produced by their competitors. JEP products are distinguishable by the "JEP" mark on their radiators.

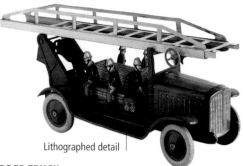
Lithographed detail

LADDER TRUCK
This tinplate fire engine bears fine lithographed detail.
$$$ • 15 in (38 cm) long

Core Collectibles

SPACE PILOT TOY GUN
Manufactured by Kobe Yoko Ltd. in the 1960s as part of their Space Pilot range, this Japanese friction-powered ray gun features a sparkling barrel and an explosive firing noise.
$$ • Box 8¼ in (21 cm) wide

Starter Buys

CLOCKWORK COAL MINE
Dating to the 1950s, this coal mine and train were made by Technofix in West Germany.
$ • 34½ in (88 cm) long

CLOCKWORK LORRY
In the Mettoy Wells style, this is a rare military truck with a driver and canvas rear-tilt.
$$$ • 9¾ in (25 cm) long

ROCKET RACER
A friction-powered Rocket Racer toy from the 1950s, with lithographed detail.
$$ • 6¾ in (17 cm) long

SCHUCO EXAMICO
This prewar Schuco Examico 4001 wind-up toy has gears and front-wheel steering.
$$$ • 5½ in (14 cm) long

HALLOWEEN CLACKER
A 1950s American Halloween tinplate clacker with a lithographed witch's face.
$ • 8¼ in (21 cm) long

You may also like… Automata & Clockwork Toys, see pp. 228–31

Toy Soldiers

The field of toy soldier collecting incorporates historical and modern military figures, both of which are hugely popular with collectors, although the secondhand market can be unpredictable.

The first commercially produced toy soldiers appeared in the late 18th century, made by French firm Lucotte. The three-dimensional figures were used by Napoleon to instruct his aspiring generals in the art of war; later, in 1885, a young Sir Winston Churchill played with them at Blenheim Palace. The company became CBG Mignot in 1928, and its toy soldiers are very sought after today.

Among the toy soldiers made in the early to mid-19th century were "flats." These were cast from tin or lead, sometimes in slate molds, and were essentially flat. In 1893, William Britain's new hollow-cast figures were cheaper and lighter, revolutionizing the industry. Prices for rare hollow-cast figures have soared in recent years while composite figures, such as the German Elastolin range, and plastic figures made by firms such as Timpo have also seen steady price rises.

Specialist toy auctions and the Internet are good hunting grounds for modern figures at low prices, but beware of Britains copies being sold online.

Miniature Rivals

John Hill & Co. was a British manufacturer of repute and a rival of Britains, producing very similar good-quality miniatures from 1906 until it ceased trading in the early 1960s. Its "Johillco" figures and sets are very collectible today, and less expensive than their Britains counterparts.

TROOPERS BOX SET
This 1A Hill & Co. Horse Guards Troopers set 253 comprises 11 pieces. An original paper-covered lid box has minor wear, and the label shows the set was purchased in the US.

$$ • 15¾ in (40 cm) wide

KEY FACTS	1730s	1893	1900	1950s	1970s
Toy soldiers marching steadily ahead	Germany is the leader in producing model soldiers, made from tin molded between two pieces of slate.	William Britain devises a new method of producing lead soldiers through hollow casting.	John Hill & Co. is founded. It emulates Britains' style of soldier-making and is its main rival.	Increased production costs and concerns about lead poisoning give rise to plastic soldier manufacture.	Hinchcliffe Models Ltd. of Yorkshire produces a collectors' handbook, including a uniform color guide.

What's Hot

Look out for:

In a market dominated by Germans, William Britain started his "hollow-cast" figure company in the face of stiff opposition. He perfected this technique of casting around 1893. The climb to popularity of Britains figures was swift, and the company soon became a household name.

Wire traces (rods connecting the horses)

Hollow-cast lead figures

Six-horse gun team with three drivers carrying whips

SKI TROOPER

A rare item, this is a Britains ski trooper no. 2037 in white coveralls and a cap.

$$ • Figure 2¾ in (7 cm) high

RARE MIGNOT SAPEUR

Perhaps a workman's model, this large-scale marching sapeur with rifle is a rare piece.

$$ • 6 in (16 cm) high

ROYAL HORSE ARTILLERY SET

One of the rarest of all gun team sets is this Britains Royal Horse Artillery, in tin helmets and khaki uniforms, c. 1939–40.

$$$$ • Gun team approx. 11¾ in (30 cm) long

What's Not

Collecting modern diecast and alloy figures and soldiers can be fun but not necessarily profitable. There are many manufacturers producing handpainted collectibles. Although Alymer is the official maker of military miniatures to the Spanish royal family, the figures are not generally investment pieces.

BRITAINS LTD. TRUCK

This rare early Britains Ltd. set no. 1643 Heavy Duty Underslung Lorry has a driver, kneeling gunners, an antiaircraft gun, 18 white wheels, and an original illustrated box.

$$ • 7¼ in (18 cm) long

HORSE ARTILLERY GUN TEAM

A Britains Royal Horse Artillery gun team, at the halt, c. 1930s. Twisted wire traces and collar harnesses are typical of pre–World War II sets; later sets had straight wires and breast harnesses.

$$$ • 11¾ in (30 cm) long

ALYMER FIGURE

An Alymer figure of Edward Plantagenet (Prince of Wales, Black Prince), one of its huge range of historical figures.

$ • 3¼ in (8 cm) high

Core Collectibles

HEAVY DUTY TRUCK
This rare Britains Heavy Duty Lorry (no. 1641) has a driver, a 10-wheel cab tractor with an 8-wheel semi-trailer, and its original card box.
$$$ • 7¼ in (18 cm) long

WWII MODEL TANK
A World War II Recognition model metal 105mm Howitzer with a cast-metal tank, in excellent to good condition.
$ • 3¼ in (8 cm) long

AMERICAN FLAG BEARER
This large-scale Elastolin American Flag Bearer has a metal sword in his right hand. The right arm has a crack and there are chips on the flag and figure. The soldier was probably made in Germany some time between 1935 and 1960.
$ • 7¼ in (18.5 cm) high

SET OF ELASTOLIN KNIGHTS
A rare selection, this set comprises five foot knights in battle with assorted weapons and two mounted charging knights. They are all tied in the original box and in excellent condition, although the horses' legs are fading and there are some rough edges. The box shows some age wear but is in good condition.
$$ • Box 7¾ in (20 cm) high

Ask the Expert

Q. Is it possible to restore missing parts on Britains toy soldiers?
A. Believe it or not, there are companies that cast spare parts for Britains figures—even new heads. With modern glues and resins the figures are not too difficult to repair. If you prefer to do a traditional job of it, insert a matchstick into the figure and pop the head back on!

Q. If Britains military vehicles come in new boxes, does this mean they're not original?
A. It's an area that can be a little hazardous for the amateur collector. Some items are restored and come with reproduction boxes; others are totally modern replicas or "reissues" with new boxes. Britains plastic "Deetail" figures are now being reproduced in China and Argentina!

Firing mechanism

MOBILE 18" HEAVY HOWITZER
This Britains set no. 9740 mobile 18" Heavy Howitzer with its original box and ammunition is mounted for field service.
$ • 5½ in (14 cm) long

SEVEN BRITAINS PIPERS

This set of seven Britains Seaforth and Gordons pipers has been later embellished with more detailed paintwork.

$ • 2¾ in (7 cm) high

MIGNOT DRAGOONS

Retied in its original box, this Mignot set of French dragoons comprises nine marching at the slope, a drummer, and an officer.

$ • Box 7¼ in (18 cm) high

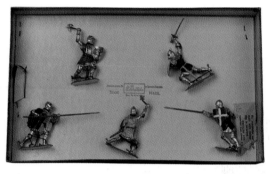

BRITAINS KNIGHTS OF AGINCOURT

A set of five Britains Historical Series Knights of Agincourt (no. 1664) foot knights, retied in the original box.

$ • Box 7¼ in (18 cm) high

Starter Buys

VALLEY FORGE SOLDIERS

Britains set no. 5872 Valley Forge soldiers in their original box and in mint condition.

$ • Box 4¾ in (12 cm) high

ELASTOLIN TOTEM POLE

This Wild West series figure is in excellent to mint condition with detailed paintwork.

$ • 4 in (10 cm) high

HERALD HORSE GUARDS

A set of unbreakable models of mounted and foot figures in their original box, c. 1950.

$ • Box 7¾ in (20 cm) high

ASTRA PHAROS HOWITZER

Made by Astra Pharos Ltd., this 12" Heavy Howitzer comes in its original box.

$ • 5 in (13 cm) long

You may also like… Dinky Toys, pp. 222–23

Bisque Dolls

Among the finest French dolls from the second half of the 19th century, both the adultlike fashion models and the bébés produced for children are highly sought after and command thousands of dollars.

The name "bisque" applies to a ceramic material with a matt surface, which is poured or pressed into a mold, fired, painted, and fired again. The best finish is translucent. Bisque doll's heads went into production in around 1860 in Europe, notably in Bavaria, Bohemia, and Limoges, and around Paris. In most cases, the dolls' bodies were made of composition. The smaller dolls were often made entirely of bisque.

The early French bisque dolls, those of the Bru, Gaultier, Huret, Jumeau, Rohmer, Schmitt, and Steiner factories, made beautiful "bébés" and "fashionable" dolls in wonderful outfits with their own trousseaux. From 1880, German firms such as Simon and Halbig, Kämmer & Reinhardt, and Armand Marseille followed suit. In 1899, many French factories amalgamated to form the Société Française de Fabrication de Bébés et Jouets (SFBJ).

By 1910, "character" dolls modeled on real children were all the rage. Other countries made and exported bisque dolls, but collectors prize the French and German models most highly.

Beautiful Baby

The value of this bisque Tête Jumeau bébé lies in her fine quality, her original mohair wig, stunning glass "paperweight" eyes—blown glass orbs resembling miniature paperweights—and her original satin and lace clothes and satin shoes. Discerning doll collectors will pay handsomely for original clothes, and the satin shoes will have the Jumeau bee incised on the sole.

JUMEAU BÉBÉ DOLL

This doll in its original fine clothes is in mint condition and has a red stamp mark that reads "Tête Jumeau." The doll dates from the high point of bébé production, around 1880.

$$$$ • 18 in (46 cm) high

KEY FACTS	1860	1870	1860–80	1900–10	1930
The glory years of bisque doll production	French and German ceramics factories start making bisque doll heads with adult faces.	The first dolls that look like children, known as "French bébés," are produced by leading French doll makers.	"Fashion" dolls, representing ladies exquisitely dressed in the fashions of the day, prove hugely popular.	German character dolls meet the huge demand for more realistic-looking child dolls.	Bisque gives way to plastic and vinyl, which are considered less fragile and more child-friendly.

What's Hot

CHARACTER BOY
This doll has a bisque socket head by Simon and Halbig, on a Kämmer & Reinhardt body. It is in good condition.
$$$$$ • 21 in (53.5 cm) high

BÉBÉ MOTHEREAU DOLL
This rare doll has threaded blue eyes and a closed mouth. Made between c. 1870–75, it has all its original clothes.
$$$$$ • 19½ in (50 cm) high

BRU BREVETE DOLL
This c. 1870 doll has an all-kid body with a swivel head on a bisque shoulder plate and sculpted hands.
$$$$$ • 15¼ in (39 cm) high

JUMEAU PORTRAIT DOLL
This very rare bisque-headed doll has a kid body with a bisque shoulder plate attached.
$$$$$ • 28 in (71 cm) high

THUILLIER BÉBÉ
This rare doll has a kid body. Its ears are pierced, and it has an original mohair wig and original shoes marked A.T.
$$$$$ • 21 in (53.5 cm) high

Look out for:

Bisque dolls made by Simon and Halbig are much sought after. What collectors look for is an "oily" bisque that is smooth to touch. This bisque doll is made more desirable by its "flirty" eyes that move from side to side.

Jointed limbs allow more movement

SIMON AND HALBIG BISQUE DOLL
This doll has a composition body and a tremble tongue. It also has a voice box. Pale bisque tends to be more sought after than darkly tinted bisque.
$$$ • 17¾ in (45 cm) high

What's Not

Parian dolls are unglazed and uncolored bisque dolls. They look rather anemic, with painted features that seem lackluster and dull, which is probably why there has been a less than enthusiastic demand for them over the past 15–20 years.

PARIAN SHOULDER DOLL
This is a Parian shoulder doll with molded hair and painted features on a very pale face. Dated c. 1870, the doll is wearing a green satin dress and is carrying a violin.
$$ • 12 in (31 cm) high

Core Collectibles

"323" GOOGLIE
This is an original German Armand Marseille "323" Googlie, dated c. 1915.
$$$ • 9¾ in (25 cm) high

BISQUE "LAUGHING BOY"
Made by Gebrüder Heubach, this c. 1910 doll has intaglio eyes. His teeth can be seen.
$$$ • 13 in (33 cm) high

ARMAND MARSEILLE ORIENTAL BABY DOLL
An Oriental "My Dream Baby" bisque doll from c. 1926 with a composition body. This Armand Marseille doll has sleeping eyes and a closed mouth, and wears a handwoven Oriental outfit.
$$$ • 15 in (38 cm) high

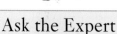

FRENCH BELTON-TYPE DOLL
This c. 1880 Belton-type doll has a swivel flange neck. The doll's accessories include a hat and a pair of red stockings.
$$$ • 9 in (23 cm) high

GERMAN LADY DOLL
Dated c. 1890, this doll has a bisque head and shoulders, and a kid body covered by a white lace dress.
$$$ • 21¼ in (54 cm) high

Ask the Expert

Q. What should I look for when choosing collectible bisque dolls?
A. The clothes and wig should be original. There should be no chips or cracks on the head.

TÊTE JUMEAU DOLL
Made c. 1880, this doll has blue eyes, and her original cotton dress.
$$$$ • 18 in (46 cm) high

Plain but original pinafore

Q. Is it better to buy a French or German doll?
A. It depends on the quality of the doll. Generally, German "character" dolls are preferred over the ordinary "dolly" faces. However, from the pre-1899 era, dolls manufactured in France are more in demand and command higher prices than the German ones.

Q. Is it a good idea to lift the doll's wig to check for damage when buying?
A. It depends on whether the dealers allow you to lift the wig. Buyers should be allowed to check for damage. If you are buying dolls at an auction, you should request to see the head under the wig before the bidding starts.

KESTNER "247" DOLL
This German doll has molded teeth and an original wig. It is dated c. 1915.
$$$ • 13¾ in (35 cm) high

SFBJ "227" BOY DOLL
This c. 1910 doll with fixed glass eyes and an open mouth is dressed in period clothes.
$$$$ • 21 in (53 cm) high

TOP TIPS

- Look closely at clothes and value more highly a doll with original, undamaged costume.
- Opt for named makers wherever possible, as these dolls are more likely to appreciate in value.
- Choose dolls for display with their original packaging if you can—this adds value.
- Clean the face of a bisque doll with a soft sponge or cotton ball and gentle soap and water. Be careful not to touch the eyes, which often have a fragile thin layer of wax on the lids and twisted cotton lashes.
- As a general rule, buy a doll that has jointed limbs rather than simple bent limbs.

JOINTED BISQUE DOLL
An Armand Marseille doll with sleeping eyes, an open mouth, and a jointed body.
$$ • 17¾ in (45 cm) high

JULES STEINER DOLL
This c. 1800 Steiner doll has long, delicate fingers. It is wearing its original clothes.
$$$$ • 24 in (61 cm) high

GERMAN CHARACTER DOLL
A rare German character doll, this has dimpled cheeks. It was made c. 1910–15.
$$$ • 5¼ in (13.5 cm) high

LIMOGES CHERIE DOLL
A Cherie doll from France with fully jointed elbows and knees, c. 1920.
$$$ • 20 in (51 cm) high

Starter Buys

FRANZ SCHMIDT & CO. DOLL
This character baby has an open mouth with two teeth.
$$ • 13½ in (34 cm) high

BRUNO SCHMIDT DOLL
A life-size doll, this is wearing a white pleated dress.
$$$ • 25½ in (65 cm) high

1910 "LAUGHING JUMEAU"
This "236" French SFBJ doll has bent limbs.
$$$ • 16¼ in (41 cm) high

SEATED DOLL WITH CHAIR
A c. 1915 French SFBJ doll seated on a chair.
$$ • 12½ in (32 cm) high

You may also like… Fabric, China & Other Dolls, see pp. 246–49

Fabric, China & Other Dolls

Over the past 400 years, dolls have been made from many materials, including cloth, wood, papier mâché, poured wax, waxed-composition, and porcelain. All these playthings have their own appeal for collectors.

Most early dolls were made by meticulous craftsmen who carved them from wood, painted their features, and fashioned their clothing. These 17th- and 18th-century carved dolls were within the budgets of only rich and aristocratic families.

The first quarter of the 19th century began with the production of carved wooden peg-jointed dolls in Austria and Germany. Then came papier mâché and waxed-papier-mâché ones, also German. By 1850, England had become famous for its poured wax doll makers. Names such as Montanari and Pierotti, Italian families who had settled in England, were adept at modeling beautiful wax dolls. Cloth was used to make cheaper dolls from the late 1890s, while early in the 20th century names such as Chad Valley, Norah Wellings, and Dean's Rag Book in England, and Art Fabric Mills in the US made dolls in all types of fabrics, including cotton, felt, and velvet.

While rare dolls in top condition command high prices, the choice of affordable dolls is huge, so most collectors tend to focus on a particular area. Some collectors may choose a specific material or manufacturer, others a certain, special era.

An Unconventional Dollmaker

Creative and versatile, Käthe Kruse was not simply a dollmaker: she was an actress, writer, photographer, and artist, as well as mother to seven children. She believed that her lifelike dolls would thrill children, fire their imaginations, and give them something to love. From the start, her dolls were admired for their artistic qualities, and that is still the case. The company now makes other toys and accessories and continues to design and make simply designed dolls and their clothes by hand.

KÄTHE KRUSE BOY DOLL
This c. 1915 Käthe Kruse doll has a molded head on a fabric body.
$$$$ • 16¼ in (41 cm) high

KEY FACTS	1600–1800	1830s	1850s	1900s	1940s
Living in a material world	Wooden dolls are made for the aristocracy, and don fine silks and satins to emulate the lady of the house.	Peg-jointed wooden dolls of all sizes are produced in Grödner Tal, Austria, and Sonneberg, Germany.	English wax modelers Montanari, Pierotti, Meech, Peck, and Marsh begin selling poured wax dolls.	German company Krammer & Reinhardt start a trend for realism with their bisque character dolls.	After WWII, doll makers started experimenting with more modern hard plastic materials.

What's Hot

PAPIER MÂCHÉ DOLL
A French papier mâché "Pauline" doll with a kid leather body, 1850–60.
$$$ • 33½ in (85 cm) high

GEORGIAN WOODEN DOLL
This is a rare large doll with elaborately carved wooden hair, c. 1830.
$$$$ • 27½ in (70 cm) high

Look out for:

The values of cloth dolls made by the Turinese firm Lenci have not only held strong during the last 20 years, they have increased more than other makes of cloth doll, with the sole exception of German maker Käthe Kruse. Sideways-glancing eyes, as seen in this example, were popular on felt dolls in the 1930s.

Typical 1930s-style boy's shorts

ITALIAN LENCI SCHOOLBOY
A c. 1930 Italian Lenci felt doll, dusty but all original.
$$$ • 17 in (43 cm) high

FRENCH CHINA DOLL
A Madame Rohmer "cup and saucer" neck china doll with a finely molded face, c. 1850.
$$$$ • 17 in (43 cm) high

PHILADELPHIA CLOTH DOLL
This painted cloth doll, in a dress and bonnet, has well-molded features, c. 1900.
$$$$ • 22 in (56 cm) high

What's Not

This so-called "Pumpkin-head" has declined in popularity in the last 10–15 years, mainly because the thin layer of wax over the base composition tends to crack.

WAX PUMPKIN-HEAD DOLL
This c. 1860 English wax pumpkin-head doll has an elaborate hairstyle, and wooden legs and hands.
$$ • 14¼ in (36 cm) high

Core Collectibles

LENCI MASCOTTE DOLL
A rare doll clad in a white lacy dress with a black velvet cape. This doll has its original label.
$$$ • 8 in (20 cm) high

"FORTUNE TELLER" DOLL
This German china shoulder doll has a skirt made of paper fortune predictions, c. 1870.
$$ • 4 in (10 cm) high

DEAN'S FABRIC DOLLS
A pair of almost life-size fabric 1940s Dutch boy and girl dolls, arms intertwined.
$$$ • Boy 31 in (79 cm) high

LIFE-SIZE DEAN'S FELT DOLL
An English felt doll by Dean's, in original contemporary clothes of the period, c. 1930s.
$$$ • 30 in (76 cm) high

"RAGGEDY ANN" DOLL
A "Raggedy Ann" doll in a rare, original dress and Georgene label, one of a pair. "Raggedy Ann" was based on a story by the American John Gruelle, whose publisher was the first to mass produce these dolls from 1918.
$$ • 12 in (31 cm) high

GERMAN PORCELAIN DOLL
A porcelain half-doll modeled as a lady in Art Deco clothes—a painted orange jacket finished with exaggerated black-lined collar and cuffs—and with a painted coiffure in typical 1920s style. The incised marks read "10039."
$ • 3 in (7.5 cm) high

Ask the Expert

Q. What type of doll is it best to look for when starting a collection?
A. Some people prefer the smaller dolls and others the very large, almost child-sized ones. The most popular seem to be of the size that fits into a glass cabinet.

AMERICAN INDIAN DOLL
Made for an exhibition of Dean's toys, this doll is in an American Indian outfit.
$$$ • 31 in (79 cm) high

Yarn wig

Q. Can the clothes of a doll be cleaned or would it harm the fabric?
A. This very much depends on the material of the clothes. For instance, a brightly colored felt dress is better left alone, because the colors will run even in cold water. A cotton dress of whatever age can be taken off and washed in mild soap suds, without any harm coming to it. Silks, satins, and taffeta should not be washed, but simply dusted and left alone.

Q. If a doll is purchased without a wig, is it easy to find the correct one?
A. It is possible to find the right wig at a doll fair rather than at an auction, but a dealer usually has spare wigs. Note that mohair wigs are imported from Germany or China.

TOP TIPS

- Choose dolls with their original clothing, wigs, shoes, and underclothes, as this adds to the value.
- Expect to pay high prices for papier mâché dolls in good condition: they are hard to find.
- Look for later wax dolls with a maker's stamp on the torso; this enhances their value.

1930S WINTER DOLL
Made in the 1930s, this doll is wearing a blue winter suit.
$$ • 21¼ in (54 cm) high

VELVET DOLL
A Norah Wellings doll from c. 1935, dressed in a grass skirt.
$$ • 11¾ in (30 cm) high

DOLL HOLDING A ROSE
A porcelain half-doll with painted facial features.
$ • 3 in (7.5 cm) high

PAPIER MÂCHÉ DOLL
A c. 1850 German doll with its original clothes.
$$$ • 8½ in (22 cm) high

EARLY GLAZED CHINA DOLL
This German doll has an oval face. It was made c. 1860.
$$$ • 13½ in (34 cm) high

PIEROTTI WAX DOLL
This c. 1860 doll has been re-dressed, reducing its value.
$$$ • 11¾ in (30 cm) high

GRÖDNERTAL DOLL
A German all-wood doll with a comb in its hair, c. 1830.
$$$ • 12½ in (32 cm) high

Starter Buys

MAID DOLL
This doll has a papier mâché head and a wooden body.
$$ • 9 in (23 cm) high

CLOTH BOY DOLL
Dated c. 1930, this is a Chad Valley brown cloth boy doll.
$$ • 24¾ in (63 cm) high

PENNY WOODEN DOLL
Made in the US, this c. 1890 doll is peg-jointed.
$$ • 11½ in (29 cm) high

MID-VICTORIAN DOLL
A wax-headed doll with a cloth body and wax legs.
$$$ • 20½ in (52 cm) high

You may also like… Soft Toys, see pp. 260–61

Plastic Dolls

From the composition or celluloid models of the late 19th century, through the hard plastic introduced in the 1940s, to the softer vinyl of the 1950s, plastic dolls have a ready market with collectors.

"Composition" is a mixture of papier mâché, chalk, sawdust, and resin, while "celluloid" is a lightweight material composed of pyroxylin, camphor, pigments, and alcohol. These dolls were cheaper to produce than traditional china and bisque ones, although they are more fragile, should not be cleaned, and, once damaged, cannot be invisibly repaired. Made in America, Japan, Germany, and France, they were widely distributed, with celluloid models bearing a maker's mark on the back of the head. Three of the

most prolific American manufacturers—Ideal from 1907, Effanbee from 1912, and Madame Alexander from 1923—made dolls first of composition, then hard plastic followed by vinyl. These companies started modeling their dolls on famous personalities and storybook characters.

Barbie made her debut in 1959, followed by Ken and others. Early Barbie and Ken dolls, if bought for investment, must be kept untouched in their original boxes or they will lose their value.

Hello, Dolly!

Born in 1934 in Ontario, Canada, the Dionne quintuplets were famous in their day, since it was so rare to have five babies survive. American doll maker Madame Alexander cleverly produced these dolls in a variety of settings— in miniature metal cribs, or simply as seen here, with a name tag on each. The company continued to reissue dolls as the girls grew up, and all are still collectible today.

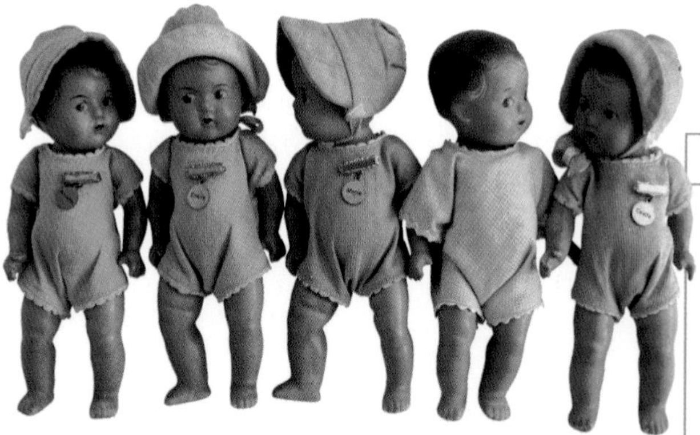

MADAME ALEXANDER TODDLERS
This rare set of five composition "Dionne Quints" toddlers was manufactured to commemorate the birth of identical quintuplets in Ontario in 1934.
$$$ • Each 7½ in (19 cm) high

TOP TIPS

- Look for dolls with makers' tags still attached, as this increases the value.
- Pick dolls with clean, unstained plastic—but watch out for those that have been damaged by too much cleaning.
- Avoid dolls whose hair has been cut, restyled, or otherwise damaged.

KEY FACTS	1907	1912	1928	1935	1959
The many faces of fantastic plastic	The Ideal Novelty & Toy Co. of Brooklyn, New York, produces composition, then plastic and vinyl dolls.	Effanbee starts making composition character dolls such as "Baby Grumps" and "Naughty Marietta."	Effanbee introduces the "Patsy" doll, who comes with a wide range of clothes and other accessories.	Madame Alexander makes "personality" dolls such as "Scarlett O'Hara" and "Judy Garland."	Mattel Inc. of Hawthorne, California, produces the adult-form Barbie doll, a cultural icon.

What's Hot

"DEFOE" DOLL
This rare Alexander "Dr. Allen Defoe" doll is dated 1937–39.
$$$ • 15 in (38 cm) high

MATTEL BARBIE NO. 1
A very rare dressed Barbie with bag and shoes, 1959.
$$$$$ • 11¾ in (30 cm) high

Look out for:
Hard plastic dolls made from 1923 onward were given names and modeled on well-known personalities. Many were dressed in elaborate costumes and even in haute couture.

Original accessories intact and in excellent condition

"MARGOT BALLERINA"
A 1953 Madame Alexander "Margot Ballerina" doll, with original clothing, hatbox, fashion award, medallion, hairnet and curlers, and box.
$$$ • 14 in (35.5 cm) high

Core Collectibles

PLASTIC "PATSY"
This plastic Effanbee "Patsy" is dated c. 1940.
$$ • 11 in (28 cm) high

"LUPINO LANE"
This 1950s doll is by Dean's Rag Book of London.
$$ • 11½ in (29 cm) high

Starter Buys

SNOW BABY DOLL
A charming German doll with sled from c. 1900.
$ • 11 in (28 cm) high

COMPOSITION "PATSY"
A 1930s Effanbee doll, wearing a green dress.
$$ • 14 in (35.5 cm) high

BOXED "PATSY"
A Chiltern English doll with box, c. 1940.
$$ • 15 in (38 cm) high

"SWEET SUE"
An all-original American character doll from the 1950s.
$$ • 15 in (38 cm) high

NORAH WELLINGS BOY
This doll has a molded felt face and velvet limbs, c. 1950.
$$ • 11 in (28 cm) high

You may also like… Fabric, China & Other Dolls, see pp. 246–49

PEZ Dispensers

Many people are astounded by the niche markets that turn into major industries, and PEZ dispensers illustrate this concept perfectly. These colorful plastic candy dispensers are collected the world over.

PEZ's status as a cultural icon—it has appeared in both blockbuster movies such as *E.T.* and hit television shows such as *Seinfeld*—has helped drive its popularity all over the world. The early full-body Santa Claus dispenser introduced in the mid-1950s has been joined today by hundreds of other character dispensers in as many head and stem variations, each of them avidly sought after by PEZ enthusiasts.

Dispensers and other PEZ-related accessories are traded through specialist dealers and at collectors' fairs, and the market is constantly replenished by limited editions and new varieties. Unsurprisingly, older models, which were produced in smaller quantities, are more valuable than current ones—and are more susceptible to being faked, too.

This is a highly accessible area for collectors, as PEZ dispensers are largely pocket-money collectibles. As such, however, big returns should not be expected.

Gold Standard

In 2002, the 50th anniversary of the company's arrival on U.S. shores, PEZ released a celebratory replica of its early-era cigarette-lighter-shaped Golden Glow Regular dispenser, presented on a matching display stand in a clear display box.

GOLDEN GLOW
This special-edition dispenser comes on a matching display base.
$ • 6½ in (16.5 cm) high

TOP TIPS

- Make sure the feet on a modern PEZ dispenser have not been shaved off to mimic the base of an older, more valuable model.
- Look to the American market for rarities. PEZ has a stronger presence there than in Europe.
- Start a basic collection by buying on the Internet, where single collections frequently come up for sale—but do your research so you aren't taken in by false claims of provenance.

KEY FACTS	Late 1940s	1955	1987	1991	2007
The little candy dispenser that could	The PEZ Box Regular is welcomed as a new and "hygienic" way to store and eat candy.	Character-head models are introduced as PEZ starts marketing to children.	PEZ begins producing candy dispensers with feet on the bottom of their stems.	The collectors' convention PEZ-A-MANIA launches in Ohio.	An Elvis PEZ set is released, with heads showing the singer at three different ages.

What's Hot

TOM DISPENSER
Dating from the 1980s, this is a footed Tom dispenser.
$ • 4 in (10 cm) high

SPACE TROOPER
This Space Trooper full-body dispenser is from c. 1955.
$$ • 3¾ in (9.5 cm) high

Look out for:
Among the many variations of Batman PEZ dispensers made available over the years, this version of the DC Comics superhero, with an attached cape, has remained a firm collector favorite. Now discontinued, this model has become even more desirable.

Movable cape

Model available in blue or black

BATMAN DISPENSER
Made in the 1960s, this Batman PEZ dispenser has a movable cape. A Batman dispenser without a cape exists as well.
$$ • 4 in (10.5 cm) high

Core Collectibles

GOOFY DISPENSER
Unusual swinging ears grace this 1970s dispenser.
$ • 4¼ in (11 cm) high

CHEERIOS DISPENSER
A promotional item for Honey Nut Cheerios cereal, 2001.
$ • 2¾ in (7 cm) high

GIANT PETER PEZ
This large-format dispenser releases entire rolls of candy.
$ • 12½ in (32 cm) high

SPEEDY GONZALES
First introduced c. 1978, this is a Looney Tunes character.
$ • 4½ in (11.5 cm) high

Starter Buys

HOMER SIMPSON
One in a family of five from the popular TV show.
$ • 5 in (12.5 cm) high

DONATELLO DISPENSER
An angry-faced variation of the cartoon character.
$ • 4¼ in (11 cm) high

You may also like… Disneyana, see pp. 322–23

Teddy Bears

The teddy bear market is one of the steadiest collecting fields, and vintage bears are always in demand. The older the bear, the more it is worth; pre-1910 bears in good condition are particularly valuable.

Teddy bears are so popular because their moving limbs, expressive features, and cuddly fur make them irresistible to young and old alike. Animals have been copied throughout history in many materials, but it was not until 1902 that a toy bear with movable limbs was invented: the movable limbs enabled the bear to sit or stand. It was given the name "Teddy" after the then US president, Theodore Roosevelt.

In 1983, when teddy bears were first offered for sale at auction, even moth-eaten and fur-worn bears were popular. Back then, the highest price was $475, paid for a bear made from black mohair plush (real fur obtained from a mountain goat) by the Ideal Toy Company of America. Today, that bear would command one, if not two, more zeros if offered for sale on the open market! Collectors are also less likely to accept worn fur these days.

Collectors prize bears by Steiff and Bing (which are rarer and therefore more desirable) most highly. British bears by such makers as Chad Valley, Chiltern, Farnell, and Merrythought also command high prices, as do those by American and French makers.

Don't I Look Cute?

In 1907 in Germany, the world's largest toymaking company, Gebrüder Bing, began making teddy bears. Although most famous for mechanical walking, skating, acrobatic, and even soccer-playing bears, Bing also produced many nonmechanical bears, which were made from high-quality materials and prized for their memorable expressions. Early bears often had a seam at the front where one bolt of plush finished and another was started. The company ceased trading in the early 1930s, so its bears are rare today.

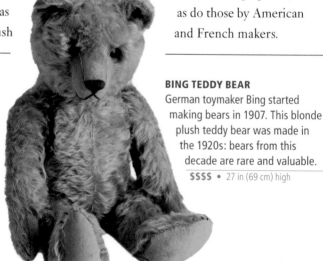

BING TEDDY BEAR
German toymaker Bing started making bears in 1907. This blonde plush teddy bear was made in the 1920s: bears from this decade are rare and valuable.
$$$$ • 27 in (69 cm) high

KEY FACTS	1902	1904	1920–40	1969	1983
The rise and rise of the teddy bear	Toy bears, hitherto rigid pull-alongs, are invented with movable joints—able to sit, stand, and hug.	Steiff starts stamping a metal button embossed with an elephant into every bear's left ear.	High-quality hand-finished bears are produced in England, France, Germany, and the US.	A book by British actor Peter Bull, on his love of bears, kickstarts a collecting fever for high-quality bears.	Sotheby's holds the first teddy bear sale in London. Christie's hosts twice-yearly bear sales from 1993 onward.

What's Hot

Look out for:

Teddy bears made by German firm Steiff are the most desirable because of their exceptional quality. The company created the first jointed bear in 1902. Early bears had distinctive hump backs, long snouts, and boot-button eyes. In 1904 the "button in ear" trademark was invented to distinguish genuine Steiff bears from fakes.

Elongated snout

Soft mohair fur

Long arms that extend past knees

WHITE STEIFF BEAR
This tagged Steiff bear, dated c. 1912, has black boot-button eyes and pad feet.
$$$$ • 17¾ in (45.5 cm) high

BLONDE STEIFF BEAR
From the 1920s, this blonde Steiff bear has glass eyes, pad feet, and a stitched nose.
$$$$ • 18 in (46 cm) high

1920S STEIFF BEAR
Made in the 1920s, this brown bear has glass eyes, pad feet, and a black stitched woolen nose.
$$$$$ • 18 in (46 cm) high

What's Not

This Merrythought bear has seen better days. He was obviously much loved, and therefore is very worn and missing one eye. While its eye can be replaced, the worn fur cannot.

STEIFF KOALA BEAR
This Steiff koala bear has pad feet and nose, and glass eyes. It also has a paper chest tag and an ear stud with raised "Steiff" logo.
$$ • 5 in (12.5 cm) high

CINNAMON STEIFF BEAR
Dated c. 1908, this is a Steiff cinnamon plush bear. It has boot-button eyes and jointed limbs. This bear also has a button fitted in its left ear.
$$$$$ • 13 in (33 cm) high

CHAD VALLEY BEAR
This 1930s British Chad Valley teddy bear is typically chunky and has large ears, black and brown eyes, a black stitched snout, and felt-covered paws. Chad Valley bears are prized by collectors.
$$$ • 19¾ in (50 cm) high

MERRYTHOUGHT BEAR
Despite having an original ear stud, this 1928 bear is less desirable because its fur is lacking.
$$ • 18 in (46 cm) high

Core Collectibles

MOHAIR STEIFF BEAR
This 1907 mohair bear comes with its original ear tag.
$$$$$ • 13½ in (34 cm) high

AMERICAN BLONDE BEAR
Made during 1906–08, this mohair bear has a wool nose.
$$$ • 11½ in (29 cm) high

CINNAMON MOHAIR BEAR
From the 1950s, this bear has orange and black glass eyes, and a pronounced muzzle.
$$ • 21¼ in (54 cm) high

CLOCKWORK TUMBLER BEAR
Made during 1909–10, this Bing bear somersaults when its left arm is wound.
$$$$ • 11½ in (29 cm) high

SCHUCO PANDA
This is a fully jointed plush panda by Schuco. Its mouth and nose have been stitched, and it has beads for eyes. Schuco pandas often have appealing facial expressions.
$$ • 3¼ in (8.5 cm) high

Ask the Expert

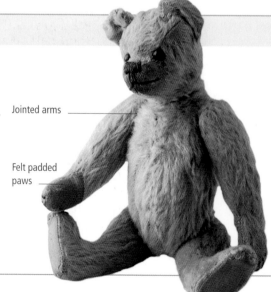

Jointed arms

Felt padded paws

Q. How can I date a bear?
A. Look at its shape—pre-1940 bears generally have long arms, mohair plush, and solid stuffing. Early eyes are almost always opaque black in color.

Q. Does it matter if the pads of my 1930s bear have been replaced?
A. Pad replacement does not affect the value: it is to be expected with older bears.

Q. How can I recognize a fake teddy bear?
A. The bears most commonly faked are those that date from before World War II. Be wary of "older" bears that look suspiciously clean.

FARNELL BEAR
A wide, rectangular, vertically stitched nose is a hallmark of British-made Farnell bears.
$$$ • 11 in (28 cm) high

ROD-JOINTED MOHAIR BEAR
This was made in 1904 of mohair plush, one of the most common early materials for fur, with a stuffing of wood shavings. It has the trademark Steiff metal button in its left ear.

$$$ • 17 in (43 cm) high

STEIFF TEDDY BABY
Although small in size, this c. 1940 Steiff bear, made of mohair, is fully jointed.

$$$$ • 8 in (20.5 cm) high

SMALL STEIFF BEAR
A small blonde bear, this Steiff has glass eyes and brown stitched nose and claws.

$$$ • 8½ in (21.5 cm) high

MOHAIR TEDDY BEAR
Made of blonde mohair, this Steiff teddy bear comes in box condition, but has no original logo button. The ribbon around the neck is original.

$$$ • 11 in (28 cm) high

GOLD MOHAIR BEAR
This rare American bear is made of gold mohair, with black boot-button eyes, card inserts for the feet, and original felt pads.

$$$$ • 24½ in (62 cm) high

HUGMEE BEAR
Manufactured in Britain, this Chiltern Hugmee bear is made of plush mohair.

$$ • 16 in (40.5 cm) high

BLONDE STEIFF BEAR
Made in the 1950s, this bear has an original peach ribbon and paper chest tag.

$$ • 7½ in (19 cm) high

GROWLER TEDDY BEAR
This 1930s Chiltern growler teddy bear is in a very good condition, and still growls.

$$$ • 25¼ in (64 cm) high

SCHUCO BERLINER BEAR
This very small, dark brown Schuco Berliner bear has a metal crown.

$$$ • 3 in (7.5 cm) high

Core Collectibles

BLONDE GERMAN BEAR
Made in Germany, this bear has black eyes and a brown stitched nose and mouth.
$$ • 20 in (51 cm) high

CHILTERN MOHAIR TEDDY BEAR
A 1930s Chiltern light golden mohair teddy bear, this has orange and black glass eyes, a pronounced clipped muzzle, a swivel head, jointed limbs with velvet pads, and a hump. Its nose and mouth have been restitched, and its pads re-covered.
$$ • 24½ in (62 cm) high

HERMANN TEDDY BEAR
This is a 1930s German Hermann open-mouth teddy bear with a growler.
$$ • 20 in (51 cm) high

CHAD VALLEY TEDDY BEAR
Manufactured in the 1930s, this bear comes with a printed metal button in the right ear.
$$$ • 21 in (53 cm) high

1950S CHAD VALLEY BEAR
This late 1950s Chad Valley golden mohair teddy bear has orange and black eyes.
$$ • 14¼ in (36 cm) high

GOLD PLUSH STEIFF BEAR
A 1950s gold plush Steiff bear, this teddy comes with its original tag, which adds value.
$$ • 6 in (15 cm) high

BLONDE CHAD VALLEY BEAR
This large Chad Valley blonde mohair teddy bear has a black stitched snout, amber glass eyes, a swivel-jointed body with rexine pads, and a label on its right foot. It is dated c. 1953.
$$$ • 30 in (76 cm) high

1920S FARNELL BEAR
This bear has black boot-button eyes and a pronounced muzzle. Its fur is badly worn.
$$ • 18½ in (47 cm) high

TOP TIPS

- Get to know the characteristics and style techniques used by different manufacturers. In general, early bears can be recognized by their long snouts, whereas bears made after World War II have flatter faces. Steiff bears, in particular, can be identified by their characteristic shapes as well as the type of button in the left ear.
- Identify pre-1950s bears by their boot-button or glass eyes, and mohair fur. Later bears more commonly have plastic eyes.
- Look for homemade bears from the World War II era, as these are increasing in popularity and value.
- Try to choose bears in shades other than the regular brown and blonde.

MERRYTHOUGHT CHEEKY BEAR

This Merrythought teddy bear has amber eyes, a typical high forehead, big flat ears with bells, and a vertically stitched pointed Draylon snout. The bear's white felt pads have also been stitched. Its label proves it is a c. 1950 original.

$$$ • 11 in (28 cm) high

1920S BLACK MOHAIR BEAR

A 1920s British black mohair teddy bear with black boot-button eyes, pronounced clipped muzzle, and stitched nose, mouth, and claws.

$$$ • 15 in (38 cm) high

Starter Buys

STEIFF TEDDY BEAR

With its flatter snout and large nose, this is not an early Steiff bear, but the button in one ear makes it genuine.

$ • 12½ in (32 cm) high

CHILTERN TING-A-LING

Made in the 1950s, this mohair bear has orange and black glass eyes and a short mohair muzzle. Its nose, mouth, and claws have been stitched and its fur is slightly worn.

$ • 11¾ in (30 cm) high

MERRYTHOUGHT TEDDY BEAR

The embroidered label identifies this mohair teddy bear as an original Merrythought creation. Although the bear's fur is worn and patchy, it is still a collectible item.

$ • 20 in (51 cm) high

You may also like... Soft Toys, see pp. 260–61

Soft Toys

Prior to the early 1900s, most soft toys were made by hand. It wasn't until the turn of the 20th century that commercial production of soft toys gained momentum with innovations by producers such as Steiff.

Vintage soft toys are a wide and varied genre encompassing domestic and exotic animals, characters from children's literature, and even rag books. Teddy bears, in their great and cuddly variety, are usually classed in a category of their own.

Toys by major makers are generally more sought after—names such as Steiff are enduringly popular, for instance—but attribution can sometimes be difficult: while many makers used labels or buttons, these are often worn away or even nonexistent, having been pulled off by child owners. Add to your collection at auctions of specialist toys, which sometimes include affordable soft toys in mixed lots.

Meanwhile, vintage toys that were handmade by resourceful parents can have an undeniable attraction. These charming naïve toys can often be found very cheaply at flea markets and garage sales.

Monkeying Around

In the 1920s, the almost legendary German toy company Schreyer & Co. (later known as Schuco) produced a range of soft toy novelty perfume bottles in a variety of forms and colors. Some variations even contained a lipstick or compact. These are highly sought after by collectors—and their value shows in the prices they command.

TOY MONKEY PERFUME BOTTLE
Designed by Schuco, this c. 1920s novelty perfume bottle with a glass tube insert is in the form of a plush fabric monkey.
$$$ • 4 in (10 cm) high

TOP TIPS

- Learn about manufacturers and styles such as J. K. Farnell, Dean's, Merrythought, Chiltern, and Chad Valley. These popular makers can still be found at reasonable prices.
- Keep informed of trends. The market for Disney soft toys and period pieces, for instance, has remained fairly strong in recent years.
- Take very special care of your collection, as the materials used to make vintage soft toys are especially susceptible to insect damage. If in doubt, seek expert advice.

KEY FACTS	1905	1920s	1932	1960	1993
A century of lovable characters	The Steiff toy company adds the famous trademark button to the ears of their soft toys and bears.	The founder of Schuco, Heinrich Müller, starts developing and patenting toy ideas from the age of 17.	Dean's Rag Book Co. Ltd. receives a license from Disney to make the first-ever Mickey Mouse soft toys.	The first Noddy soft toy is produced. Original versions by Merrythought are now very collectible.	Ty Warner introduces Beanie Babies at the World Toy Fair in New York, setting off a veritable craze.

What's Hot

Look out for:

Steiff remains a magical name for toy collectors. Here, the combination of Steiff's reputation and a famous character is bound to excite the serious collector. Original 1930s examples are much sought after.

Clean, unfaded, and in excellent condition

MERRYTHOUGHT MOUSE
"Jerry," a velveteen Merrythought mouse with its label attached, c. 1930.
$$ • 9 in (23 cm) high

SCHUCO MONKEY
This rare orange plush Schuco monkey is dressed in green felt trousers.
$$$ • 3¼ in (8.5 cm) high

STEIFF MICKEY MOUSE
This fine example of the largest of the Steiff Mickeys has an original tag in its ear.
$$$ • 18 in (45.5 cm) high

Core Collectibles

MERRYTHOUGHT PIGLET
A 1950s Merrythought plush piglet with a label.
$$ • 9 in (23 cm) high

STEIFF PENGUIN
Unmarked, this toy has a hole where the button used to be.
$ • 4 in (10 cm) high

Starter Buys

MERRYTHOUGHT MONKEY
A mohair plush monkey with a cloth face, paws, and feet.
$$ • 22 in (56 cm) high

GOLLY
Dating from c. 1930, this is an unmarked British Golly.
$$ • 14 in (35.6 cm) high

STEIFF REINDEER
This Steiff reindeer with mottled fur dates from c. 1950.
$$ • 8 in (20 cm) high

TOY BEAR PERFUME BOTTLE
Concealed in this Schuco bear is a perfume bottle, c. 1920s.
$$$ • 5 in (12.5 cm) high

STEIFF RABBIT
Made by Steiff, this stretching rabbit is from the 1950s.
$ • 4¼ in (11 cm) long

STEIFF TERRIER
A terrier with a Steiff button in its ear, dating to the 1940s.
$ • 3½ in (9 cm) high

You may also like… Tinplate Toys, see pp. 236–37

Board Games & Puzzles

From ancient Egyptian senet to chess and checkers, games have entertained us throughout history. Commercially published for a wide audience since 1800, games and puzzles are attractive to collectors.

Because of the huge variety of games and puzzles, most collectors specialize in specific areas: antique wooden puzzles, playing card sets, chess, solitaire, and 1970s board games are some examples.

There is great demand for classic antique sets of games such as checkers and chess, especially if they are exquisitely fashioned from rare or fragile materials. Prime examples can be worth thousands. Yet there is something for everyone in this field, and plenty of quality, handcrafted items to go around. Victorian and Edwardian parlor games are popular, often because of their attractively illustrated boxes. Travel, war, and exploration themes are common, and games such as Aerito, L'Attaque, Invasion of Europe, and British Empire can still be found today.

Garage sales, flea markets, and secondhand stores can be good hunting grounds for vintage games, which are those dating from the postwar period. Popular games such as Monopoly are generally of low value due to the very high volume of production.

Treasure Trove

This Victorian burr walnut games compendium has been custom made to fit a leather folding chess/backgammon board, two lift-out trays with cards, a cribbage board, turned ivory checkers, bezique score markers, treen dice shakers, carved ivory markers, chess pieces, and bone dominoes.

GAMES COMPENDIUM
This has a brass plaque inscribed "H. Rodricues, 42 Piccadilly. London." Its registration lozenge is for November 29, 1869.

$$$$ • 14¼ in (36.5 cm) wide

KEY FACTS	1700s	1840s	1890s	1935	1979
Game inventions	Dominoes first appear in Europe in the courts of Venice and Naples; John Spilsbury invents the jigsaw puzzle.	The world's leading chess player, Howard Staunton, organizes the first international chess tournament.	Snakes and Ladders, based on an ancient Indian game, is introduced to Victorian England.	Game designer Charles Darrow sells his Monopoly patent to Parker Brothers and becomes a millionaire.	Finding some Scrabble pieces missing, two newspaper editors invent a new game, Trivial Pursuit.

What's Hot

INDIAN FIGURAL CHESS SET
This fine Indian painted ivory figural chess set is from Rajasthan, c. 1790. Many such sets were produced as decorative objects and were never really meant to be played with.

$$$$$ • 5½ in (14 cm) high

ENGLISH BOXWOOD CHESS SET
Dating from the early 18th century, this is a rare English boxwood chess set in a later-era box. It is missing a rook and four pawns, a condition that adversely affects its value.

$$$ • King 3¾ in (9.5 cm) high

ENGLISH IVORY CHESS SET
This boxed English ivory chess set, c. 1840, with some re-carved pawns, is in the style of Lund, a London retailer who sold an array of stationery, corkscrews, chess sets, and other items.

$$$ • King 3½ in (9 cm) high

Look out for:
Napoleonic "prisoner of war" work is highly collectible, as captured French soldiers were adept at fashioning rather complicated mechanical novelties, ships, and other items using very basic tools. Domino sets, such as this one made from scraps of bone, were quite common. They were often sold to prison visitors as a way of raising money.

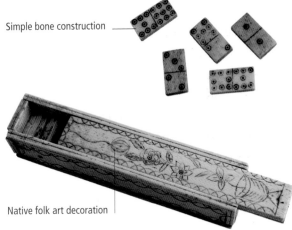

Simple bone construction

Native folk art decoration

CARVED DOMINO BOX
A carved and painted bone prisoner-of-war domino box set with mildly erotic painting on the inner lid. Hidden themes such as the erotic decoration on this example can bolster the value.

$$ • 5½ in (14 cm) long

What's Not

Merchandise associated with 1970s and '80s TV shows, especially those that have acquired cult status, can be collectible if well made, but this product, a cheaply produced jigsaw puzzle with no intrinsic quality, remains at the low end of the market.

"CHARLIE'S ANGELS" PUZZLE
This jigsaw puzzle features Jaclyn Smith, one of the stars of the TV series, c. 1970s.

$ • Box 10 in (25 cm) wide

Core Collectibles

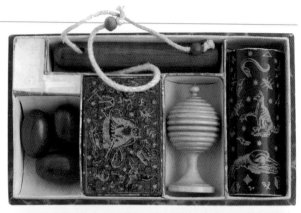

FRENCH GAMES COMPENDIUM

Made by A. Giroux & Co, Paris, this French rosewood games compendium contains two packs of 19th-century playing cards (dated 1816 and 1853), and bone or ivory counters, c. 1825.

$$$$ • 12 in (30 cm) wide

VICTORIAN MAGICIAN'S SET

The Little Conjurer is a Victorian magician's set for children. It comes in a faux tortoiseshell card box with a printed cover, enclosing turned wood implements.

$$ • 6¾ in (17 cm) wide

Ask the Expert

Q. Is it OK to actually play the games in my board game collection?

A. It depends. Many people collect in this area because they enjoy playing the games or using old gaming trays like those on the right. However, if you are collecting by value and buy games in excellent condition, with intact packaging, it makes sense to keep them in a good state.

Q. What kind of games are worth collecting?

A. Gamages' (the most popular toy store of its day) Christmas catalog for 1913 has 32 pages of board and parlor games. Many games from this period are simplistic, but they are often worth collecting for their boxes alone, especially if they have wonderful lithographed covers.

Painted detail

Worn lacquer

REGENCY CARD TRAYS

A pair of Regency lacquer card trays, one decorated with a king and queen, the other with the word "GAME."

$$ • 4½ in (11.5 cm) long

MAP OF THE WORLD PUZZLE
Made by Gall and Inglis, Edinburgh, this Victorian puzzle map of the world has a box with a printed sliding cover and is marked, "A new series of dissected maps by J. Passmore."

$$ • 10 in (25 cm) high

ILLUSTRATED PERIOD BUILDING BLOCKS
A set of early paper-on-wood building blocks in excellent condition. The detailed, colorful illustrations depict animals, and children in costumes of the day.

$$ • Largest 4 in (10 cm) high

PAPIER MÂCHÉ SKITTLE SET
This 19th-century painted papier mâché skittle set comprises a cabbage-shaped container holding nine skittles in the form of various vegetables, each with an amusing painted face.

$$$ • Each 10¼ in (26 cm) high

GAME OF WORDS SET
Made by the Cincinnati Game Co., Cincinnati, in 1903, each card in this American educational Game of Words is lithographed with a school scene and a letter of the alphabet.

$ • 5 in (12 cm) high

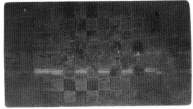

ESCALADO HORSE RACING GAME
A 1940s or '50s horse racing game by Chad Valley, in which mechanical horses race across a vibrating course.

$$ • Box 11 in (28 cm) wide

CANADIAN GAME BOARD
This is a rare wooden Canadian game board with its original paint and finish still intact, dating from c. 1900.

$$ • 26 in (66 cm) high

OSCAR BOARD GAME
A complete Oscar board game that has Hollywood stars competing for fame, made by Henry Hirst & Son, England.

$ • Board 25½ in (65 cm) wide

Core Collectibles

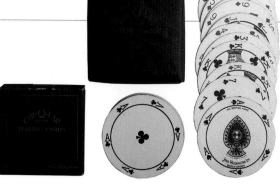

MURANO GLASS CHESS SET

A 20th-century Murano large glass "bust" chess set made in Venice, with figures representing the *commedia dell'arte*.

$$$$ • Largest approx. 4½ in (11.5 cm) high

ROUND PLAYING CARDS

This 1930s set of Waddington's Cir-Q-Lar round playing cards comes complete with a maroon box and carrying pouch.

$ • Box 3½ in (9 cm) square

"ERBACH" CHESS SET

From the 20th century, this German carved ivory "Erbach" chess set consists of white and bronze-colored figures.

$$$$ • Largest approx. 3½ in (9 cm) high

MACAO-TYPE CHESS SET

Probably Cantonese, this fine ivory Macao-type "bust" chess set has an inlaid wooden box with a hinged lid, c. 1830.

$$$$ • King 4½ in (11.5 cm) high

BURMESE-STYLE IVORY SET

An ivory set dating from c. 1840. The chess pieces, in white and stained red, have been elaborately carved in the Burmese style.

$$$ • King 4 in (10 cm) high

DUTCH BOXWOOD CHESS SET

Comprising distinctive and delicately fashioned bone-mounted boxwood pieces, this is a 19th-century Dutch set.

$$$ • 4¼ in (11 cm) high

FRENCH BONE CHESS SET

This French "bust" chess set is from Dieppe, Normandy, a well-known center for bone and ivory carvers, c. 1790.

$$$$$ • King 3¼ in (8.5 cm) high

19TH-CENTURY STAUNTON CHESS SET

An English Jaques Staunton ivory chess set from the 19th century with "Jaques London" stamped on the base of the white king.

$$$$ • King 3½ in (9 cm) high

"SILLY SYMPHONY" CARDS

A pack of Walt Disney *Silly Symphony* Snap cards, featuring Disney's best-loved cartoon characters. The cards were made by Chad Valley during the 1930s.

$ • Box 4 in (10 cm) high

Starter Buys

KER PLUNK

This game of sticks and marbles was produced by Ideal in 1967.

$ • 18 in (45 cm) long

PHENOLIC CHESS SET

Dating from the 1930s, this boxed and carved phenolic chess set with two-dimensional pieces was made by Grays of Cambridge. It is in good condition but missing a pawn.

$ • Box 1½ in (4 cm) high

ASTRONAUTS PUZZLE

This 1968 Astronauts puzzle, celebrating a new era of space travel, contains 20 pieces.

$ • 4½ in (11.5 cm) high

"BONANZA" RUMMY GAME

A 1964 NBC-licensed *Bonanza* Michigan Rummy game by Waddington's.

$$$ • 14¼ in (36.5 cm) wide

DONKEY KONG

Produced by Milton Bradley, this is a Donkey Kong board game made in c. 1983. It is based on a Nintendo arcade game in which the hero must save a fair maiden from a giant ape.

$ • Box 19 in (48.5 cm) wide

"STAR WARS" MONOPOLY

A sealed collectors' edition of *Star Wars* Episode One Monopoly by Hasbro.

$ • Box 15 in (38 cm) wide

You may also like… Computers & Games, see pp. 362–65

Money Boxes & Banks

Fanciful, inventive, humorous—money boxes abound in a variety of shapes and materials. This major industry caters for everyday collectors while offering many options for the discerning collector of antique items.

Think of a material, then think of a subject. It's almost certain that at some point in the last 200 years someone has made a money box in that form, be it a pottery pig, a cast-iron building, or a tinplate coffin.

It's rare to find money boxes that predate the late 18th century, though potteries of this period sometimes produced small, dated pieces decorated with simple glazes and sgraffito. Generally bell-shaped and often topped with a bird, these are popular with collectors of early pottery, and can sell for more than $2,000.

In the early 19th century there began to be an increase in the selection of money boxes, including pearlware pieces in the form of buildings, again often named and dated, and similarly collectible. Cast-iron American money boxes from this period are popular, with designs based on cultural icons of the time, and some can sell for colossal amounts. Beware when collecting in this field, however, as the market is rife with fakes and poor reproductions.

"Thank You Very Much"

A collectors' favorite, this Tammany Bank caricatures William M. Tweed, a corrupt leader of Tammany Hall in 19th-century New York. A coin placed in the right hand drops into a "pocket" slot on the left, and causes the head to nod in gratitude.

TAMMANY BANK

A painted cast-iron Tammany Bank by the J. & E. Stevens Co, with a nodding head mechanism patented in 1873.

$$$ • 6 in (15 cm) high

TOP TIPS

- Search hard for ceramic money boxes from the 18th and 19th centuries, scarce today as many were smashed to retrieve the coins. They will certainly appreciate in value.
- Look out, too, for postwar Japanese banks, which are cheap and worth collecting if in good condition and with the original packaging.
- Avoid NatWest piggy banks, which are over-hyped and unlikely to increase in value.

KEY FACTS	1843	1870	1920s	1950s	1983
Following the money (box) trail	J. & E. Stevens Co of Connecticut is founded, the earliest cast-iron toymaker in the US.	The company expands to the stage where it is producing over 1000 different tinplate toys.	Ellgreave Pottery, Staffordshire, produces "Mr. Pig" ceramic money boxes for children.	Banks warring for new customers begin offering free money boxes to depositors.	NatWest piggy banks become available for the first time.

What's Hot

JOCKEY BANK
From the early 20th century.
A coin placed in the jockey's
mouth makes the horse buck.

$$$ • 10½ in (26.5 cm) long

UNCLE SAM BANK
Coins dropped into the "US
Treasury" purse cause Uncle
Sam's beard to move, 1886.

$$$ • 11½ in (29 cm) high

Look out for:
This Darktown Battery money box by the J. & E. Stevens
Co. is a prime example of a high-value American bank.
A coin placed in the pitcher's hand is thrown to the
batter, and caught in the catcher's breastplate.

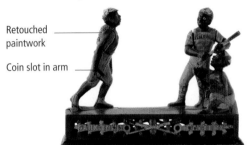

Retouched
paintwork

Coin slot in arm

DARKTOWN BATTERY BANK
This painted cast-iron money bank produced in 1888 is in very
good condition, with a working mechanism.

$$$ • 9¾ in (25 cm) long

Core Collectibles

"SNOWMAN" MONEY BANK
A ceramic Royal Doulton
"Snowman" money bank,
with a green hat and scarf.

$$ • 8½ in (21.5 cm) high

LUCKY WHEEL BANK
The wheel of this c. 1929 tin
bank by Jacob & Co, England,
spins when a coin is inserted.

$$ • 7½ in (19 cm) high

Starter Buys

MR MONEY BANK
A Tomy toy that "swallows" a
coin placed in its hand, c. 1987.

$ • 6 in (15 cm) wide

ACCOUNT BOOK MONEY BOX
This is a 1940s piece by
Pearson, Page, Jewsbury & Co.

$ • 4½ in (11.5 cm) high

BANTHRICO MONEY BANK
This die-cast money bank by
Banthrico bears an inscription
reading, "Save your money."

$$ • 7¾ in (19.5 cm) long

PASCAL'S MONEY BOX
A 1920s money box in
the shape of a chocolate-
dispensing machine.

$$ • 5¼ in (13.5 cm) high

GLASS PIGGY BANK
This 1950s glass bank features
a card pig on a rainy day.

$ • 7 in (18 cm) high

CHIPMUNK MONEY BANK
A porcelain SylvaC money
bank, stamped "5105."

$ • 6¼ in (16 cm) high

You may also like… Tinplate Toys, see pp. 236–37

CHAPTER

6

Fashion

Vintage for All

Retro and vintage fashion has never been so popular. Society as a whole spends more on fashion than it ever has before, and shopping has become a recreational pastime fueled by cheaper products and a greater style consciousness.

In the past, keeping up with the fashion of the day was principally the province of an elite minority; these people were from the privileged classes and their fashions reflected their status. Over the centuries the situation has changed, and keeping up with the latest fashions is now a mass-market preoccupation. Closely linked to all other aspects of daily life, from architecture to automobiles, and advertising to air travel, fashion today reaches more people than ever, and fashions from the past, or "vintage," are highly sought-after collectibles.

Fashion is the product of centuries of cultural and physical influences. It reflects not only status, but also taste, tradition, occupation, and climate. Ancient art, the arrival of silk in Europe, the first exploration of East Asia—all of these factors have affected fashion

Yellow Lucite handbag, see Core Collectibles, p. 297.

Biba cosmetics containers, 1970, see Starter Buys, p. 301.

and style, and the industry continually looks for new and exciting references and materials. The business still operates at an elite level, but now we can all benefit. Catwalk styles filter down to the shopping mall, and if Karl Lagerfeld says that shorts are "in" this season, then stores respond by selling their own versions. The branding of accessories cleverly deals with our desire to enter this elite world: sunglasses, jewelry, bags, cosmetics, and shoes all offer affordable access to a brand, and the label can speak volumes about how you perceive yourself, and how you want others to perceive you.

Collecting fashion may seem a strange notion. Most people "buy to wear" and amass vast quantities, therefore becoming collectors. Does having 70 pairs of shoes make you a shoe collector? What is certain is that the market for antique, vintage, retro, and modern fashion is buoyant. Whether we consider an 18th-century Spitalfield's silk waistcoat or a Vivienne Westwood punk T-shirt, everything from couture to street fashion can offer the collector great pleasure and perhaps even great financial reward.

People choose vintage clothing for a variety of reasons, such as nostalgia, uniqueness, the pleasure of collecting, interest in specific style periods, cost, and the look and feel of vintage clothing. If you're searching for vintage clothes on the Internet, you'll come across a plethora of shopping resources and sites, but secondhand shops and neighborhood rummage sales offer happy hunting grounds and rich pickings.

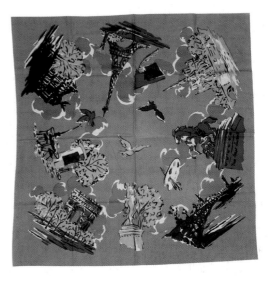

Demi-parure, c. 1885, see Starter Buys, p. 275.

Emilio Pucci dress, see Core Collectibles, p. 289.

Yves Saint Laurent scarf, c. 1970, see Core Collectibles, p. 291.

Victorian Jewelry

The great advantage in collecting 19th-century jewelry is the diversity of material, at prices that can range from a few dollars for a modest silver locket to six-figure sums for a formal diamond corsage brooch.

Much Victorian jewelry is judged unfashionable today, which means that a discerning collector can choose from a huge range of designs, many of which are affordable. While modern jewelry can be repetitive and quickly passes out of fashion, a well-carved antique cameo brooch or French enameled gold locket is stylish, timeless, and original.

Jewelry in the Victorian era can be divided into three periods: Romantic (1837–60), Revival style (1860–85), and Aesthetic (1885–1901). Jeweled serpents, nature and naturalism, and the art of the Middle Ages typified the 1840s and '50s. The mid-Victorian period was characterized by jewels in bold colors and designs inspired by the Renaissance. The late Victorian era saw industrialization of jewelry manufacture, which allowed mass production, although a simple bar brooch can still be charming.

Victorian jewelry offers a near inexhaustible supply of durable and creative designs in a category that is bound to rise in value as demand increases.

Diamonds for the People

Diamonds were prohibitively expensive in the early Victorian period, but after the opening of South Africa's diamond mines in 1870, they became affordable for the middle classes, who often wore them in cluster rings.

CLUSTER RING
Dating from 1880, this is a sapphire and diamond cluster ring with a 3.7-karat sapphire set on a gold band.
$$$$ • Approx. ¾ x ½ in (2 x 1.5 cm)

TOP TIPS

- Check that brooches have their original C-shaped clasps; if these have been replaced, the value will be affected.
- Jewelry engraved with names, initials, or dates is more collectible.
- Early gold Victorian items were all 18–22-karat. After 1854, gold content was standardized at 9, 12, or 15 karats, and had to be hallmarked and stamped.

KEY FACTS	1837	1861	1884	1890	2008
Victoriana then and now	Victoria comes to the throne. In the US, jewelry company Tiffany & Co. is founded in New York.	Victoria is often seen wearing jet mourning jewelry after the death of Prince Albert, starting a new fashion.	Bulgari is founded in Italy, another step away from patronage by the rich to independent studio production.	The growth of the industrial revolution allows a new middle class to grow, with a taste for jewels.	English Heritage buys a Victorian silver factory in Birmingham's Jewelry Quarter.

What's Hot

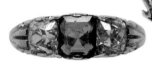

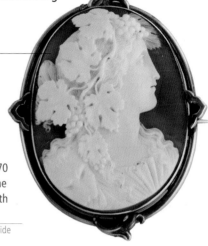

THREE-STONE RING
A 1.21-karat emerald and 1.71-karat diamond three-stone ring from 1900.
$$$$$ • ½ x ¼ in (1.5 x 0.5 cm)

FROG BROOCH
This is a late Victorian brooch set with rose-cut diamonds and garnets.
$$$$ • 1 in (2.5 cm) long

Look Out For:
Cameos were very popular in the Victorian era. They were mostly carved from shells in Italy, or from layered stone such as agate. Look for even color in the background and carving in high relief.

Reddish shell background

Core Collectibles

CRESCENT BROOCH
Set with opals and pairs of old-cut diamonds, this brooch has an inscription dated 1911.
$$$ • 1½ in (3.5 cm) in diameter

ENAMEL RING
Made in 1880, this is a gold and turquoise enamel ring set with split pearls.
$$ • ½ x ¼ in (1.6 x 0.5 cm) long

CAMEO BROOCH
This brooch from 1870 has an 18-karat frame and shows a lady with grapes in her hair.
$$$$ • 2¼ in (6 cm) wide

Starter Buys

DEMI-PARURE
This is a Victorian-cased demi-parure with a hinged bangle, brooch, and earrings.
$$$ • Bangle 2¼ in (5.5 cm) wide

ENGRAVED LOCKET
An 1881 Aesthetic Movement engraved silver locket, made in Birmingham.
$$$ • 2½ x 1½ in (6.2 x 3.5 cm)

GOLD EARRINGS
A pair of pink gold pendant earrings from c. 1880. Copper gives the pink tint.
$$$ • 2 in (5 cm) long

DIAMOND SET BROOCH
An opal- and rose-cut diamond-set brooch dating from c. 1885.
$$$ • 1¾ in (4.5 cm) long

VICTORIAN RING
A Victorian gold and coral ring with diamond sparks set around the coral.
$$$ • 1½ x ¼ in (.5 x 0.5 cm)

You may also like… Costume Jewelry, see pp. 280–83

Art Nouveau Jewelry

Jewels from the Art Nouveau period reflect the incredible creative energy of the era and the mastery of its jewelers. For many collectors, these distinctive pieces are miniature works of art.

The Art Nouveau movement brought jewelry design into the 20th century. Its style was radically different and hugely imaginative. Nature was the dominant theme, with sensuous animal, plant, and female forms interwoven in curved fluid lines.

Materials were chosen to complement the design, rather than for their intrinsic value, and colors exploded with a variety of enameling techniques sometimes combined with semiprecious stones or glass. *Pliqué à jour* enamel, applied without backing so light can shine through, resembling stained glass, was particularly characteristic of the time.

The list of exponents is endless, but includes luminaries such as René Lalique, Georges Fouquet, and Louis Comfort Tiffany. Today, a fine gold jewel with *pliqué à jour* enamel might fetch around $20,000, but simple French brooches and pendants can still be bought for less than $1,000.

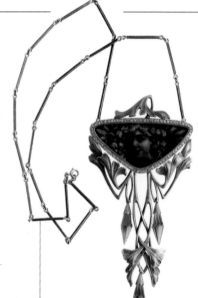

Enameler Extraordinaire

Sculptor Lucien Hirtz (1864–1928) was one of the most famous enamelers of his day. He worked for over 30 years for jeweler Frédéric Boucheron, whose patrons included royalty and society hostesses, and who remained popular until the 1930s.

PENDANT NECKLACE
Attributed to Lucien Hirtz, this 18-karat gold necklace has a diamond-framed triangular panel enameled with the head of a young girl amid flowers, bordered with leaf motifs.
$$$$$ • Pendant 4¾ in (12 cm) long

TOP TIPS

- Beware of fakes. Telltale signs include: uniform, sharp enameling with little or no shading; sharp edges with little wear and tear; and an absence of filing or polishing marks. Take a hallmarking book with you to check dates.
- Look for designs by Liberty & Co.—they were designed by artists but made using modern manufacturing techniques and tend to be more affordable.

KEY FACTS	1890	1895	1900s	1905	1979
The flourishing of a movement in jewelry	Art Nouveau designs begin to take shape, closely influenced by the German Jugendstil movement.	German art dealer Siegfried Bing opens a gallery in Paris called L'Art Nouveau, which names the movement.	Iconic designer and craftsman René Lalique becomes famous for his era-defining Art Nouveau work.	After a brief efflorescence, simpler modernist styles start to edge out the period's extravagance.	A diamond-studded Lalique dog-collar makes a record sale for Christie's in Geneva for $98,694.

What's Hot

LAPORTE-BLAIRSY PENDANT
This Leo Laporte-Blairsy piece has a carved ivory head, looped leaves, and flowers.
$$$$$ • 3 in (7.5 cm) long

FLORAL MOTIF NECKLACE
Liberty & Co. necklace of gilt metal set with blue, green, and turquoise enamels, c. 1900–05.
$$$$ • 14¾ in (38 cm) long

Look out for:
Enamel jewelry is particularly sought after. If, as here, it is still in its original case or box or has its paperwork proving authenticity, this will add to its value.

Three-dimensional enamel

LIBERTY & CO. SILVER AND ENAMEL BUTTONS
This set of six Liberty & Co. buttons in an original case was designed by Archibald Knox. Each circular button has a whiplash motif enameled in shades of green, blue, and yellow.
$$$$ • Each button 1 in (2.5 cm) in diameter

Core Collectibles

TWO-PIECE BUCKLE
This 1900 Liberty & Co. silver buckle with a turquoise matrix is attributed to Oliver Baker.
$$$$ • 2¾ in (7 cm) wide

FLORAL PENDANT
An enameled Art Nouveau pendant of curved flower-head form with an oval pearl.
$$ • 1½ in (4 cm) wide

Starter Buys

QUEENSWAY BROOCH
An Art Nouveau brooch with enamel leaves and pearls.
$$ • 2 in (4.8 cm) wide

SILVER PENDANT
Silver and enameled pendant in the Art Nouveau style.
$$ • 2 in (5 cm) long

BELT BUCKLE
Pair of Kerr & Co. goldwashed silver buckles from the 1900s in the form of peacocks.
$$$ • 3½ in (9 cm) wide

GOLD BROOCH
Liberty & Co. brooch by Archibald Knox with sinuous interwoven tendrils, 1905.
$$$ • 1½ in (3.5 cm) wide

SILVER BELT BUCKLE
This buckle by Howard & Co. is dated 1885–1900.
$$ • 3¼ in (8.25 cm) long

JADE RING
The oval mount is silver with marquisates.
$ • Approx ¾ x ½ in (2 x 1.5 cm)

You may also like… René Lalique Glass, see pp. 94–95

Art Deco Jewelry

The Art Deco era was one of the formative periods in the history of jewelry design. Demand in this area has been strong for the past 20 years, and prices range from modest to stellar.

Art Deco was a groundbreaking style of design that blossomed during the 1920s and '30s. It emerged in a new industrialized age that saw the rise of machinery and speed and the advent of the Charleston and rebellious young "flappers." With its striking, aerodynamic forms, Art Deco epitomized elegance and sophistication.

Designers used many materials, from rubies and pearls to plastic and steel, with large stones being less important than unusual colors and combinations.

Platinum was the most popular luxury metal, while geometric diamond cuts like the baguette and emerald were used for the first time. In Europe, designers like Cartier and Van Cleef & Arpels were at the forefront of the movement; in the United States, Harry Winston and Tiffany & Co. were known for their iconic style.

A revival of interest in the Art Deco period means that this is a popular area of collecting, but there is still plenty to suit all tastes and budgets.

Elegant Emeralds

Paris was the trendsetter in the Deco period. French jewelers like Cartier and Charles Jacqueau used the finest materials and most innovative designs to create their stylish works of art. This articulated platinum bracelet is studded with high-quality diamonds and has five large carved emeralds set along its center.

DIAMOND & EMERALD BRACELET
This late-1920s French platinum bracelet is set with diamonds and emeralds.
$$$$$ • 6¾ in (17.5 cm) long

TOP TIPS

- Authentic Art Deco items should show signs of wear; if it looks too new, don't buy.
- Check for any dents, deep scratches, missing stones, and evidence of repairs, such as unlikely solder joints.
- If you are willing to accept flaws and imperfections, you stand a better chance of being able to afford an almost-perfect piece.

KEY FACTS	1890–1914	1914–18	1919	1926	1933
Style and substance	La Belle Époque—as the Edwardian period is known in France—sees a last flash of period extravagance.	The horrors of the Great War sweep away luxury living, and many materials became scarce.	The end of the first World War ushers in a new austerity in fashion, yet also daring designs.	Flapper fashion is truly out in force in the Roaring '20s, and Art Deco complements the Jazz Age lifestyles.	The pioneering Bauhaus school, famed for its simplified forms, is closed down by the Nazis.

What's Hot

RING & BAR PIN
A diamond platinum rectangular brooch made by Mappin & Webb, London.
$$$$ • 2 in (5 cm) wide

FUR CLIP
One of a pair of diamond-encrusted French fur clips with three emerald-cut stones.
$$$$$ • 2½ in (6 cm) wide

Look out for:
The bright white of platinum provided the perfect contrast for stones like rubies, emeralds, and sapphires and helped to define the Art Deco style. Today, rings from the period are becoming highly sought after as engagement rings, with prices rising to reflect this popularity. Diamonds, as in this example, enhance the visual appeal.

Core Collectibles

Geometric cut ⎯⎯⎯⎯⎯⎯

RECTANGULAR BROOCH
This diamond plaque brooch has mille grain set throughout with old-cut diamonds.
$$$ • 1½ in (4 cm) wide

DIAMOND BROOCH
A diamond and platinum rectangular brooch by Mappin & Webb, London.
$$$ • 2 in (5 cm) wide

RUBY RING
Art Deco platinum ring set with an oblong ruby and a diamond.
$$$$ • Approx ¾ x ½ in (2 x 1 cm)

Starter Buys

SILVER PIN
This pin has a ruby-red paste and clear crystal rhinestones.
$$ • 2 in (5 cm) wide

SAPPHIRE AND DIAMOND BRACELET
A platinum, white gold, sapphire, and diamond bracelet composed with a scalloped navette-shaped center.
$$$$ • 7 in (17.5 cm) long

ART DECO SILVER BRACELET SET
Late 1920s French bracelet with crossed and interlaced bands of clear crystal rhinestones and ruby-colored paste cabochons.
$$$ • 7½ in (19 cm) long

SILVER PENDANT
An English Art Deco sterling silver pendant necklace with clear crystal rhinestones from the 1930s.
$$$ • 1½ in (4 cm) long

ENGLISH SILVER BRACELET
This bracelet has openwork decoration in stylized floral and foliate motifs with jade-green glass cabochons, 1920s.
$$$ • 7 in (18 cm) long

You may also like… Fashion Accessories, see pp. 300–01

Costume Jewelry

Paste or glass jewels have existed since the 1700s, but it was only in the 1920s that costume jewelry really came into its own, championed by the likes of Coco Chanel. It has grown in popularity ever since.

While it looks like the real thing, costume jewelry is made from relatively inexpensive materials such as paste, plastics, and base metals. The most popular items for collectors date from between 1920 and 1950, because these tend to be affordable, obtainable, and above all fashionable. It was during this era that movie stars began to achieve the sort of celebrity that we recognize today, and they were often seen wearing costume jewelry, which only added to its appeal.

Pre-1930 examples, especially good-quality ones, are more difficult to find and therefore more valuable. Complete sets or signed pieces are also rising in value, particularly those by notable designers such as Boucher, Hagler, Eisenberg, Miriam Haskell, and Trifari. Bakelite jewelry is also sought after. But for those on a budget, fun pins and brooches from the 1950s and '60s can be had for as little as $10.

Double Whammy

Duettes, enameled tremblers, and whimsical designs by Adolph Katz for the Coro jewelry company are highly collectible today. Founded in New York in 1901 by Emanuel Cohn and Gerald Rosenberg (the company name comes from the first letters of their surnames), at one time Coro made half of all the jewelry sold worldwide. Its ranges spanned cheap and cheerful pins to more exclusive high-end items.

CORO CRAFT DUETTE PIN
A 1930s glass, enamel, and diamanté duette pin. Coro used many different marks; the name "Coro Craft" was used from 1937, originally on higher-quality items.
$$$ • 3 in (7 cm) long

KEY FACTS	1926	c. 1930	1940	1945	1979
All that glitters	Miriam Haskell opens her New York City store, selling her jewelry of unique organic design.	Alfred Phillippe becomes the head designer at Trifari. The company's distinctive look is born.	Alexandra Korda promotes the movie *The Thief of Baghdad* with jewelry based on that worn on set.	Actor Steve Brody and Dan Staneskieu found Cadoro jewelers, catering to the rich and famous.	After almost 80 years, Coro goes out of business, which increases the value of its jewelry.

What's Hot

SWAN PIN

This very rare 1940s swan pin was made by famous American costume jeweler Trifari.

$$$ • 3 in (7 cm) wide

JOMAZ COLLECTION

Here is a glittering set by Jomaz of New York, with bracelet, pin, and earrings.

$$$ • Pin 1½ in (4 cm) long

Look out for:

Marcel Boucher was born in Paris in 1898. He did his apprenticeship with Cartier in Paris and then worked as a designer for Mazer Brothers in New York in the 1930s. Signatures increase the value of costume jewelry, and Boucher almost always signed and numbered his pieces, making them very easy to identify.

Diamanté choker

Gold-colored faux pearl

Tubular glass flowers

FLORAL BANGLE

A gold-plated bangle by Stanley Hagler with glass bead floral motifs.

$$$ • 7 in (19 cm) in circumference

BOUCHER PIN

Made in the 1950s, this is a Boucher glass and diamanté pin with a stamped signature.

$$$ • 2¼ in (5.5 cm) high

FAUX PEARL NECKLACE

A rare Marcel Boucher poured glass, diamanté, and faux pearl pendant necklace from the 1940s.

$$$$ • 5 in (12 cm) wide

What's Not

This Napier bracelet is not very desirable, as its design lacks inspiration. The gilding is also very dull, and will wear quickly if the bracelet is worn. Napier jewelry is still mass-produced today.

ROBERT PIN

A pin from the 1940s made by Robert, well known for its elaborate, expensive pieces.

$$$ • 3 in (7 cm) long

SANDOR PIN

Dating to the 1930s, this is a Sandor pin with three yellow flowers in a green pot.

$$$ • 3 in (7 cm) long

NAPIER BRACELET

A Napier bracelet, period unknown, with white metal leaf shapes.

$ • 7 in (19 cm) long

Core Collectibles

FLOWER PIN
A 1950s flower pin in yellow, amber, and cream lucite on a silver filigree backing.
$$ • 5½ in (14 cm) wide

NAPIER BRACELET
This Napier bracelet has a ribbed ring design and is marked "STERLING."
$ • 8 in (20 cm) long

HOBE BIB COLLECTION
Dating to the 1950s–60s, this is a Hobe "Bib" necklace, bracelet, pin, and earrings parure in gilt metal with strings of faceted faux topaz and red beads, with overlaid blue and pink glass beads.
$$$ • Bib and pin 2½ in (6 cm) wide; bracelet 6½ in (16.5 cm) circumference

WING BROOCHES
A pair of American sterling silver- and gold-plated wing brooches from the 1940s.
$$ • 3¼ in (8.5 cm) long

EISENBERG EARRINGS
A pair of Eisenberg earrings: Eisenberg used only Swarovski crystal rhinestones.
$$$ • 2 in (5 cm) long

SCHREINER SET
A 1950s Schreiner pin and earrings with rhinestones and amethyst-colored cabochons.
$$$ • Pin 2½ in (6 cm) in diameter

CRAB-SHAPED CLIP
Nettie Rosenstein signed 1940s fur clip with silver, enamel, and gold plating.
$$ • 2 in (5 cm) long

Ask the Expert

Q. How do you clean costume jewelry?
A. The safest way is to use a soft dry cloth or toothbrush to remove any dirt from the surface and between the claws or the settings.

COPPER PIN
This 1940s Rebajes copper pin has looped and coiled wire decoration.
$ • 2½ in (6.5 cm) wide

Keep in airtight bag to avoid tarnish

Q. How do I begin collecting costume jewelry?
A. This depends on your budget, but keep a few things in mind: buy complete pieces; inspect jewelry in a good light, if possible with a 10x loupe; consider building up jewelry sets—it is a good idea to invest in popular pieces or a full set; also, buy what you would like to wear.

Q. How important are signatures to pieces?
A. Not all costume jewelry pieces are signed, but when they are, it can add significant value. Identifying fake signatures is important, as is recognizing different signatures: Francisco Rebajes (1932–67) used "Rebaj," "Rebaje" and also "Rebajes" (with the "s" known as a "fish mark").

PEARL SET
This striking Miriam Haskell pearl pin and earrings set dates from the 1960s.

$$ • 3½ in (9 cm) long

BOUQUET OF FLOWERS PIN
Cristobal poured glass pin with rhinestones in a brass wire frame, from the 1990s.

$$$ • 3½ in (9 cm) high

CRISTOBAL NECKLACE
This 1950s necklace, decorated with amber and topaz rhinestones in a ruthinium-plated casting, was made by Cristobal London in the late 1990s.

$$ • 15½ in (39 cm) in circumference

TRIFARI PIN
Trifari "Jelly Belly" chick in egg pin. Trifari jelly bellies are highly coveted today.

$$$ • 2 in (5 cm) long

DUET PIN
Trifari gold-toned duette pin from the 1930s with pale green stones.

$$$ • 3 in (8 cm) wide

ENGLISH BROOCH
An unmarked 1930s English silver paste onyx and simulated pearl brooch.

$$ • 2¼ in (5.5 cm) long

CHRISTMAS TREE PIN
A 1960s Stanley Hagler pin, hand-wired on gold-plated filigree setting.

$$ • 3¾ in (8.5 cm) high

Starter Buys

BAR PIN
Carved stylized leaf bar pin in cherry-red bakelite.

$$ • 3 in (7 cm) wide

BUTTERFLY PIN
Cristobal butterfly pin from the late 1990s.

$$ • 5¼ in (13.5 cm) wide

"SCOTTY" DOG PIN
A black lucite "Scotty" dog pin dating to the 1930s.

$$ • 3 in (7 cm) long

FLOWER EARRINGS
1940s Miriam Haskell gilt and diamanté flower earrings.

$$ • 1½ in (4 cm) long

You may also like… Handbags & Purses, see pp. 294–99

Designer Clothing

Collecting designer clothing continues to be a growth market. From the prewar vintage chic of Chanel to the sometimes outrageous designs of Vivienne Westwood, this is an interesting market to explore.

Haute couture has driven the retail fashion market since the early 1900s. For most of us, it's an area of the market that bears no relation to what we wear, mainly because of the huge expense of such clothes. This is where secondhand clothing comes into its own: sales of "vintage" clothing have grown over the years, fuelled by major museum exhibitions, specialty shops, and auction sales. "Street" fashion, too, continues to be a growth market.

Of course, one of the main attractions for collectors is the wearing of these items. Does this make them collectors or shoppers? Whatever the term, your "vintage" Pucci, Gucci, Prada, Christian Dior, Courrèges, or other designer items will tend to find a market. Saleability may depend on current or future trends, but fashion is notorious for revisiting past styles and reinventing old looks.

Utilize the usual hunting grounds: secondhand stores or consignment shops know their labels these days but can still be relatively well priced. Look for one-time sales or charity events—increasingly popular, including online auctions—where donated designer clothing or celebrity pieces subsidize good causes.

Back to the Future

Born in Italy in 1922, Pierre Cardin has enjoyed a long and varied career: in the mid-1940s, he studied architecture in Paris and worked with Schiaparelli and Dior before founding his own fashion house in 1950. His diverse output includes car interiors, film work, and toiletries, and he remains one of the 20th century's most respected and innovative designers. Though Cardin's trademark geometric space-age designs have always been avant garde, the most sought-after Cardin designs generally date from the 1960s, when his designs, as seen in this dress, were at their most futuristic.

"SPACE AGE" DRESS
A rare Pierre Cardin couture "Space Age" green and black block dress from the 1960s.
$$$ • 41 in (105 cm) long

KEY FACTS	1883	1905	1920s	1960s	c. 1971
Fashions of the day	Gabrielle "Coco" Chanel is born in Saumur, France, and goes on to set up a millinery shop in 1910.	Christian Dior is born. His "New Look" silhouette will revolutionize women's fashion in the 1940s.	Chanel launches the boyish *garçon* look, followed in 1923 by the classic Chanel suit.	Mary Quant pushes the mini skirt to the micro skirt. The first Biba store opens in London's Kensington.	Vivienne Westwood begins to sell the now-famous and highly collectible Punk Seditionaries range.

What's Hot

Look out for:

Andy Warhol's Campbell's Soup design is one of the most iconic 20th-century images. His paper dress was marketed in the early 1960s for a mere $1.25. Today, one in good condition could probably be worth $1,400–$2,400.

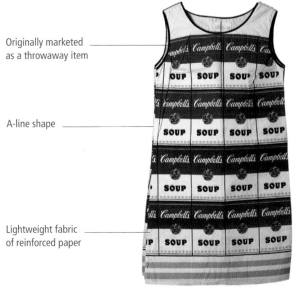

Originally marketed as a throwaway item

A-line shape

Lightweight fabric of reinforced paper

PUCCI TROUSERS
A pair of silk trousers in a characteristically flamboyant Pucci print, 1960s.
$$$ • 41 in (105 cm) long

COURRÈGES MAXI SKIRT
Appliqué daisies embellish this Courrèges museum-quality couture maxi skirt.
$$$$ • 40 in (102 cm) long

"THE SOUPER DRESS"
Collected in major museums around the world, "The Souper Dress" is an iconic pop culture design by Andy Warhol. It is made of paper reinforced with cellulose and cotton.
$$$ • 38 in (96 cm) long

What's Not

Cut, cloth, and style are of paramount importance. Old-fashioned clothes or those aimed at the middle-class market, such as this overcoat, are less desirable.

STRAWBERRY SUIT
Dotted with red strawberry designs, this rare Ossie Clark three-piece pantsuit was exhibited in 2004 at the V&A Ossie Clark retrospective.
$$$$ • Jacket 17¼ in (44 cm) long

OSSIE CLARK BLOUSE
This is a rare Ossie Clark Art Deco floral blouse in rust, brown, and cream. Clark often used ruffles to break up a garment's surface.
$$$ • 33 in (83 cm) long

1960S PEGGY COAT
A Peggy French Couture blue coat in a 1960s style for the middle-class market.
$ • 31½ in (80 cm) long

Core Collectibles

TAILORED RED JACKET
Edged with black velvet trim, this 1950s tailored junior red jacket is in size "S."
$$ • 23½ in (60 cm) long

EDITH FLAGG COAT
Dating from the 1960s, this floral printed cotton coat is an Edith Flagg creation.
$ • 54 in (138 cm) long

1950S COTTON SKIRT
A flowing cotton skirt with an all-over printed pattern in the 1950s style.
$ • 54 in (138 cm) long

PUCCI DRESS
This 1960s Pucci Saks Fifth Avenue dress in size 12 is teamed with a belt. Pucci's distinctive silks, printed with psychedelic patterns, were very much in vogue at the time.
$$$ • 54 in (138 cm) long

COURRÈGES JACKET
Futuristic material gives this Courrèges turquoise jacket a wet look.
$$$ • 21¾ in (55 cm) long

Ask the Expert

Q. I would like to have some vintage designer outfits altered so that I can wear them. Will this affect their value?
A. It very much depends on how well it's done and whether it changes the look or line of the garment. If it's a valuable designer piece, think twice.

Q. I still have a Vivienne Westwood "Pirate" shirt, which I bought in the late '80s. Is it worth anything?
A. Yes! The Japanese market is particularly strong, but all early Westwood items, including bodysuits, are in demand. A shirt like yours in good condition will be worth hundreds of dollars.

Westwood's orb and satellite hallmark

VIVIENNE WESTWOOD BODYSUIT
This navy blue bodysuit bears a repeated pattern in pale pink of Westwood's now-familiar orb motif, which has been in use for her clothing since 1987.
$$ • *28 in (71 cm) long*

MARY QUANT SLACKS & TOP
This black-and-white-striped two-piece is a rare 1960s Mary Quant design.
$$ • 50 in (126 cm) long

VERSACE TWO-PIECE
Black, yellow, and purple pants and a matching top make up this Versace outfit.
$$$ • Top 17¾ in (45 cm) long

BIBA CHECK DRESS
Brown and white in color, this check dress was designed by Biba in the 1960s.
$$ • 54 in (138 cm) long

TAFFETA BALL GOWN
Gold sequins add luster to this 1950s halter-neck rayon taffeta ball gown.
$ • 56 in (142.5 cm) long

1940S SILK DRESS
A 1940s silk dress decorated with red, yellow, and purple carnations on a cream ground.
$$ • Approx. 57 in (145 cm) long

1950S SHIRT DRESS
This 1950s blue cotton pleated shirt dress has white polka dots and buttons.
$ • Approx. 40 in (101.5 cm) long

SONIA RYKIEL DRESS
A Sonia Rykiel creation, this red and black knit sweater dress has long sleeves.
$$ • 41 in (105 cm) long

OSSIE CLARK FLORAL DRESS
With its Birtwell print, this cream dress is a distinctive 1960s Ossie Clark design.
$$$ • 57 in (145 cm) long

Core Collectibles

FLORAL MINI DRESS
In a 1960s Mary Quant style, this dress has a white floral print on a black background.

$ • 32 in (81 cm) long

1950S FLORAL DRESS
A red bodice ribbon offsets the full skirt of this 1950s red and green dress printed with floral sprays. It has a buckle belt of the same material, and fits size 10–12.

$ • 33½ in (85 cm) long

MISSONI DRESS
This classic clingy Missoni dress is in orange and red, with a long tie belt.

$$$ • 46 in (117 cm) long

BALMAIN SILK DRESS
Yellow and black in color, this 1960s Balmain silk dress has pockets on each side.

$$ • 37 in (93 cm) long

PUCCI PRINTED DRESS
An early Pucci design, this dress and belt are printed with blue and green flowers.

$$$ • 44 in (111 cm) long

TULIP BOW DRESS
This Vivienne Westwood dress is from the Pagan I collection and Westwood's own archive.

$$$ • 36 in (92 cm) long

JEAN PATOU TRIM COAT
A rare Jean Patou design, this blue leather trim coat has a matching dress (not shown).

$$$$ • 43 in (110 cm) long

TOP TIPS

- Beware of copies and period homemade pieces. Patterns for designer-style clothing were very popular in the 1960s and '70s. "Handmade" doesn't mean "couture."
- Think twice before buying a worn-out or stained piece. Condition is very important.
- Consider out-of-fashion garments as potential investments if they represent a certain "look" or period.

EMILIO PUCCI DRESS
Trimmed with orange lace, this turquoise dress is an Emilio Pucci design.
$$ • 53 in (134 cm) long

SILK VELVET OPERA COAT
The scalloped cuffs and hem mark this 1920s embroidered opera coat in pink silk velvet.
$$$ • 37½ in (95 cm) long

1960S WOOL COAT
This 1960s Lilli Ann wool coat has a wide collar embroidered with black beads.
$$ • 39½ in (100 cm) long

NAVY CREPE DRESS
Dating to the 1930s, this crepe size 12 dress bears a ruffle detail on its printed bodice.
$ • 38½ in (98 cm) long

Starter Buys

SUSPENDER BELT & BRA
This lace-trimmed suspender belt and bra, a matching set, are designed by Extasy.
$$ • Top 17 in (43.2 cm) wide

RIBBON JACKET
A cropped ribbon jacket in the style of 1960s First Lady Jackie Kennedy.
$$ • 13½ in (34 cm) long

CIRCLE SKIRT
Trimmed with lace, this full circle skirt is made of red and white gingham.
$ • 19¾ in (50 cm) long

RAIN JACKET
Iridescent pink in color, this tie-belted rain jacket is a Byblos creation.
$$ • 23½ in (60 cm) long

You may also like… Handbags & Purses, see pp. 294–99

Hats & Headscarves

The myriad designs of hats and headscarves and the variety of historical and designer pieces offer ample choice to the collector. Well-made pieces that stand the test of time will add value to a fun collection.

The hat and the headscarf have both long been adopted for special treatment by the great fashion houses and designers of the world. While some of the big designers in contemporary society used hats as a starting point—Coco Chanel, for example, started her career in millinery—others are known specifically for their work with hats. Philip Treacy and Stephen Jones, for instance, are already represented in museums alongside the classic "shock value" hats of designers such as

Elsa Schiaparelli. Meanwhile, fashion houses such as Hermès and Chanel have made headscarves a luxury decorative item, just as often framed and displayed as a work of art as worn on the head or around the neck.

This can be a fun genre to collect and wear if the mood takes you. Good sources include secondhand stores, while more exotic headwear, such as military helmets and hats, can be found at auctions. There is something for almost all budgets in this collecting area.

Hat, Hat, Hooray!

The fedora is an enduring icon in popular culture, and this example, designed for a woman, plays with gender stereotypes in a fashionable way. As such, this jaunty 1960s design—made small to sit on the top of the head— retains a contemporary feel.

BELLINI STRAW HAT
This woven straw hat with a grosgrain band and orange trim was designed by Bellini in the mid- to late 1960s.
$$ • 11½ in (29 cm) wide

TOP TIPS

- Learn to distinguish what makes a hat stylish and potentially more valuable.
- Consider hatpins as a good sideline to a hat collection.
- Start a scarf collection by choosing commemorative editions, as they are not prohibitively expensive.
- Keep a lookout for sought-after wartime propaganda-print scarves.

KEY FACTS	1910	1928	1930s	1960s	1997
Famous hats for famous heads	The house of Chanel is founded in Paris, with her "back to basics" designs becoming icons of elegance.	The first Hermès silk scarf is marketed in Paris. Today, one is sold somewhere every 25 seconds.	Schiaparelli works with Surrealist artist Dalí to produce hats in the shapes of giant shoes and lamb chops.	Jackie Kennedy first sports her signature pillbox hat, boosting the career of then-milliner Roy Halston.	Philip Treacy's muse, Isabella Blow, buys the entire graduation fashion collection of Alexander McQueen.

What's Hot

Look out for:

Good-quality examples of popular Hermès scarves are especially sought after. This scarf's horse print is testament to the firm's equestrian heritage.

PUCCI SILK SCARF
This 1960s scarf bears typically Pucci bright colors and geometric patterns.
$$ • 35 in (89 cm) square

DERBY SCARF
A scarf from the Winners of the Derby series by Welsh Margetson & Co., 1953.
$$ • 34 in (86.5 cm) square

HERMÈS SCARF
Designed and signed by Jacques Eudel, this "Grand Apparat" silk twill scarf has hand-rolled edges, c. 1970s.
$$ • 35 in (89 cm) square

Core Collectibles

WOVEN STRAW CLOCHE
A silk-lined chocolate brown cloche hat with a satin band from the 1920s.
$$ • 5¼ in (13.5 cm) high

SCHIAPARELLI HAT
Designed by Elsa Schiaparelli, this three-color woven straw hat is from the 1940s.
$ • 9 in (22.5 cm) wide

YSL SILK SCARF
This bright Yves Saint Laurent silk scarf is decorated with whimsical representations of Parisian monuments. In excellent condition, it dates from c. 1970.
$$ • 35 in (89 cm) square

Starter Buys

COTTON POODLE SCARF
Dating from the 1950s, this printed cotton scarf is decorated with poodles.
$ • 18 in (45.5 cm) square

1970S SILK SCARF
A red-and-white Paisley-patterned silk scarf from Liberty of London, 1970s.
$ • 26½ in (67 cm) square

WOOL FELT HAT
A 1950s burgundy wool felt hat with applied silk flowers.
$ • 7½ in (19 cm) wide

DAISY HAT
Decorated with daisies, this hat is from the 1950s.
$ • 8 in (20 cm) wide

You may also like… Fashion Accessories, see pp. 300–01

Shoes

Shoes are not just about fashion—they are culturally interesting and historic items that offer a perspective on customs and craft, often illustrating a design lineage that weaves through the centuries.

Shoes are frequently regarded as art forms and objects of veneration, and models by big-name designers such as Manolo Blahnik or Jimmy Choo have become cultural icons—every girl's dream, and with price tags to match.

Like couture clothing designs, most people wear shoes that are influenced by the giants of fashion, but in a world where even secondhand Nike athletic shoes can sell for hundreds of dollars, it can be difficult to define the collecting of shoes.

Generally, shoe buyers or collectors wear their purchases. Antique shoes are a different matter and are not a high profile collectible, but vintage shoes form a market fueled by passion and a sometimes unfathomable desire.

Vintage footwear can be found in secondhand stores and flea markets, consignment shops, and on the Internet. It's surprising how well a skilled cobbler can renovate and restore vintage shoes, but beware—this can be expensive.

Westwood Ho!

These precipitous "super-elevated Ghillie" platform shoes, by the original "Queen of Punk," Vivienne Westwood, were first shown at the Anglomania collection in 1993. They gained notoriety as the shoes from which Naomi Campbell fell while striding down the catwalk. The original "mock-croc" pair is now in the Victoria & Albert Museum.

"SUPER-ELEVATED" PLATFORM SHOES
A pair of red patent leather platforms designed by Vivienne Westwood.
$$$ • Heel 9 in (22.5 cm) high

TOP TIPS

- Search out shoes by important designers or those encapsulating a particular design period.
- Be careful not to crush shoes; they deform easily and are best stored on shoe "lasts" (wooden formers) or in their boxes. Avoid damp environments: mold grows easily on shoes that have been worn.

KEY FACTS	1898	1920s	1960	1978	1998
Footprints through time	Birth of Salvatore Ferragamo, the renowned shoemaker to high society and Hollywood stars.	The Flappers of the interwar years sport short skirts, short hair, and daring footwear and attitudes.	R. Griggs begins the manufacture of the famous Dr. Martens brand air cushioned sole, still in production.	Miuccia Prada takes over the family firm, expanding its repertoire to include luxury fashion items such as shoes.	*Sex and the City* hits TV screens, and shoe designer Manolo Blahnik becomes a pop culture icon.

What's Hot

DIAMANTÉ STILETTOS
A pair of 1950 diamanté sandals with Lucite heels.
$$ • 9¾ in (25 cm) long

CARVED HEEL SHOES
These hand-embroidered shoes have an unusual heel.
$$ • 11 in (28 cm) long

Look out for:

Trends in fashion often revisit earlier epochs, and 1970s style has become very prominent at the shopping mall and on the catwalk. Shoes by famous designers of the era, such as Terry de Havilland, are highly desirable and are even being reproduced.

Core Collectibles

EMBROIDERED SANDALS
A pair of handpainted and embroidered sandals with stiletto heels.
$$ • 9¾ in (25 cm) long

SLINGBACK STILETTOS
These plastic Guildmark stilettos have faux leather and faux pearl decoration.
$ • 9½ in (24 cm) long

High wooden platforms characteristic of Glam Rock era

PLATFORM SANDALS
A pair of 1970s sandals with wooden platforms and plastic uppers decorated with cherries.
$$ • 11 in (28 cm) long

Starter Buys

STRAW MULES
A pair of straw mules from the 1950s. These dainty shoes have been embroidered with small silver and white beads, on both uppers and heels.
$$ • 9½ in (24 cm) long

EDWARDIAN LEATHER SHOES
A pair of Edwardian glacé-finished kid leather shoes with eyelet and ribbon made by Lord and Taylor of New York.
$$$ • 9¾ in (25 cm) long

PANDORA DEVORÉ SHOES
This pair of lilac Pandora shoes dates from the 1950s.
$$ • 9¾ in (25 cm) long

SUEDE STILETTOS
These asymmetrical stilettos were made by Herbert Levine.
$$ • 11 in (28 cm long

LEATHER STILETTOS
Made in the 1950s, these have a patented "springalator."
$$ • 9½ in (24 cm) long

1970S PUMPS
A pair of Clarks "Intrigue Skyline" lace pumps.
$ • 9¾ in (25 cm) long

You may also like… Hats & Headscarves, pp. 290–91

Handbags & Purses

Fashion gurus say that accessorizing is the key to looking good, but discerning buyers understand that increasingly collectible vintage or designer handbags and purses are much more than mere accessories.

The handbag or purse is one of the most expensive accessories a woman is likely to buy. There are many cheaper bags available, but for serious collectors there are those that are venerated in the fashion world as cultural icons. The Hermès Kelly bag was made iconic by Grace Kelly in the mid-1950s when she appeared carrying it in *Life* magazine. The Birkin, codesigned by Jane Birkin, is an Hermès bag with similar status. Chanel's double "C" logo graces many a classic. These bags cost thousands of dollars each and have long waiting lists.

However, it's not all about designers. There is a strong market for American pre- and postwar novelty bags, evening purses, and clutches made from materials including plastics and wicker. Edwardian celluloid bags have continued to gain in value, particularly the strong Art Deco and Art Nouveau designs. Beaded and petit-point bags have been popular since the early 19th century and the intricate work is still reflected in prices paid by collectors today.

Doggy Bag
This bag is decorated with appliquéd sequins in a poodle design and dates from the mid- to late 1960s. It was originally sold as a craft kit, and would have been hand-decorated by the purchaser. Although many examples were sold, the poodle design is among the most popular and commands higher prices. Other popular materials used to make bags during this period were raffia and wood. Decorations were lavish and could also be made of beads or shells.

POODLE BAG
A mid- to late-1960s poodle sequin bag, sold as a craft kit for the purchaser to complete.
$$ • 10½ in (26.5 cm) high

KEY FACTS	1920s	1955	1956	1960s	1981–84
20th-century handbags	Celluloid bags with detail in materials such as mother-of-pearl and enamel come into fashion.	Chanel introduces the classic quilted 2.55 bag named after its introduction in February 1955.	Grace Kelly appears in a copy of *Life* magazine carrying an Hermès bag; it has borne her name ever since.	Genuine reptile and silk handbags become popular; Givenchy, Chanel, and Pucci are favored designers.	A new Hermès bag is named after actress Jane Birkin. Today these can command $20,000 and up.

What's Hot

TELEPHONE HANDBAG
This 1940s example was made as a VIP gift for residents of the Hôtel Ritz in Paris.

$$$$ • 8¼ in (21 cm) high

WICKER PARASOL PURSE
A rare American wicker parasol purse with no maker's mark, dating from 1955.

$$$ • 25¼ in (64 cm) high

Look out for:
Emilio Pucci is one of the most distinctive and highly sought-after designers of the 20th century. His bold and brilliant designs stormed the catwalks of the '60s and '70s, and are still worn by celebrities such as Madonna. He invented Capri pants and even designed a car for Ford.

Chunky handles

BEADED POODLE PURSE
Dating from 1955, this is a very rare American Walborg beaded poodle purse.

$$$$ • 13½ in (34 cm) high

PUCCI HANDBAG
From the 1950s or '60s, this Pucci handbag is made of black, purple, and blue swirled velour fabric. It has a leather interior, and is accented with gold-tone handles and a gold-tone clasp.

$$ • 7½ in (19 cm) wide

TORTOISESHELL BAG
Rare and highly sought-after, this 1950s Lucite oblong bag with filigree edging is by Tyrolean NY.

$$ • 7¾ in (19.5 cm) wide

LUCITE BEEHIVE HANDBAG
This 1950s American beehive bag in ribbed and pearlized white Lucite is inset with gold-plated bee motifs.

$$$ • 5½ in (14 cm) high

What's Not

The common bag shapes of the 1950s and '60s, which were usually rectangular in style and made for the mass market in black vinyl with poorer quality mounts, have low resale value. With few redeeming features, they tend to be associated with an older generation.

THREE-WAY CONVERTIBLE BAG
A three-way convertible bag from the 1950s with a detachable reversible cover. This has cream and gold on one side and black on the other.

$ • 9 in (23 cm) wide

Core Collectibles

PLAYING CARDS HANDBAG

This 1940s playing cards handbag is made of black buckskin and has gold club, spade, heart, and diamond motifs and an ivory dice clasp. It was made in the 1940s by the Parisian designer Anne-Marie.

$$$ • 11½ in (29 cm) wide

BLACK ALLIGATOR BAG

An unmarked 1950s American black alligator bag with a gold-tone clasp and fastening.

$$ • 12 in (31 cm) high

VANITY HANDBAG

This hard-cased vanity handbag in pearlized white dates from the 1950s.

$$ • 6½ in (16.5 cm) wide

WOODEN OCTAGONAL HANDBAG

With butterfly and floral decoupage and a Lucite handle, this octagonal handbag is made of wood. It has a gold-tone clasp and feet, and dates from the 1960s or '70s.

$$ • 7 in (18 cm) wide

Ask the Expert

Q. Are plastic handbags worth collecting?
A. It depends on the quality. Rigid plastic bags were first made in the 1940s, and those made in New York, and in novelty shapes, are highly desirable. Always check the material for nicks and crazing, as these are signs of degradation that will affect value.

Q. A vintage Chanel leather handbag has been kept in its protective material bag, which has now stuck to it. It has left white fluff adhering to the leather. Can the bag be cleaned?
A. It sounds as though you may have kept your bag in a damp or humid environment. It's best to give it to a professional to restore it.

Q. Can I risk using my vintage Gucci clutch bag?
A. Part of the fun of collecting vintage fashion is using a piece every once in a while. Just make sure you take good care of it!

Resin handles in good condition

HARD-CASED RESIN BAG
This resin bag with interior compartments was produced in the 1950s.
$$ • *6½ in (16.5 cm) wide*

JOLLES HANDBAG
This 1950s Jolles bag has a black velvet body and a feather owl with glass bead eyes.
$$ • 17 in (43.5 cm) high

PLEATED EVENING BAG
A 1930s pleated black silk bag with a carnelian-, onyx-, and marcasite-studded frame.
$$$ • 8¾ in (22.5 cm) wide

PLASTIC BOX BAG
Made of mottled plastic, this gray bag has a circular handle, moiré silk lining, and pockets.
$$ • 9½ in (24 cm) high

BASKET-SHAPED HANDBAG
This Lucite bag from the 1950s is shaped like a basket with a wavy ruff and gold filigree detailing. A superior type of plastic, Lucite can be manufactured in opaque or translucent colors.
$$$ • 13 in (33 cm) high

TAPESTRY BAG
Probably made in the 1920s, this tapestry petit-point bag has an enamel clasp.
$$ • 9½ in (24 cm) wide

1950S LUCITE BAG
A red Lucite handbag with a bronze flowered opening clasp from the 1950s.
$$$ • 8½ in (21.5 cm) wide

YELLOW LUCITE HANDBAG
In the 1950s, Lucite bags were all the rage and were sold in upscale department stores. This fine period piece comes in a desirable yellow color, with a clear Lucite top.
$$ • 9¼ in (23.5 cm) wide

DIAMANTÉ EVENING BAG
A silk bag with diamanté detailing and a black Bakelite frame and clasp, c. 1930.
$$ • 8 in (20.5 cm) long

Core Collectibles

COMPACT EVENING BAG
This 1930s compact evening bag has a gold mesh wrist strap. It is in fine condition.

$$ • 5 in (12.7 cm) wide

CASKET HANDBAG
A 1950s handbag with a black Lucite body and an abstract gold-on-black decoration.

$$ • 6¾ in (17 cm) long

EMBROIDERED BAG
A 1950s embroidered bag highlighted with applied varicolored glass beads.

$$ • 12½ in (32 cm) wide

SILK DUFFEL HANDBAG
This American silk "duffel" handbag has a striped pattern with embroidered flowers and an ivorine frame with a carved ivorine clasp of an Asian figure. It dates from the early 1930s.

$$$ • 8 in (20.5 cm) wide at base

HAND-DECORATED BAG
Hand-decorated, this 1950s bag with a Bakelite handle is by Soure NY.

$$ • 13¾ in (35 cm) wide

CONFETTI BAG
This transparent 1950s bag could be lined with material to match a woman's outfit.

$$ • 9½ in (24 cm) wide

1930S SUEDE CLUTCH
Made of black suede, this early-1930s French clutch has a Paisley-pattern frame, a white and beige glass bead trim, and a small Paisley-print enamel cameo.

$$$ • 13½ in (34 cm) wide at base

GUILD CREATIONS FELT BAG
A 1950s bag with a cathedral-type frame and a clasp with multicolored stones.

$$ • 11 in (28 cm) wide

SPLIT OAK BAG
An unusual split oak bag with a jeweled lid, by Jolles NY.
$$ • 7½ in (19 cm) diameter

BASKETWORK FROG HANDBAG
This American handbag, a popular, frivolous piece, dates from the late 1950s.
$$$ • 14¼ in (36 cm) long

TOP TIPS

- Be very careful when buying online—a high percentage of designer bags offered for sale are fake.
- Check the condition of a bag carefully—some materials, such as Lucite, cannot successfully be repaired if badly cracked.
- Keep an eye out for pieces by designers such as Lulu Guinness, as they are likely to gain ground in years to come.
- Be aware that some bags and purses are made from materials that are banned from import into the US and Canada. This includes crocodile skin.

Starter Buys

WOVEN BASKET
Colorful felt fruit baskets are attached to this 1950s white woven basket.
$$ • 8½ in (22 cm) wide

WICKERWORK HANDBAG
Made in Hong Kong, this bag has a gold-plated rope handle and dates from the 1950s–60s.
$$ • 15 in (38 cm) wide

SATIN CLUTCH BAG
This 1930s olive green clutch decorated with beadwork was made in France for Coblentz.
$$ • 7½ in (19 cm) long

CARON OF TEXAS BAG
Hand-decorated with beaded butterflies, costume jewels, and gold embroidery, this bag is made by the famed American handbag designer Caron of Houston, Texas.
$$ • 11½ in (29 cm) high

WOVEN TOTE BAG
This cotton pink, purple, and orange psychedelic tote bag is from the 1970s.
$ • 13 in (33 cm) high

You may also like… Hats & Headscarves, see pp. 290–91

Fashion Accessories

Accessories encompass a broad category that attracts true collectors and fashionistas alike—whether it's a compact, a pair of sunglasses, or a belt, vintage pieces can be original additions to any wardrobe or collection.

Cosmetics-related items have remained strong in recent years. The Internet continues to provide a platform for lower-value but readily collected items. Compacts and scent bottles are collected worldwide, but vintage sunglasses are rarely expensive and are generally good buys. As with all genres, there are degrees, and a solid gold Cartier compact will find a different market from its poorer mass-produced cousin, just as a pair of

Courrèges sunglasses will be more likely to find a collector than an everyday wearer. This is the nature of the antiques and collectors market.

Secondhand stores are one place to start looking, but nowadays good items seem to be spread more thinly. Certain shops or neighborhoods have always had a reputation for supplying collectors; investigate the "scene" in big cities to find out where such specialists congregate.

Crafty Eyewear

These folding silver spectacles date from the early 19th century, during the reign of George III. The looped terminals could be used to attach a string or safety chain. This pair has a particularly fine tortoiseshell case with a silver inlaid cartouche for engraving the owner's name or initials. These were not a poor man's accessory: the silver and the quality of the case denote them as having belonged to a gentleman.

TOP TIPS
• Look for the quirky and original. A 1950s tiepin in the shape of a rocket will always be more collectible than the more traditional riding crop shape.
• Try not to accumulate too many mediocre items. Be prepared to pay a little extra to gain more in the long run.
• Negotiate with traders—a deal can always be struck!

FOLDING SPECTACLES
This pair of silver spectacles with a tortoiseshell case was made by F. Hedley, Richmond.
$$ • Case 5 in (12.7 cm) long

KEY FACTS	1804	1909	1920s	1960s	1964
Fashionable additions	Napoleon promotes the French economy by barring ladies from wearing the same outfit twice at court.	Famous Parisian jeweler and watchmaker Cartier establishes its first branch in New York.	Flapper girls dominate the interwar years' fashions, and elegant powder compacts become all the rage.	First Lady Jackie Kennedy creates an entire eyewear culture with her oversized sunglasses.	The first Biba store opens in London, its young fashions always sold with matching accessories.

What's Hot

CARTIER COMPACT
Designed by Cartier, this gold and black Art Deco compact has a silver clasp.
$$$$ • 2½ in (6.5 cm) wide

SILVER COMPACT
A Norwegian silver compact with purple flowers and gold detail, dating from c. 1920.
$$$ • 2½ in (6.5 cm) diameter

Look out for:

Soir de Paris, also known as Evening in Paris, is perhaps one of the best-known scents of the 20th century. Introduced in the late 1920s, it became a dime-store favorite in the United States.

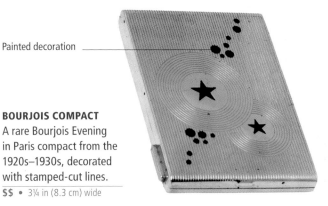

Painted decoration

BOURJOIS COMPACT
A rare Bourjois Evening in Paris compact from the 1920s–1930s, decorated with stamped-cut lines.
$$ • 3¼ in (8.3 cm) wide

Core Collectibles

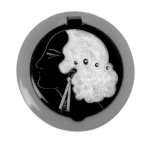

POWDER PUFF COMPACT
René Lalique designed this powder compact for the French perfumier Coty, c. 1930.
$ • 2 in (5 cm) diameter

BAKELITE COMPACT
This Bakelite Art Deco compact is decorated with a woman's profile, c. 1930.
$$ • 3¼ in (8.3 cm) diameter

MUSICAL COMPACT
A 1950s "Kissing Couples" musical compact with lipstick compartment, by Thorens.
$$ • 4 in (10 cm) wide

LOVEBIRD COMPACT
Dating from c. 1925, this French Art Deco compact features a lovebird motif.
$$ • 3 in (7.5 cm) wide

Starter Buys

CAT'S-EYE SPECTACLES
Laminated spectacles with metal and rhinestone inserts.
$ • 5½ in (14 cm) wide

ART DECO COMPACT
This green and silver Art Deco compact dates from c. 1930.
$$ • 3 in (7.5 cm) diameter

ANSICO COMPACT
This 1950s compact has a mother-of-pearl cover.
$ • 2 in (5 cm) wide

BIBA CONTAINERS
A set of cosmetics containers from cult brand Biba, 1970.
$ • Larger approx. 3½ in (9 cm) wide

You may also like… Shoes, see pp. 292–93

Cie Gle TRANSATLANTIQUE
French Line
Cie Gle TRANSATLANTIQUE
NORMANDIE
COUPE LONGITUDINALE
DU PAQUEBOT
NORMANDIE
79.280 Tonneaux

CHAPTER

Entertainment, Sports & Travel

The Wonderful World of Entertainment

Life is full of heroes and villains, and our desire to come close to these people is manifested in the amazing array of objects featured in this chapter. These form some of the most popular fields in current collecting.

In many respects, the subjects covered in this category are often closely interlinked, covering glamour and achievement, to name just two. The cult of celebrity easily crosses from one category to another—be they famous race car drivers, female aviators, glamorous movie stars, intrepid explorers, or record-breaking athletes, the possession of artifacts or memorabilia provides a tangible link for the collector. An autograph, a trophy, or a piece of clothing can bring a person or an event to life. The intensity of that "connection" can be hard to describe in words, but it is often manifested as a desire to

Snow White figurine, 1950s, see Core Collectibles, p. 323.

Talking Dalek, with original box, see What's Hot, p. 329.

collect. Of course, the market has many facets, and personally associated items are often more expensive. However, there is a whole gamut of other material that provides a wide choice for anyone with an interest in collecting. Sensitive objects such as a lifebelt from the *Lusitania* or a small piece of a metal strut from the *Hindenburg* have an inherent poignancy that is valued by collectors. Recent record results for items from the *Titanic* prove the strength of this market. This is the nature of collecting and the historical relationship between politics, technology, natural disaster, and tragic loss of life continue to fascinate many.

The motivation to buy in any one area can be driven by countless variables—a sense of nostalgia, childhood memories of steam travel, a favorite television program, or the effect of a ground-breaking cinematic first, such as *Star Wars*. New movies over the decades draw in new generations of fans and then collectors.

Many of us seek out memorabilia from the formative events or defining moments in both our own and others' lives—the market continues to grow very strongly in these areas. Collectors who grew up in the 1960s in the heyday of pop music may be interested in focusing on groups such as the Beatles, who have left a wealth of collectible items behind them. This includes not just the instruments they played, but literally tons of merchandising items, album covers, concert tickets, fanzines, and posters. Other stars, such as the Rolling Stones and Elvis Presley, have also left rich trails of collectibles.

Disney movies have been top of their field for several decades, and they leave a vast range of collectible promotional products, such as posters, lunchboxes, and pencil cases in their wake for those who hold fond childhood memories of Snow White or, of course, Mickey Mouse.

The Beatles *Yellow Submarine* quad poster, see Core Collectibles, p. 308.

Francis Rossi's Flying V guitar, see Core Collectibles, p. 313.

Soccer ball autographed by Pelé, see Core Collectibles, p. 339.

The Beatles

Memorabilia connected with the Fab Four is among the hottest in the music collecting market, with many longstanding fans willing to pay large sums for rare or unusual pieces of Beatles history.

The Beatles are by far the most popular band for collectors, and prices at auction can exceed $200,000 for the Beatles' hand-written lyrics, musical instruments, and automobiles.

There are several reasons for this exceptional interest. The Beatles were without doubt the most popular band of the 20th century, and many of the baby boomer generation who grew up with the Beatles are now in a financial position to pay considerable sums to acquire major items of music memorabilia. Photographs signed by all four members of the band are highly prized, as are original sealed albums, while many of the early concert posters and flyers command a premium. Even a signed Pan Am in-flight menu fetched almost $20,000 at a Christie's auction in 2003.

Beatlemania left in its wake an avalanche of merchandise, movie posters, concert tickets, signatures, and personal effects. So even in a market that is continually rising, there is plenty to buy.

A Show to Remember

In 1963, the Beatles toured Europe with American rock 'n' roll star Roy Orbison, who had enjoyed a string of hits on both sides of the Atlantic. The Beatles were as yet unknown in America and it was Orbison who encouraged them to visit the States. He became lifelong friends with the band, especially John Lennon and George Harrison, with whom he later recorded in the Traveling Wilburys.

TICKET STUB
A rare concert ticket stub for the Beatles and Roy Orbison show in Ipswich in May 1963. The ticket cost just eight shillings and sixpence (about $1.50); the stub is worth 20 times that today.

$$ • 3 in (8 cm) high

KEY FACTS	1962	1964	1967	1969	1970
The Beatles' wonder years	The Beatles' first single, "Love Me Do," is released. It eventually reaches No. 17 in the UK and No. 1 in the US.	The Beatles' first movie, *A Hard Day's Night*, opens. The band enjoys superstardom in America.	Brian Epstein dies, Apple Corps is born, and *Sgt. Pepper's Lonely Hearts Club Band* changes the face of pop history.	John marries Yoko, Paul marries Linda, and bickering between the band members begins to take its toll.	The Beatles release two more albums and shock fans worldwide by announcing their breakup.

What's Hot

LENNON'S TOBACCO BOX
This 1960s tobacco box has a leather-covered barrel with metal lining and gilt-metal hookah pipe handles.
$$$$$ • 10 in (25.5 cm) high

MCCARTNEY'S DRUM
A tom-tom drum owned by the teenage Paul McCartney. This drum formed part of the first kit used by the Beatles.
$$$$ • 12 in (30.5 cm) in diameter

"SGT. PEPPER'S LONELY HEARTS CLUB BAND" ALBUM COVER
This album cover was created using a total of 62 photographic enlargements of people the Beatles admired as a backdrop to the band, who were dressed in bright military-style outfits.
$ • 12 x 12 in (30 x 30 cm)

LENNON'S GUITAR STRAP
Used by John Lennon, this embroidered cloth guitar strap is signed on the inside with the words, "To Tex Love Jock Lennon Thanks for the Memories."
$$$$ • Approx. 87 in (144 cm) long

Look out for:
Here are all the hallmarks of a great piece of music memorabilia: clear, early, and original signatures from members of the world's leading pop group, and in good condition. A dedication can reduce the value, unless, in this case, your name happens to be Carol.

Dedication

Clear signatures

LENNON MANUSCRIPT
Hand-written by John Lennon, this is a lyric manuscript for "All You Need is Love." It comprises 12 lines in black ink written during the *Our World* satellite broadcast on June 25, 1967, together with a letter of authenticity from the woman who attended the performance.
$$$$$ • Approx. 9¾ in (25 cm) high

ORIGINAL BEATLES' AUTOGRAPHS
A promotional postcard from the Star Club, Hamburg, with a rare and early set of the Beatles' signatures, dated 1962.
$$$$$ • Approx. 4 in (10 cm) high

Core Collectibles

BEATLES PHOTOS
Two unpublished photographs of the Beatles at Zurich airport, June 7, 1964.

$$ • 9½ in (24 cm) wide

ODEON THEATRE HANDBILL
Featuring the Beatles in their trademark mop-tops, this Welsh flyer dates from 1963.

$$$ • 10¼ in (26 cm) high

"YELLOW SUBMARINE" POSTER
A 1968 UK quad teaser poster for the animated film *Yellow Submarine*, starring the Fab Four. The innovative movie, released in July 1968, incorporated the varied graphic styles of the era.

$$$$ • 40 in (101.5 cm) wide

SHOW PROGRAM
The program for *Another Beatles Christmas Show* 1964/65 at the Hammersmith Odeon, together with the original ticket stub for a second performance on Friday, January 8, 1965. The drawings are by John Lennon.

$$ • 11¾ in (30 cm) high

AUTOGRAPH BOOK
This autograph book from the year 1967 has been signed by Paul McCartney, "John F. Lennon," "George O'Harrison," and Ringo Starr (by Harrison), as well as Nat Jackley and Peter Noone.

$$$$ • 4¼ in (11 cm) wide

Ask the Expert

Q. Is memorabilia relating to one of the Beatles more desirable than that of another band member?
A. Memorabilia relating to John Lennon nearly always commands a higher price.

Silver-colored, damaged cover

SHOW PROGRAM
A program for "The Beatles Show" with a poor cover but good contents.

$ • *Approx. 11¾ in (30 cm) high*

Q. Is condition an important factor when buying Beatles memorabilia?
A. Condition always has a marked effect on the value of music memorabilia. The program (at left) has a badly damaged cover, so is worth perhaps a quarter of what one in good condition would fetch.

Q. How can I tell an original signature from one done by facsimile printing?
A. One tip is that facsimiles are often printed in the same color, underneath the glaze. Hold at an angle to the light to check.

PRESS KIT

A 1963 press kit with a laminated cover, including a review of "Love Me Do."

$$$ • Approx. 11¾ in (30 cm) high

RICHARD AVEDON POSTERS

Two posters from a set of four by acclaimed American photographer Richard Avedon from a 1967 issue of the German magazine *Stern*.

$$$ • Approx. 12½ in (32 cm) high

LENNON'S HOOKAH PIPE

John Lennon owned this hookah pipe in the late 1960s.

$$$$$ • 10 in (25.5 cm) long

ORIGINAL LP

Introducing the Beatles was the first album to be released in the US, on January 10, 1964.

$$$ • 11¾ in (30 cm) high

CAMPAIGN BOOK

This five-page "Let it be" exhibitors' campaign book is from United Artists.

$$ • 12½ in (32 cm) high

"THE BEATLES BOOK MONTHLY"

A complete set of the original 77 issues of *The Beatles Book Monthly* magazines dating from 1963 to 1969. These original editions were republished between 1977 and 1983.

$$$ • 8 in (20 cm) high

Starter Buys

"SUBMARINE" LUNCHBOX

A 1968 *Yellow Submarine* metal lunchbox and matching thermos flask.

$$$ • 8½ in (22 cm) wide

"BEATLES FOR SALE"

This 1964 *Beatles for Sale* promo flat features the front cover of the mono album.

$$ • 12 in (31 cm) wide

"BIG 6" GUITAR

Manufactured in the 1960s by Selcol (UK), this "Big 6" six-string toy guitar bears facsimile autographs and a sticker of the group on the plastic body.

$$ • 31¾ in (80.5 cm) high

You may also like… Rock & Pop Memorabilia, see pp. 310–15

Rock & Pop Memorabilia

The market for rock and pop memorabilia has taken off over the past 30 years as new enthusiasts seek out reminders of their childhood. Almost any item connected with a well-known star is collectible.

Although the Beatles are the premier band for collectors, there are many more groups and individual pop and rock stars whose memorabilia is avidly collected by enthusiasts. These include greats such as Elvis Presley, Jimi Hendrix, the Rolling Stones, the Who, the Sex Pistols, the Grateful Dead, Bob Dylan, and Eric Clapton. These stars' effects can command extremely high prices at auction. There are also many hundreds of fan clubs that support the collecting of souvenirs of lesser-known groups and individual acts, all of which can easily be found on the Internet.

Although memorabilia can often be sourced from specialist dealers and auction houses, there is nothing better than obtaining a signed photograph directly from the group or individual when attending a concert. In general, it is better to acquire signatures on an album cover or photograph in ink, avoiding felt-tip that can fade and become illegible over time.

JIMI HENDRIX'S STRATOCASTER
A left-handed sunburst Fender Stratocaster (serial number L-38705) used by Jimi Hendrix. This guitar comes in its original hard case, with a hand-written letter of authenticity, dated 1986, from a sound engineer at Hendrix's Electric Lady Studios in New York.

$$$$$ • Scale 25½ in (64.8 cm) long

Electric Performances

The Fender Stratocaster guitar, often called a "Strat," was designed in 1954 and, having been played by some of the world's best-known guitarists, can be heard on many historic recordings. In the early 1960s it was championed by Hank Marvin of The Shadows and in the '70s it was strummed by the likes of David Gilmour of Pink Floyd, Eric Clapton, and Mark Knopfler. Strats are highly collectible, especially if they have been played by a rock legend.

KEY FACTS	1954	1970	1972	1975	1978
Moments in music history	Elvis Presley, a 19-year-old truck driver, records "That's All Right, Mama" at Sun Studios in Memphis.	Jimi Hendrix dies in London. One of his Stratocasters later fetches $168,000 at auction in 2006.	David Bowie creates Ziggy Stardust, the first of his many exotic personae; glam rock is well and truly launched.	Bob Marley becomes an international reggae star after his first hit with the Wailers, "No Woman, No Cry."	Dire Straits goes multi-platinum with their first album, promoting a more stripped-down rock sound.

What's Hot

LOCK OF ELVIS'S HAIR
The lock of hair is mounted alongside a photograph of Elvis getting his army haircut.

$$$$ • 9½ in (24 cm) high

SEX PISTOLS FLAG
Owned by Steve Jones, this "God Save the Queen" Sex Pistols flag was used in many Pistols gigs and also featured in the movie about the band, *The Great Rock 'n' Roll Swindle*.

$$$$$ • Approx. 48 in (122 cm) wide

Look out for:
Led Zeppelin's December 2007 sellout concert in London proved that the rock band still has a huge following. This poster would make a fabulous addition to the collection of anyone who attended the August 11, 1979 show.

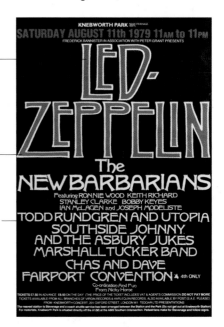

Red and white print on black

Striking typography

Lists support acts

LED ZEPPELIN CONCERT POSTER
This promotional poster is for an all-day concert at Knebworth Park headlined by Led Zeppelin on Saturday, August 11, 1979.

$$ • 26 in (66 cm) high

What's Not

While rare Presley items command a premium, pictures of "the King" were produced by the millions and are only of interest to die-hard fans.

KEITH RICHARDS' GUITAR
A 1957 sunburst-finish Gibson ES350T semiacoustic guitar used by Keith Richards.

$$$$$ • 17 in (43 cm) wide

JIMI HENDRIX RECORDS
This is a unique collection of nine Reprise Record acetates featuring Jimi Hendrix.

$$$$$ • Each 10 in (25.4 cm) wide

ELVIS PHOTOGRAPH
A clip-framed picture of Elvis taken early on in his journey to meteoric success.

$ • Approx. 11¾ in (30 cm) high

311

Core Collectibles

ELTON JOHN POSTER
This March 1973 Elton John UK concert poster is a rare original silkscreen poster for gigs at Leeds University Union, in blue and fluorescent print on white ground. It is in excellent condition.

$$ • 28 in (71 cm) high

JACK BRUCE'S SPEAKER CABINET
A Marshall 4x12 angle-fronted speaker cabinet, model 1960A, used by Cream band member Jack Bruce. It is accompanied by a letter confirming its provenance, c. 1967–68.

$$$$ • 11¾ in (30 cm) high

ELTON JOHN JACKET
Part of an original collection of Elton John promotional items belonging to Phonogram Records, this pale blue casual tour jacket has "Elton Live" and an outline of Australia embroidered on the front.

$$ • Approx. 45 in (114 cm) wide

JIMI HENDRIX'S SUEDE VEST
This brown handmade suede vest with eyelet decoration was possibly made by Omar's of the Village, NYC, and given to Jimi Hendrix by Steve Paul, a club owner.

$$$$ • Approx. 42 in (107 cm) wide

LED ZEPPELIN POSTER
A Led Zeppelin "Tour over Europe 1980" poster that lists European venues, printed in red, white, and black. The poster is framed and glazed.

$$ • 26 in (66 cm) high

MONSTERS OF ROCK POSTER
Listing rock legends AC/DC, Van Halen, and Ozzy Osbourne, this poster publicizes the August 18, 1984, Monsters of Rock festival.

$$ • 59 in (150 cm) high

ELTON JOHN JUKEBOX
Once owned by Elton John, this is a miniature Wurlitzer 1015 jukebox complete with micro cassettes. It comes in its original box.

$$ • Box 13 in (33 cm) high

JIMI HENDRIX ALBUM COVER
The album cover for *Are You Experienced* by the Jimi Hendrix Experience, signed by Jimi Hendrix, Noel Redding, and Mitch Mitchell.

$$$$ • 11¾ in (30 cm) wide

GRAND OLE OPRY SIGNED ACOUSTIC GUITAR
This blonde Gibson SJ20AN guitar was signed by various country & western artists, including Shania Twain and the Dixie Chicks, at the Grand Ole Opry, Nashville, Tennessee, in 1999.
$$$$$ • Scale 25½ in (64.8 cm) long

ROGER MCGUINN'S REGAL GUITAR
A 12-string Regal spruce-top acoustic guitar, owned by Roger McGuinn, lead singer of the Byrds, together with a letter of authenticity from country music star Hoyt Axton, dated c. 1957.
$$$ • Scale 24¾ in (63 cm) long

FRANCIS ROSSI'S FLYING V GUITAR
Status Quo's Francis Rossi used this Gibson Flying V guitar, serial number 550953.
$$$$ • Scale 24¾ in (63 cm) long

ALEXIS KORNER'S GUITAR
Owned and much used by pioneering blues musician Alexis Korner, this hand-built acoustic guitar dates from the 1950s. It is accompanied in its hard case by a photograph of Korner playing the guitar with a young Mick Jagger as the front man, Dick Heckstall Smith on saxophone, Jack Bruce on double bass, and Cyril Davis on harmonica.
$$$$ • Scale approx. 24¾ in (63 cm) long

DIRE STRAITS SALES AWARD
The Dire Straits multi-album "Pinball" presentation sales award from 1989.
$$ • 37 x 29 in (94 x 74 cm)

Ask the Expert

Q. Is there a current group whose memorabilia will increase in value in the future?
A. Forecasting who will be famous and venerated in the future is an impossible task. Collect the group you are most passionate about and enjoy the material rather than worrying about making an investment.

Q. There are many prints and photographs that are sold as limited editions. Are these worth buying?
A. Always check the number of the total edition. If this runs into the thousands then the edition is hardly limited. Check, too, whether the artist signed the print or photograph, as this will add to the value.

Visual record of the band in its prime

Stars' signatures

ABBA PHOTO
This color laser print of the Swedish supergroup at the height of their fame in the mid-70s is signed by all four members.
$$ • *Approx. 7¾ in (20 cm) high*

Core Collectibles

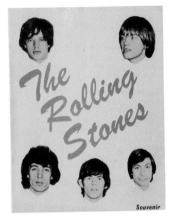

RONNIE WOODS PHOTOS
Two black-and-white photographs (only one shown) of Ronnie Woods, signed and doodled with a gold pen.

$$ • Approx. 15¾ in (40 cm) high

JOHN LENNON AND MICK JAGGER PHOTO
This photograph of John Lennon and Mick Jagger was taken by Michael Randolph during the filming of *The Rolling Stones Rock and Roll Circus* in 1968. The TV special was not screened at the time because the Stones were not happy with it.

$$ • 17¼ in (44 cm) wide

STONES PROGRAM
An original program for the Rolling Stones at Romford ABC Cinema, with two ticket stubs for the second performance.

$$ • Approx. 11¾ in (30 cm) high

PHILIP TOWNSEND PRINTS
Four limited-edition prints of the Rolling Stones taken by seminal '60s photographer Philip Townsend in early 1963. These are among the very first shots of the Stones.

$$$ • Largest 24 in (61 cm) high

ROLLING STONES PHOTOS
Black-and-white photographs showing Keith Richards and Mick Jagger backstage.

$$ • Each 24 in (61 cm) wide

Starter Buys

KYLIE PHOTO AND SINGLE
These items of Kylie Minogue memorabilia are accompanied by a certificate of authenticity.

$ • Single approx. 10 in (25 cm) wide

ABBA SOAP
A boxed bar of cassette tape-shaped soap from the 1970s.

$ • 4 in (10 cm) long

TOP TIPS

- Search for well-priced 1970s memorabilia, which is avidly collected because of its nostalgic appeal.
- Keep an eye out for items from the golden era of rock 'n' roll, as they are scarcer than those from later decades.
- Start your collection with posters relating to important concerts—they are among the most affordable pieces of rock and pop memorabilia, by comparison.
- Note that a simple signature on a sheet of paper is normally worth less than a signed document, photo, or letter.

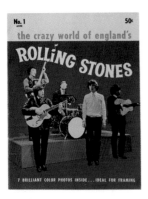

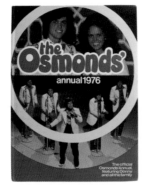

ROLLING STONES BOOKLET
This American souvenir program dates from 1964.

$ • Approx. 11¾ in (30 cm) high

CLIFF RICHARD PROGRAM
A late 1950s program for "Oh Boy! It's Cliff Richard."

$ • Approx. 11¾ in (30 cm) high

OSMONDS ANNUAL
Osbro Productions' 1976 annual starring the Osmonds.

$ • 10¾ in (27.3 cm) high

ELTON JOHN PROGRAM
From 1993, a concert program for Elton John's UK tour.

$ • Approx. 11¾ in (30 cm) high

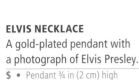

ELVIS NECKLACE
A gold-plated pendant with a photograph of Elvis Presley.

$ • Pendant ¾ in (2 cm) high

ELVIS COLOGNE
Elvis cologne authorized by the Presley estate, c. 1991.

$ • 2½ in (6.5 cm) high

You may also like… Cult TV, see pp. 330–33

Movie Posters

Movie posters were never intended to be sold to the public, yet today rare and original examples are in great demand. They are tangible souvenirs of favorite films and characters we fell in love with.

Printed in limited quantities for a single use in theaters screening the movie, the film poster had a sole purpose: advertising. In the 1930s, posters were relatively scarce because there were only a few movie theaters. For this reason, they are very rare and valuable today—a world record price of nearly $336,600 was paid in 2007 for the only known copy of Universal's 1935 *Bride of Frankenstein* poster.

As a general rule, the most popular and valuable posters are pre-1950s, with classics, horror, and science fiction genres leading the pack. But the market is constantly expanding as today's "new" buyers collect their nostalgia from the 1960s and '70s, and prices in some areas are still modest. The artwork itself is also an important consideration; artists such as Saul Bass, Anselmo Ballester, Roger Soubie, and Ercole Brini are names to look out for.

A Classic Bar None

"Casablanca" posters were created with varying imagery for publicity campaigns around the world. Posters made for Japan, Sweden, Yugoslavia, and Argentina are coveted for their slightly kitsch appeal, but it is a Belgian poster showing Bogart and Bergman cheek to cheek that is perhaps the most famous. Paper shortages and other restrictions during the war mean that posters of this era are now hard to come by.

GERMAN "CASABLANCA" POSTER
This is a German poster advertising the 1942 Oscar-winning classic. The film was eventually released in Germany in 1946 but the word "Nazi" was never spoken in the film and about 20 minutes of footage was cut.

$$$ • 34 in (86.5 cm) high

KEY FACTS	1939	1943	1947–48	1969	1978
Milestones in film history	*Gone with the Wind*, *The Wizard of Oz*, and *Wuthering Heights* are released during this notable year.	Initially a middle-of-the-road success, *Casablanca* rockets to stardom with three Academy Awards.	Britain imposes a 75 percent tax on Hollywood films: US studios boycott the British market.	Dennis Hopper's low-budget *Easy Rider* signals a new wave of independent film-making in Hollywood.	Controversial Vietnam-era films begin to appear, including *The Deer Hunter* and *Apocalypse Now*.

What's Hot

"GOLDFINGER"
The US poster of the third Bond film, *Goldfinger*, starring Sean Connery, 1965.
$$$ • 41 in (104 cm) high

"PSYCHO"
The US poster of Alfred Hitchcock's classic thriller movie, *Psycho*, 1960.
$$$$ • 41 in (104 cm) high

Look out for:
Very little original material relating to the *Harry Potter* series is available on the market, so a Daniel Radcliffe–signed poster becomes a desirable collectible.

Signature in blue ink

"HARRY POTTER" TEASER
This poster is a teaser for *Harry Potter and the Philosopher's Stone*, the first film in the popular series based on the books by J. K. Rowling. It is signed by its young star, Daniel Radcliffe, and is accompanied by a sheet of his own headed note paper.
$$ • 23 in (59 cm) high

"NOTORIOUS!"
A US poster of the 1946 horror and suspense film *Notorious!*, starring Cary Grant and Ingrid Bergman and directed by Alfred Hitchcock. Claude Rains was nominated for an Academy Award for best supporting actor.
$$$$ • 41 in (104 cm) high

SCI-FI POSTER
This is a US poster for *The Day the Earth Stood Still*, a black-and-white sci-fi movie produced in 1951 at the start of the Cold War and the time of the first atomic bombs. This movie strongly addressed issues of violence and politics.
$$$$$ • 41 in (104 cm) high

What's Not

An unremarkable poster design with Spanish text and cut-off borders make this movie poster less desirable.

"BUNNY LAKE" POSTER
A 1965 Spanish poster for the psychological thriller *Bunny Lake Is Missing*, now considered a cult classic.
$$ • 39 in (99 cm) high

Core Collectibles

"SOME LIKE IT HOT"
A rare US soundtrack poster of the 1959 comedy *Some Like It Hot* with Marilyn Monroe.
$$$ • 25 in (63.5 cm) high

"BLACK LAGOON" POSTER
A stone-lithographed 1954 Argentine poster of *Creature from the Black Lagoon*.
$$$$ • 43 in (109 cm) high

"GILDA"
A stone-lithographed poster of *Gilda* to accompany the film's 1946 Argentine release.
$$$$ • 43 in (109 cm) high

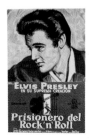

"JAILHOUSE ROCK"
This 1957 stone-lithographed poster was for the Argentine release of *Jailhouse Rock*.
$$$ • 43 in (109 cm) high

"THE ADVENTURES OF ROBIN HOOD"
A rereleased 1950s UK poster of the 1938 swashbuckler, *The Adventures of Robin Hood*. Reissue posters are still original movie posters, but are worth less than an original release.
$$$$ • 40 in (102 cm) high

Ask the Expert

Q. Is there a way of acquiring modern movie posters on a limited budget?
A. Make friends with the manager of your local movie theater. Posters used to promote a film are often thrown away after the run and rescuing them will ensure your collection grows without involving a large financial outlay.

"THE HAUNTED HOUSE OF HORROR"
A teaser for the 1960s British horror film.
$ • 43 in (109 cm) high

Q. Can crease marks on a movie poster be made less obvious before the poster is framed?
A. The best way to loosen crease marks is to have the poster professionally laid down on linen. Although quite costly, this preserves the paper and makes the poster look more attractive.

Folds can be a sign of authenticity

"LE MANS"
The 1971 US one-sheet poster for *Le Mans*, featuring the actual Le Mans rally in 1970.
$$$ • 41 in (104 cm) high

"IT'S A WONDERFUL LIFE"
A US one-sheet poster for the rerelease of the 1950s classic *It's a Wonderful Life*.
$$$$ • 41 in (104 cm) high

"CAPTAIN MARVEL"
An Argentine poster of the 1941 film serial *The Adventures of Captain Marvel*.
$$$ • 43 in (109 cm) high

"GLADIATOR"
This US one-sheet poster from 2000 has been signed by the actor Russell Crowe.
$$$ • 42 in (106 cm) high

"REBEL WITHOUT A CAUSE"
James Dean plays a rebellious teenager in this 1956 movie.
$$$$ • 41 in (104 cm) high

"SIDEWALKS OF NEW YORK"
An Australian one-sheet stone-lithographed poster.
$$$$ • 41 in (104 cm) high

"TRIPLE-O-SEVEN" POSTER
A triple-bill poster advertising three Bond movies: *Octopussy*, *For Your Eyes Only*, and *Thunderball*.
$$ • 30 in (75 cm) high

"HIGH NOON"
An Argentine poster of *High Noon*, the 1952 Western starring Gary Cooper.
$$$ • 43 in (109 cm) high

"AN AMERICAN IN PARIS"
A US poster for the 1951 musical *An American in Paris*, starring Gene Kelly.
$$$ • 41 in (104 cm) high

"EASY RIDER"
This striking example is the UK quad poster for the iconic road movie *Easy Rider*, released in 1969 and starring Peter Fonda and Dennis Hopper.
$$ • 30 in (76 cm) high

Core Collectibles

"THE MANCHURIAN CANDIDATE"
Based on the thriller by Richard Condon, *The Manchurian Candidate* was released in 1962.
$$$ • 30 in (76 cm) high

"AMERICAN GRAFFITI"
This is a 1973 UK quad poster for *American Graffiti*, the coming-of-age comedy drama directed by George Lucas.
$$$ • 30 in (76 cm) high

"CASINO"
A 1995 poster that has been autographed and framed.
$$$ • 46 in (116 cm) high

"BLADE RUNNER"
This 1982 US poster features artwork by John Alvin.
$$$ • 41 in (104 cm) high

"TERMINATOR"
This is a 1984 Czech poster of *The Terminator* starring Arnold Schwarzenegger.
$$ • 41 in (104 cm) high

INDIANA JONES POSTER
A US one-sheet poster for the first film in Steven Spielberg's Indiana Jones series.
$$ • 41 in (104 cm) high

"THE MAN WITH THE GOLDEN ARM"
Based on Nelson Algren's novel, *The Man with the Golden Arm* depicts the life of card shark and heroin addict Frankie (Frank Sinatra). This iconic 1954 poster was designed by Saul Bass.
$$$$ • 41 in (104 cm) high

"MY FAIR LADY"
This is a 1964 poster for the Italian release of *My Fair Lady*, with artwork by Nistri.
$$ • 28 x 13 in (71 x 33 cm)

"DIRTY HARRY"
A green and monochrome Australian poster for *Dirty Harry*, dated 1971.
$$ • 30 x 13 in (76 x 32 cm)

"TERROR" POSTER
This is a US poster for the 1958 science-fiction film *Terror from the Year 5000*.
$$$ • 41 x 27 in (104 x 69 cm)

Starter Buys

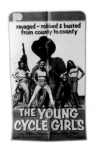

"NEVER SAY NEVER AGAIN"
This is a 1983 German one-sheet poster for the Bond film *Never Say Never Again*.
$ • 16 in (40.5 cm) high

"THE YOUNG CYCLE GIRLS"
Dated 1977, this *Young Cycle Girls* poster accompanied the US release.
$ • 16 in (40.5 cm) high

"FINDERS KEEPERS"
A framed 1966 poster of the film starring Cliff Richard and the Shadows.
$$ • 41 x 31 in (104 x 79 cm)

"CARRY ON" POSTER
This is a poster for *Carry On Round the Bend* (known in the UK as *Carry On at Your Convenience*), the first box office failure in the series.
$ • 41 x 27 in (104 x 69 cm)

"PULP FICTION"
A *Pulp Fiction* poster signed by stars John Travolta, Samuel L. Jackson, Tim Roth, Uma Thurman, Harvey Keitel, and Quentin Tarantino.
$$$ • 41 x 27 in (104 x 69 cm)

You may also like… Autographs, see pp. 192–95

Disneyana

Enduringly lovable characters and a broad, well-developed range of merchandise make the Walt Disney Company a fertile source of collectible items produced from the 1930s to the present day.

Disney collectibles commemorate some of the seminal moments in the development of modern entertainment. The most desirable items are original hand-drawn production celluloids (cels), on which character animations were drawn. Celluloid is extremely flammable and prone to decomposition, making originals from the earlier films hard to come by. Cels from the iconic cartoons *Snow White and the Seven Dwarfs* (1932), *Pinocchio* (1940), and *Dumbo* (1941) are especially valuable. A very few of these were personally signed by Walt

Disney to be given as gifts to friends and colleagues. These are exceptionally rare, and can command five-figure sums at auction.

More affordable are the posters, toys, and merchandise relating to films produced later in the 20th century. Crafty merchandising deals meant that many high-end items were produced in numbered limited editions, with a collecting market in mind. Such items continue to be manufactured on the release of each new Disney production, providing an easy starting point for a collection.

Perfect in Every Way

Front-of-house stills (or "lobby cards") are often collectible in their own right, and examples from Disney films doubly so. This complete set of 12 cards from the original 1964 release of "Mary Poppins" is an unusual and lovely item, recalling the golden age of live-action Disney films released in Walt Disney's last years.

FRONT-OF-HOUSE STILLS
One of a set of 12 original UK front-of-house stills from the 1964 live-action movie *Mary Poppins*.

$$ • 8 in (20 cm) high

TOP TIPS
• Look for Disney's copyright marks and details to help date pieces.
• Seek rare Disney-licensed merchandise produced especially for the European market.
• Steer away from computer-generated animation cels. Pricier hand-drawn cels are sure to hold their value, whereas computer-generated cels can be easily mass-produced.

KEY FACTS	1923	1928	1938	1950s	1989
Of mice (and dwarfs and mermaids) and men	Brothers Walt and Roy Disney found a small animation studio in California.	Mickey Mouse is born with the release of a short film called *Steamboat Willie*.	*Snow White and the Seven Dwarfs* is Disney's first full-length animated feature.	Disney branches into live-action films, starting with *Treasure Island* in 1950.	*The Little Mermaid* revives Disney's fortunes after Walt Disney's death in 1966.

What's Hot

SNOW WHITE BUTTON
A 1938 lithographed Snow White Jingle Club pin button on linen backing.
$ • 1½ in (3.5 cm) diameter

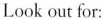

"BAMBI" POSTER
A 1942 stone-lithographed poster from the Argentine release of *Bambi*.
$$$$ • 43 in (109 cm) high

Look out for:
Vintage Mickey Mouse watches, first produced in 1933, are famously desirable. One example in mint condition recently sold for around $6,000.

Face prone to chips and scratches

Inset dial counts seconds

Core Collectibles

MICKEY MOUSE WATCH
Ingersoll Mickey Mouse watch with original strap. This one does not work, reducing its value.
$$$ • Face 1 in (2.5 cm) diameter

MICKEY MOUSE PIN
This 1960s Mickey Mouse pin, issued in the UK, features the "Yoo Hoo" catchphrase.
$$ • 3½ in (9 cm) diameter

SNOW WHITE FIGURE
This 1950s ceramic Snow White figurine is stamped "Walt Disney Prod, Japan."
$ • 7¼ in (18.4 cm) high

Starter Buys

CERAMIC FIGURES
These limited-edition musical figurines of Mickey and Minnie Mouse are by Schmid.
$$ • 14 in (36 cm) high

MICKEY AND MINNIE BARREL ORGAN
A 1940s Charbens and Salco diecast model of a barrel organ, with its original box and a musical mechanism.
$$ • 3½ in (9 cm) high

PRINTED LAMPSHADE
A Walt Disney lampshade from the 1950s.
$ • 8½ in (21.5 cm) high

MICKEY MOUSE FIGURE
This 1970s plastic figurine has poseable limbs.
$ • 7 in (17.8 cm) high

You may also like… Movie Posters, see pp. 316–21

Star Wars

The market for *Stars Wars* collectibles is insatiable, as both trilogies of movies continue to attract new generations of fans. This means that rarer, hard-to-find items are fetching increasingly high prices.

The scope of *Star Wars* collectibles is immense, spanning over 30 years and making it probably the largest single themed collecting field in existence.

The rarity of early items is largely thanks to the franchise's humble beginnings. The first film was conceived as a one-time novelty by studio executives and toy producers, and the original merchandise range was produced in small quantities. As the franchise grew, later ranges were produced in bulk,

and the so-called "expanded universe" of authorized books, games, and toys continues to provide a fertile area for collectors.

With the second trilogy of movies complete, it is uncertain whether the *Star Wars* market will continue to grow. However, the attraction of these collections is less their investment potential than their character, variety, and the thrilling universe of action and adventure that they evoke.

Designing the Future

Original dyeline concept drawings for the series are very rare. These four drawings of an X-Wing spacecraft by Joe Johnston are dated 1977, during the planning stages of the first movie. Concept drawings like these were used by George Lucas and Norman Reynolds to design models for filming, and these particular pages were shown during initial negotiations with Fox to drum up funding for the film. The top left page is signed by Johnston.

 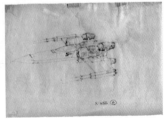

CONCEPT DRAWINGS
Four original hand-annotated dyeline concept drawings showing various elevations of an X-Wing and its interior.
$$$$ • Each sheet 18 in (46 cm) wide

KEY FACTS	1977	1977–85	1982	1995 onwards	1999–2005
"A galaxy far, far away… "	The first *Star Wars* movie is released, followed by sequels in 1980 and 1983.	The original action figures are produced by Kenner in the US and Palitoy in the UK.	The first *Star Wars* computer games are released, originally on the Atari 2600.	Kenner, now owned by Hasbro, restarts production of *Star Wars* toys.	The second trilogy of movies is released, attracting a new generation of fans.

What's Hot

"STAR WARS" POSTER
This poster was drawn by Drew Struzan and Charles White III for the second US release of *Star Wars* in the summer of 1978. It is very popular with collectors.

$$$ • 41 in (104 cm) high

YAK FACE FIGURE
A figure from the "Power of the Force" range, released in 1985. This version is packaged for sale in Canada, and comes with intact backing card and collector's coin.

$$$$ • Figure 3¾ in (9.5 cm) high

TATOOINE SKIFF
This *Return of the Jedi* Tatooine Skiff by Kenner is from the "Power of the Force" range, 1985. The back of the box demonstrates the toy's special features.

$$$ • Box 15½ in (39.5 cm) long

DEATH SQUAD COMMANDER
Action figures from the original *Star Wars* movie were released in the UK by Palitoy in 1978. This Death Squad Commander comes with all original packaging intact.

$$$ • Figure 3¾ in (9.5 cm) high

Look out for:
Star Wars figures were originally produced as toys, but as collecting fever caught on, many were bought for keeping rather than playing. Play-worn figures without original packaging are much less desirable than items like this one, in pristine condition with all packaging intact.

Card backing undamaged

Image not faded or torn

Plastic bubble free from dents

HAN SOLO FIGURE
Dated 1981, this action figure by Palitoy depicts Han Solo from *The Empire Strikes Back*, the second movie in the series.

$$ • Figure 3¾ in (9.5 cm) high

What's Not

This Imperial Biker Scout from *Return of the Jedi* is one of the more popular figures released in 1983, to tie in with the third *Star Wars* movie. However, it is still widely available, and examples like this one without their original packaging are not high in value.

IMPERIAL BIKER SCOUT
This Biker Scout action figure comes with a gun and has articulated joints.

$ • 3¾ in (9.5 cm) high

Core Collectibles

IMPERIAL AT-AT
The Empire Strikes Back model AT-AT ("All Terrain Armored Transport"), by Palitoy, 1980.
$$ • Box 18 in (45.5 cm) high

VINYL-CAPED JAWA
This red plastic figure was replaced by a cloth-caped toy soon after launch—very rare.
$$ • 2½ in (6.5 cm) high

CLOUD CITY PLAYSET
This 1980 *Empire Strikes Back* Cloud City playset by Kenner is sealed in its box.
$$$ • Box 12 in (30.5 cm) wide

RANCOR MONSTER
This *Return of the Jedi* Rancor monster has a moving jaw and limbs. The "tri-logo" range, with the film logo in three different languages, was released across Europe and the UK from 1984.
$$ • Figure 9 in (22.5 cm) high

DAGOBAH PLAYSET
A Dagobah action playset from *The Empire Strikes Back*, released by Kenner in 1981.
$$ • Box 13 in (33 cm) high

HAN SOLO FIGURE
"Power of the Force" series Han Solo figure in trench coat, made by Kenner in 1985.
$$$ • Figure 3¾ in (9.5 cm) high

DARTH MAUL AND SITH SPEEDER
This Hasbro 1998 *The Phantom Menace* action figure is a sales sample without markings. The larger size marked a departure from the 3¾-in (9.5-cm) standard.
$$ • 9 in (22.5 cm) high

GREEDO FIGURE
Dated 1979, this is a Greedo action figure by Kenner from the original *Star Wars* movie.
$$$ • Figure 3¾ in (9.5 cm) high

TROOP TRANSPORTER
An Imperial Troop Transporter made by Palitoy in 1977 to tie in with the first *Star Wars* movie.
$$ • Box 10 in (25.5 cm) wide

LUKE SKYWALKER FIGURE
An unboxed Luke Skywalker from the original range, 1978.
$$ • 3¾ in (9.5 cm) high

TOP TIPS
• Start by heading for a *Star Wars* convention, where a huge range of merchandise is usually on sale.
• Check the Internet for details of collecting societies, which offer social events for collectors, as well as networks for finding and trading collectibles.
• Look for items in original packaging, which can sell for up to ten times the price of the item alone.
• Don't count on your collection being an investment for the future—collect things you will enjoy owning.

SCOUT WALKER VEHICLE
This is a 1980 *Empire Strikes Back* Scout Walker by Kenner, with original box.
$$ • Box 12 in (30.5 cm) high

Starter Buys

DROID FIGURE
This Death Star Droid action figure is from Kenner's 1979 range of characters from the first film. The lack of original packaging reduces its value.
$ • 3¾ in (9.5 cm) high

TIE FIGHTER VEHICLE
This *Star Wars* Imperial TIE Fighter by Palitoy, 1978, is rarer than the Kenner version.
$$ • Toy 10½ in (26.5 cm) wide

JABBA THE HUTT PLAYSET
A Jabba the Hutt playset, by Kenner, in a rare Sears mail-away box, dated 1983.
$$ • Box 13 in (33 cm) wide

SENATOR PALPATINE
A 1998 Hasbro talking figure from *Star Wars Episode 1*.
$ • 3¾ in (9.5 cm) high

DARTH SIDIOUS
Star Wars Episode 1 talking figure by Hasbro, from 1998.
$ • 3¾ in (9.5 cm) high

You may also like… Movie Posters, see pp. 316–21

Doctor Who

Doctor Who first materialized on British TV screens in November 1963. Since then the series has become a part of Britain's television culture, with generations of fans watching from behind the sofa.

Many fans of the original series have grown up to become avid collectors of *Doctor Who* memorabilia. The combination of picturesque heroes, dastardly villains, and hideous monsters makes this a colorful and appealing area for collectors.

Unusually, older items are not necessarily more collectible. The huge popularity of the program during the 1960s and '70s meant that memorabilia from that era were generally mass-produced, and

are often still easy to come by. However, with the series in limbo during the 1990s, merchandise production slowed, and key items from that period are rare.

The ultimate collectibles are, of course, original costumes and props used in filming. Very few survive from the early series, and those that do are highly valued. An original Dalek sold for $62,000 at auction in 2005, while, in 2007, Tom Baker's frock coat and striped scarf sold for an incredible $50,000.

The Doctor in Action

Issued in 1964 by Cadet Sweets, this set of trading cards depicts the first Doctor, played by William Hartnell. Vivid, colorful action scenes are accompanied by story elements printed on the back of the cards.

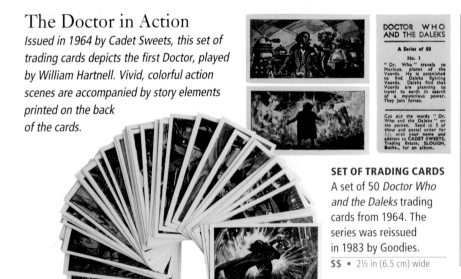

DOCTOR WHO AND THE DALEKS

A Series of 50

No. 1

" Dr. Who " travels to Marinus, planet of the Voords. He is astonished to find Daleks fighting Voords. Daleks find that Voords are planning to travel to earth in search of a mysterious power. They join forces.

Cut out the words " Dr. Who and the Daleks " on the packet. Send in 5 of these and postal order for 1/- with your name and address to CADET SWEETS, Trading Estate, SLOUGH, Bucks., for an album.

SET OF TRADING CARDS
A set of 50 *Doctor Who and the Daleks* trading cards from 1964. The series was reissued in 1983 by Goodies.

$$ • 2½ in (6.5 cm) wide

TOP TIPS

- Look for items produced at the start of the series: there is much less of it around and it therefore commands high prices.
- Avoid worn and damaged goods. Buy items that are in mint condition, and come with the original packaging and instructions.
- Note that interest in the early '80s Doctors is growing, so this could be a good area to collect.

KEY FACTS	1963	1963–89	1989	1996	2005
Tracking the Doctor	The very first *Doctor Who* episode airs on British television on November 23.	The Doctor enthralls the nation during 26 seasons, and a broad range of merchandise is produced.	The BBC suspends the show because of falling viewer figures.	US Fox Network co-produces a *Doctor Who* television movie with the BBC.	The Doctor returns to British screens, renewing interest in related collectibles.

What's Hot

Look out for:

The Daleks were the Doctor's most recognizable adversary. Intact models such as this one are very collectible, especially if the speech mechanism is still operational.

Fragile arms rarely found intact

VIDEO GIFT PACK
This gift pack from 1990 includes a video of *The Five Doctors* and a Dalek figurine.
$$ • 10 in (25.5 cm) wide

GIVE-A-SHOW PROJECTOR
This projector, made by Chad Valley in 1965, has a complete set of slides and original box.
$$ • Projector 9¼ in (23.5 cm) long

TALKING DALEK
A talking Dalek by Palitoy with original packaging, produced c. 1975.
$$ • 7 in (18 cm) high

Core Collectibles

SENSORITE FIGURE
A model of a Sensorite alien from the first series, made by Classic Moments in 2002.
$ • 7 in (18 cm) high

DRACONIAN FIGURE
A statuette of a Draconian from series 10, made by Classic Moments in 2002.
$ • 7 in (18 cm) high

"ICE WARRIORS" BOX SET
Issued by the BBC in 1998, this box set contains two videos, a book, and a CD.
$ • 7½ in (19 cm) high

SERIES GUIDE
This is a reference guide to the earliest series, published by Virgin Books in 1992.
$ • 12 in (30 cm) high

Starter Buys

2001 CALENDAR
A 2001 *Radio Times* calendar in its original packaging.
$ • 12 in (30.5 cm) wide

ROLL-A-MATICS DALEKS
A set of toys from 2002 with pull-back motors.
$ • 2½ in (6.5 cm) high

SIGNED TRADING CARD
A trading card by Cornerstone, signed by Colin Baker.
$ • 3½ in (9 cm) wide

"GET WELL SOON" CARD
This greeting card features Tom Baker as the Doctor.
$ • 7¼ in (18.5 cm) high

You may also like... *Star Wars*, see pp. 324–27

Cult TV

It's tricky to define what makes a cult TV series. Whether it's science fiction, crime, or comedy, the cult status of any TV show is marked by a fanatical following, and a correspondingly active market for collectibles.

Fans fall in love with the characters and settings of cult shows, and a collection of related items can provide a real thrill, nostalgic or otherwise.

This is a large-scale industry: props and costumes, merchandise and memorabilia, books, magazines, videos, and DVDs all play a part in the cult TV collectibles market. New and reissued merchandise tends to be very common, making short-term profits rare for collectors. Although the wide variety of merchandise available allows collectors of every budget to participate, collecting in a major cult area such as *Star Trek*, for instance, means competing with the most fanatical of fans, who can drive prices for key items sky-high.

Ultimately, original props, costumes, posters, and memorabilia will always remain collectible, but these are often pursued to lofty heights, and amateur collectors may do better simply collecting items they enjoy. After all, a good box set of *The Phil Silvers Show* will offer hours of timeless entertainment.

Supermarionation Hero

Happy childhood memories of classic 1960s "supermarionation" shows such as "Joe 90," "Stingray," and "Thunderbirds" have forged a strong core of collectors for Gerry Anderson memorabilia, including the "TV21" comics and annuals of the 1960s and '70s. The comics featured a newsy, stop-press style, telling stories in the manner of real-life journalism, and sold more than a million copies a week at their height. This annual is in good condition, and promises stories from all the favorite Anderson shows of the era.

"TV21" ANNUAL
The 1969 *TV21* annual features adventures of *Captain Scarlet*, *Fireball XL5*, *Thunderbirds*, *Stingray*, and *Zero X*. Early editions of the comic, from 1965–68, carry the title *TV Century 21* and tend to fetch higher prices than later printed Anderson material.

$ • 12 in (30 cm) high

KEY FACTS	1950	1960s	1966	1970s	2006
Making TV history	*Andy Pandy*, one of the earliest dedicated children's shows, appears on screens for the first time.	The "spy-fi" genre takes off with shows such as *The Prisoner* and *The Avengers*.	*Star Trek* is launched in the US, and *Dad's Army*, the archetypal British comedy, in the UK.	Cop shows take center stage with series such as *Columbo*, *Kojak*, and *The Sweeney*.	A model starship used in the original *Star Trek* is auctioned for $576,000.

What's Hot

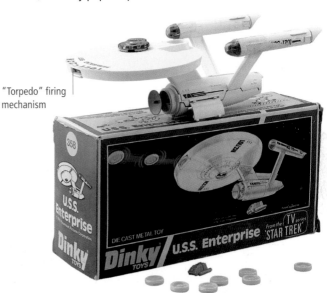

Look out for:

Merchandising is part and parcel of the success of most cult TV shows. This is particularly true of science fiction. Both Corgi and Dinky are renowned for their television tie-in models, and the Dinky USS *Enterprise*, first issued in 1977, is a very popular piece.

"Torpedo" firing mechanism

"AVENGERS" SWORD STICK

This display card for a 1960s *Avengers* sword stick by Lone Star becomes very collectible if paired with the stick.

$$ • 6¼ in (16 cm) wide

DYLAN FIGURINE

A plastic figure by Corgi of the character from *The Magic Roundabout*, originally shown in the 1960s and '70s.

$ • 2 in (5 cm) high

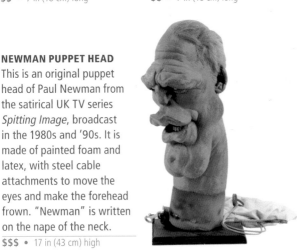

"STARSKY & HUTCH" CAR

This *Starsky & Hutch* Ford Torino, Corgi model 292, is in excellent condition and comes with its original box.

$$ • 7 in (18 cm) long

"KOJAK" BUICK

A Corgi *Kojak* Buick in its original box. Both toy and box are in mint condition, making this very desirable.

$$ • 7 in (18 cm) long

DINKY USS ENTERPRISE

This Dinky *Star Trek* USS *Enterprise*, model 358, comes in its original box. The toy has a built-in firing mechanism, and the set includes disk-shaped missiles as well as a plastic shuttle.

$ • 9½ in (24 cm) wide

What's Not

The resurgence of many classic shows has seen the market flooded with new and rereleased merchandise. Original items will always command the highest prices, and it will be some time before new products find a stable and reliable market.

NEWMAN PUPPET HEAD

This is an original puppet head of Paul Newman from the satirical UK TV series *Spitting Image*, broadcast in the 1980s and '90s. It is made of painted foam and latex, with steel cable attachments to move the eyes and make the forehead frown. "Newman" is written on the nape of the neck.

$$$ • 17 in (43 cm) high

"STINGRAY" SUBMARINE

A Matchbox *Stingray* submarine, made in 1993. It is one of a range of classic Matchbox action figures reissued in recent years.

$ • 12 in (30 cm) long

Core Collectibles

"FLINTSTONES" ASHTRAY
An ashtray showing Betty and Barney Rubble, made by Arrow Houseware of Chicago.

$$ • 5½ in (14 cm) high

RUBBER NODDY AND CAR
This flexible rubber toy of Noddy in his car is from the 1970s. The Enid Blyton character first appeared on British TV screens in 1955 in *The Adventures of Noddy*.

$ • 10½ in (26.5 cm) long

SOOTY PUPPET
Made by Chad Valley, this puppet of Sooty the bear is from the 1960s.

$ • 8¾ in (22 cm) high

TARGET RANGE GAME
A *Starsky & Hutch* target range game, c. 1977, made by Arco, in its original box.

$ • Box 18 in (46 cm) wide

"MY MAGIC ROUNDABOUT" POP-UP BOOK
Published in 1975 by Dean, this pop-up book by Serge Danot is one of the many items of memorabilia from the well-loved television series of the 1960s and '70s.

$ • 9¼ in (23.5 cm) wide

BACK PACK RADIO
A Kenner back pack radio, c. 1973, from the TV series *The Six Million Dollar Man*.

$ • Box 12 in (30 cm) high

1973 "STAR TREK" ANNUAL
The *Star Trek* annuals included stories from Gold Key comics not available in the UK.

$ • 10½ in (27 cm) high

"DUKES OF HAZZARD" WATCH
A boxed *Dukes of Hazzard* LCD quartz watch from c. 1981. The watch face shows the Dukes' recognizable orange Dodge Charger, named General Lee, in a high-speed car chase.

$ • Box 10¼ in (26 cm) wide

SECRET SAM SPY CASE
Made by De Luxe Toys, this James Bond-esque Secret Sam weapons case is dated c. 1969.

$$ • 18¾ in (48 cm) wide

"KNIGHT RIDER" GAME
Dated c. 1982, this *Knight Rider* racetrack game in its original box is by the German toy car company Darda.
$ • Box 25½ in (65 cm) wide

"THE MONKEES" DISPLAY
This late-1960s *Monkees* bubble gum card display box is by A&BC. With its original lid, its value could triple.
$ • 16 in (40 cm) long

KERMIT THE FROG FIGURE
A flexible toy of the well-loved Muppet, with indistinct marks, c. 1970.
$ • 8½ in (21.5 cm) high

Starter Buys

"LOGAN'S RUN" ANNUAL
A 1979 *Logan's Run* annual. The TV series aired for just one season, 1977–78.
$ • 12 in (30 cm) high

"SPACE 1999" ANNUAL
This hardcover 1976 *Space 1999* annual was produced by World Distributors.
$ • 12 in (30 cm) high

"FLOWERPOT MEN" BOOK
A 1950s book starring the TV characters Bill and Ben the Flowerpot Men.
$ • 11 in (28 cm) high

PARTRIDGE FAMILY ALBUM
A 1972 Bell Records *Partridge Family Shopping Bag* vinyl LP, with a real shopping bag.
$ • 12¼ in (31 cm) wide

BIONIC BEAUTY SALON
This *Bionic Woman* bionic beauty salon toy made by Kenner is dated c. 1976.
$ • Box 14 in (36 cm) long

FONZ BUTTON
Made in the US, this 1970s Fonz button features the wisecracker from *Happy Days*.
$ • 1 in (2.5 cm) diameter

You may also like… Rock & Pop Memorabilia, see pp. 310–15

Fishing Memorabilia

There are several auctioneers and dealers specializing in fishing-related items and, with both the diversity of material and the large number of collectors, it is likely that the piscatorial market will continue to flourish.

With more than 4 million anglers in the UK alone, it is perhaps no surprise that vintage and collectible fishing tackle enjoys the attention it does. But it's not just anglers who count themselves among the scores of collectors—the history and innovative technology behind the sport and its equipment continue to entice new enthusiasts to the genre.

The core collector market tends to be for reels and rods, with rare versions and those by famous makers such as Hardy and Farlow commanding top prices. Premium prices can certainly cause a big splash: in 2005, a limited-edition Hardy fishing reel from the 1930s sold for a record-breaking $17,000. The market for cased fish is strong as well—here, prices range from a few hundred to several thousand dollars, depending on the rarity, condition, size, and provenance of the model.

Fishing fans with smaller budgets may be interested in exploring the many other accessories the sport offers—lures and flies and their boxes, gaffs, fly-tying equipment, and angling books are all good places to start.

Come Fly with Me

Tackle boxes and fly reservoirs hold fascinating and often extensive collections of an angler's necessary accoutrements. This handsome example has an ivorine strip in its front door to prevent warping in wet conditions.

HARDY FLY CABINET
A Hardy Bros. unique mahogany brass-mounted fly cabinet with a recessed brass handle. The interior has nine sliding trays with ivorine handles and name plates.
$$$$ • 9 in (23 cm) high

TOP TIPS

- Choose items by known makers such as Allcocks. They may cost more but will always be more sought after than unnamed pieces.
- When considering split cane rods, be sure to buy those in original condition. Their value drops sharply if restoration work has been done.

KEY FACTS	c. 1770	1872	1890s	1970s	2004
Hook, line, and sinker	By this period, rods with reels as we recognize them today are in standard use, especially in America.	Hardy Bros. is founded in Alnwick, England, and eventually builds a reputation for the finest fishing tackle.	Reel design improves. Farlow and Co. market George Kelson's Patent Lever Winch and Hardy introduces the Perfect.	Bamboo rods begin to be replaced with fiberglass, becoming shorter and lighter while still strong.	A c. 1910 Roller Back Coxon Aerial fishing reel sells at auction for $11,400. This record is broken a year later.

What's Hot

MARQUIS NO. 2 REEL
This Hardy Marquis No. 2 salmon fly reel comes with two spare spools.
$$ • 4 in (10 cm) diameter

FISHERMAN PORTRAIT
The Young Fisherman, a signed oil painting by Esther Blaikie Mackinnon.
$$$$ • 30 x 17¾ in (76 x 45 cm)

Look out for:
The Marquis fly reel, introduced by Hardy in 1968, was *the* classic workhorse reel—and was often copied by other makers—for some three decades before it was retired in 1999.

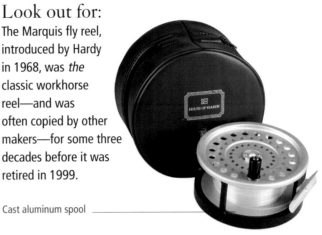

Cast aluminum spool

HARDY MARQUIS FISHING REEL
A Hardy Marquis 9/10/11 disk reel with its original case. The reel came in a variety of sizes for different line weights, suitable for fishing anything from small trout to salmon.
$$ • 4 in (10 cm) diameter

Core Collectibles

MAHOGANY FISHING REEL
A mahogany and brass coarse fishing reel with some line left on the spool.
$$ • 4½ in (7 cm) diameter

HARDY BRASS REEL
This brass reel, stamped "Hardy Bros., Alnwick," shows some signs of age.
$$ • 2½ in (6.5 cm) diameter

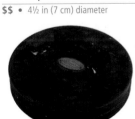

METAL CAST BOX
A felt-lined metal cast box with a makers' plaque reading "Hardy Bros Ltd."
$ • 4 in (10 cm) diameter

TELESCOPIC GAFF
This telescopic gaff made of brass was manufactured by Hardy, c. 1900.
$$$ • 29½ in (75 cm) long

Starter Buys

FLY FISHING CLASSIC
A copy of F. M. Halford's 1899 *Dry-Fly Fishing*. Halford devoted his life to fishing for trout using only dry flies.
$ • 9 in (23 cm) high

HARDY PERFECT REEL
The classic Hardy fly reel—one of the most collectible.
$$ • 3¼ in (8 cm) diameter

ANGLER'S TACKLE BOX
A zinc tackle box, c. 1900, containing some line and flies.
$$ • 6 in (15 cm) wide

You may also like… Sporting Memorabilia, see pp. 338–39

Golfing Memorabilia

Dating back to the 15th century, golf has a very long tradition, and it is one of the few sports to have a truly global appeal. As a result, there is a myriad of golfing memorabilia to satisfy collectors across the world.

For fans of the game, the chance to own a piece of its history is hard to pass up. The best pieces provide a sense of connection with fellow enthusiasts from centuries gone by.

Recent market history provides a salutary reminder that collectors should buy for love of their subject rather than investment value. In the 1980s, a number of Japanese collectors entered the golfing memorabilia market, driving up prices. However, when the East Asian stock markets fell a few years later, the value of golf memorabilia plummeted.

The most buoyant items on the current market are competition medals and trophies, particularly those awarded in the 19th century and before. But unsurprisingly, the most common items to appear on the market are golf clubs and balls.

Age is a significant factor in determining value. Early "featherie" balls, made from goose feathers encased in a leather cover, are currently much sought after, fetching as much as $60,000. "Long nose" wooden-headed clubs from the late 19th century are also very popular.

Down to a Tee

In their heyday, in the early 20th century, lead soldiers by William Britain were collected by thousands of schoolboys all over the country. This model of a golfer is a more unusual figure, but like all Britain figures is well painted and of good quality.

LEAD GOLFER FIGURE

This painted lead golfer was manufactured in the early 20th century by W. Britain, marking a departure from their range of military toys.

$$ • 2¼ in (5.5 cm) high

TOP TIPS

- Look out for 19th-century clubs made by Hugh Philip, Robert Forgan, and David Robertson.
- Don't limit yourself to golfing equipment: golf-related prints, books, and even tableware from the right era can all have value.
- With the exception of valuable early and rare equipment, items tend to be most valued in their country of origin.

KEY FACTS	1603	1905	1931	1973	2007
Gutties and putters through the ages	William Mayne is appointed as royal golf club maker to King James I.	Haskell and Taylor design a rubber-cored, dimpled golf ball, still used in essence today.	Billy Burke is the first player to win a major tournament using clubs with steel shafts.	Carbon fiber replaces wood and steel as the material of choice for golf club shafts.	An 18th-century Andrew Dickinson putter sells at auction for $181,000.

What's Hot

SCOTTISH GOLFING MEDAL
From c. 1873, this medal is from the Edinburgh Burgess Golfing Society.
$$$$ • 3 in (8 cm) high

GOLF CALENDAR
This 1900 golf calendar features illustrations by Edward Penfield.
$$$$ • 19 in (48 cm) high

Look out for:
This delightful image appeals to three markets: golf, cats, and the works of Louis Wain. Wain's pictures were widely forged in the 1970s and '80s, so buyers should consult a specialist.

Compositor's notes

LOUIS WAIN, "MISSED"
This Louis Wain cartoon, entitled "Missed," has the artist's signature and penciled notes for the journal typesetter.
$$$ • 21 in (53.5 cm) high

Core Collectibles

GOLFING COOKIE JAR
A cookie jar made by Arthur Wood & Sons, probably in the 1930s.
$$$ • 5½ in (14 cm) high

"FEATHERIE" BALL
Early golf balls like this were made from leather stuffed with goose down.
$$$$ • 1½ in (4 cm) diameter

Starter Buys

GOLFING MUG
This 1950s mug was made by Arthur Wood & Sons.
$$ • 5¼ in (13 cm) high

A HISTORY OF GOLF
A 1952 first edition of *A History of Golf in Britain*.
$$ • 11 in (27.5 cm) high

SCOTT CLUB
A persimmon wood club from the early 20th century, made by A. H. Scott, Elie.
$$ • 36 in (91.5 cm) long

MORRIS PUTTER
This 19th-century wooden putter bears the stamp of maker Tom Morris.
$$$$ • 35 in (89 cm) long

SET OF SILVER SPOONS
A set of six silver spoons with golf-club-styled handles.
$$ • Each 4 in (10 cm) long

GOLF-BALL MATCH HOLDER
This match holder is styled as a gutta-percha ball (or "guttie").
$ • 1¾ in (4.5 cm) diameter

You may also like… Sporting Memorabilia, see pp. 338–39

Sporting Memorabilia

Opportunities to own a piece of sporting history can be as fiercely contested as the events themselves. It is small wonder, then, that sporting memorabilia, in its many forms, is so popular among collectors.

With the 1864 Wisden *Cricketers' Almanack* selling for $200,000, Pelé's shirt from the 1970 World Cup final going for $232,000 and key baseball memorabilia fetching hundreds of thousands of dollars, you clearly need a very deep pocket to become involved in the top end of the sporting memorabilia market. However, don't despair if you're starting out on a limited budget, as many interesting items can still be purchased for sums below $200.

If you are just starting out as a collector, take some time to study the market. One essential caveat is that the market for signed photographs, shirts, and so on is rife with forgeries, so be sure to check the provenance and authenticity of your purchase. Always go for the best quality you can afford, and be patient: the potential of this market is enormous and the rewards can be considerable.

SIGNED PHOTOGRAPH
Autographed by Sir Geoff Hurst, this is a photograph from the 1966 World Cup final with the quote "They think it's all over… It is now!"
$$ • Photo 6 in (15 cm) wide

"They Think It's All Over… "
Kenneth Wolstenholme's commentary as Geoff Hurst hurled the ball into the back of the net in the dying seconds of the 1966 World Cup final is now part of soccer folklore. Hurst is the only player to have scored a hat trick in a World Cup final. This is a picture that any fan would be proud to own.

TOP TIPS
• Stick to memorabilia from a sport followed by your country. Cricket collectors might struggle in the US!
• Study the market, sit through a few auctions, and look at some dealers' websites before you make a purchase.

KEY FACTS	1864	1896	1966	1999	2002
Milestones in sporting history	The first edition of John Wisden's *Cricketers' Almanack* or "The Bible of Cricket" is published.	The first modern Summer Olympic Games are held in Athens, Greece.	England wins the Soccer World Cup, beating West Germany in a dramatic final.	The baseball hit by Mark McGwire for his 70th home run sells for $2,700,000.	Match-winner Pelé's 1970 World Cup final football shirt sells for $232,000 at auction.

What's Hot

CIGARETTE CASE
An enameled cigarette case decorated with a scene of soccer players.
$$$ • 3½ in (9 cm) long

YORKSHIRE CHALLENGE CUP
This 9kt gold medal is from the 1921 Yorkshire Football Challenge Cup.
$$$ • Box 3 in (7.5 cm) long

Look out for:
To date, cycling has been a fairly quiet collecting area. But with the recent successes of British cyclists in the Olympic Games and World Championships, the popularity of cycling memorabilia is set to rise, and items such as this Olympic ticket may well increase in value.

Antiforgery paper stock

OLYMPIC EVENT TICKET
A ticket for the cycling tournament at the 1932 Los Angeles Summer Olympics, held on the evening of August 3.
$ • 3¼ in (8 cm) wide

Core Collectibles

WINTER OLYMPICS BADGE
A badge from the 1936 Winter Olympics, held in Garmisch-Partenkirchen, Germany.
$$ • 2 in (5 cm) high

TENNIS TROPHY
This late-Victorian dinner gong is supported by crossed tennis rackets on an oak base.
$$$ • 13 in (33 cm) wide

Starter Buys

CRICKETING TOAST RACK
A Victorian silver-plated toast rack shaped as cricket bats.
$$ • 6 in (15 cm) long

DON BRADMAN–SIGNED BAT
This cricket bat is signed by Australian Donald Bradman.
$ • 33½ in (85 cm) long

RUGBY JUG
This Copeland pottery jug is decorated with scenes from a rugby game.
$$ • 6 in (15 cm) high

PELÉ-SIGNED SOCCER BALL
This soccer ball was signed by Pelé during the 1998 FIFA World Cup in France.
$$$ • Inflated 12 in (30 cm) diameter

LA BASEBALL CAP
A cap with "Sam the Eagle," the 1984 Olympic mascot.
$ • 8 in (20 cm) wide

1932 OLYMPICS PIN
A participant's pin from the 1932 Olympics.
$ • ½ in (1 cm) high

You may also like… Golfing Memorabilia, see pp. 336–37

Marine Memorabilia

This is a market that encompasses the ancient and the modern. Humans have plied the oceans for thousands of years; given the unpredictability of the sea, they have also left a legacy prized by many collectors.

Just like the motor vehicle and the aircraft, the ship has had many applications throughout history, both civil and military. Related material often comes to the marketplace, and historical relics from vessels such as the *Titanic* or Nelson's flagship, the *Victory*, will always be placed at the top end of the market.

There are many specialist auction houses dealing with shipping and maritime articles. A quick online search will help to find them. Some higher-profile houses stage special auctions, and it is worth noting that an anniversary, such as the *Titanic* centennial in 2012, is usually accompanied by a release of related memorabilia onto the market. This can, however, prove a more expensive way of buying, as such sales usually generate high interest.

For those with shallower pockets, there are various artifacts to be purchased in antique stores and at flea markets and garage sales. These can range from postcards to menus and cruise souvenirs, many at quite moderate prices.

"SOS!"

The sinking of RMS "Titanic" on April 15, 1912, during its maiden voyage, was one of the greatest maritime disasters in history, and has gained an almost mythical status. Collectors stop at nothing to acquire related items. Photographs, correspondence, menus from the restaurant, personal effects, even material from related vessels such as the RMS "Carpathia," which rescued over 700 survivors, have all become highly collectible. Indeed, anything with a hint of a connection seems to find a market.

RMS "TITANIC" PHOTOGRAPH, 1912
A photo from the original negative.
$$$ • 21½ in (54.5 cm) wide

TOP TIPS

• Treat unprovenanced artifacts, often found on the Internet, with caution. Many items are illegally removed from wrecks or other sites of archaeological interest.

• Watch out for fake and imitation maritime items, particularly brassware, which have flooded the market in recent years.

KEY FACTS	1545	1912	1967	1997	2000
Making waves in maritime history	Henry VIII's flagship, *Mary Rose*, sinks off Portsmouth Harbor, with the loss of about 500 lives.	The "unsinkable" RMS *Titanic* strikes an iceberg and sinks on its maiden voyage to America.	The famous Cunard liner *Queen Elizabeth II*, named after the Queen Mother, is launched.	Causing the Queen to shed a tear, the 83rd Royal Yacht *Britannia* is decommissioned in Edinburgh Harbor.	The *Hunley*, the first submarine to sink a surface ship, is recovered 136 years after its sinking.

What's Hot

AMERICAN DIORAMA
This is a late 19th-century carved and painted model of the ship *Lily of Philadelphia*.
$$$ • 32 in (81.5 cm) wide

SOUVENIR CUP
An RMS *Queen Mary* cup and saucer, marking the ship's maiden voyage in May 1936.
$$ • Saucer 5½ in (14 cm) diameter

Look out for:
The glamour of ocean liner travel in the 1920s and '30s was captured in the superb artwork of posters and other printed material.

Iconic design and artwork

DECK PLAN
A deck plan for the famous 1930s French liner *Normandie*.
$$ • 12¾ in (32 cm) high

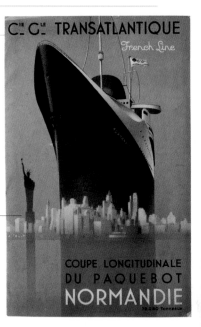

Core Collectibles

JIGSAW PUZZLE
This RMS *Queen Mary* souvenir jigsaw puzzle is dated 1936.
$ • Box 9½ in (24 cm) wide

GLASS DECANTER
Dated c. 1910, this decanter is engraved on its front with the logo of the P&O line.
$$ • 7 in (18 cm) high

Starter Buys

TEA STRAINER
A 1950s tea strainer from RMS *Andes*.
$ • 6 in (15 cm) long

"ARCADIA" EGGCUP
This 1950s P&O eggcup was made by Mappin & Webb.
$ • 3¼ in (8 cm) high

PINCUSHION
A rare item from RMS *Australia*, this pincushion is dated c. 1900.
$$ • 5¼ in (13.5 cm) wide

SURGEON'S MORTAR
This c. 1700 surgeon's mortar for mixing medicines is from the wreck of HMS *Association*.
$$$ • 4¼ in (11 cm) high

LINEA C ASHTRAY
A Linea C ship's funnel ashtray from the 1930s.
$ • 3½ in (9 cm) high

SAILING SCHEDULE
A 1938 sailing schedule for the Dutch line KPM.
$ • 9¾ in (24 cm) high

You may also like… Aeronautica, see pp. 348–49

Railwayana

The age-old romanticism of steam travel continues to attract a large community of collectors. This is a market kept alive by a deep sense of nostalgia and history.

Railwayana encompasses almost everything to do with railroads, ranging from rail spikes to schedules, from diesel and electric mainline memorabilia to pieces relating to narrow gauge and mining tracks.

Many collectors pursue their specialty through professional railwayana auctioneers and countless specialist dealers. Items can often be found in general auctions, with books and ephemera such as schedules and tickets easily sourced from bookstores. Besides scouring the Internet, it's always worth looking in the local press for news of swap meets and sales, particularly in areas that have a strong railroad heritage.

A love of railwayana often goes hand-in-hand with a love of rail travel, and serious collectors will traverse the world looking for experiences on the great railroads or on fast-disappearing steam lines in far-flung countries.

"KENYA" NAMEPLATE
This nameplate comes from a William Stanier-designed LMS Jubilee Class locomotive built at Crewe railway works in 1934.
$$$$$ • Approx. 27 in (69 cm) long

What's in a Name?
One of the most expensive items a railwayana collector can find is the locomotive nameplate. The age of steam trains has an unequaled nostalgia, and its attraction cannot be denied. Nameplates and cabsides—many, such as GWR plates, shaped to the curve of the "wheel splashers"—are often the most important "relics" surviving from locomotives and carry a weight of history.

TOP TIPS

- Keep an eye out for rare totem signs still in circulation today. One such oddity is "Besses o' th' Barn," which is the only totem with lower-case letters on it.
- Look for early railroad prints, deeds, documents referring to 19th-century rail company land purchases, and so on. They can be fun to research, and financially rewarding.

KEY FACTS	1847	1934	1948	1960s	1964
Chugging along on tracks old and new	The first *Bradshaw's Continental Railway Guide* is published, reaching 1,000 pages in later editions.	*The Flying Scotsman*, built in 1923, becomes the first steam locomotive to record a speed of 100 mph.	All railroads in England are nationalized according to the Transport Act of 1947.	Expansion of UK road networks results in the "Beeching Axe" rail closures and a flood of memorabilia.	Shinkansen, the Japanese bullet train, starts running, achieving speeds of more than 130 mph.

What's Hot

ENAMEL DOORPLATE
Bearing early-era lettering, this is a British Railways (Southern) doorplate.

$$$ • 18 in (45.5 cm) wide

CERAMIC TEAPOT
This rare Canadian Pacific Railway Co. teapot is stamped "JAPAN" on the base.

$$$ • 4¼ in (11 cm) high

Look out for:
Many British collectors' memories of steam travel are most likely epitomized by the once-humble "totem" station sign, adopted soon after nationalization in 1948.

Color-coded by region   Enameled metal construction

"AMBERGATE" TOTEM
This maroon "Ambergate" totem is from a former Midland Railway mainline station between Derby and Chesterfield.

$$$ • 36 in (91.5 cm) long

Core Collectibles

BOOKING HALL SIGN
This Midland Railway enamel sign has its original frame and wrought-iron support bracket.

$$ • 21 in (53.5 cm) wide

OIL SIGNALING LAMP
A rare Lancashire and Yorkshire Railway oil lamp with a bull's-eye lens.

$$ • 4½ in (11.5 cm) diameter

Starter Buys

PEAKED CAP
This is a rare London, Midland, and Scottish Railway cap.

$ • 9¾ in (25 cm) wide

SOUVENIR PLATE
A souvenir plate from the South African Railways Blue Train.

$ • 8 in (20 cm) diameter

WARNING SIGN
Unrestored and showing signs of outdoor use, this is a metal Midland Railway notice.

$ • 16 in (40 cm) wide

SIGNAL ARM
From Great Eastern Railway, a rare wooden fixed distant signal arm and mono spectacle.

$ • 55 in (140 cm) long

HOTEL TARIFF
A London and North Western Railway Euston Hotel tariff.

$ • 7¼ in (18.5 cm) high

RAILWAY GUIDE
Published by Cassell, this is an illustrated railroad guide.

$$ • 6¼ in (16 cm) high

You may also like… Trains & Steam Toys, see pp. 232–35

Automobilia

Collectors of automobilia are driven by nostalgia for the golden age of motoring in the early 20th century, when motoring was a fairly elite pursuit tinged with daring, glamour, and decadence.

Automobilia from the prewar period up to the mid-1930s always curries favor with collectors, but it's a varied market covering all aspects, from fabulously expensive hood ornaments to low-value key rings.

Whether considering the rarest Bugatti or a humble Austin, many collectors are fanatical about cars and the accessories associated with them. Racing memorabilia, military vehicles, original sales brochures, land-speed souvenirs, wicker picnic hampers, and grille badges are just a few of the items that can see their prices soar to enormous heights. Many collectors focus on just one area of automobilia—the Michelin Man and his vast variety of merchandise, for example, have a strong international following.

There are several prestigious auctioneers that hold frequent motoring and automobilia sales as well as a strong online market for buying and selling, and events such as the annual International Autojumble at the National Motor Museum at Beaulieu attract tens of thousands of visitors. This is a well-documented market but one that affords a chance to every would-be collector and every budget.

Bird on the Wing

Frederick Bazin is recognized as one of the best of the various French sculptors who included bronze hood ornaments among their works. He designed ornaments for Isotta, produced by Marvel, in addition to his "Flying Stork" for Hispano-Suiza. Marvel of Paris offered collectors a range of more than 150 different accessory ornaments with which to personalize their cars during the 1920s. It was another French company, A. E. Lejeune, who became the world's largest manufacturer of ornaments, however. They too employed some of the finest sculptors of the day.

HISPANO-SUIZA ORNAMENT
A 1919 Hispano-Suiza hood ornament in silvered bronze, designed by Frederick Bazin.
$$$$ • 5¼ in (13.5 cm) high

KEY FACTS	1885	1886	1908	1997	2008
Decorating the need for speed	Gottlieb Daimler invents what is regarded as the prototype of the modern gasoline engine.	Karl Benz, father of Mercedes Benz, receives the first patent for a gasoline-powered car.	The first Ford Model T is produced in Detroit, heralding the beginning of affordable mass-production motoring.	A land speed record of 766 mph is set in a turbo jet car by Andy Green, breaking the sound barrier.	The Bugatti Veyron is the most expensive production car in the world at approximately $1.5 million.

What's Hot

Look out for:

Brooklands is known as the birthplace of British aviation and motor sport. Opened in 1907, it was the first custom-built auto racing circuit in the world. Items associated with Brooklands and British motor racing are highly collectible. The speed badges are particularly sought after.

Vitreous colored enamels on chrome-plated brass

Mounted for display as a desk accessory

NATIVE AMERICAN ORNAMENT
A kneeling hood ornament with a snake and hatchet, designed by Frederick Bazin, 1920.
$$$$ • 5½ in (14 cm) high

ROLLS-ROYCE ORNAMENT
This "Flying Lady" hood ornament is from a Rolls-Royce Silver Ghost, c. 1912.
$$$$ • 6¼ in (16 cm) high

BOXED BADGES
A box of Brooklands Racing Club's annual-entry member's and guests' badges, 1920.
$$$ • 4 in (10 cm) wide

"MICKEY MOUSE" ORNAMENT
Depicting a smiling Mickey, this hood ornament was made by the Desmo Co., c. 1930.
$$$ • 4½ in (11.5 cm) high

BROOKLANDS SPEED BADGE
This highly coveted Brooklands Automobile Racing Club speed badge was awarded, in June 1938, to a driver who had covered a lap of the track at an average speed of 130 mph or more.
$$$ • 3½ in (9 cm) high

What's Not

It is a fact of life that supply and demand govern most prices realized, and a relatively common AA membership certificate will never be in the realms of valuable automobilia. Most would regard it as a curious keepsake from a bygone era when AA men used to salute the members!

"SPEED HEAD" ORNAMENT
This very rare 1929 Red Ashay hood ornament in glass was based on Lalique's *Victoire*.
$$$$ • 4½ in (11.5 cm) high

BERGMAN ORNAMENT
A c. 1910 hood ornament by Bergman, depicting a nude riding a broomstick.
$$$$ • 6 in (15 cm) high

MEMBERSHIP CERTIFICATE
An Automobile Association membership certificate in a personalized wallet.
$ • 3 in (7.6 cm) wide

Core Collectibles

SILVER WRAITH ORNAMENT
This Rolls-Royce "Silver Wraith" hood ornament dates to the 1930s–40s.

$$$ • 4½ in (11.5 cm) high

RAC CAR BADGE
A limited-edition RAC centennial commemorative badge, dated 1997.

$$ • 4¾ in (12 cm) high

ASTON MARTIN CAR CLUB BADGE
An enameled post–World War II Aston Martin Owners' Club badge. Such badges—from clubs for owners of luxury performance cars—are consistently sought after.

$$ • 5¾ in (14.5 cm) wide

DASHBOARD TIMEPIECE
Formerly installed in the interior of the car, this time-piece has a gilt metal case.

$$ • 5½ in (14 cm) diameter

ROLLS-ROYCE ORNAMENT
This 1991 Silver Cloud "Spirit of Ecstasy" hood ornament was designed by Charles Sykes.

$$$ • 5¼ in (13.5 cm) high

BARC CAR BADGE
A 1930s Brooklands Automobile Racing Club committee members' badge.

$$$$ • 3½ in (9 cm) high

RACING CLUB BADGE
This British Automobile Racing Club car badge is dated to the 1950s–60s.

$$ • 4¾ in (12 cm) high

HOOKED RUG
An American hooked rug mounted for hanging, c. 1930, showing a 1906 Cadillac.

$$$ • 24 in (61 cm) high

CRYSTAL PALACE POSTER
A mid-1950s Crystal Palace motor racing poster illustrated by Raymond Groves.

$$ • 29¾ in (75.5 cm) high

ROLLS-ROYCE ASHTRAY
This 1980s chrome-plated ashtray was a presentation piece for a retiring employee.

$$$ • 4¾ in (12 cm) long

FERRARI CLUB CAR BADGE
An enameled Ferrari Owners' Club grille badge with the characteristic prancing horse.

$$ • 3¼ in (8.5 cm) high

BUGATTI CLUB BADGE
This is an enameled and chromed Bugatti Owners' Club motor vehicle badge.

$$ • 3¾ in (9.5 cm) high

1920S BENTLEY ORNAMENT
A 1920s nickel-plated Bentley "B" hood ornament with outstretched wings. The "Flying B" logo has been attributed to Frederick Gordon Crosby.

$$$ • 2 in (5 cm) high

TOP TIPS

- Hold on to items produced in small runs for regional auto clubs, as their comparative rarity helps retain and even increase their value.
- When buying key rings or other memorabilia, look for unusual or obscure clubs, or makes no longer in existence.
- Cast your research net wide. Besides the wealth of books and online sources available, racing clubs and vintage rallies provide a huge and inspirational resource.
- Don't ignore general auctioneers, who often sell a good smattering of automobilia as parts of larger, mixed lots.

RACE-CAR TEAPOT
A Saddlers race-car teapot with cover, glazed in yellow with silvered highlights.

$$ • 8¾ in (22 cm) long

BENTLEY ORNAMENT
From the 1930s, this is a winged, forward-leaning Bentley "B" hood ornament.

$$$ • 3½ in (9 cm) wide

MEMBERS' BADGE
This is a popular 1930s–40s National Motorists Association members' badge.

$$ • 5½ in (14 cm) high

RAC CAR BADGE
A limited-edition Golden Jubilee commemorative car badge, dated 2002.

$$ • 3½ in (9 cm) high

Starter Buys

MOTORING MAGAZINE
A 1937 issue of *The Modern Motor Car* magazine with Maurice Beck on the cover.

$ • 13½ in (34.5 cm) high

SPEED TRIALS POSTER
A 1996 poster for the popular motoring competition still held today in Brighton.

$ • 31 in (80 cm) high

CAR CLUB KEY FOB
This is a Ferrari Owners' Club leather key fob with a chromed and enameled logo.

$ • 1½ in (4 cm) high

CAR BADGE
A "Morgan's Finest Hour" Le Mans commemorative car badge, June 23–24, 1962.

$ • 3¾ in (9.5 cm) wide

You may also like… Dinky Toys, see pp. 222–23

Aeronautica

Throughout history, humanity's struggle to overcome the law of gravity has produced amazing feats of endurance. Even the humblest item of aeronautica stands testament to human courage and ingenuity.

In 1909, Frenchman Louis Blériot became the first person to fly a heavier-than-air machine across the English Channel. He went on to design the fighters used by the Allies in World War I. So great was his fame that even today a humble period postcard of a Blériot monoplane can sell for $200.

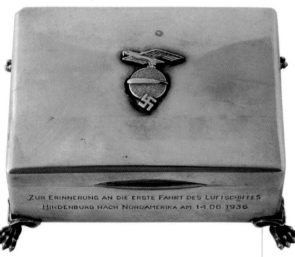

COMMEMORATIVE SILVER BOX
This silver cigar box commemorates the *Hindenburg*'s first flight from Germany to the United States in 1936. It carries an applied enamel plaque and an inscription in German.
$$$$ • 4¾ in (12 cm) wide

Tales like this sum up what is so exciting about aeronautica. The field covers some of the defining moments of the last century, during which aerospace technology developed at an incredible pace. Within 40 years the industry progressed from the biplane to the jet engine, changing the face of modern travel.

Collecting big-ticket items can be expensive, but given the profusion of material from more than a century of aviation, the market operates at all levels.

Triumph and Tragedy

The "Hindenburg" and its sister ship the "Graf Zeppelin II" were the largest aircraft ever built. On May 6, 1937, coming to land at Lakehurst, New Jersey, the "Hindenburg" burst into flames and crashed, killing 36 people. Its destruction spelled the end of the lighter-than-air era. Zeppelin memorabilia are always highly collectible, but pieces from the doomed "Hindenburg" are especially poignant.

TOP TIPS

- Look out for online auctions and aviation flea markets that often carry diverse items from around the United States.
- Rather than buying a lot of high-value but unrelated items, try to build a coherent, themed collection.

KEY FACTS	1874	1903	1930s	1969	2008
The history of mechanical flight	The Montgolfier brothers ascend to more than 3,000 ft (900 m) in a hot-air balloon.	Orville and Wilbur Wright achieve the first sustained powered flight.	Frank Whittle is granted a patent for the turbo jet engine, which makes its first flight in 1939.	The *Concorde* makes its first test flight, and goes supersonic for the first time.	Richard Branson's Virgin Airlines trials the first airplane to run partly on biofuel.

What's Hot

AOA POSTER
A 1946 poster for American Overseas Airlines, designed by Jan Le Witt and George Him.
$$$$ • 40 in (101 cm) high

BROOKLANDS CLUB BADGE
Made by H. A. Shelley, this is a 1930s members' badge from the Brooklands Flying Club.
$$$$ • 4½ in (11.5 cm) high

Look out for:
Items linked to record-breaking events are a must for any collector. The Schneider Trophy was awarded between 1911 and 1931, greatly advancing the development of aircraft.

Rolls-Royce logo

SCHNEIDER HOOD ORNAMENT
This model Supermarine S6B seaplane was presented to Flt. Lt. J. Boothman, winner of the 1931 Schneider Trophy, by Rolls-Royce, whose engines powered the record-breaking plane.
$$$ • 4 in (10 cm) long

Core Collectibles

SOUTH COAST CLUB BADGE
A 1930s painted alloy membership badge for the South Coast Flying Club.
$$ • 3 in (8 cm) high

BSAA POSTER
This 1948 poster for British South American Airways was designed by Pat Keely.
$$$ • 40 in (101 cm) high

Starter Buys

ZEPPELIN PHOTOGRAPHS
A set of 12 photographs of the first *Graf Zeppelin*, from 1928.
$ • 3½ in (9 cm) wide

AIR FRANCE ASHTRAY
This is a plastic Air France ashtray from the 1960s.
$ • 6 in (15 cm) long

ONYX ASHTRAY
A World War II–era onyx ashtray with an airplane on top of a chrome-plated globe.
$$ • 8¼ in (21 cm) long

GIFFARD BALLOON MEDAL
This bronze medallion from 1878 depicts the flight of Henri Giffard's hot air balloon.
$$ • 2 in (5 cm) in diameter

BOAC ASHTRAY
A 1970s BOAC blue ceramic ashtray by Wade.
$ • 10¼ in (26 cm) long

TWA ASHTRAY
A Trans World Airlines souvenir ashtray from the 1950s.
$ • 4¾ in (12 cm) wide

You may also like… Railwayana, see pp. 342–43

Science, Technology & Timepieces

Collectibles for the Technologically Minded

We accept technological advance and evolve with it, sometimes marveling but rarely questioning where it will take us. We love to reminisce about past advances, and this chapter illustrates our desire to preserve our recent history.

In the 20th century we saw unprecedented advances in technology, creating what was truly a technological revolution—noteworthy inventions included many things that we now take for granted, such as the television, the home computer, and the cell phone. It's of little consequence to most people that their cell phones carry more computing power than the whole Apollo 11 mission, but, amazingly, it's true. Where, you may think, will all this lead? How can technological advances be measured in the future? It's extraordinary to think that all forecasts

Grandstand Munchman, see Core Collectibles, p. 364.

Limited-edition Rolex, see What's Hot, p. 377.

Videosphere television, 1970s, see What's Hot, p. 361.

predict even greater advances in science and technology than before, with progress in the next 25 years surpassing all those made in the last hundred.

With such rapid change, the vogue for nostalgia is even more prevalent. It's easy to lament the death of the video cassette or proudly proclaim that you still own a record turntable and a full set of vinyl records to play on it! The change is tangible and fast. Life without the Internet, cell phones, PCs, video games, digital cameras, and LCD flat-screen televisions is recent history and yet we wonder how we ever existed without them.

For collectors, it's often all about owning the first thing of its kind. One example of this is the Sinclair ZX Spectrum home computer. This tiny 16 KB precursor to our present "memory monsters" cost a whopping $185 in 1982, but is still held in a great deal of affection by its fans. It now has a firmly established place in the history of home computing and is therefore classified as a collectible.

Sometimes the nostalgic element seems somewhat perverse. Who would have thought that it was sensible to reintroduce LED watches 30 years after they were first invented? The inconvenience of pressing a button every time you want to look at your watch makes little sense, but it's interesting how design, technology, and fashion are all inextricably intertwined. We continually try to look into the crystal ball of the future, but at the same time we are also constantly harking back to the past for further sources of ideas and inspiration. This has never been more evident than in the technologically advanced but retrogressive designs of recent years, and this is a major premise for fueling this area of the collectors' market.

Longcase clock, c. 1900,
see What's Hot, p. 371.

Olympus Pen F camera, 1963,
see What's Hot, p. 359.

Telephones & Cell Phones

The collectors' market for cell phones is in its infancy. As the technology is still young, even the so-called "classic" phones can be easily purchased. Vintage domestic telephones are also readily available.

Vintage telephones have become widely desirable objects for interior decoration. However, the price of Bakelite GPO (General Post Office) telephones has dropped in recent years, and this may be due to a shift in decorating fashions toward sleeker, more modern designs.

Classic telephones—such as the sleek Ericofon, made for more than two decades, or the rosewood Trub phone, a Swiss design classic from the 1970s—are also popular with collectors. Many classic telephones are reproduced by contemporary

companies. Countless copies of vintage phones, usually made in East Asia, can be found on the market. This results in reduced prices in some areas.

Cell phones are not widely collected and remain affordable. Some, such as the early "brick phones" by Motorola, are bought as "anti-fashion" accessories, though not all phones will work on modern networks. Secondhand stores and garage sales are good hunting grounds for these items.

An Elegant Black Number

Before the days of mass consumerism and cheap electronic products, telephones were often rented. The rental cost would vary depending on the model or color. As a result, red, ivory, and green Bakelite models are less common than black ones. Changes in fashion and an influx of cheap reproductions have affected the market for such phones.

BAKELITE 200 SERIES TELEPHONE
This phone is the genuine article, but fakes from East Asia are common. Run a finger over the numbers on the handset bar. If they are not crisp, the phone is a remolded reproduction.

$$ • 8 in (20 cm) wide

KEY FACTS	1876	1940s	1973	1979	1985
Telephones through history	Alexander Graham Bell makes the first "phone call" to his assistant in the room next door.	Basic cell phone technology exists later in the decade but the work of allocating frequencies is slow.	Dr. Martin Cooper of Motorola invents the first cell phone handset and makes his first call to his rival, Joel Engel.	The first commercial cellular telephone system commences operation in Tokyo.	Cellnet opens for business with just one transmitter on top of London's BT Tower for all of Greater London.

What's Hot

PHILIPPE STARCK'S "OLA"
This classic blue plastic Thomson "Ola" phone was designed by Philippe Starck in 1996.
$ • 11 in (28 cm) long

AMPER EXPLORER
This is a gray model of the Motorola Amper Explorer phone—an upright brick analog icon.
$ • 7¾ in (19.5 cm) long

Look out for:

The Ericofon is a classic modern phone made by Ericsson in the late 1940s. It was a revolutionary piece of plastic industrial design, anticipating the evolution of the typical cordless phone by decades. It went global in 1956 and was a great success. Though production in America was discontinued in 1972, Ericsson continued to produce a rotary dial version until 1980.

Sleek handset

Speaker sits above dial

MOTOROLA 6800
A Motorola 6800 with a base battery unit and an aerial.
$ • 9½ in (24 cm) long

SONY CRM-R111
This Sony CRM-R111 phone has a flip-arm microphone.
$ • 4¼ in (11 cm) long

1970S ERICOFON TELEPHONE
This plastic cream-colored Ericofon is a stylish one-piece design. The phone's dial is located in its base.
$$ • 8¼ in (21 cm) high

GFELLER TELEPHONE
A wooden Trub phone from the 1970s, designed by Gfeller.
$$ • 8¼ in (21 cm) wide

STARTAC GSM
This Motorola Startac GSM cell phone is dated c. 1998.
$ • 3¾ in (9.5 cm) long

What's Not

Cell phones become obsolete at an alarming rate, and people change them very frequently. Nokia phones from the mid-'90s are a good example of this. They are very common and of low value to collectors.

NOKIA NHE-5NX
Equipped with a fixed aerial, this set has illuminating keys.
$ • 7 in (18.5 cm) long

Core Collectibles

NOKIA 2110 MOBILE
A walnut-colored Nokia ETACS mobile, this phone was manufactured c. 1994.
$$ • 6½ in (17 cm) long

SONY GSM
Also called the "Mars Bar" due to its size, this phone comes with a sliding earpiece.
$ • 6¾ in (17.5 cm) long

MOTOROLA PERSONAL
A "personal phone" from Motorola, this does not have an LCD or digital display.
$ • 6½ in (16 cm) long

VODAFONE EB2602/7
Made in c. 1990, this mobile weighs almost 5 lb (2 kg) and has a base battery unit.
$$ • 9¼ in (23.5 cm) wide

SONY CMD-X2000
This phone has an extendable aerial and jog wheels.
$ • 6½ in (17 cm) long

NORTEL CLARET
A brown Nortel Claret with an extendable aerial.
$ • 6 in (15 cm) long

PIONEER PCC730
An analog mobile with a flip cover, c. 1993.
$ • 6¾ in (16.5 cm) long

EH97 HOTLINE ETACS
This model was Ericsson's first handheld phone.
$ • 7 in (18 cm) long

Ask the Expert

Q. What do the letters ETACS on a cell phone mean?
A. ETACS stands for Extended Total Access Control System. It was an expanded version of TACS, a 1980s "patchwork" of base stations arranged in a cellular pattern that allowed for a higher number of subscribers. Both are now obsolete.

Q. Is it true that there are lots of reproductions of vintage phones?
A. Yes, foreign copies of more recent phones are common, as are reproduction parts for old phones. If your purchase is too pristine, be suspicious.

NEC 22A MOBILE
A British phone with no aerial. It dates from c. 1993.
$$$ • 7 in (18 cm) long

Genuine wear and tear

Q. Could a "cradle" phone be worth less now than it was a few years ago?
A. Markets do change. In recent years, prices have declined for many classic designs. This is due partly to changes in fashion, and also to the large number of later-made versions and cheap copies on the market.

L. M. ERICSSON TELEPHONE
Manufactured c. 1910, this is an L. M. Ericsson telephone with crank.
$$ • 13 in (33 cm) high

RELIANCE TELEPHONE
This red plastic telephone, with a retro rotary dial, was made by Reliance Telephone Co. in the 1960s.
$$ • 5 in (12.5 cm) wide

TOP TIPS

- Collecting cell phones is a long-term investment area. Buy unusual phones and be sure they are in mint condition to maximize returns.
- Consider phones with a design element, as they may have potential. Names such as Philippe Starck or Jacob Jensen are likely to add value.
- Look for telephones produced by Swatch. The company, well known for maintaining value in mass-produced goods through their well-marketed and often collectible watches, also produced a range of telephones in the 1980s. Pieces in mint condition are known to change hands for reasonable sums.

Starter Buys

HOT LIPS TELEPHONE
A plastic Hot Lips phone made in the 1980s.
$ • 8½ in (21.5 cm) wide

BAKELITE 300
This black Bakelite 300 phone comes with its original cord.
$$ • 6 in (15 cm) wide

MOTOROLA MR1 FLIPHONE
Made c. 1994, this black Motorola PCM phone has an extendable aerial.
$ • 6 in (15 cm) long

PINK PEOPLE'S TELEPHONE
This Japanese CTN7000 ETACS cell phone was manufactured c. 1995.
$ • 6½ in (17 cm) long

SIEMENS S6 GSM
A 1996 black Siemens Classic GSM cell phone with a hi-fi loudspeaker earpiece.
$ • 7½ in (19 cm) long

MAXON SL500
This phone was developed by Maxon in the form of a walkie-talkie.
$ • 8 in (20 cm) long

You may also like… Radio, TV & Record Players, see pp. 360–61

Cameras

The camera market remains buoyant for good names and rare models but also provides a platform for the beginner or novice, with many affordable cameras available, particularly in the online marketplace.

The history of photography has been a growth market for collectors for some time. Vintage images remain popular, but the technical side has also seen rising interest, with rare cameras reaching ever-higher prices at auction. In particular, key models by manufacturers such as Leica, Nikon, and Canon, who were at the forefront of camera development throughout the 20th century, are firm favorites among collectors today.

Specialist auctions for photographic equipment are fairly common, with listings available through photography magazines, clubs, and websites. Many camera retailers also sell older collectible items alongside modern equipment.

Collectors of vintage photographic equipment can expect to discover not just ingenious design and engineering, but also seminal moments in the history of mass media and popular art.

A Private Eye

The Ticka subminiature camera was developed by a Swede, Magnus Neill, and produced in England by Houghton's from 1904. It was an excellent seller, with later versions including a watch face for better disguise.

WATCH POCKET CAMERA
A nickel-plated Ticka novelty camera, c. 1904, in its box, with box of film. The camera lens is concealed in the watch winder.

$$ • 2¼ in (5.5 cm) in diameter

TOP TIPS

- Vintage cameras often carry military insignia, but beware of fake engravings added by unscrupulous dealers.
- Avoid common cameras in poor condition. Instead, look for special editions or unusual colors, or concentrate on collecting a set.
- Buy to use: Russian Leica copies such as the Zorky can still produce good photos on a reasonable budget.
- Consider using vintage cameras as decoration. Large mahogany-cased cameras look very attractive.

KEY FACTS	1839	1900	1913	1990	2001
Taking pictures through the ages	Louis Daguerre creates the Daguerreotype, the first widely adopted form of photography.	The first Kodak Brownie camera allows mass-market home photography.	The Homeos is the first widely-produced camera to use 35mm film, setting the standard for decades.	Dycam Model 1 is released, the first commercially available digital camera.	A unique 1946 Phantom camera is auctioned at Christie's for $207,000.

What's Hot

GOMZ LENINGRAD CAMERA
The Russian-built Leningrad camera, 1956, took the Grand Prix at the 1958 World Fair.
$$ • 6 in (15 cm) wide

ENSIGN SPECIAL REFLEX
A 1930s plate camera, with brass-bound teak body and leather bellows.
$$$ • 5 in (13 cm) wide

Look out for:
The Olympus Pen range, released between 1959 and 1981, was designed to be as portable and easy to use as a pen. The most popular model was the Pen F, now a highly collectible item.

Slim design

Removable lens

OLYMPUS PEN F CAMERA
Released in 1963, the Olympus Pen F is one of the smallest SLR cameras ever made, using mirrors rather than a prism for a compact design. This piece has a 38mm removable lens.
$$ • 5 in (13 cm) wide

Core Collectibles

CHILD'S CAMERA
A plastic "Sun Ray" camera with original blue straps and *Howdy Doody Show* branding.
$ • 4½ in (11 cm) wide

IKONTA CAMERA
A Zeiss "Baby" Ikonta 520, known as the Ikomat in the US, with a rare Tessar lens.
$$ • 4½ in (11 cm) high

Starter Buys

BILORA RADIX CAMERA
This 1950s German camera comes with its original tin.
$$ • Camera 5 in (13 cm) wide

MINOLTA "A" CAMERA
An early 35mm rangefinder camera from 1955.
$$ • 5 in (13 cm) wide

ECHO 8 NOVELTY CAMERA
This 1951 Japanese "Zippo" camera was popularized by the movie *Roman Holiday*.
$$$ • 1½ in (4 cm) wide

LEICA I MODEL C
The first Leitz camera with interchangeable lenses, the Model C was released in 1931.
$$$ • 5½ in (14 cm) wide

REFLEX KORELLE CAMERA
Developed by Kochmann in 1935, the Reflex Korelle was one of the first SLR cameras. It used 120 format film.
$$ • 4¾ in (12 cm) wide

You may also like… Vintage Photography, see pp. 190–91

Radio, TV & Record Players

The huge impact of radio and television on the modern world has led to early designs of this technology becoming cultural icons. As a result, vintage examples can be very collectible.

Early radio and television combined milestone advances in technology, materials, and design in a remarkable evolutionary period. Collectors can potentially own historical objects from crucial moments in both scientific and artistic development. These are investment pieces of the future, featured as design icons in museums around the world.

The most collectible pieces demonstrate the work of both important designers, such as Wells Coates and Braun's Dieter Rams, and pioneering scientists like Leo Baekeland, inventor of Bakelite. It's easy to get started since mass-produced classics such as the Bush DAC90 radio set are often available at very affordable prices, even in working order.

Many specialist dealers focus exclusively on design-based collectibles. There are auction houses that run dedicated sales based on modern design, technology, and mechanical music, and collectors' fairs and antique markets often have sections specifically for collectible technology.

The iPod of the 1930s

The Excelda, by Swiss manufacturer Thorens, was one of several compact portable gramophones manufactured in the 1930s. Introduced in 1931, it mimicked the shape and design of the Kodak folding vest camera. It was one of the most successful gramophones of its type and remained in production until the mid-1940s.

MINIATURE GRAMOPHONE
A compact 1930s Excelda record player. Its needle arm and winding handle stow inside the case.
$$ • 5 in (12.5 cm) long

TOP TIPS

- Explore transistor radios, which are currently a relatively cheap area. Classics such as the Panasonic R-70 are particularly worthwhile.
- Be careful when using vintage electrical goods. It's imperative that an electrician check out any secondhand electronic appliances before they are used.

KEY FACTS	1877	1895	1920s–30s	1936	1997
Powerful transmissions	Thomas Edison stuns the world with his invention of the phonograph, a device to record and play sound.	Guglielmo Marconi transmits a radio signal over a distance of a mile. He wins the Nobel Prize in 1909.	The Art Deco movement and mass-production make design-led technology widely available.	On November 2, a BBC TV station opens at Alexandra Palace, the world's first regular public TV service.	Almost 33 million people in the UK watch TV coverage of the funeral of Diana, Princess of Wales.

What's Hot

SINCLAIR FTV1
This 1983 Sinclair miniature television has a 2-in (5-cm) black-and-white screen.

$ • 5½ in (14 cm) wide

PORTABLE TELEVISION
A National Commando 505 portable transistor television with earpiece from the 1970s.

$ • 12 in (30 cm) high

Look out for:

Manufactured by JVC (Victor Company of Japan, Ltd), the Videosphere television was introduced in 1970 and is regarded as a classic pop item.
The space-helmet design had broad appeal after the success of the 1969 Moon landing.

Space-helmet visor design

VIDEOSPHERE TV SET
This spherical 1970s JVC TV set is complete with base and hanging chain.

$$ • 12½ in (32 cm) high

Core Collectibles

EKCO AC85
A 1934 radio with a Bakelite case, designed by Wells Coates for Ekco.

$$ • 23 in (58.5 cm) wide

1950S RECORD PLAYER
This 1950s record player by Decca Dansette is decorated with nursery rhyme scenes.

$$ • 13½ in (34.5 cm) wide

TABLE TV SET
A Bush TV62 television set from 1956. The Bakelite case is in good condition.

$$ • 12 in (30 cm) high

TOOTALOOP BANGLE RADIO
This 1970s Panasonic radio is worn, when closed, like a bangle around the wrist.

$ • 6 in (15 cm) in diameter (closed)

Starter Buys

ELECTRIC TURNTABLE
This 1950s Dansette turntable has built-in speakers.

$$ • 12½ in (32 cm) wide

"PANAPET" RADIO
An early-1970s Panasonic R-70 radio with original box.

$ • 5 in (12.5 cm) in diameter

TRANSISTOR RADIO
A Bush TR103 transistor radio from 1959.

$ • 11 in (27 cm) high

RECORD PLAYER
A 1970s Penny 45rpm record player by Mangiadischi, Italy.

$$ • 9 in (23 cm) wide

You may also like… Cameras, see pp. 358–59

Computers & Games

Technology has advanced so rapidly over the past quarter-century that early computers and games now seem positively archaic. Yet the trend for collecting "retro" games is relatively new.

For many people, a sense of nostalgia prompts the desire to collect old-fashioned technology. The early Sinclair ZX Spectrum home computers, released in 1982, had only 16 or 48KB of RAM but remain popular with their "Specky" fans despite their limits. Early electronic arcade games such as Space Invaders or Asteroids remind us of times past, and now seem positively Stone Age in comparison to current game consoles and PCs.

This is still a fledgling market and a very affordable area in which to collect. Predictions of astronomical price rises still remain optimistic, but may well be realized over the next decade or so as these older pieces become more difficult to source.

Garage sales are good for buying old consoles and software. The Internet remains the best source for dealing with avid collectors.

Gaming for Two

The first Videomaster Superscore system was released in 1976 and could be purchased ready-built or as a self-assembly kit. The original advertising slogan, "Superscore is super fun," says it all! The version pictured here is the Compendium set, supplied with two paddles so that two people could play alongside each other. It cost around $55 when first retailed. Its current value is about the same but may rise if, as some predict, vintage technology becomes the next big thing. Possible sources include garage sales, secondhand stores, and the Internet.

SPY VIDEO GAME
This Videomaster Superscore system is the Compendium version, c. 1978. It comes in a spy briefcase-style box with an additional paddle for two-player games, and a light gun.

$$ • 13½ in (34 cm) wide

KEY FACTS	1837	1958	1962	1974–77	1996
From scarcity to ubiquity	Charles Babbage develops the first programmable mechanical computer.	Jack Kilby and Robert Noyce patent the integrated circuit, otherwise known as the microchip.	Steve Russell invents the first computer game, involving warring spaceships firing torpedoes.	The first home computers come on to the market; names include Scelbi, Altair, IBM 500, and Apple 1.	The first Tomb Raider game is released, starring Lara Croft. She becomes a cultural icon.

What's Hot

DONKEY KONG MK-96
A Nintendo Donkey Kong Circus MK-96 Panorama series Game and Watch from c. 1984.
$$ • 3¾ in (9.5 cm) wide

DONKEY KONG CJ-93
The Nintendo Donkey Kong Jr. CJ-93 Panorama series Game and Watch, c. 1983.
$$ • 3¾ in (9.5 cm) wide

Look out for:
The Sovereign calculator was the last calculator design marketed by Clive Sinclair before his company concentrated on home computers. No one can deny Sinclair's contribution to the field of electronics and computing, or his flair for unique ideas, innovation, and design. Also available with a black-painted or silver-plated body, this classy-looking slimline model, here with a gold-plated cover, cost a staggering $80 in 1977.

Gold-plated cover

Pressed-steel case

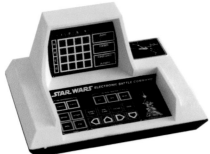

"STAR WARS" BATTLE COMMAND
A Kenner *Star Wars* Electronic Battle Command tabletop game, c. 1979; a space exploration game with LED grid coordinates.
$$ • 8¼ in (21 cm) wide

POCKET CALCULATOR
A gold-plated Sinclair Sovereign calculator, c. 1977.
$$ • 5½ in (14 cm) long

What's Not

The Prinztronic Tournament IV system has limited capability and has remained fairly static in price. It provided six simple sports games, but all were essentially very similar, and the system was known to mark TV screens with prolonged use.

VERMIN GAME & WATCH
This Nintendo Vermin MT-03 Game and Watch in a white casing is from c. 1980.
$$$ • 3¾ in (9.5 cm) wide

SPITBALL SPARKY
A Nintendo Spitball Sparky BU-201 Supercolor series Game and Watch, c. 1984.
$$ • 5¾ in (14.5 cm) high

PRINZTRONIC GAMES SYSTEM
This Prinztronic Tournament IV system from c. 1978 came with six simple games.
$ • 11¾ in (30 cm) wide

Core Collectibles

ASTRO WARS
The Grandstand Astro Wars classic electronic tabletop game, by Tomy, c. 1981.

$ • 5¾ in (14.5 cm) wide

THE EXTERMINATOR MT-03
An alternate version of Vermin released by Nintendo for the North American market.

$$ • 3¾ in (9.5 cm) wide

VECTREX GAMES SYSTEM
An MB Vectrex games console, with an elongated monitor in an arcadelike black case, dating from c. 1983.

$$ • 9½ in (24 cm) wide

BAMBINO SAFARI
In this c. 1980 Bambino Safari tabletop game, the player has to capture animals to score; points are deducted for misses.

$ • 9½ in (24 cm) wide

MISSILE INVADER
This Bandai Missile Invader handheld game in blue casing with orange controls dates from c. 1978.

$ • 3½ in (9 cm) wide

GRANDSTAND MUNCHMAN
A Grandstand Munchman tabletop game with a multi-colored fluorescent display, c. 1981, also sold as Pacman.

$ • 7¾ in (20 cm) wide

Ask the Expert

Q. What are the main factors affecting value?
A. Rarity, condition, and functionality determine the value of collectible computers and computer games. The original packaging and instruction booklets also boost the price, but look out for corrosion in battery compartments and nonfunctioning controls.

Q. What might be worth looking for in terms of a future investment?
A. It would be best to look for interesting design elements and media tie-ins. Take the Tomy *Tron* tabletop game based on the Walt Disney film of the same title. It uses key elements from the film (which was a groundbreaking hit). It has a smoky see-through case and simulated internal circuitry, all very reminiscent of the film's design concept. It's a game that has acquired cult status!

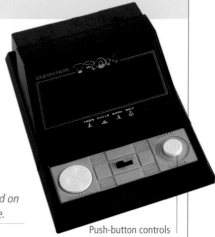

TOMY "TRON" GAME
A tabletop game based on the 1982 Disney movie.
$$ • *6 in (15 cm) wide*

Push-button controls

VIRTUAL BOY
The Nintendo Virtual Boy 3D game system, c. 1995.

$$ • 8½ in (22 cm) wide

TOP TIPS

- Avoid battered and malfunctioning pieces—they may be cheap but do not constitute a good investment.
- Search out games produced solely for the Japanese market, as these are avidly sought after—but make sure they can be played without mastery of the language!
- Learn about milestones in technology to help you make astute buys for the future. You should know, for instance, that the most popular retro games date from the 1980s.

Starter Buys

RACETRACK GAME
This handheld Toytronic Racetrack game is from c. 1980.

$ • 3½ in (9 cm) wide

SPEAK & SPELL
A Texas Instruments Speak & Spell, with original box, c. 1978.

$ • 15½ in (37.2 cm) high

ATARI HOME COMPUTER
This Atari 800 XL home computer, designed to look like a friendly typewriter, has an expandable system of two easily accessible cartridge ports under the front cover, c. 1983.

$$ • 15 in (38 cm) wide

GALAXY TWINVADER
This CGL Galaxy Twinvader tabletop game is from c. 1981.

$ • 6½ in (17 cm) wide

SUPER MARIO BROS.
A Nintendo YM-105, c. 1988, in the New Widescreen series.

$ • 4¼ in (11 cm) wide

MATTEL ARMOR BATTLE
Mattel Armor Battle handheld game, c. 1978.

$ • 3½ in (9 cm) wide

SINCLAIR CALCULATOR
This was Sinclair's second calculator, c. 1973.

$$ • 2 in (5 cm) wide

MASTER-BLASTER STATION
A handheld Bambino UFO Master-Blaster game, c. 1980.

$ • 5 in (13 cm) wide

POCKET SIMON
A late 1970s/early 1980s MB Electronics Pocket Simon.

$ • 7 in (18 cm) high

You may also like… Telephones & Cell Phones, see pp. 354–57

Mantel & Carriage Clocks

While mantel clocks have pendulums and need to be kept on a stable surface, carriage clocks are designed to be portable. Both are popular with collectors because of their size and affordability.

Mantel clocks come in many different guises—figural, architectural, and technical. Designed to sit on the mantelpiece, they were made from a variety of materials, including different types of wood, porcelain, and gilded metal. Throughout the 1700s, the earliest period in the development of these clocks, the best quality and most innovative were produced by English clockmakers.

Carriage clocks tended to be made of brass and became very popular by the mid-19th century. Most were made in France for the very lucrative English market.

Decorative carriage clocks had prettily painted porcelain panels, while technically interesting examples featured calendar work and unusual striking tones. A small number of English carriage clocks were made in London in the 19th century, and these tended to be of better quality than their more numerous French counterparts. Today, standard French carriage clocks can be worth between $100 and $20,000, while English versions can fetch from $2,000 up to $400,000.

Reliable Companion

In the mid-19th century, a carriage clock was considered an important part of the upper classes' traveling luggage. Its revolutionary lever escapement ensured reliable timekeeping on bumpy carriages and trains. One of France's foremost clockmakers, Louis Breguet, is credited with the invention of the "pendule de voyage" in around 1795. He reportedly sold his first carriage clock to Napoleon Bonaparte in 1798.

EARLY CARRIAGE CLOCK
This c. 1840 brass-cased carriage clock by Auguste, Paris, has a twin train movement with lever platform escapement and an enameled dial with Roman chapters. The mechanism is enclosed within a heavily engraved case with a hinged carrying handle.
$$$$ • 7 in (17 cm) high

KEY FACTS	1700s	1800s	1890s	1950s	1960s
History of carriage clocks	Carriage clocks are invented as traveling clocks, and are first made in France in the late 18th century.	With the advent of reliable coach and shipping services, their manufacture increases exponentially.	After the Industrial Revolution, the French export mainly to Britain and then to the booming US market.	The popularity of antique carriage clocks revives as collectors appreciate their intricacy and design.	Quartz timekeepers spell the end for mechanical clocks as they are reliable even on the move.

What's Hot

Look out for:

French carriage clocks from the second half of the 19th century are fairly common. This example, however, has beautifully painted porcelain panels and a matching painted porcelain dial. Of crucial importance is the fact that the porcelain is almost perfect (chips and cracks can halve the price). This piece deserves its value of $8,000–12,000.

Engraved columns _____

Gilt bronze feet _____

MANTEL TIMEPIECE
An early Victorian maple-cased mantel timepiece by James McCabe, London.
$$$$ • 9 in (23 cm) high

GLOBE CLOCK
A Louis XVI-style ormolu and marble clock with naked nymphs and floral drapes.
$$$$ • 24 in (61 cm) high

MANTEL REGULATOR
This mahogany regulator with arched case has a silvered dial with large minute chapter ring, a subsidiary hours and seconds ring, and a detached escapement. It is signed "Dalgety's patent."
$$$$ • 19 in (49 cm) high

FRENCH CARRIAGE CLOCK
This late 19th-century porcelain-mounted French carriage clock was made for Tiffany & Co., New York. The circular dial has Roman chapters on a Sèvres-style turquoise ground.
$$$$ • 7 in (19 cm) high

What's Not

A late 19th-century gilt metal clock may look exciting at an estate sale, but it will never rise in value. Such items were produced in large quantities and are of poor quality, which makes them of little interest to serious collectors.

EMPIRE ORMOLU CLOCK
The twin train movement in this clock strikes the half hours on a steel bell.
$$$$ • 13 in (33 cm) high

NEO-CLASSICAL CLOCK
This very rare brass and ormolu mounted mantel clock depicts George Washington.
$$$$$ • 16 in (40.5 cm) high

ALABASTER CLOCK
A 19th-century French gilt metal and alabaster clock with enamel dial marked "Ray & Niles," Paris.
$$ • 12 in (30 cm) high

Core Collectibles

PEWTER AND ENAMEL CLOCK
This "Tudric" clock by Archibald Knox was made for Liberty & Co.

$$$$ • 8 in (20 cm) high

MANTEL CHRONOMETER
A burr walnut-cased mantel chronometer by Thomas Mercer, St. Albans.

$$$$ • 9½ in (24 cm) high

BRONZE MANTEL CLOCK
An early 19th-century French gilt clock with a white enamel dial and Roman numerals; the movement, with silk suspension and outside count wheel, strikes on a bell.

$$ • 10 in (25 cm) high

STRIKING CLOCK
This striking carriage clock with an alarm is by E. Maurice & Co., Paris.

$$$$ • 6 in (15 cm) high

ENAMEL MANTEL CLOCK
French 19th-century ormolu and champlevé clock stamped "Japy Frères et Cie."

$$$$ • 18 in (45 cm) high

TORTOISESHELL CLOCK
With silver-inlaid tortoiseshell panels, this timepiece is hallmarked c. 1910.

$$$ • 5 in (12 cm) high

BRASS TIMEPIECE
This French gilt timepiece has a lever escapement and a circular white enamel dial.

$$ • 5½ in (14 cm) high

JUMP TIMEPIECE
This small tortoiseshell and gilt clock by Jump of London has a silvered dial.

$$$$ • 7 in (18 cm) high

BLACK FOREST CLOCK
A large Wherle trumpeter musical mantel clock with skeletonized movement.

$$$$ • 29 in (72 cm) high

LYRE-SHAPED CLOCK
This Louis XVI-style marble and ormolu mounted clock was sold by Tiffany & Co.

$$$$ • 19 in (48 cm) high

PORCELAIN MANTEL CLOCK
Late 19th-century decorative clock with a harbor scene.
$$$ • 18 in (45 cm) high

SILVER TIMEPIECE
This clock has a wooden frame and a 1910 hallmark.
$$$ • 14 in (36 cm) high

TOP TIPS

- Make sure the clock is actually working.
- If there are metal mounts on the case, check that there are none missing or damaged.
- If the dial is enameled or painted, make sure it is not chipped or badly restored.
- Look out for clocks by important makers such as France's Breguet, Garnier, Drocourt, Jacot, and Margaine, and England's Vulliamy, Jump, McCabe, and Frodsham.
- When dating, note that carriage clocks with one-piece cast brass frames usually date to pre-1850; after this time brass frames tended to be constructed from several pieces.

Starter Buys

ANNIVERSARY CLOCK
American eight-day, half-hour strike cathedral gong clock.
$$ • 9 in (23 cm) high

TRAVEL CLOCKS
Two Art Deco travel clocks, both with working alarms.
$$ • 3 in (7 cm) high

FRENCH MANTEL CLOCK
An ebonized and walnut-cased mantel clock from 1890.
$$ • 12 in (30 cm) high

BRASS CARRIAGE CLOCK
A small brass-cased repeating carriage clock.
$$ • 6 in (15 cm) high

LACQUERED MANTEL CLOCK
An early Georgian-style red lacquered mantel timepiece.
$$ • 9 in (23 cm) high

OAK MANTEL CLOCK
This carved clock has a silvered chapter ring.
$$ • 15 in (38 cm) high

WALNUT MANTEL CLOCK
This late 19th-century mantel clock has an enameled dial.
$$ • 8 in (20 cm) high

1940S MANTEL CLOCK
A walnut-cased mantel clock from the 1940s.
$$ • 11 in (28 cm) high

You may also like… Fob & Pocket Watches, see pp.374–75

Wall & Bracket Clocks

Many of the most desirable and valuable clocks belong to these varieties of clocks. As a rule of thumb, 18th-century clocks tend to be of better quality than 19th-century ones.

Wall clocks have enjoyed a renaissance in the past few years, with prices rising by as much as 50 percent. This is particularly the case for late 18th-century English dial clocks, which can be worth from $10,000 to $40,000. Later Victorian dial clocks are less desirable but make excellent kitchen clocks and are worth between $1,000 and $10,000.

The term "bracket clock" is a misnomer: only a few were made to sit on specially made wall brackets, while the vast majority were meant to sit on a table. Somehow the name "bracket clock" has stuck nonetheless. The most sought after are English table clocks from 1660–1700. The pendulum clock was only invented in 1657, and London clockmakers were quick to capitalize on this great innovation. Clocks by Thomas Tompion are the most desirable and can sell for up to $5 million, but clocks by lesser makers can be had for $10,000 upward. Table clocks from the 19th century are still relatively inexpensive at $2,000–$10,000.

A Light in Time

"Lantern" clocks were so called because of their distinctive lantern shape. The earliest models, from the 15th and 16th centuries, were called "chamber" clocks, and were incredibly rare but poor timekeepers. One of the earliest recorded examples in the English royal court is the Anne Boleyn clock, which was made c. 1533 and is still in the royal collection. Because of their simple design, lantern clocks continued to be made right through to the 20th century.

LANTERN CLOCK
Made of brass, this lantern clock has a replaced chain fusee movement. The Roman chapter ring enclosing the subsidiary alarm dial has the inscription "John Ebsworth." The case was made in about 1670 but the original movement has been replaced, reducing the value.
$$$ • 14 in (35 cm) high

KEY FACTS	1500s	1600s	c. 1800	1841	1840s
Important dates for clock times	In roughly 1560, the first use of an (inaccurate) second hand on a clock is recorded.	The invention of the pendulum in 1657 enables clocks to keep much better time.	Smaller spring-driven "carriage clocks" with a carrying handle are developed in France, to be used while traveling.	Scottish clockmaker Alexander Bain patents the electric clock, changing the face of clockmaking.	Skeleton clocks, which show all the internal wheels through a glass dome, become very popular.

What's Hot

Look out for:

This tavern clock is one of the rarest examples of its type. Made in about 1745, it is decorated with black lacquer and raised chinoiserie gilt figures. The dial is octagonal and there is a glass lenticle in the base of the trunk through which the pendulum can be seen swinging back and forth.

Maker's name

Gilt chinoiserie scene

Glass lenticle in base

STRIKING TABLE CLOCK
A late 17th-century ebony clock with engraved backplate inscribed "Nicolas Masey."
$$$$$ • 15 in (38 cm) high

LONGCASE CLOCK
This Victorian inlaid mahogany longcase clock is dated c. 1900.
$$$$$ • 96 in (245 cm) high

EBONY STRIKING CLOCK
This George III bracket clock, number 279, is by Matthew and Thomas Dutton.
$$$$$ • 17 in (43 cm) high

CHIMING BRACKET CLOCK
A George III mahogany and gilt brass-mounted clock, signed "Spencer & Perkins London."
$$$$$ • 26 in (66 cm) high

PARLIAMENT TIMEPIECE
This George II black-lacquered and gilt-decorated Parliament timepiece is by John Merrigeot, London. Its dial has Arabic and Roman chapters and elaborate pierced brass bands.
$$$$$ • 60 in (150 cm) high

What's Not

Modern clocks made to look like period timepieces have not really risen in value for the past 10–15 years. Although decorative, as an investment they are bad news.

WALL TIMEPIECE
A mahogany-cased timepiece by Jonathan Rowland, Sherrard Street, St. James's, with single train fusee movement, c. 1820.
$$$$ • 14 in (36 cm) in diameter

REGENCY TABLE CLOCK
A rosewood double-fusee striking clock by James McCabe of Royal Exchange, London, number "2376."
$$$$ • 17 in (43 cm) high

ORNATE BRACKET CLOCK
This 20th-century tortoiseshell veneered and gilt clock is by Tiffany & Co., New York, in the style of the 18th century.
$$$ • 21 in (56 cm) high

Core Collectibles

BELL TOP BRACKET CLOCK
This late-18th-century mahogany bracket clock is by John Carter, London.
$$$$$ • 22 in (55 cm) high

BELL TOP BRACKET CLOCK
A c. 1770 mahogany verge escapement clock with an engraved backplate.
$$$$$ • 18 in (45 cm) high

SCOTTISH LONGCASE CLOCK
A 19th-century mahogany eight-day longcase clock by R. Cunninghame, Edinburgh.
$$$$ • 88 in (220 cm) high

SKELETON CLOCK
With a glass dome, this Victorian brass clock has a silvered brass chapter ring.
$$$ • 11 in (28 cm) high

EBONIZED BRACKET CLOCK
This George II clock has a five-pillar bell-striking movement and inverted bell top, c. 1740.
$$$$$ • 18 in (45 cm) high

MAHOGANY CLOCK
A George III clock, twin train fusee movement striking on a bell, by J. Y. Hatton, London.
$$$$$ • 19 in (47 cm) high

BOULLE WALL CLOCK
A French tortoiseshell 19th-century clock with twin train movement striking on a gong.
$$$$$ • 55 in (140 cm) high

Ask the Expert

Q. What's the best way to clean an antique clock?
A. The only cleaning you should do is to dust the clock with a soft brush or cloth. Don't be tempted to touch or clean the mechanism itself or you may damage it. Get it cleaned and checked by a professional at least every five to ten years.

Q. Is it true that tavern clocks are particularly collectible just now?
A. Tavern clocks have always been popular, partly because of their quality—being public service clocks, they had to be able to keep good

Chinoiserie decoration

Wooden case for wall-mounting

time—and partly because they are so decorative. They were also known as Parliament clocks in an erroneous link to the five-shilling tax levied on every clock in 1797.

PARLIAMENT CLOCK
Dated c. 1770, this fine tavern clock is by William Allam, London.
$$$$$ • *57 in (145 cm) high*

TOP TIPS

- Check whether the clock is in working order before you buy it if you wish to use it as a functional clock.
- Keep an eye out for English precision clocks, such as regulators—they are most unusual.
- Make sure the glass dome is intact when buying decorative simple Victorian skeleton timepieces.
- Consider late-Victorian dial clocks for the kitchen—they are relatively inexpensive.

FOUR-GLASS CLOCK

This late 19th-century French ormolu and champlevé four-glass clock, so called because of the glass panel on each side of the clock face, was sold by Tiffany and Co. Its oval-shaped base encloses a white enamel dial painted with flowers within a paste-set bezel. It has a paste-set pendulum enclosing a miniature on ivory of an 18th-century lady. It is flanked by champlevé columns.

$$$$ • 14 in (35 cm) high

DOUBLE FUSEE CLOCK

This mahogany double fusee bracket clock has a white convex dial within a lancet case with ebony moldings.

$$$$ • 20 in (51 cm) high

DROP DIAL CLOCK

A mahogany William IV wall clock with fan-shaped angle brackets and brass inlay, by "M. Bartley, Bristol."

$$$$ • 11 in (28 cm) wide

Starter Buys

DIAL CLOCK

This is a good-quality, early 20th-century mahogany-cased fusee dial clock.

$$$$ • 12 in (30 cm) diameter

ROSEWOOD BRACKET CLOCK

From c. 1820, this Regency clock has a stepped top with an acorn finial.

$$$$ • 14 in (35 cm) high

BRASS SKELETON CLOCK

A clock with silvered chapter ring, anchor escapement, and single chain fusee movement.

$$$ • 13 in (33 cm) high

FRENCH CARTEL CLOCK

This 19th-century French gilt metal cartel clock is in the late-18th-century style.

$$$$ • 27½ in (69 cm) high

You may also like… Kitchenalia, see pp. 170–73

Fob & Pocket Watches

Once hidden within a person's clothing, pocket watches evolved to become beautifully crafted ornaments that spoke volumes about the wearer's style and status long before the invention of the wristwatch.

The term "fob watch" is a bit of a misnomer. The fob was a pocket in a man's waistcoat for holding bits and pieces. However, after it became fashionable in the 18th century to hang watches on a ribbon or chain from a person's clothing, fob watches came to describe small ladies' pocket watches worn inside or hung from the outside of their garments.

Simple pocket watches were made as early as the 15th century by blacksmiths who forged them in steel, but these were very poor timekeepers. In the late 16th and early 17th centuries, German watchmakers led the field and their creations are now among the most valuable. When spiral hairsprings were introduced in the 1670s, accuracy was greatly increased and watches could give the time correct to the nearest few minutes. In the 18th century, English makers came to the forefront of the industry, adding gem stones to the tivots.

Today, good quality pre-1700s pocket watches are very rare. Easier to find and very collectible are English and French watches from the 19th century, up to the late 1800s when Swiss and American machine-made watches were introduced.

The Earlier the Better

With the advent of the wristwatch fashion in the 20th century, hundreds of thousands of pretty ladies' fob watches from the late 19th century were simply put away for safekeeping. Usually in finely engraved silver or gold cases with precise Swiss movements, most are worth less than $200 today. Far more valuable are pieces like this, crafted by makers of repute.

AUTOMATON POCKET WATCH
A quarter-repeating 18kt yellow-gold pocket watch by Le Roy of Paris, c. 1820.
$$$$$ • 2¼ in (5.5 cm) in diameter

TOP TIPS

- Condition is important, so check the case and dial are not damaged or repaired.
- It is expensive to repair a watch movement, so make sure it works before buying.
- For a budget collection, start with easily-available silver 18th-century watches.

KEY FACTS	1500s	1800s	1965	1999	2006
The right time in a pocket	With the invention of the spring-driven clock, the first portable watches are made, to hang around the neck.	The development of railroads results in the more widespread professional use of pocket watches.	The first American Watch Fob Collector's meeting is held in Norwalk, Ohio.	A world record price for a pocket watch is set when a Patek Philippe model sells for $12,000,000.	A vintage pocket watch from the *Titanic* goes on sale, its hands frozen at 2:19 am.

What's Hot

PLATINUM POCKET WATCH
This Patek Philippe pocket watch has an unusual diamond-set dial, c. 1940.
$$$$$ • 2 in (5 cm) in diameter

SPLIT SECOND WATCH
A Patek Philippe 18kt-gold watch with double-handed stopwatch mechanism.
$$$$$ • 2 in (5 cm) in diameter

Look out for:

A good chain doubles the value of what would otherwise be a fairly common gold-cased pocket watch. In fact, gold chains are often worth more than the watch itself!

Blue enamel Roman numerals on the outer case

CASED POCKET WATCH
This gentleman's 18kt-gold half hunter cased pocket watch has a yellow-gold guard chain with keyless wind and a locket.
$$$ • 2 in (5 cm) in diameter

Core Collectibles

MASONIC POCKET WATCH
A 1930s silver-cased triangular pocket watch with a mother-of-pearl face.
$$$ • Case 2 in (5 cm) long

LADY'S FOB WATCH
This is an American gold-cased lady's fob watch by J. E. Caldwell & Co.
$$$$ • 1¼ in (3 cm) in diameter

Starter Buys

HUNTER POCKET WATCH
This lever hunter pocket watch is made of 18kt gold. It has a Swiss 21-jewel movement.
$$$ • 2 in (5 cm) in diameter

TORTOISESHELL WATCH
Dated 1818, this is a silver pair-cased watch overlaid with tortoiseshell.
$$$ • 2 in (5 cm) in diameter

ENAMELED FOB WATCH
This 1920s lady's cloisonné enameled spherical watch has a 17-jewel movement.
$$$ • 2 in (5 cm) long

SWISS FOB WATCH
This 18kt-gold watch has an engraved monogram.
$$$ • 1¾ in (4.5 cm) in diameter

J. W. BENSON WATCH
An open-faced keyless pocket watch made of 18kt gold.
$$$ • 2 in (5 cm) in diameter

You may also like… Writing Tools, see pp. 180–83

Wristwatches

Initially designed as decorative bracelets for ladies, wristwatches took over from the pocket watch as a way of personal timekeeping after World War I, when soldiers found them easier to use in battle.

The most sought-after name in the world of wristwatches is that of Swiss company Patek Philippe: their watches regularly fetch world-record prices. Vintage Rolex, Cartier, Audemars Piguet, and Vacheron & Constantin also often sell for very large sums. The golden period of watchmaking was between 1940 and 1970, and the most desirable watches are those with complex movements, such as calendar and chronograph (stopwatch) facilities, or limited editions of particular watches that are enhanced by having an unusual style of case or dial.

Toward the lower end of the market, some early pieces by lesser makers from the 1930s and 1940s can be bought relatively cheaply; examples with pretty enamel dials and simple silver and gold cases can be bought for less than $2,000.

Ladies' gem-set watches are an entirely different market in which value is largely determined by the quality and quantity of precious stones rather than the watch itself. Vintage Cartier watches, for example, are regarded as items of jewelry in their own right and are very collectible.

Memorable First-timers

In 1927, Rolex made the first real waterproof watch, the "Oyster." It had a screw-down winder with a rubber seal to keep the movement dry. The company was also the first to produce a commercial automatic wristwatch. Called the "Bubbleback," it had a rotor fixed to the back of the movement that wound the spring with every movement of the owner's arm. The original rotor was quite large, so the back of the case had to be bowed out to accommodate it—hence the name "Bubbleback." Rolex was founded by the German Hans Wilsdorf in 1905. On his death in 1960, it became a nonprofit trust and today remains one of the great names in Swiss watch-making history.

"BUBBLEBACK" WRISTWATCH
A c. 1940 18kt-gold Rolex "Bubbleback" wristwatch with a thunderbird bezel.
$$$$$ • 1¼ in (3 cm) wide

KEY FACTS	1884	1914–18	1927	1940s	2005
Portable timepieces for rich and poor	Founded in 1839, the famous Swiss company Patek Philippe introduces its first wristwatch.	Wristwatches replace pocket watches as the most popular timepieces for soldiers in the trenches.	The first waterproof wristwatch is produced by Rolex and survives an attempt to swim the English Channel.	Breitling adds a circular slide rule to the bezel of its chronograph models for use by airline pilots.	A Patek Philippe wristwatch sells at auction for a record-breaking $4,000,000.

What's Hot

CHRONOGRAPH WATCH
Finished in 18kt gold, this
1939 Patek Philippe piece
is highly valued by collectors.
$$$$$ • 1½ in (4 cm) wide

ROLEX DAYTONA
This is a rare version of the
18kt-yellow-gold Rolex
Daytona from 1978.
$$$$$ • 1¾ in (4.5 cm) wide

Look out for:

In the 1970s, a small number of Rolex "Sea Dweller"
watches were issued to Comex, a French marine
engineering company. Without "Comex" on the dial,
the watch would be worth around $6,000–$8,000, but
with the marking, it is worth ten times that figure.

Stainless-steel bracelet

Black enamel dial

Comex insignia

PATEK PHILIPPE WATCH
The first automatic watch
made by Patek Philippe, this
wristwatch dates to 1955–60.
$$$$$ • 1½ in (4 cm) wide

CUSHION-CASE WATCH
This early Patek Philippe
18kt-gold wristwatch has a
fragile enamel dial, c. 1920.
$$$$$ • 1¼ in (3 cm) wide

LIMITED-EDITION ROLEX
A 1970s stainless steel Rolex
Comex "Sea Dweller" with a
plastic face. This limited-edition
version was made exclusively for the
Comex Oil Company's deep-sea divers.
$$$$$ • 1¾ in (4.5 cm) wide

What's Not

Gem-set watches aren't always
worth as much as people think.
The majority are set with low-
quality stones and are worth
less than $2,000—especially
with a damaged dial, as here.

TONNEAU WATCH
A c. 1920 Patek Philippe
platinum-cased wristwatch
with a two-tone dial.
$$$$$ • 1 in (2.5 cm) wide

CARTIER DIAMOND WATCH
This 1920s Cartier dress watch
has a diamond-set bezel and
Roman numerals on the dial.
$$$$$ • ¾ in (2 cm) wide

BEUCHE GIROD WATCH
A gentleman's wristwatch
made of platinum, gold,
lapis lazuli, and diamonds.
$$$ • 1¼ in (3 cm) wide

Core Collectibles

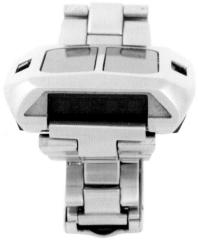

TIFFANY & CO. WATCH
A 1930s Tiffany & Co. triple-calendar gentleman's wristwatch cased in 14kt gold, with movement by Movado. The band is also made of 14kt gold.

$$$$ • 1½ in (4 cm) wide

HAMILTON YELLOW-GOLD WATCH
A Hamilton gentleman's 14kt-yellow-gold wristwatch with silver-colored indexes and dauphine hands, attached to a brown leather band.

$$$ • 1½ in (4 cm) wide

SOLAR-POWERED WATCH
Designed in 1973 by Roger Riehl, a pioneer of LED wristwatch development, this is a Synchronar 2100 solar-powered watch with LED readout and a stainless-steel bracelet.

$$$ • 1¾ in (4.5 cm) wide

"BUBBLEBACK" WATCH
This stainless-steel Rolex "Bubbleback" wristwatch has an Arabic dial and a black leather strap that contrasts with its white face. It dates from the 1940s.

$$$$ • 1½ in (4 cm) wide

VACHERON & CONSTANTIN WATCH
Fitted with an original engine-turned *guillouche* dial, this is a late-1940s/early-1950s, 18kt-gold oversized round watch by Vacheron & Constantin.

$$$$$ • 1½ in (4 cm) wide

OYSTER PERPETUAL
This 1950s Rolex Oyster Perpetual gentleman's wristwatch is cased in 18kt gold, with gilt baton markers and an engine-turned and chased bezel.

$$$$ • 1½ in (4 cm) wide

HAMILTON WHITE-GOLD WATCH
A 14kt-white-gold American gentleman's wristwatch by Hamilton, with subsidiary seconds on the dial and Roman numerals on the chapter ring.

$$$ • 1½ in (4 cm) wide

SPACEVIEW WRISTWATCH
A rare mid-1960s Bulova Accutron Spaceview wristwatch with a stainless-steel bezel and visible battery movement, on a black leather strap.

$$$ • 1½ in (4 cm) wide

WWI MILITARY ROLEX
A silver military Rolex with a black dial, white numerals, and luminous green hands.

$$$$ • 1½ in (4 cm) wide

GRUEN WRISTWATCH
This Swiss nickel-cased Gruen wristwatch from the 1930s has radium hands and dial.

$$$ • 1½ in (4 cm) wide

1950S GOLD WATCH
This 1950s 18kt Patek Philippe watch with its original dial was first retailed by Gobbi of Milan.

$$$$$ • 1½ in (4 cm) wide

LORD ELGIN WATCH
A 14kt-white-gold Dunbar gentleman's wristwatch by Lord Elgin, c. 1951.

$$$ • 1¼ in (3 cm) wide

HEUER CHRONOGRAPH WATCH
A 1970s Monaco automatic gentleman's wristwatch by Heuer, with a calendar, left-hand crown, and blue twin register dial within a brushed steel case.

$$$ • 1¾ in (4.5 cm) wide

Ask the Expert

Q. What is the world record price paid for a wristwatch?
A. $4 million was once paid for a Patek Philippe platinum wristwatch.

Q. Where can I get my wristwatch repaired?
A. See the American Watchmakers-Clockmakers Institute website.

Q. Are quartz watches valuable?
A. Most are worth less than $100, but examples by Patek Philippe have sold for $10,000 and more. The watch must be in working condition, though.

Roman numerals

CALATRAVA WRISTWATCH
A Patek Philippe stainless-steel Calatrava from the 1940s.

$$$$$ • 1¼ in (3 cm) wide

Q. Why are some wristwatches so valuable?
A. It's all about quality, innovation, and rarity. The upper end of the market is dominated by the Swiss firm Patek Philippe, which made some of the most complicated, technologically advanced watches between 1920 and 1960, and in limited numbers.

Core Collectibles

JAEGER REVERSO WATCH
An Art Deco–style 1940s Jaeger Reverso watch. The dial can be protected by swiveling the watch 180° in its case.
$$$$ • 1 in (2.5 cm) wide

ROLEX OYSTER
An early cushion-case Rolex Oyster in 9kt yellow gold with an enamel dial. Oysters were the first waterproof watches.
$$$$ • 1¼ in (3 cm) wide

OYSTER PERPETUAL GMT MASTER
Sporting a blue and red enamel rotating bezel, this Rolex stainless-steel watch has luminous markers.
$$$$ • 1¾ in (4.5 cm) wide

Starter Buys

HAMILTON WATCH
This Hamilton 14kt-gold gentleman's wristwatch with 19-jewel movement is stamped "M73549."
$$ • 1 in (2.5 cm) wide

OMEGA CONSTELLATION
A steel and gold-plated Omega Constellation automatic gentleman's wristwatch with dauphine hands.
$$$$ • 1½ in (4 cm) wide

GOLD-CASED TIFFANY WATCH
This is a 14kt-gold-cased Tiffany & Co. gentleman's wristwatch from the 1930s with Longines movement.
$$$$ • 1¼ in (3 cm) wide

OYSTER PRECISION WATCH
A late 1950s Rolex Oyster Precision gentleman's wristwatch with white baton dial and a milled outer bezel.
$$$ • 1½ in (4 cm) wide

LIP WATCH
This 1970s Lip wristwatch has a brown plastic bezel, a brown dial, white Arabic numerals, and a brown suedette strap.
$$ • 1¼ in (3 cm) wide

SILVER ROLEX
A 1930s silver-cased lady's Rolex with a white enamel full-figure dial, luminous hands, and a hinged case back.
$$$ • 1¼ in (3 cm) wide

1950S ROLEX WATCH
This 1950s Rolex gentleman's watch with a circular white dial has a manual movement and a black leather strap.
$$$ • 1½ in (4 cm) wide

LONGINES WATCH
A 1950s 18kt-gold Longines gentleman's wristwatch with full, handsome numerals on a plain dial.
$$$ • 1½ in (4 cm) wide

1958 LONGINES WRISTWATCH
Dating from 1958, this 14kt-gold Longines wristwatch on a fabric strap is inscribed and dated on the back.
$$$ • 1½ in (4 cm) wide

PIAGET WATCH
This 18kt, 18-jewel-movement Piaget gentleman's wristwatch has its original strap and a gold buckle.
$$$ • 1¼ in (3 cm) wide

JAEGER–LECOULTRE WRISTWATCH
A 1960s stainless-steel wristwatch by Jaeger–LeCoultre, with Arabic quarter numerals on a silvered dial.
$$$ • 1½ in (4 cm) wide

LONGINES GOLD-FILLED WATCH
This is a 1950s 10kt-gold-filled Longines gentleman's wristwatch with an unusual case.
$$$ • 1¼ in (3 cm) wide

MOVADO WATCH
A Movado triple-calendar stainless-steel gentleman's wristwatch with day and month apertures on the dial.
$$$$ • 1½ in (4 cm) wide

You may also like… Art Deco Jewelry, see pp. 278–79

Swatches

The Swatch was launched in 1983 as a fun, affordable fashion accessory. It was instantly popular and, as arty limited editions and one-of-a-kind specials were issued, collectors soon became hooked.

As the Swiss watch market declined during the 1970s in the face of stiff competition from other countries, notably Japan, the Swatch Group rose to the challenge. It made a plastic watch with only 51 components, which, like many other successful collectibles, was both cheap and well made. The watch was a phenomenal success—in its first 21 months some 3.5 million were sold. By its 20th birthday, the figure had reached around 300 million.

The watches came in bright colors and unique, eye-catching designs that caught the public's imagination, particularly at their peak in the mid-1980s. There are now around 2,500 models and new styles are introduced each season, giving collectors huge scope. Rare examples and limited editions have fetched large sums at auction, with those designed by artists such as Keith Haring and Kiki Picasso commanding the highest prices.

Swatch sales declined in the 1990s but new innovations such as the Paparazzi series, an Internet-connected watch that can download stock quotes, news, weather reports, and other data, keep interest in the brand alive.

Watch This Space…

The world record price for a Swatch was just under $32,000 paid in 1995 for an example designed by Kiki Picasso. Nostalgia for the 1980s has fueled interest in Swatches from this era, when one of the fads was to wear several on the wrist at the same time.

"YAMAHA RACER" WATCH
Numbered GJ 700, from the Coral Reef series, this is a Swatch "Yamaha Racer" from 1985.
$$ • 1¼ in (3.3 cm) diameter

TOP TIPS

- Buy items you like rather than to invest. The market is not what it was 10 years ago, and prices are deflated.
- Check the Internet for price records before you buy.
- There are fakes of the more valuable examples—beware!
- Condition is paramount—once you wear a Swatch, its value is dramatically reduced.

KEY FACTS	1960s	1983	c. 1985	c. 1995	1996–2004
From a gap in the market to a collector's item	Japanese companies such as Seiko market aggressively; high-end digital watches take over the market.	Swatches enter the Swiss market, in an attempt to boost sales of entry-level analog watches.	Swatches become a fashion statement and the brand often collaborates with artists such as Keith Haring.	Swatch diversifies extensively, producing new ranges, specialized models, and seasonal themes.	Swatch is the official timekeeper for three Summer Olympic Games in a row.

What's Hot

"NICHOLSON" WATCH
Swatch "Nicholson" watch
from 1985, number GA 705,
from the Plaza series.
$$ • 1¼ in (3.3 cm) diameter

"X-RATED" WATCH
GB 406 "X-Rated" wristwatch
with black ribbed strap from
the 1987 Neo Geo series.
$$$ • 1¼ in (3.3 cm) diameter

Look out for:
Condition is absolutely
crucial when collecting
Swatches. It is imperative
that they come with their
original packaging and
papers, and that if they
have been worn there is
little or no sign of wear.

Scratches reduce value

Core Collectibles

"RUFFLED FEATHERS" WATCH
Swatch GF 100 Kiva series
"Ruffled Feathers" wristwatch
from 1986, with brown strap.
$ • 1¼ in (3.3 cm) diameter

"TIME & STRIPES" WATCH
Number SAN 105 from 1993
with skeleton back, window
face, and striped strap.
$$ • 1½ in (3.6 cm) diameter

"12 FLAGS" WATCH
A 1984 Swatch "12 Flags" number
GS 101 wristwatch from the Skipper series.
$$$ • 1¼ in (3.3 cm) diameter

Starter Buys

"RAVE" WATCH
This is a DJ Ten Strikes series
"Rave" watch from 1991.
$ • 1¼ in (3.3 cm) diameter

"DAN JANSEN" WATCH
Commemorative item from
the 1996 Atlanta Olympics.
$ • 1½ in (3.8 cm) diameter

"HEARTSTONE" WATCH
With a brushed chrome-plated
case, this is a 1998 wristwatch
from the Heavy Metal series.
$$ • 1¼ in (3.3 cm) diameter

"BLACK MAGIC" WATCH
Numbered LB 106, from the
Carlton series, this is a "Black
Magic" ladies' watch.
$$ • 1 in (2.5 cm) diameter

"GLOWING ARROW" WATCH
MOCA series wristwatch,
number GX 109, from 1989.
$ • 1¼ in (3.3 cm) diameter

"CALAFATTI" WATCH
From the Vienna Deco series,
a 1987 "Calafatti" watch.
$ • 1¼ in (3.3 cm) diameter

You may also like… Computers & Games, see pp. 362–63

CHAPTER

Militaria

Serving the Nation

The brutal and bloody reality of battle is often seen as glamorous and romantic by those not involved, and there still remains a huge fascination for collecting anything relating to wars.

Not a year has gone by in the last two centuries without a war or battle taking place somewhere in the world, many involving the European or US powers. It is surprising, therefore, that, far from being weary of war, the Western world has far more collectors of militaria than any other part of the world. Although it is not unknown for women to collect militaria, it is more usually a masculine hobby, possibly brought about as an extension of playing soldier games as a boy, or listening to tales told by old soldiers. Many collectors start their hobby by being given a badge or button, sparking a latent collecting instinct, which, in some, grows to massive proportions, taking over house and home.

Medals from World War I,
see Core Collectibles, p. 390.

Fortunately, whatever the budget, there is an area of militaria to suit. At the cheaper end are medal ribbons, cartridge cases, and buttons—there are thousands of these to find and some collectors devote a lifetime to specializing in a single narrow field.

Even if you have little to spend, you could try a more economical project, such as photographing every Civil War battlefield and monument. It would prove a difficult job and probably take a lifetime, as there are significant sites in at least 28 states, but it would be a highly satisfying project. For those with deeper pockets, there are edged weapons, flintlock and percussion guns, and armor, which can cost anything from a few hundred to tens of thousands of dollars.

The majority of militaria is anonymous so it can be hard to relate objects to the actual soldiers they once belonged to. However there are certain items that can give a fascinating insight into individuals and the lives they led. At the cheaper end are World War I postcards that were sent home to loved ones, costing just a few pounds. At the other end are medals. Prior to World War II most were named and can be traced to the records of their original owner. There are many details available on the Internet, and it can prove exciting and satisfying to build up a complete picture of the recipient's life.

Militaria collectors are often accused of glorifying war, but being interested in the history of an object is not to approve of the conflict it may have seen. Indeed, to forget history is to fail to learn its lessons, and even to risk repeating it.

Victorian helmet plate, see What's Hot, p. 389.

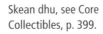

Skean dhu, see Core Collectibles, p. 399.

A rifle from the Boer War, see Core Collectibles, p. 395.

Medals, Badges & Insignia

As symbols of heroic action, loyal service, and accomplishment, all medals tell a story. The greater the service and more illustrious the recipient, the higher the value of the medal, badge, or insignia.

The award of a medal for exceptional service has a long history. In the second century BC, Alexander awarded a gold button to Jonathon the High Priest for leading the Jews into battle. In Britain, however, it wasn't until the 19th century that medals started to be awarded in large numbers.

Collecting medals can be a fascinating hobby and can suit varied budgets from a few dollars to well over $200,000 for the rarest Victoria Cross (Britain's highest military award for valor). In addition to medals, which are generally meant to be pinned on the breast, the term also includes medallions, which

are often found in little boxes and commemorate events such as coronations or exhibitions, and prize medals for competitions. Badges and insignia refer to identification symbols, normally of metal, which are worn on a uniform to indicate which regiment or unit the person belongs to.

Those with a limited budget could go for a small group of World War II medals for less than $50. These are mostly unnamed, but World War I medals are nearly always named around the edge, giving more personal interest. Documents relating to the recipient add significantly to the value.

Bravery and Service
The center pair of these medals are the WWI Victory Medal (second from left) and the British War Medal. The Military Medal (right) was awarded to NCOs and other ranks for bravery. This recipient, having served in World War I, was probably too old to fight in World War II, so the Defence Medal (left) was probably awarded for serving in Civil Defence.

MEDALS FROM TWO WORLD WARS
Four military medals, as they might be found in an antiques market, awarded to a member of the East Lancs regiment.

$$$ • 6½ in (16.5 cm) wide

KEY FACTS	1847	1856	1899–1902	1919	1990–91
Medals in history	The Naval General Service Medal (NGS) is instituted with an astonishing 230 clasps.	The Victoria Cross is instituted as the foremost award for gallantry of any rank.	The Queen's South Africa medal is awarded in huge numbers during the Boer War.	The Treaty of Versailles marks the official end of World War I, although the armistice ended fighting in 1918.	The UK's Gulf Medal commemorates continuous service during the Iraqi invasion of Kuwait.

What's Hot

OFFICER'S BELT PLATE
An Argyll and Sutherland Highlanders officer's gilt-plated shoulder belt plate.
$$$ • Approx 4 in (10 cm) high

LLOYDS MEDAL
The Lloyds medal for bravery at sea was instituted in 1940 by the Lloyds Committee.
$$$ • 1⁷⁄₁₆ in (3.6 cm) in diameter

Look out for:

Medals are sought-after items in themselves, but documents or photographs relating to them can add to their value. It was popular for families to have medals framed with a photograph of the recipient. Anything on paper that relates to a medal is called "ephemera." The value is further enhanced if the recipient was an important personality or if any of the medals were awarded for valor.

Photograph of John Bostock

Companion of the Order of the Bath badge, Military version (far left)

Gwalior star (center), made from the metal of captured guns

SHOULDER BELT PLATE
Made of brass, an other-ranks shoulder belt plate of the Strathspey Fencibles, 1793–99.
$$$ • Approx 3½ in (9 cm) high

INDIAN MUTINY MEDAL
This two-clasp medal was awarded for service in the Indian Rebellion of 1857.
$$$ • 1⁷⁄₁₆ in (3.6 cm) in diameter

FRAMED MEDALS AND PHOTOGRAPH
The Order and medals of John Ashton Bostock (1815–1895), C.B., Deputy Surgeon-General of the army and Hon. Surgeon to Queen Victoria. He served in India and in the Crimea.
$$$$ • Medals 5⅛ in (13 cm) long

What's Not

Although quite collectible, QSA medals tend to be inexpensive because of the large number awarded (around 178,000), and can be found for as little as $150.

VICTORIAN HELMET PLATE
An officer's gilt and silver-plated helmet plate of the York and Lancaster Regiment.
$$$ • Approx 4¼ in (9 cm) high

CRIMEA MEDAL
Three clasps for fighting in the battles at Alma, Inkermann, and Sebastopol, c. 1856.
$$$ • 1⁷⁄₁₆ in (3.6 cm) in diameter

QUEEN'S S. AFRICA MEDAL
A three-clasp campaign medal awarded following the Second Boer War of 1899–1902.
$$$ • 1⁷⁄₁₆ in (3.6 cm) in diameter

Core Collectibles

OFFICER'S CAP BADGE
Made of gilt metal and silver, this cap badge belonged to an officer of the Northamptonshire Imperial Yeomanry.

$$$ • Approx. 1½ in (4 cm) high

GLENGARRY BADGE
An other-ranks white metal badge of the 4th–7th Battalions of the Black Watch.

$$$ • Approx. 2 in (5 cm) high

OTHER-RANKS CAP BADGE
A scarce gilding metal cap badge of the 3rd County of London Imperial Yeomanry (Sharpshooters).

$$$ • 2 in (5 cm) high

MINIATURE BOER WAR MEDALS
Miniature Victoria Cross, Queen's South Africa, King's South Africa, Army Long Service, and Good Conduct medals.

$$$ • Approx. 3⅛ in (8 cm) long

SHOULDER BELT PLATE
A 78th Foot (Highland Regt) officer's gilt and plated shoulder belt plate.

$$$ • Approx. 4 in (10 cm) high

WORLD WAR I GROUP
Four WWI medals: the British War Medal, Victory Medal, Military Medal, and the 1914–15 Star, awarded to Sgt. W. Barr.

$$$ • Medals each 1⁷⁄₁₆ in (3.6 cm) in diameter

OFFICER'S HELMET PLATE
A Victorian officer's silver-plated helmet plate, worn by the Cheshire Regiment.

$$$ • Approx. 4¼ in (11 cm) high

QUEEN'S SUDAN MEDAL
The ribbon of this silver medal symbolizes the desert, British forces, and Sudan.

$$$ • 1⁷⁄₁₆ in (3.6 cm) in diameter

INDIAN MUTINY MEDAL
This medal for the battle at Lucknow was awarded to T. Ledsham, 2nd Dragoon Guards.

$$$ • 1⁷⁄₁₆ in (3.6 cm) in diameter

SOUTH AFRICA MEDAL
An "1879" one-clasp medal from the Zulu wars, awarded to Cpl. G. Beck, 2–21st Foot.

$$$ • 1⁷⁄₁₆ in (3.6 cm) in diameter

CRIMEA MEDAL
Only Crimea Medals bear the atypically ornate clasp shaped like oak leaves with acorns.

$$$ • 1⁷⁄₁₆ in (3.6 cm) in diameter

OFFICER'S HELMET PLATE
Bearing the central monogram "VR," this is a Victorian silver-plated helmet plate of the Royal Westmoreland Light Infantry Militia.

$$$ • Approx. 4¼ in (11 cm) high

TOP TIPS

• Specialize in a particular subject, such as military medals from a particular campaign, life-saving medals, coronation medals, Commonwealth medals, or Territorial Service medals.
• If you can't afford full-size military medals, go for miniatures.
• Unless they are very rare, don't buy medals that are heavily polished.
• In general, the fewer the medals or clasps awarded, the more valuable the medal. In addition, medals awarded to officers rather than enlisted men are scarcer.

OTHER-RANKS HELMET PLATE
A Victorian brass helmet plate of the Royal Marines Light Infantry in good condition, with one resoldered lug.

$$ • Approx 4¼ in (11 cm) high

CAP BADGE AND COLLARS
A white metal cap badge and pair of collars of 28th County of London Battalion (Artists Rifles) depicting Mars and Minerva. The collars are stamped "Mappin & Webb."

$$ • Approx 1½ in (4 cm) high

PLAID BROOCH
Depicting a wreath bearing South African battle honors surrounding the Glengarry badge, this white metal plaid brooch belonged to a member of the Highland Light Infantry.

$$$ • Approx 3½ in (10 cm) in diameter

Starter Buys

WORLD WAR I MEDALS
This is a fine trio of Military (George V first type), British War, and Victory medals.

$$$ • 1⁷⁄₁₆ in (3.6 cm) in diameter

OFFICER'S CAP BADGE
A badge of the Chota Nagpur Regiment, marked "S" on the reverse, made by J. R. Gaunt.

$$ • Approx 2 in (5 cm) high

KHEDIVE'S SUDAN MEDAL
Originally instituted by the khedive of Egypt, with clasps inscribed in English and Arabic.

$$$ • 1⁹⁄₁₆ in (3.9 cm) in diameter

POUCH BELT BADGE
This silver-plated badge was worn by an officer of the 2nd Essex Rifle Volunteers.

$$ • Approx 2¼ in (5.6 cm) high

You may also like… Swords & Edged Weapons, see pp. 396–99

Antique Guns

Collecting antique guns is a well-established pastime today, and wonderfully crafted examples of vintage firearms can be found in most museums and many respected private collections.

A good collection of antique guns (generally, those made before 1899) can be acquired without a license, so anyone can start a collection. The earliest gun that beginners will commonly come across is the flintlock. Perfected by the early 1600s, it uses a flint against steel to make a spark, which ignites the gunpowder and fires the gun. A more reliable method was invented by Scottish Reverend A. J. Forsyth in 1807. His percussion method of ignition gave rise to tiny copper caps filled with a highly sensitive explosive mixture that ignited when struck.

The percussion-cap system gave way to the modern breech-loading system after the American Civil War. In recent years the trend has been for flintlock gun prices to rise faster than those for percussion. A small flintlock pocket pistol in good condition will cost perhaps twice as much as a percussion version.

Gun accessories are also very popular collectibles. A good copper powder flask made to hold the black powder for a shotgun can be purchased for less than $40, and there are hundreds of different patterns to collect.

Fire Power

An English revolver can be worth twice as much if, like this example, it is in its original case with accessories. Although gun shops were more common in England in the 19th century than they are today, it was essential for the owner to be able to cast his own bullets. A bronze mold would always be included with a cased set along with a small copper powder flask, a tin of percussion caps, patches, and a cleaning rod.

ADAMS REVOLVER
This is a cased five-shot 54-bore Adams model 1851 self-cocking percussion revolver with London proofs. It is in its original oak case, which also contains a double-cavity bronze bullet mold, powder flask, loading/cleaning rod, pewter oil bottle, wad punch, cap tin, turnscrew, and a leather bag containing bullets.

$$$$ • Barrel 6¼ in (16 cm) long

KEY FACTS	1517	1807	1836	1866	1947
Names in firearm history	Johann Kiefuss of Nuremburg develops the first automated firing system.	Reverend Forsyth uses mercury fulminate for ignition, laying the path to the self-contained cartridge.	Samuel Colt patents his Colt revolver in the US; it has a revolving cylinder and innovative cocking device.	American Colonel Boxer and English Colonel Berdan invent the modern center-fire cartridge.	Mikhail Kalashnikov invents the AK-47 assault rifle, which becomes the Soviet Army's standard issue.

What's Hot

SEA SERVICE BELT PISTOL
Made in 1800, this flintlock belt pistol has a walnut full stock with brass mounts and belt hooks.
$$$$ • 18½ in (47 cm) overall, barrel 12 in (30.5 cm) long

DOUBLE-BARRELED PISTOL
Each Damascus twist barrel in this flintlock pistol has a sliding safety catch and roller on a frizzen spring.
$$$$ • 9¾ in (24.5 cm) long

BRACE OF FLINTLOCK DUELING PISTOLS
Made by W. Dupe of Oxford, these pistols (one shown) have "saw-handled" grips and octagonal barrels.
$$$$$ • Barrels 9¾ in (24.5 cm) long

SMITH & WESSON RUSSIAN REVOLVER
This scarce .44 revolver is a first-model Russian single-action pistol. It has the Russian Imperial eagle on its sighting rib.
$$$ • 12 in (30 cm) long

Look out for:
In recent years cased percussion revolvers from around the 1850s and '60s have risen in price, sometimes dramatically. In particular, look for original condition and accessories, such as tins and reloading accessories.

Green baize-lined case   Pistol caps

SELF-COCKING TRANTER PATENT REVOLVER
This is an 80-bore ("bore" was used to describe gun calibers at the time) percussion revolver with accessories in a mahogany case. The revolver retains most of its original finish.
$$$$ • 9 in (23 cm) overall, barrel 4½ in (11.5 cm) long

What's Not

Belgium had a huge arms manufacturing industry in the 19th century. They copied many makes of English guns, sometimes under official license, but often without permission. Often their product was of lesser quality than similar English examples.

BELGIAN ADAMS REVOLVER
This is a Belgian-made five-shot, 48-bore Adams model 1856 revolver in fair condition.

$$$ • 12½ in (31.5 cm) long

Core Collectibles

GAME RIFLE
This fine military-style 12-bore flintlock game rifle by E. London has Baker-type 8-groove rifling and a breech with a platinum vent, c. 1830.
$$$$ • 48 in (122 cm) overall, round barrel 32 in (81.5 cm) long

PIN-FIRE REVOLVER
A Belgian six-shot 7-mm double-action pin-fire revolver, with folding knife beneath the barrel.
$$$ • 7½ in (19 cm) long

COLT ARMY REVOLVER
A percussion Colt 1860 model Army revolver, with military proof marks.
$$$ • Barrel 8 in (20 cm) long

CANNON BARRELED PISTOL
A mid-18th-century silver-mounted Queen Anne–style 22-bore flintlock pistol.
$$$ • 12 in (30 cm) long

BRASS POCKET PISTOL
A mid-18th-century flintlock boxlock turn-off barrel pocket pistol by Hampton.
$$$ • 5½ in (14 cm) long

MILITARY FLINTLOCK HOLSTER PISTOL
A Belgian 14-bore pistol with a slightly rounded lock and swan neck cock, c. 1790.
$$$ • Barrel 9 in (23 cm) long

BOXLOCK POCKET PISTOL
A 120-bore percussion boxlock pocket pistol.
$$$ • 5½ in (14 cm) long

CIVILIAN PATTERN SEA SERVICE PISTOL
A .56-in percussion pistol with Birmingham proofs, engraved "Beckwith, London."
$$$ • 11½ in (29 cm) overall, barrel 6 in (15 cm) long

POWDER FLASK
A leather-covered 19th-century flask for a sporting gun.
$$$ • 7 in (18 cm) long

"APACHE" REVOLVER
A six-shot 7-mm pin-fire "Apache" combination revolver, brass knuckles, and dagger.
$$$$ • 9 in (23 cm) long

SOLID FRAME REVOLVER
A Remington New Model Army percussion revolver.
$$$$ • 14 in (35.5 cm) long

PERCUSSION REVOLVER

Included in this green velvet-lined mahogany case are a four-shot 46-bore percussion pepperbox revolver, steel pincer mold, loading/cleaning rod, pewter oil bottle, screwdriver, and keys to the case. The piece was made by William Needler of Hull c. 1850.

$$$$ • 7 in (18 cm) long

TOP TIPS

- Before buying, inspect the inside of the barrel with a bore-light for any pitting caused by rust.
- Look for original blue or black finish on the barrel and action of a gun. Condition is key to their value.
- Don't dismiss damaged guns, as they can be cheaper, and there are gunsmiths who specialize in reproduction spare parts.

WESTLEY RICHARDS IMPROVED MARTINI HENRY RIFLE

This Boer .577/450in underlever military pattern rifle with Birmingham proofs is stamped "Henry Rifling-Westley Richards & Co." and dated 1897.

$$$ • 49½ in (126 cm) overall, barrel 33½ in (85 cm) long

DOUBLE-BARRELED POCKET PISTOL

A double-barreled 80-bore over-and-under tap action flintlock boxlock pocket pistol, c. 1815.

$$$$ • 5¾ in (14.5 cm) long

Starter Buys

PEPPERBOX PISTOL

A mid-19th-century percussion six-barreled revolving pistol.

$$$ • 8½ in (21.5 cm) long

DOUBLE-ACTION PERCUSSION REVOLVER

A five-shot 120-bore closed wedge frame revolver with two-piece walnut grips.

$$$ • 10½ in (26.5 cm) long

WORLD WAR II SPIKE BAYONETS

These spike bayonets are probably the best known of the WWII bayonets (No. 4 Mk I or II).

$$ • Blades 7½ in (19 cm) long

BOXLOCK POCKET PISTOL

A 50-bore flintlock boxlock pistol by Clarke, Dublin.

$$$ • 5 in (14 cm) long

COPPER POWDER FLASK

This large copper gunpowder flask is embossed with foliage and a stag's head. These flasks were popular in the 19th century.

$$ • 7½ in (19 cm) long

PERCUSSION PISTOL

A pistol with sprung bayonet.

$$ • 8½ in (21.5 cm) long

You may also like… Swords & Edged Weapons, see pp. 396–99

Swords & Edged Weapons

From Georgian swords—the last to be carried by gentlemen on a daily basis—to World War I military daggers, edged weapons constitute a diverse, fascinating field that's not for the fainthearted.

It was during the Bronze Age that metal was first cast and made into swords and knives. Once iron was discovered, blades became more durable, but it was not until the Roman period that steel was developed and used to make weapons.

Swords and edged weapons have been used in battle for thousands of years, and changes in tactics and technology dictated the style of their design, from the huge double-handed heavy broad sword used by armored knights, to the fine, razor-sharp scimitars used in warmer climates.

With armor starting to fall out of favor in Europe in the 16th century, swords became more refined and were carried daily for self-protection. Swords were, and still are, also worn to show rank and importance, particularly in the armed and civil services.

This vast collecting area spans centuries of history around the globe. Important swords go for $100,000 and up at auction, but there are examples to suit most budgets. British Army swords are a good bet, while bayonets cost as little as $40. Penknives are also an affordable starting point.

Lethal Weapon

The Mameluke sword (a type of scimitar) became popular with British officers fighting Napoleon in Egypt. A sword with a curved blade and a distinctive cross-shaped hilt, with grips frequently made of ivory, it was styled after the shamshir, a type of sword carried by the brave Egyptian Mameluke warriors. Look for blades in good original condition without corrosion or refinishing, and ivory grips without any cracks.

GEORGIAN MAMELUKE SABER
This officer's saber belonging to General Sir James Russell, KCB, has a curved blade with false edge, a silver engraved crosspiece, swollen foliate terminals with pommel and grip rivets, and silver chain with ball. It has black polished horn grips.
$$$$ • 27½ in (67 cm) long

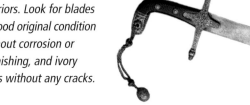

KEY FACTS	1788	1798	Early 19th century	2008
Cut-and-thrust of weapons of war	A "universal" sword pattern is adopted, the most collected being the 1796 Pattern Light Cavalry sword.	Napoleon invades Egypt and fights the mighty Mameluke warriors, whose shamshir influences sword fashions of the day.	Swords begin to lose their role in personal defense, but play a role in Western warfare until the end of WWI.	A gold-encrusted sword once owned by Napoleon sells in France for a record $6,534,000.

What's Hot

WWII GERMAN DAGGER

With a yellow celluloid grip and eagle and swastika crosspiece, this German Wehrmacht officer's dagger has its original plated scabbard.

$$$ • 10¼ in (Blade 26 cm) long

PERSIAN SWORD

An Indo-Persian sword tulwar with fine "Ladder of the Prophet" pattern watered blade engraved with Indian inscription in Kanada script.

$$$$ • Blade 26 in (65 cm) long

GEORGIAN NAVAL OFFICER'S DIRK

Etched with trophies of arms, this c. 1800 dirk has a broad curved single-edged blade with floral and foliate devices, blued and gilt decoration, and ivory and gilt hilt.

$$$$ • Blade 12 in (30 cm) long

FAIRBAIRN-SYKES FIGHTING KNIFE

Made by Wilkinson Sword Co. Ltd, London, this all-metal knife has a diced grip and recurved crossguard, and a brown leather sheath with nickel-plated chape and two securing tabs.

$$$$ • Blade 7 in (18 cm) long

Look out for:

Most Bowie knives were manufactured in the 19th century by the large firms of cutlers in Sheffield and exported to the US. They were used by trackers, woodsmen, and hunters. Originals are very sought-after these days, especially those stamped with the maker's name.

Maker's name stamped near crosspiece

Two-piece grip

Engraved pommel

BOWIE KNIFE

An Edwardian Bowie knife with a shallow diamond-section blade, a nickel crosspiece, two-piece pommel engraved with flowering foliage, and two-piece mother-of-pearl grip scales. The knife is in its original leather sheath.

$$$ • Blade 9 in (23 cm) long

What's Not

This type of short sword, often with a wavy blade, is known as a kris. Although frequently well-made, with beautiful "pattern welded" blades, they are currently unfashionable. You might pick up a good one at auction for under $200.

JAVANESE KRIS

With straight watered blade and carved wooden hilt, this kris has a sheath covered in white metal.

$$ • 20 in (52 cm) long

Core Collectibles

SILVER-MOUNTED DHA DAGGER
Burmese dha dagger with a curved single-edged blade, ivory hilt, and silver sheath.
$$ • Blade 12½ in (31.5 cm) long

MILITARY DAGGER
A scarce WWI French dagger with diamond-section blade.
$$ • Blade 6 in (15 cm) long

MIDSHIPMAN'S DIRK
This c. 1800 midshipman's dirk has an ivory grip with lion mask gilt metal finial.
$$$ • Blade 11 in (28 cm) long

NAVAL OFFICER'S SWORD
An 1827 pattern sword with a slightly curved blade, pronounced clipped back tip, and flat backstrap etched with a crown.
$$$ • 30 in (76 cm) long

ARMY OFFICER'S SWORD
Victorian officer's sword of the 18th Hussars by Wilkinson, No. 26726 (supplied in 1885), with leather-covered scabbard.
$$$ • 34 in (85 cm) long

RIVER PIRATES' SWORDS
Chinese 19th-century period swords with shallow diamond-section double-edged blades.
$$$ • 18 in (45.5 cm) long

SCOTTISH STEEL SWORD
A 17th-century Scottish basket-hilt sword.
$$$$ • 31 in (78.5 cm) long

NAZI SS OFFICER'S SWORD
This rare sword with hallmarked silver hardware has a plain blade by Pet Dan Krebs Solingen.
$$$ • 33½ in (85 cm) long

Ask the Expert

Q. How can you tell a fake modern knife from the genuine article?
A. There are hundreds of convincing replicas out there, so distinguishing an original is difficult. Buy from a reputable dealer or auction.

BOWIE KNIFE COPY
This well-made copy has a white metal crosspiece with large leaf-shaped quillons and white metal gripstrap and mounts.
$$$ • *Blade 10 in (25.5 cm) long*

Leather sheath

Broad double-edged blade

Q. How can you prevent rusty fingerprints from developing on a blade?
A. Moisture on our hands is acidic and salty and will rust blades that aren't oiled. Avoid touching a blade and always wipe it with an oily cloth before putting it away.

SGIAN DUBH
A silver-mounted sgian dubh of the Argyll & Sutherland Highlanders.

$$$ • Blade 4 in (10 cm) long

INDIAN KATAR
This 18th-century weapon has a blade with a thickened armor-piercing point.

$$$ • Blade 10 in (25.5 cm) long

MARK I DRUMMER'S SWORD
A scarce Victorian Gothic brass-hilted drummer's sword with a straight double-edged blade, brass hilt with strung bugle device to center panel, and a brass-mounted leather scabbard.

$$$ • 18 in (45 cm) long

Starter Buys

EASTERN DAGGER
A late-19th-century Moroccan silver-mounted dagger with an all-metal scabbard.

$$ • Blade 9 in (23 cm) long

KHUKRI
An Indian-made khukri, the traditional knife used by the Gurkhas.

$$ • 14 in (36 cm) long

SUMATRAN KRIS
This unusual kris has an early wavy blade of distinct pattern, with carved stylized grip.

$$$ • Blade 14 in (35.5 cm) long

FOLDING HUNTING KNIFE
An Edwardian knife with clipped-back blade and white metal crosspiece and mounts.

$$$ • Blade 7 in (18 cm) long

FOLDING KNIFE
This 19th-century Spanish sailor's navaja has a curved blade with foliage in red lacquer, a horn hilt inlaid with brass wire, brass zigzag against a pink foil ground, and engraved brass mounts.

$$$ • Blade 10 in (25.5 cm) long

You may also like… Toy Soldiers, see pp. 238–41

Auction Houses

ALABAMA
Flomaton Antique Auctions
P.O. Box 1017, 320 Palafox Street, Flomaton,
AL 36441
251 296 3059
www.flomatonantiqueauction.com

CALIFORNIA
Aurora Galleries International
30 Hackamore Lane, Suite 2, Bell Canyon,
CA 91307
818 884 6468
www.auroragalleriesonline.com

Bonhams
220 San Bruno Avenue, San Francisco,
CA 94103
415 861 7500
www.bonhams.com

Butterfield & Butterfield
7601 Sunset Boulevard, Los Angeles, CA 90046
323 850 7500
www.butterfields.com

Butterfield & Butterfield
220 San Bruno Avenue, San Francisco,
CA 94103
415 861 8951
www.butterfields.com

Christie's
360 North Camden Drive, Beverly Hills,
CA 90210
310 385 2600
www.christies.com

Malter Galleries
17003 Ventura Blvd, Encino, CA 91316
818 784 7772
www.maltergalleries.com

Poster Connection Inc
43 Regency Drive, Clayton, CA 94517
925 673 3343
www.posterconnection.com

Profiles in History
110 North Doheny Dr, Beverly Hills, CA 90211
310 859 7701
www.profilesinhistory.com

San Rafael Auction Gallery
634 Fifth Avenue, San Rafael, CA 9490
415 457 4488
www.sanrafael-auction.com

CONNECTICUT
Alexander Autographs
100 Melrose Avenue, Greenwich, CT 06830
203 622 8444
www.alexautographs.com

Norman C. Heckler & Co
79 Bradford Corner Road, Woodstock Valley,
CT 0682
860 974 1634
www.hecklerauction.com

Lloyd Ralston Gallery
350 Long Beach Blvd, Stratford, CT 016615
203 386 9399
www.lloydralstontoys.com

DELAWARE
Remember When Auction Inc
302 436 4979
www.history-attic.com

FLORIDA
Auctions Neapolitan
995 Central Avenue, Naples, FL 34102
941 262 7333
www.auctionsneapolitan.com

Burchard Galleries
2528 30th Avenue N, St. Petersburg, FL 33713
727 821 1167
www.burchardgalleries.com

Kincaid Auction Company
3809 East CR 542, Lakeland, FL 33801
800 970 1977
www.kincaid.com

Sloan's Auction Galleries
8861 Northwest 19th Terrace, Suite 100,
Miami, FL 33172
305 751 4770
www.sloansandkenyon.com

GEORGIA
Great Gatsby's
5070 Peachtree Industrial Blvd, Atlanta, GA
770 457 1903
www.gatsbys.com

My Hart Auctions Inc
P.O. Box 2511, Cumming, GA 30028
770 888 9006
www.myhart.net

ILLINOIS
Leslie Hindman Inc
122 North Aberdeen Street, Chicago, IL 60607
312 280 1212
www.lesliehindman.com

Joy Luke
300 East Grove Street, Bloomington, IL 61701
309 828 5533
www.joyluke.com

Mastronet Inc
10S 660 Kingery Highway, Willobrook, IL 60527
630 471 1200
www.mastronet.com

INDIANA
Curran Miller Auction & Realty Inc
4424 Vogel Rd, Suite 400, Evansville, IN 47715
812 474 6100
www.curranmiller.com

Kruse International
5540 County Road 11A, Auburn, IN 46706
800 968 4444
www.kruseinternational.com

Lawson Auction Service
P.O. Box 885, North Vernon, IN 47265
812 372 2571
www.lawsonauction.com

Stout Auctions
529 State Road 28 East, Williamsport,
IN 47993
765 764 6901
www.stoutauctions.com

IOWA
Jackson's Auctioneers & Appraisers
2229 Lincoln Street, Cedar Falls, IA 50613
319 277 2256
www.jacksonauction.com

Tom Harris Auctions
2035 18th Avenue, Belle Plaine, IA 52208
319 444 2413 / 319 444 0169
www.tomharrisauctions.com

KANSAS
Manions International Auction House
P.O. Box 12214, Kansas City, KS 66112
913 299 6692
www.manions.com

CC Auctions
416 Court Street, Clay Center, KS 67432
785 632 6021
www.cc-auctions.com

Brian Spielman Auctions
P.O. Box 884, Emporia, KS 66801
620 341 0637
www.kansasauctions.net/spielman

KENTUCKY
Hays & Associations Inc
120 South Spring Street, Louisville, KY 40206
502 584 4297
www.haysauction.com

Steffens Historical Militaria
P.O. Box 280, Newport, KY 41072
859 431 4499
www.steffensmilitaria.com

LOUISIANA
New Orleans Auction Galleries
801 Magazine Street, New Orleans, LA 70130
504 566 1849
www.neworleansauction.com

MAINE
James D. Julia Auctioneers Inc
P.O. Box 830, Fairfield, Maine 04937
207 453 7125
www.juliaauctions.com

Thomaston Place Auction Galleries
P.O. Box 300, 51 Atlantic Highway,
US Route 1 Thomaston, ME 04861
207 354 8141
www.thomastonauction.com

MARYLAND
Guyette & Schmidt
P.O. Box 1170, St. Michaels, MD 21663
410 745 0485
www.guyetteandschmidt.com

Isennock Auctions & Appraisals
4106B Norrisville Road, White Hall, MD 21161
410 557 8052
www.isennockauction.com

MASSACHUSETTS
Eldred's
P.O. Box 796, 1483 Route 6A, East Dennis,
MA 02641
508 385 3116
www.eldreds.com

Grogan & Co
22 Harris Street, Dedham, MA 02026
800 823 1020
www.groganco.com

Simon D. Hill & Associates
420 Boston Turnpike, Shrewsbury, MA 01545
508 845 2400
www.simondhillauctions.com

Skinner Inc
The Heritage on the Garden, 63 Park Plaza,
Boston, MA 02116
617 350 5400
www.skinnerinc.com

Willis Henry Auctions
22 Main Street, Marshfield, MA 02050
781 834 7774
www.willishenry.com

MICHIGAN
DuMouchelles
409 East Jefferson Avenue, Detroit, MI 48226
313 963 6255
www.dumouchelles.com

MINNESOTA
Buffalo Bay Auction Co
825 Fox Run Trail, Edmond, OK 73034
405 285 8990
www.buffalobayauction.com

Rose Auction Galleries
3180 County Drive, Little Canada, MN 55117
615 484 1415 / 888 484 1415
www.rosegalleries.com

MISSOURI
Ivey-Selkirk
7447 Forsyth Boulevard, Saint Louis, MO 63105
314 726 5515
www.iveyselkirk.com

MONTANA
Allard Auctions Inc
P.O. Box 1030 St Ignatius, MT 59865
406 745 0500
www.allardauctions.com

Cope Sports Collectibles
2504 Suite D, West Main, Bozeman, MT 59718
406 587 1793
www.copesportscollectibles.com

NEW HAMPSHIRE
Northeast Auctions
93 Pleasant St, Portsmouth, NH 03801-4504
603 433 8400
www.northeastauctions.com

NEW JERSEY
Bertoia Auctions
2141 Demarco Drive, Vineland, NJ 08530
856 692 1881
www.bertoiaauctions.com

Dawson & Nye
128 American Road, Morris Plains, NJ 07950
973 984 6900
www.dawsonandnye.com

Rago Modern Auctions LLP
333 North Main Street, Lambertville,
NJ 08530
609 397 9377
www.ragoarts.com

NEW MEXICO
Manitou Gallery
123 West Palace Avenue, Santa Fe, NM 87501
800 986 0440
www.manitougalleries.com

Parker-Braden Auctions
P.O. Box 1897, 4303 National Parks, Highway,
Carlsbad, NM 882200
505 885 4874
www.parkerbraden.com

NEW YORK
Bonhams
580 Madison Avenue, New York, NY 10022
212 644 9001
www.bonhams.com

Christie's
20 Rockefeller Plaza, New York, NY 10020
212 636 2000
www.christies.com

TW Conroy
36 Oswego Street, Baldwinsville, NY 13027
315 638 6434
www.twconroy.com

William Doyle Galleries
175 East 87th Street, New York, NY 10128
212 427 2730
www.doylenewyork.com

Guernsey's Auctions
108 East 73rd Street, New York, NY 10021
212 794 2280
www.guernseys.com

Phillips, De Pury & Luxembourg
450 West Street, New York, NY 10011
212 940 1200
www.phillips-dpl.com

Sotheby's
1334 York Avenue, New York, NY 10021
212 606 7000
www.sothebys.com

Swann Galleries Inc
104 East 25th Street, New York, NY 10010
212 254 4710
www.swanngalleries.com

NORTH CAROLINA
Robert S. Brunk
P.O. Box 2135, Asheville, NC 28802
828 254 6846
www.brunkauctions.com

Historical Collectible Auctions
24 NW Court, Square Suite 201, Graham,
NC 27253
336 570 2803
www.hcauctions.com

OHIO
The Cincinnatti Art Galleries
225 East 6th Street, Cincinnati, OH 4502
513 381 2128
www.cincinnatiartgalleries.com

Cowans Historic Americana
673 Wilmer Avenue, Cincinnati, OH 45226
513 871 1670
www.historicamericana.com

DeFina Auctions
1591 State Route 45 South, Austinburg,
OH 44010
440 275 6674
www.definaauctions.com

Garth's Auctions
26909 Stratford Road, Box 369, Delaware,
OH 43015
740 362 4771
www.garths.com

PENNSYLVANIA
Alderfer Auction Gallery
501 Fairgrounds Road, Hatfield, PA 19440
215 393 3000
www.alderferauction.com

Dargate Auction Galleries
214 North Lexington, Pittsburgh, PA 15208
412 362 3558
www.dargate.com

Freeman's
1808 Chestnut Avenue, Philadelphia, PA 19103
610 563 9275
www.freemansauction.com

Hunt Auctions
75 East Uwchlan Avenue, Suite 1, 30 Exton,
PA 19341
610 524 0822
www.huntauctions.com

Morphy Auctions
2000 North Reading Street, Denver PA
717 335 3435
www.morphyauctions.com

Pook & Pook Inc
463 East Lancaster Avenue, Downington,
PA 19335
610 269 4040
www.pookandpook.com

Skinner's Auction Co
170 Northampton Street, Easton, PA 19335
610 330 6933
www.skinnersauction.com

Stephenson's Auctions
1005 Industrial Boulevard, Southampton,
PA 18966
215 322 618
www.stephensonsauction.com

RHODE ISLAND
WebWilson
P.O. Box 506, Portsmouth, RI 02871
800 508 0022
www.webwilson.com

SOUTH CAROLINA
Charlton Hall Galleries Inc
912 Gervais Street, Columbia, SC 29201
803 799 5678
www.charltonhallauctions.com

TENNESSEE
Berenice Denton Estate Sales
2209 Bandywood Drive, Suite C, Nashville,
TN 37215
615 292 5765
www.berenicedenton.com

Kimball M. Sterling Inc
125 West Market Street, Johnson City,
TN 37604
423 928 1471
www.sterlingsold.com

TEXAS
Austin Auctions
8414 Anderson Mill Road, Austin,
TX 78729-4702
512 258 5479
www.austinauction.com

Dallas Auction Gallery
1518 Socum Street, Dallas, TX 75207
213 653 3900
www.dallasauctiongallery.com

Heritage Galleries
3500 Maple Avenue, Dallas, TX 75219
214 528 3500
www.heritagegalleries.com

VERMONT
Eaton Auction Service
Chuck Eaton, 3428 Middlebrook Road, Fairlee,
VT 05045
802 333 9717
www.eatonauctionservice.com

VIRGINIA
Ken Farmer Auctions & Estates
105A Harrison Street, Radford, VA 24141
540 639 0939
www.kfauctions.com

Phoebus Auction Gallery
14-16 East Mellen Street, Hampton, VA 23663
757 723 2280
www.phoebusauction.com

Signature House
407 Liberty Avenue, Bridgeport, WV 25330
304 842 3386
www.signaturehouse.net

WISCONSIN
Schrager Auction Galleries
2915 North Sherman Blvd, P.O. Box 100043,
Milwaukee, WI 53210
414 873 3738
www.schragerauction.com

CANADA
Bonhams
20 Hazelton Avenue, Toronto M5R 2E2
416 462 9004
www.bonhams.com

Maynards Fine Art & Antique
Auction House
415 West 2nd Avenue, Vancouver V5Y 1E3
604 876 6787
www.maynards.com

Pinneys Auctions Les Encans
2435 Duncan Road, Montreal H4P 2A2
514 345 0571
www.pinneys.ca

Ritchies
288 King Street East, Toronto,
Ontario M5V 1K4
416 364 1864
www.ritchies.com

Waddington's Auctioneers & Appraisers
111 Bathurst Street, Toronto, Ontario M5V 2R1
416 504 9100
www.waddingtons.ca

Specialist Dealers

CERAMICS
Blue and White Dinnerware
4800 Crestview Drive, Carmichael, CA 95609
916 961 7406

Charles & Barbara Adams
By appointment only,
289 Old Main Street, South Yarmouth,
MA 02664
508 760 3290

Faye Landes Antiques
593 Hansell Road, Wynnewood, PA 19096
610 658 0566

Greg Walsh
P.O. Box 747, Potsdam, NY 13676-0747
315 265 9111
www.walshauction.com

The Perrault-Rago Gallery
333 North Main Street, Lambertville, NJ 08530
609 397 1802
www.ragoarts.com

Keller & Ross
47 Prospect Street, Melrose, MA 02176
781 662 7257
www.members.aol.com/kellerross

Ken Forster
5501 Seminary Road, Suite 1311,
South Falls Church, VA 22041
703 379 1142

Mellin's Antiques
P.O. Box 1115, Redding, CT 06875
203 938 9538

Mark & Marjorie Allen
300 Bedford Street, Suite 421, Manchester,
NH 03101
603 644 8989
www.antiquedelft.com

www.adantiques.com
www.alexisantiques.com
www.carltonware.biz
www.chinasearch.co.uk
www.commemorabilia.co.uk
www.decorative-antiques.com
www.perfectpieces.co.uk
www.pooleroom.co.uk

GLASS
Betty and Larry Schwab
The Paperweight Shoppe, 2507, Newport Drive,
Bloomington, IL 61704-4525
309 662 1956

Block Glass Ltd
203 556 0905
www.blockglass.com

Glassfinders
32040 Mount Hermon Road, Salisbury,
MD 21804
410 546 5881

Jeff E. Purtell
P.O. Box 28, Amherst, NH 03031-0028
603 673 4331

Paul Reichwein
2321 Hershey Avenue, East Petersburg,
PA 17520
717 569 7637

Paul Stamati Gallery
1050 Second Avenue, New York, NY 10022
212 754 4533
www.stamati.com

Suzman's Antiques
P.O. Box 301, Rehoboth, MA 02769
508 252 5729

Walk Memory Lane (Fenton Glass)
www.walkmemorylane.com

www.abstracta-art.com
www.circaglass.co.uk
www.cranberryglass.co.uk
www.glasgalerie-zindel.nl
www.glasscottage.net
www.great-glass.co.uk
www.glassfairs.co.uk
www.20thcentury-glass.com
www.retromoderndesign.com
www.thestudioglassmerchant.co.uk
www.sweetbriar.co.uk

HOUSEHOLD ACCESSORIES
David Nishimura
Vintage Pens, P.O. Box 41452, Providence,
RI 02940-1452
401 351 7607
www.vintagepens.com

Dee Battle
9 Orange Blossom Trail, Yalaha, FL 34797
352 324 3023

Malabar Enterprises
172 Bush Lane, Ithaca, NY 14850
607 255 2905

Gary & Myrna Lehrer
16 Mulberry Road, Woodbridge,
CT 06525-1717
203 389 5295
www.gopens.com

Jazz'e Junque
1648 West Belmont Avenue, Chicago, ILL60657
773 472 6450
www.jazzejunque.com

Krazy Cat Collectibles
P.O. Box 1192, Emmitsburg, MD 21727
301 271 9851
www.krazycatcollectibles.com

Phil & Karol Atkinson
713 Sarsi Tr, Mercer, PA 16137 (May-Oct)
724 475 2490
7188 Drewry's Bluff Road, Bradenton,
FL 34 203 (Nov-Apr)
941 755 1733

Village Green Antiques
Port Antiques Center, 289 Main Street,
Port Washington, NY 11050
516 625 2946

www.advertisingarchives.co.uk
www.bunnys-place.com
www.guinntiques.com
www.hanspens.com
www.antiquebottles-glass.com
www.huxtins.com
www.rubylane.com
www.uniquebottles.co.uk
www.vintagepens.co.uk

BOOKS, MAGAZINES & EPHEMERA
Abebooks
www.abebooks.com

Aleph-Bet Books
85 Old Mill River Road, Pound Ridge, NY 10576
914 764 7410
www.alephbet.com

Autographs of America
P.O. Box 461, Provo, UT 84603-0461
www.autographsofamerica.com

Bauman Rare Books
535 Madison Avenue, between 54th & 55th
Streets, New York, NY 1002
212 751 0011
www.baumanrarebooks.com

Carl Bonasera
A1-American Comic Shops, 3514 West 95th
Street, Evergreen Park, IL 60642
708 425 7555

The Comic Gallery
4224 Balboa Avenue, San Diego, CA 92117
619 483 4853

De Wolfe and Wood
P.O. Box 425, 2 Waterboro Road (Route 202),
Alfred, Maine 04002
www.dwbooks.com

Metropolis Collectibles Inc
873 Broadway, Suite 201, New York, NY 10003
212 260 4147
www.metropoliscomics.com

Million Magazines
221 East 6th Street, #125 (rear), Tucson,
AZ 85705
800 877 9887

Mori Books
141 Route 101A, Amherst, NH 03031
603 882 2665
www.moribooks.com

Platt Autographs
P.O. Box 135007, Clermont, FL 34711
352 241 9164
www.ctplatt.com

www.applebybooks.net
www.autographcollection.co.uk
www.beatbooks.com
www.metropoliscomics.com
www.postcardworld.co.uk
www.remainstobeseen.com
www.sppf.co.uk
www.theweeweb.co.uk

TOYS, DOLLS & TEDDY BEARS
Atomic Age
318 East Virginia Road, Fullerton, CA 92831
714 446 0736

Harper General Store
10482 Jonestown Road, Annville, PA 17003
717 865 3456
www.harpergeneralstore.com

Litwin Antiques
P.O. Box 5865, Trenton, NJ 08638-0865
609 275 1427

Marion Weis
Division Street Antiques, P.O. Box 374, Buffalo,
MN 55313-0374
612 682 6453

Memory Lane
18 Rose Lane, Flourtown, PA 19031-1910
215 233 4094

Memory Lane
45-50 Bell Boulevard, Suite 109, Bayside,
NY 11361
www.tias.com/stores/meminny

Milezone's Toys
4025 South Franklin Street, Michigan City,
IN 46360
219 874 6629
www.milezone.com

Neet-O-Rama
93 West Main Street, Somerville, NJ 08876
908 722 4600
www.neetstuff.com

Gary Doss
Burlingame Museum of PEZ Memorabilia
214 California Drive, Burlingame, CA 94010
650 347 2301
www.burlingamepezmuseum.com

Treasure & Dolls
518 Indian Rocks Road, North Belleair Bluffs,
FL 33770
727 584 7277
www.treasureanddolls.com

www.1853dollhouse.com
www.antiquedollworld.co.uk
www.bearsofwindyhill.co.uk
www.bygonevintageboardgames.com
www.coolcollectibletoys.co.uk
www.diecast-model-car.co.uk
www.dinkycollector.com
www.dollshouse.com
www.oldrockinghorses.com
www.lolli-dollies-online.co.uk
www.luckbears.com
www.magictoybox.co.uk
www.vintagehornby.net
www.oldbear.co.uk
www.traditional-tin-toys.co.uk
www.tortoys.co.uk
www.toysandhobbies.net
www.toydreams.co.uk
www.vintage-toybox.co.uk

FASHION
Andrea Hall Levy
P.O. Box 1243, Riverdale, NY 10471
646 441 1726

Aurora Bijoux
www.aurorabijoux.com

Barbara Blau
c/o South Street Antiques Market,
615 South 6th Street, Philadelphia,
PA 19147-2128
215 739 4995/592 0256

Baubles
c/o South Street Antiques Market,
615 South 6th Street, Philadelphia,
PA 19147-2128
215 487 0207

The Junkyard Jeweler
www.junkyardjeweler.com

Mod-Girl
c/o South Street Antiques Market,
615 South 6th Street, Philadelphia,
PA 19147-2128
215 592 0256

Terry Rodgers & Melody LLC
30 & 31 Manhattan Art & Antique Center, 1050
2nd Avenue, New York, NY 10022
212 758 3164

Colette Donovan
98 River Road, Merrimacport, MA 01860
978 346 0641

Fayne Landes Antiques
593 Hansell Road, Wynnewood, PA 19096
610 658 0566

Lucy's Hats
1118 Pine Street, Philadelphia, PA

Neet-O-Rama
93 West Main Street, Somerville, NJ 08876
908 722 4600
www.neetstuff.com

Vintage Clothing Company
P.O. Box 20504, Keizer, OR 97307-0504

Vintage Eyeware of New York
646 319 9222

Yesterday's Threads
206 Meadow Street, Branford, CT 06405-3634
203 481 6452

www.1860-1890.com
www.absolutevintage.co.uk

www.bjantiquejewellery.co.uk
www.brightthingsrevisited.com
www.thefrock.com
www.antique-fashion.com
www.the-way-we-were.com
www.vintagetextile.com

ENTERTAINMENT, SPORTS & TRAVEL
Classic Rods & Tackle
P.O. Box 288, Ashley Falls, MA 01222
413 229 7988

Dunbar's Gallery
54 Haven Street, Milford, MA 01757
508 634 8697
www.dunbarsgallery.com

George Baker
CollectorsMart, P.O. Box 580466, Modesto,
CA 95358
290 537 5221
www.collectorsmart.com

George Lewis
Golfinana, P.O. Box 291, Mamaroneck,
NY 10543
914 698 4579
www.golfiana.com

Golf Collectibles
P.O. Box 165892, Irving, TX 75016
800 882 4825
www.golfforallages.com

The Hager Group
P.O. Box 952974, Lake Mary, FL 32795
407 788 3865

Heinz's Rare Collectibles
P.O. Box 179, Little Silver, NJ 07739-0179
732 219 1988

Larry Fritsch Cards Inc
735 Old Wassau Road, P.O. Box 863,
Stevens Point, WI 54481
715 344 8687
www.fritschcards.com

MuseumWorks
525 East Cooper Avenue, Aspen, CO 81611
www.mwhgalleries.com

Norma's Jeans
3511 Turner Lane, Chevy Chase,
MD 20815-2313
301 652 4644

The Nostalgia Factory
Charlestown Commerce Center,
50 Terminal Street, Building 2, Boston,
MA 02129
www.nostalgia.com

Peter DeNevai
20th C. Aviation Collectibles, HC63 Box 5,
Duchesne, UT 84021-9701

Poster America
138 West 18th Street, New York,
NY 10011-5403
212 206 0499
www.posterfair.com

Tod Hutchinson
P.O. Box 915, Griffith, IN 46319-0915
219 923 8334

Tom & Jill Kaczor
1550 Franklin Road, Langhorne, PA 19047
215 968 5776

ShipShape
1041 Tuscany Place, Winter Park,
FL 32789-1017
407 644 2892
www.shipshape.com

Sign of the Tymes
Mill Antiques Center, 12 Morris Farm Road,
Lafayette, NJ 07848
973 383 6028
www.millantiques.com

The Space Source
P.O. Box 604, Glenn Dale, MD 20769
301 871 6367
www.thespacesource.com

STARticles
58 Stewart Street, Studio 301, Toronto, Ontario,
M5V 1H6, Canada
416 504 8286

Vintage Poster Works
P.O. Box 88, Pittsford, NY 14534
585 381 9355
www.vintageposterworks.com

Vintage Sports Collector
3920 Via Solano, Palos Verde Estates,
CA 90274
310 375 1723

Wonderful World of Animation Art
51 East 74th Street, Suite 1R, New York,
NY 10022
www.animationartgallery.com

www.antiquegolf.com
www.atthemovies.co.uk
www.aviationcollectibles.co.uk
www.beatlesmarketplace.com
www.disneyana.com
www.disneyanaexchange.com
www.fa-premiersignings.co.uk
www.thefootballmuseum.net

www.locomobilia.com
www.memorabilia-uk.co.uk
www.oldnautibits.com
www.rugbyrelics.com
www.sportcasts.co.uk
www.sportsmemorabilia.com
www.sportingantiques.co.uk
www.tracks.co.uk
www.vinylrecords.co.uk

SCIENCE, TECHNOLOGY & TIMEPIECES
AndHow! Antique Telephones
www.andhowantiques.com

Catalin Radios
419 824 2469
www.catalinradio.com

Early American Watch Club
P.O. Box 81555, Wellesley Hills,
MA 02481-1333

George Glazer Gallery
28 East 2nd Street, New York, NY 10021
212 535 5706
www.georgeglazer.com

Mark Laino
c/o South Street Antiques Market,
615 South 6th Street, Philadelphia,
PA 19147-2128

**National Association of
Watch & Clock Collectors**
514 Poplar Street, Columbia, PA 17512-2130
717 684 8261
www.nawacc.org

The Olde Office
68-845 Perez Road, Suite 30, Cathedral City,
CA 92234
760 346 8653
www.thisoldeoffice.com

Jane Hertz
www.breker.com

www.antique-watch.com
www.candlestickandbakelite.co.uk
www.davewestclocks.co.uk
www.finesse-fine-art.com
www.pasttimesradio.co.uk
www.retrobrick.com
www.telephonelines.net
www.vintagecameras.co.uk

Collectors' Clubs & Societies

CERAMICS
Carlton Ware World Wide
www.carltonwareworldwide.com

Ceramic Review
www.ceramicreview.com

Chintznet
www.chintznet.com

Clarice Cliff Collectors Club
www.claricecliff.com

Collecting Doulton and Beswick Collectors Club
www.collectingdoulton.com

Craft Potters Association
www.cpaceramics.co.uk

Crazed Collector (Chintz)
www.crazedcollector.net

Crown Devon Collectors Club
www.fieldingscrowndevclub.com

Friends of Blue
www.fob.org.uk

Moorcroft Collectors Club
www.moorcroft.com

Myott Collectors Club
www.myottcollectorsclub.com

The Pendelfin Family Circle
www.pendelfin.co.uk

Poole Pottery Collectors Club
www.poolepotterycollectorsclub.co.uk

Staffordshire.org
www.staffordshire.org

The Staffordshire Collectors Club
www.staffordshirecollectorsclub.co.uk

Studiopottery.co.uk
www.studiopottery.co.uk

The Susie Cooper Information Site
www.susiecooper.net

SylvaC Collectors Circle
www.sylvacclub.com

Wade Collectors Club
www.wadecollectorsclub.co.uk

The Wedgwood Society
020 7628 7268

GLASS
Association for the History of Glass
www.historyofglass.org.uk

Carnival Glass
www.carnival-glass.net

The Carnival Glass Society
www.carnivalglasssociety.co.uk

The Early Glass Collector
www.earlyglass.com

The Glass Association
www.glassassociation.org.uk

The Glass Circle
www.glasscircle.org

International Carnival Glass Association
www.internationalcarnivalglass.com

National Depression Glass Association
www.ndga.net

The Northern Paperweight Society
www.northernpaperweightsociety.co.uk

Paperweight Collectors Circle
www.paperweightcollectorscircle.org.uk

Whitefriars
www.whitefriarsorg.org

Whitefriars Glass Collectors Club
www.whitefriars.com

World Art Glass
www.worldartglass.com

HOUSEHOLD ACCESSORIES
Advertising Antiques
www.advertisingantiques.co.uk

Antique Bottle Collector
www.abc-ukmag.co.uk

Antique Pot Lid Gallery
www.deantiques.com/PLG

Bottle Bills Bottle Dump
www.thebottledump.co.uk

The Coca-Cola Collectors Club
www.cocacolaclub.org

The Federation of Historical Bottle Collectors
www.fohbc.com

Plastics Historical Society
www.plastiquarian.com

The Thimble Society
www.thimblesociety.com

The Writing Equipment Society
www.wesonline.org.uk

BOOKS, MAGAZINES & EPHEMERA
Antiquarian Booksellers Association
www.aba.org.uk

The British Rare Book Society
www.rarebooksociety.org

The Cartophilic Society of Great Britain
www.csgb.co.uk

The Clique
www.theclique.co.uk

The Ephemera Society
www.ephemera-society.org.uk

Photographic Collectors' Club of Great Britain
www.pccgb.com

Postcard Pages
www.postcard.co.uk

Rare Books and Manuscripts Section
www.rbms.info

Rarebooks.info
www.rarebooks.info

Rare Book Review
www.rarebookreview.com

TOYS, DOLLS & TEDDY BEARS

**Antique Dolls Collectors
Online Advisors**
www.antiquedolls-collectors-onlineadvisors.com

Barbie Collector
www.barbiecollector.com

British Model Soldier Society
www.btinternet.com/~MODEL.SOLDIERS/

**The British Smurf Collectors
Club**
www.kittyscavern.com

Collecting Pez
www.collectingpez.com

Diecast Car Collectors Zone
www.diecast.org

The Dinky Collector
www.dinky-collector.co.uk

The Followers of Rupert Bear
www.rupertthebear.org.uk

**The Historical Model
Railway Society**
www.hmrs.org.uk

The Old Toy Guide
www.theoldtoyguide.com

Pedal Cars Collectors Club
www.brmmbrmm.com/pedalcars

The Piggy Bank Page
www.piggybankpage.co.uk

Steiff Club
www.steiffusa.com

The-toy.net
www.the-toy.net

The Train Collectors Society
www.traincollectors.org.uk

Transformers Collectors Club
www.transformerclub.com

FASHION

Antique Jewelry Online
www.antiquejewelryonline.com

**British Compact Collectors
Society**
www.compactcollectors.co.uk

The Costume Society
www.costumesociety.org.uk

The Fan Circle International
www.fancircleinternational.org

The Lace Guild
www.laceguild.org

Scottish Textiles Heritage
www.scottishtextileheritage.org.uk

ENTERTAINMENT, SPORTS & TRAVEL

Billiards and Snooker Archive
www.billiardsandsnookerarchive.co.uk

Golf Collectors Society
www.golfcollectors.com

The Historical Maritime Society
www.hms.org.uk

National Fantasy Fan Club
www.nffc.org

**The National Fishing Lure
Collectors Club**
www.nflcc.org

The Railwayana Page
www.railwayanapage.com

Richard Who
www.richardwho.com

Rugby Memorabilia Society
www.rugby-memorabilia.co.uk

Starfleet
www.sfi.org

Universal Autograph Collectors Club
www.uacc.org

SCIENCE, TECHNOLOGY & TIMEPIECES

**Antique Telephone Collectors
Association**
www.atconline.com

Antiques Wireless Association
www.antiquewireless.org

British Vintage Wireless Society
www.bvws.org.uk

The British Horological Institute
www.bhi.co.uk

The Horology Source
www.horologysource.com

MPP Users' Club
www.mppusers.freeuk.com

**Photographic Collectors' Club of
Great Britain**
www.nanites.co.uk/pccgb

Scientific Instrument Society
www.sis.org.uk

Swatch Forum
www.swatchforum.co.uk

**The Telecommunications
Heritage Group**
www.thg.org.uk

Telephone Collectors International
www.telephonecollectors.org

Vintage Camera Online
www.vintage-camera-online.com

MILITARIA

Arms and Armour Society
www.armsandarmour.net

**The Orders and Medals
Research Society**
www.omrs.org.uk

Victorian Military Society
www.victorianmilitarysociety.org.uk

Index

Acknowledgments

The publisher would like to thank the following for their kind permission to reproduce their photographs:

(Key: a-above; b-below/bottom; c-center; f-far; l-left; r-right; t-top)

BBC Antiques Roadshow: 12bl, 12clb, 13bl; **Bunny Campione:** 12cl; **DK Images:** Design20c 332bc, 361bl, 361fcrb, 365fbr; Judith Miller 50ftl, 77bc, 90, 107br, 107cra, 107tl; Judith Miller / 20th Century Glass 5bl; Judith Miller / 333 Auctions LLC 105bc, 127c, 297tr; Judith Miller / 70s Watches 378br, 378tc, 380bc; Judith Miller / Adrian Grater 79bl; Judith Miller / Albert Amor 18cb (left), 18cb (right); Judith Miller / Andrew Lineham Fine Glass 20tr, 69tl, 92br, 94c, 103bl, 103tl, 105tc, 121bl, 123bc, 124cl, 125c, 125fcl, 323br; Judith Miller / Antique Glass - Frank Dux Antiques 107bc, 107cl, 123br; Judith Miller / Antiques of Cape May 344cb, 345bl, 345cl, 345fbl, 345ftl; Judith Miller / Art Deco Etc 49cr, 50tr, 51br, 51cl, 51cr, 52tl, 79fbl, 158cb, 159tl; Judith Miller / Atlantique City 19br, 221br, 251c, 255cl, 255cr, 255tc, 255tl, 256cr, 256tr, 257bl, 257tr, 283fclb, 323fcl, 323ftl, 339cra, 339fbr, 339fcl; Judith Miller / Atomic Age 142c, 147bl, 221bl, 251tc, 253cl, 253cra, 253tc; Judith Miller / Auktionhaus Dr Fischer 92bc, 104c, 141bl; Judith Miller / Automatomania 229fbl, 229ftl, 230tl; Judith Miller / Barbara Blau 149c, 282tc, 301cr; Judith Miller / Baubles 281br, 282bc; Judith Miller / Bauman Rare Books 203bl, 203c, 203fbl, 203ftl, 204cl, 204cr, 205tl, 205tr; Judith Miller / Bébés & Jouets 244cr, 244ftl, 245fbr, 247tr, 251cl, 251crb, 255bl, 257cl, 257fbl, 257tl, 258tr, 261cl, 261fcrb, 261tl; Judith Miller / Below Stairs of Hungerford 151cr, 171cr, 172br, 173br, 173c, 173cl, 173cr, 174, 174cl, 174cr, 174tl, 175cla, 175tl, 269bl, 335bl, 335fbr, 335fcl; Judith Miller / Bertoia Auctions 227bl, 227cl, 227cra, 229tr, 231cr, 231fcl, 243tl, 243tr, 247bl, 247fbl, 269fbl; Judith Miller / Beth 47fcrb, 175bl; Judith Miller / Beyond Retro 339br; Judith Miller / Biblion 197bl, 197br, 198c, 198cl, 198tr, 198tl, 199c, 199cl, 199tl, 199tr, 203r, 204br, 204tr, 205ftl, 207bc, 207bl, 207br, 207c, 207cl, 207cr, 343fbr; Judith Miller / Biblion / The Estate of

Cicely Mary Barker 199cr; Judith Miller / Bonhams 70c, 141br; Judith Miller / Bonny Yankauer 281cr, 282tr; Judith Miller / Branksome Antiques 110cb, 111bc, 111bl, 111br, 111c, 111cl, 111cr, 111fbl, 111fcl, 111tr, 300cb; Judith Miller / Brightwells Fine Art 39cl; Judith Miller / Bucks County Antique Center 147, 175cra; Judith Miller / Bucks County Antiques Center 148tc, 174bc, 237cr, 261fbl, 265tr; Judith Miller / Bucks County Antiques Center 229cl; Judith Miller / Burstow & Hewett 77fbl; Judith Miller / Cad Van Swankster at The Girl Can't Help It 149cr, 215cl, 333br; Judith Miller / Carlton Antiques 188cb, 189bl, 189c, 189fbl, 189fcr, 217bl, 217br, 217cl, 217fbl, 217fbr, 217fcl, 217fcrb; Judith Miller / Cheffins 35fcla, 368fcl, 369ftl; Judith Miller / Cheryl Grandfield 277br, 277fbl; Judith Miller / China Search 31br; Judith Miller / Chisolm Larsson 368tr; Judith Miller / Chiswick Auctions 59cr, 75fbl, 112cb, 113bc, 113bl, 113br, 113c, 113cl, 113cr, 113cra, 113tc, 113tl, 123bl, 125cr; Judith Miller / Christina Bertrand 177, 177br, 178ca, 178cra, 179tc; Judith Miller / Christine Wildman Collection 89fcl, 96cb, 97fcl, 151br, 332tl, 341br, 346br, 349br, 349fbl, 349fbr, 349fcrb; Judith Miller / Christopher Seidler 393tl; Judith Miller / Christopher Sykes Antiques 163bc, 163bl, 163br, 163c, 163cl, 163cr, 164cl, 164ftl, 164tc, 165bc, 165bl, 165c, 165cr, 165fbl; Judith Miller / Classic Automobilia & Regalia Specialists 145br, 180cb, 345cr, 345fcl, 345tl, 346cl, 346cr, 346fbr, 346fcr, 346ftl, 346tl, 346tr, 347bl, 347br, 347cl, 347cr, 347fbr, 347fcr, 347tc, 349fcl, 349fcra, 349tl; Judith Miller / Claude Lee at The Ginnel 71ca; Judith Miller / Clevedon Salerooms 35bl (Ram and Ewe Spill Vase), 47br, 71br, 334, 335br, 335fbl, 373fcra; Judith Miller / Cloud Cuckoo Land 285br, 286, 286cl, 286tl, 287bl, 288tl, 289bl, 289cra, 289crb, 291br, 291cr, 291tl, 292cra, 292tc, 292tl, 293c, 293cl, 293clb, 293fbr; Judith Miller / Cobwebs 302, 341bl, 341cl, 341cr, 341fbl, 341fbr, 341fcl, 341ftr, 341tl, 343fcr, 345fbr, 348cl, 349bl; Judith Miller / Colin Baddiel 223crb, 223fbr, 225cr, 229br, 230b, 230fcl, 231cl; Judith Miller / Collectors Cameras 358cb, 359bl, 359cl, 359fbl; Judith Miller / Cooper Owen 7bl, 181br, 181tc,

182br, 182ca, 182cla, 182tc, 182tl, 183bc, 183ca, 183cr, 183cra, 263bl, 263cl, 263tl, 266bl, 266br, 266cl, 266clb, 266cr, 266crb, 266tl, 305bc, 307bl, 307br, 307cl, 307tc, 307tl, 307tr, 308cr, 308ftl, 308tl, 309cl, 309cr, 309crb, 309fbl, 309fcl, 309ftl, 309tr, 310, 311bl, 311cl, 311cr, 311fbl, 312bl, 312br, 312cl, 312cr, 312fbl, 312fbr, 312tl, 312tr, 313br, 313c, 313cl, 313cr, 313tl, 313tr, 314b, 314tc, 314tl, 317br, 317cr, 319cr, 319ftr, 320bl, 320fcl, 321bl, 321fcr, 322, 324, 331bl; Judith Miller / Cottees 56br, 59bl, 89cra, 167bl, 189bc, 189br, 189tl, 189tr, 265cr, 266tr; Judith Miller / Cristobal 271ca, 281cl, 282cr, 282tl, 283crb, 283fcr, 283tc, 283tr, 295bc, 295tl, 296tc, 297ca, 297tl, 298bc, 298ca, 298tr, 299cr, 299tc; Judith Miller / David Midgley 252c, 253bl, 253br, 253c, 253fbl, 253fbr, 253tl; Judith Miller / David Rago Auctions 94cb, 95bc, 95bl, 95bc, 95cr, 95cra, 95fbl, 95fcl, 95tc, 95tl, 97cl, 101bc, 101cl, 260cb, 261bl; Judith Miller / Design20c 365fcr; Judith Miller / Dickins Auctioneers 182c, 182cr, 367fbr, 369fbr, 369fcl; Judith Miller / DODO 144br, 147tl, 148tr, 149br, 151fbl, 349cl; Judith Miller / Donay Games 265bl, 267tc; Judith Miller / Dreweatt Neate 153c, 153cl, 153tl, 154, 154br, 154cl, 154cr, 154tc, 154tl, 154tr, 155bc, 155br, 155c, 155cl, 155tl, 155tr, 156bc, 156bl, 156c, 156tc, 156tr, 157bc, 157bl, 157c, 157cb, 157cl, 157cla, 157clb, 157tc, 157tl, 177cl, 179clb, 182cl, 182fcl, 183bl, 372cl; Judith Miller / Dreweatt Neate, Bristol 45br; Judith Miller / Dreweatt Neate, Tunbridge Wells 27bc (My Garden Vases), 152crb, 156cr, 156tl, 373tl, 390cl; Judith Miller / Dreweatte Neate 25cb, 27bl (Pierced Roundel), 41br, 41fbl, 69cl, 70bl, 73c, 258bc; Judith Miller / Dynamite Antiques & Collectibles 347fcl; Judith Miller / Fantiques 294c, 295bl, 295br, 298bl, 298br, 298cl, 298cr, 299cb, 299tl; Judith Miller / Feljoy Antiques 60cb, 60cl, 61bc, 61bl, 61cra, 61fbl, 61fcl, 61tc, 61tl; Judith Miller / Fellows & Sons 74bc, 148cl, 223fcrb, 231fbl, 233br, 234cr, 235bl, 235br, 235fbr, 244tl, 246, 248cr, 249ftl, 249tl, 249tr, 251bl, 259tl, 323bl, 323crb, 331cr, 347ftl, 375fcl, 379cra, 380bl, 380br, 381tl; Judith Miller / Festival 31bl; Judith Miller / Fragile Design 48br; Judith Miller / Freeman's 21ca, 21tc, 25cr, 47crb,

68br, 97bc, 97c, 97cra, 99bl, 101crb, 127bl, 127tl, 129br, 203tl, 270c, 279tc, 279tl, 285cr, 341ftl, 346fbl, 369cl, 372ftl, 373bl, 375fbr, 378bc, 380cl, 381cl; Judith Miller / Gallery 1930 Susie Cooper 29bc, 29bl, 29br, 29c, 29cl, 29cr, 29tc, 29tl, 30bc, 30cl, 30fcl, 30fcr, 30ftl, 30tl, 30tr, 31c, 31cl, 31cr, 31fbl, 31fbr, 31tc, 31tl; Judith Miller / Gardiner Houlgate 368br, 371bl, 373cra, 375fbl, 375fcrb, 378bl, 379tl, 380c, 380tr, 381bl, 381br, 381c; Judith Miller / Gary Grant 79cr; Judith Miller / Gloucestershire Worcestershire Railwayana Auctions 342c, 343bl, 343br, 343cr, 343cra, 343fbl, 343fcl, 343ftl, 373fbl; Judith Miller / Goodwins Antiques Ltd 279c; Judith Miller / Gorringes 74tl, 75cl; Judith Miller / Gorringes, Bexhill 43br; Judith Miller / Gorringes, Lewes 25tr, 28cb, 30cr, 35bl, 39br, 39c, 40bc, 40fcr, 41bl, 41cr, 41tr, 42bl, 42cra, 43bc, 45cl, 47c, 52cl, 61cb, 69bc, 70br, 70cl, 71bc, 71fbl, 71fcl, 71tc, 77bl, 101br, 131tr, 141cb, 141crb, 141fbl, 150tc, 181cr, 183tc, 243br, 244tr, 245fcl, 245tl, 248tl, 249fbr, 255c, 261crb, 346fcl, 350, 367tl, 368fcrb, 369bl, 369br, 369fbl, 373br, 397tl, 398tr; Judith Miller / Graham Cooley 15ca, 79fcl, 108cb, 109fbl, 115fbl, 117cl, 117tl, 118tr, 119c, 119tc, 129c, 129tc, 137bc, 137bl, 137c, 137cl, 137cr, 137bfbl, 137tc, 137tl, 137tr, 138cb, 139bc, 139crb, 139fcrb, 139tl, 159bc, 159c, 159cra, 159fcrb, 159tc, 355bl, 355cb, 355br, 355fcl, 355tl, 356br, 356cl, 356cr, 356fcl, 356fcr, 356ftl, 356ftr, 356tl, 356tr, 357bl, 357br, 357fbl, 357fbr; Judith Miller / Grays 54cl, 55bc, 55bl, 55br, 55c, 55cr, 55cra, 55fbl, 55fcl, 55ftl, 55tc; Judith Miller / Guernsey's Auctions 141cr, 141fcl; Judith Miller / Halcyon Days 153cr; Judith Miller / Hamptons 87fcl, 233cla; Judith Miller / Harpers General Store 254c, 256tc, 256tl, 257cc, 258bl, 261tc; Judith Miller / Harpers General Store 229tl, 230fcr; Judith Miller / Harpers General Store 230cl; Judith Miller / Hope and Glory 16bl, 84crb, 85bc, 85br, 85cr, 85tc, 86cb, 86cl, 86fcl, 86ftl, 86tc, 86tl, 86tr, 87bl, 87br, 87c, 87cl, 87cr, 87fbl, 87tc, 87ftl, 88cb, 89bc, 89br, 89cb, 89tc; Judith Miller / Hugo Lee-Jones 267bc, 352bl, 362cb, 363bl, 363br, 363cl, 363fbl, 363fcra, 363ftl, 363tl, 364br, 364cl, 364cla,

364cr, 364cra, 364tl, 364tr, 365bl, 365br, 365cl, 365cra, 365crb, 365fbl, 365fcrb, 365tl; Judith Miller / Huxtins 3cb, 89fbl, 144bl, 146cb, 146tc, 147br, 147cl, 147cr, 148cr, 148ftl, 149tc, 149tl, 149tr, 150bc, 150bl, 150cb, 150cl, 150tr, 151bc, 151bl, 151fcl, 151tl, 175cl, 237bl, 237cl, 267cr, 269cl, 269fcrb, 272br, 301fbr, 341fcr, 347fbl, 349crb; Judith Miller / Huxtins 230ftl; Judith Miller / HY Duke and Son 375cra; Judith Miller / Imperial Half Bushel 164cl; Judith Miller / Ingram Antiques 265bc; Judith Miller / James Bridges Collection 166c, 167br, 168c, 168cb, 168cl, 168cr, 168fcl, 168tl, 168tr, 169bc, 169bl, 169br, 169ca, 169cla, 169cra, 169crb, 169tc, 183crb, 267c; Judith Miller / Jean Scott Collection 177bc, 177tc, 177tl, 178, 178cl, 178cla, 178cr, 178fcl, 178tc, 178tl, 178tr, 179bl, 179br, 179cl, 179crc, 179cra, 179crb, 179tl; Judith Miller / Jeanette Hayhurst Fine Glass 109cl, 121c, 122c, 122tc, 122tr, 123cl, 123cr, 124bc, 124tc, 124tr, 125bc, 125br, 125cl, 164fcl, 165cl, 165fcl; Judith Miller / Jill Fenichell 20fcr; Judith Miller / John Bull Silver 164c, 181c, 301tl; Judith Miller / John Howard @ Heritage 33bl, 33cl, 33cla, 33cr, 33tl (left), 33tl (right), 34cr, 34ftl, 35c, 35cr; Judith Miller / John Nicholsons 40fcl, 42tl, 45tl, 46tc, 70cra, 76cl, 77tl, 105bl, 105c, 105tl, 145bl, 152tc; Judith Miller / Jonathan Horne 32crb, 33bc, 33c, 34tc, 35tr, 85c, 85tl; Judith Miller / Joseph H Bonnar 10, 274c, 275bl, 275br, 275c, 275fbl, 275fbr, 279cr; Judith Miller / Karl Flaherty Collectables 325br, 325clb, 325cr, 325fcl, 325fclb, 325tl, 326bc, 326bl, 326br, 326ca, 326cl, 326cr, 326tl, 326tr, 327bc, 327br, 327c, 327cl, 327cr, 327fbr, 327tc, 327tl; Judith Miller / KCS Ceramics 17bl, 49c, 50bc, 50tc, 51tc, 52bc, 52bl, 52tl, 52tr, 53bc, 53bl, 53cr, 53fbl, 53tc, 53tl; Judith Miller / Larry & Dianna Elman 149fbl; Judith Miller / Law Fine Art Ltd. 20fcl, 21c, 34fcl, 35bc (Glazed Cottage), 35tl, 37bl, 53br, 69cr, 71cl, 183clb, 277fbr, 279cl, 375br, 398c; Judith Miller / Lawrence's Fine Art Auctioneers 80cb, 81bc, 81bl, 81br, 81c, 81cl, 81cr, 81fbl, 81fcl, 81tc, 81tl, 81tr, 141tl, 361fbl, 361bl, 367fcl, 369cr, 389bl, 389cl, 390fbr, 393cla, 393clb, 395br; Judith Miller / Lights, Camera, Action 193br, 194tc, 194tl, 195c, 311tl; Judith

415

Miller / Lucy's Hat 290c, 291br (Wool felt hat), 291cl; Judith Miller / Luna 143ca, 151cl, 269crb, 351, 354crb, 355cr, 355ftl, 355ftl, 357cl, 357cr, 357tc, 361ftl, 361tl; Judith Miller / Lyon and Turnbull Ltd. 7bc, 24cr, 24tr, 26ftl, 26tr, 27bl, 37cl, 39bc, 40cl, 40tc, 41bc, 41ca, 42tc, 43bl, 43c, 43cr, 43fbl, 44cb, 45cr, 45tc, 46bl, 46cl, 47bc, 47tc, 51bc, 51tl, 52br, 57clb, 58cl, 58fbl, 59cra, 59crb, 59fcla, 77tr, 78cb, 95cl, 97br, 97cr, 99bc, 103c, 103cl, 103fcl, 146bc, 153bc, 154fcl, 177bl, 265cl, 277cl, 277cr, 277fcrb, 335tl, 337bl, 337cl, 337fbl, 337bcr, 337bcl, 337fbcrb, 337ftl, 337ftr, 337tl, 339cl, 352br, 353bl, 361cra, 366cb, 367fbl, 367ftl, 368tl, 369fcr, 370cb, 371cr, 371fbl, 372cr, 372fcra, 372tr, 373fbr, 394cra, 395clb; Judith Miller / Manic Attic 361br, 361cl, 361crb, 361fbr; Judith Miller / Mark Hill Collection 93bl, 115tc, 139fbl, 167bc, 167c, 167cr, 167tc, 167tl, 168ftl, 168tc, 169clb, 169fbl, 169tl, 175br; Judith Miller / Mark Laino 378tl, 379c, 379tc, 380cr, 381bc, 381tc; Judith Miller / Mary Ann's Collectibles 100cb, 103tc, 111tl, 276c, 277tl, 368ftl; Judith Miller / Mary Cooper at The Ginnel 296br, 296c; Judith Miller / Mary Wise and Grosvenor Antiques 220br, 264cla; Judith Miller / Mendes Antique Lace and Textiles 297cr; Judith Miller / Metropolis Collectibles, Inc. 186br, 212, 213cl, 213fbl, 213fbr, 213ftl, 213tl, 213tr; Judith Miller / Mick Collins 62crb, 63bc, 63bl, 63bcr, 63c, 63cl, 63cr, 63tc, 63tl, 64bc, 64c, 64cl, 64cr, 64tc, 64tl, 64tr, 65bc, 65bl, 65br, 65ca, 65cl, 65cr, 65tl, 65tr, 66bc, 66bl, 66br, 66c, 66cl, 66cr, 66fbl, 66tc, 66tl, 66tr, 67bc, 67bl, 67br, 67ca, 67cb, 67cl, 67cra, 67fbl, 67tl, 269fbr; Judith Miller / Mike Weedon 92bl, 101cb, 101tc, 101tl, 103bc, 103cr, 103tr; Judith Miller / Mod-Girl 291c; Judith Miller / Mostly Boxes 152cl, 155cr; Judith Miller / Mum Had That 79c, 79cl, 109bc, 117bl, 117cr, 120cb, 124br, 126cb, 127, 127bc, 127br, 127cr, 127tc, 128cb, 129bl, 129cl, 131bl, 131br, 131c, 131cr, 131fbl, 133bc, 133bl, 133br, 133c, 133crb, 133fbl, 135br, 135c, 135cr, 135tl, 135tr, 136cb, 137br, 159bl, 159cl, 159crb; Judith Miller / N. Bloom & Son Ltd. 275cr, 277tc, 278clb, 301ftl; Judith Miller / Nigel Benson 109tl, 118cb, 119bc, 119bl, 119br, 119cl, 119crb, 119crb, 119tl, 131bc; Judith Miller / Noel Barrett Antiques & Auctions Ltd 6bl, 218c, 219ca, 227fbl, 229bl, 230cr, 230tr, 231br, 231crb, 231t, 233tl, 237tl, 261cra, 269cra; Judith Miller / Noel Barrett Antiques & Auctions Ltd 229cla; Judith

Miller / Otford Antiques and Collectors Centre 74br, 74fcl, 121br, 122cr, 124tl, 157ca, 172tc, 174bl, 175cr, 257br, 257fbr, 258cl, 261br, 261fbr, 353br, 357tl, 359br, 359cra, 359crb, 359fcrb, 359ftl, 359tl, 360cb, 369tl; Judith Miller / Patricia Stauble Antiques 249br; Judith Miller / Pendulum of Mayfair 372bc, 372tl; Judith Miller / Petersham Books 204ftl, 204ftr, 204tl; Judith Miller / Pook and Pook 171cl, 269tc, 367bl, 371tl; Judith Miller / Posteritati 305bl, 308tr, 316, 317bl, 317cl, 317ftl, 317tl, 318cl, 318cra, 318fcl, 318ftl, 318tl, 319bl, 319bc, 319c, 319fbl, 319cl, 319ftl, 319tl, 319tr, 320cl, 320crb, 320fbl, 320tl, 320tr, 321ftl, 321tl, 321tr, 323tl, 325ftl; Judith Miller / Potteries Specialist Auctions 17br, 37br, 37c, 37cb, 37cr, 37fbl, 37tl, 46tr, 47bl, 47cra, 47fcra, 47tl, 59fclb, 72crb, 73bl, 73br, 73cl, 73cr, 73tc, 73tl, 74bl, 74c, 74cl, 74cr, 74fbl, 74tc, 74tr, 75bc, 75bl, 75br, 75c, 75ca, 75cr, 75fcl, 82cb, 83bc, 83bl, 83br, 83cb, 83cl, 83cra, 83crb, 83fbl, 83fcl, 83tc, 83tl, 264br, 269fcl; Judith Miller / RBR Group at Grays 54cb; Judith Miller / Reasons To Be Cheerful 251fbr, 303, 304bl, 323cl, 323fbr, 331tl, 332c, 332tc, 332tr, 333cra; Judith Miller / Rennies 273br, 291bl, 291crb, 291tc, 291tr, 349ftl; Judith Miller / Richard Gibbon 277bl, 279bl, 279br, 279cb, 279crb, 282fcl, 282fcr, 283cr, 295c, 295tc, 296cl, 299bl; Judith Miller / Rick Hubbard Art Deco 58ftl, 59br, 61br, 61crb; Judith Miller / Rogers de Rin 153bl, 153tc, 155bl, 156br, 156fbl, 263cr; Judith Miller / Rosebery 19cl, 41cl, 73bc, 77br, 77c, 79bc, 105cl, 105cra, 105fbl, 233cra, 243bl, 264cra, 265tl; Judith Miller / Roxanne Stuart 107c, 172tr, 280cr, 281c, 281tl, 283br, 283cl, 283fbl, 283tl, 297bl, 297cl; Judith Miller / Royal Commemorative China 85cl, 89cl; Judith Miller / Rumours 14c, 38clb, 39bl, 39cra, 39tc, 39tl, 40cr, 42bc, 42br, 43tl; Judith Miller / Sara Covelli 289tl; Judith Miller / Seaside Toy Center 1bc, 309clb; Judith Miller / Sheila Cook 293bl; Judith Miller / Sidney Gecker 269tl; Judith Miller / Sign of the Tymes 5br, 147bc, 147tc, 149bc, 149cl, 150cr, 237br, 237tc, 257cr; Judith Miller / Sloan's 99c, 99cl, 99tl, 103br, 125tl, 141cl, 141tc, 164cr, 171bl, 238cl, 239br, 239cl, 239tl, 240br, 240tc, 240tr, 241bl, 241br, 241cla, 241clb, 241cra, 241crb, 241tr, 279clb, 371fbr, 372fcl, 377br, 378tr, 394br, 394cla, 395crb, 399cr; Judith Miller / Sloans & Kenyon 97cl, 99tc, 101bl, 101cra, 101fcl, 103fbl, 202, 268c, 367cr;

Judith Miller / Somervale Antiques 121cr, 121tc, 121tl, 122bc, 122cl, 122ftl, 122tl, 123fbl, 123tc, 123tl, 123tr, 124bl, 124cr, 125tc, 145bc, 162cb; Judith Miller / Somlo Antiques 374, 375cl, 375ftl, 375tl, 376, 377bl, 377cl, 377fbl, 377fcl, 377tl, 378cl, 379bc, 380tc; Judith Miller / South Street Antiques 382, 383bl, 383br, 383cl, 383crb, 383fbl, 383fbr, 383fcl, 383fcra, 383fcrb, 383ftl, 383tl; Judith Miller / Sparkle Moore at The Girl Can't Help It 272bl, 289clb, 293bc, 293crb, 293fcrb, 296cr, 297bc, 299cl, 301br, 301fbl, 315bl, 315br; Judith Miller / Special Auction Services 160cb, 161bl, 161br, 161cl, 161crb, 161fbl, 161fbr, 161fcl, 161fcrb, 161tc, 161tl, 161tr, 225fcl, 256c, 258br, 258cr, 258tc, 258tl, 259bc, 259cr, 267br, 323tr, 331cl, 331fcl, 333crb, 337cr, 339fbl, 346bl; Judith Miller / Steinberg and Tolkien 273bc, 284c, 285cb, 285clb, 285tc, 285tl, 286bc, 286c, 286tc, 287br, 287fbr, 287ftl, 287tl, 287tr, 288bl, 288br, 288fbl, 288fbr, 288tr, 289br, 289ftl; Judith Miller / Sue Scrivens 170c, 171br, 171cla, 171tl, 172, 172bc, 172bl, 172cl, 172tl, 174tr, 175clb, 175crb, 175tr; Judith Miller / T W Conroy 151c, 173tc, 173tl, 173tr, 174br, 174tc; Judith Miller / Tagore Ltd 163tc, 181bc, 181bl, 339ftl; Judith Miller / Take-A-Boo Emporium 183, 375bl; Judith Miller / Tennants 335cl, 335cr, 335ftl, 335tr, 337br, 339crb, 339fcrb, 339tl; Judith Miller / Tenth Planet 328, 329bl, 329c, 329cr, 329fbl, 329fcl, 329fcr, 329ftl; Judith Miller / Terry & Melody Rodgers 281bc, 281bl, 281tc, 282cl, 283fcl; Judith Miller / The Blue Pump 343tl; Judith Miller / The Country Seat 109bl, 109br, 109c, 109cr, 109fcl, 109tc; Judith Miller / The Design Gallery 57tc, 91ca, 99cra, 287fbl, 297br, 298tl, 301bl, 301cl, 301cra, 301fcl, 301fcr; Judith Miller / The Doll Express 244cl, 248cl, 248ftl, 250c, 251br, 251cra, 251fbl, 251tl, 261c; Judith Miller / The Glass Merchant 105br, 106cb, 107bl, 115bl, 115br, 115c, 115cl, 115crb, 115fbr, 115fcrb, 117br, 117tc, 129cra, 129crb; Judith Miller / The Multicoloured Time Slip 267bl, 299br, 315cr, 315tc, 329fbr, 330cb, 332bl, 333fcrb; Judith Miller / The Silver Fund 256bc; Judith Miller / The Watch Gallery 352bc, 377cr, 377tl, 378cr, 379cl, 380tl; Judith Miller / Thos. Wm. Gaze & Son 21bl, 37bc, 50cl, 51ftl, 52ftl, 53cl, 77tc, 79cra, 87bc, 89crb, 107crb, 107tc, 116cb, 117bc, 117c, 117fbl, 141bc, 193cl, 195crb, 223br, 223fbl, 223ftl, 225br, 225fbr, 237bc, 259bl, 259br, 265br, 304br,

305br, 306, 308bc, 308cl, 309tc, 311br, 314tr, 315cl, 315fcl, 315fcr, 315tl, 318bc, 321cl, 321cr, 321fcl, 329cra, 338, 339bl; Judith Miller / Titus Omega 102cb; Judith Miller / Tony Moran 269br; Judith Miller / Toy Heroes 148tl, 263br, 267cl, 329tl, 331br, 331ftl, 332br, 332cl, 332cr, 333cla, 333clb, 333fbl, 333fclb, 333tl; Judith Miller / Toy Road Antiques 149bl, 150c, 150tl; Judith Miller / Van Den Bosch 270fcl, 277fcl; Judith Miller / Victoriana Dolls 221bc, 242, 243c, 243cl, 243tc, 244b, 245bl, 245br, 245cl, 245cr, 245fbl, 245fcr, 245ftl, 247br, 247ftl, 247tl, 248b, 248ftr, 248tr, 249bl, 249cl, 249cr, 249fbl, 249fcl, 249fcr; Judith Miller / VinMagCo 184c, 213bl, 213br, 213fcr, 215bl, 215br, 215fbl, 215fbr, 215fcr, 215ftl, 215tc, 215tr; Judith Miller / Vintage to Vogue 6br, 287ftr, 288tc, 289fcra; Judith Miller / W.H. Peacock 227tl; Judith Miller / Wallis and Wallis 7br, 89tl, 140cb, 153br, 164bc, 165br, 181cl, 220bl, 222, 223cl, 223cra, 223fcl, 223tl, 224, 225bl, 225cl, 225fbl, 225ftl, 225tl, 226, 227br, 227crb, 227fbr, 227fcl, 227fcr, 227ftl, 228, 231fclb, 231fcr, 232, 233clb, 233fbl, 234br, 234tl, 234tr, 235cl, 235cla, 235cr, 235cra, 235fcla, 235ftl, 235tl, 236c, 237clb, 238cr, 239bl, 239cra, 239ftl, 240tl, 336, 340cb, 343cl, 359fcl, 384, 385, 386, 387bc, 387bl, 388, 389br, 389cr, 389fbl, 389fcl, 389ftl, 389r, 389tl, 390bl, 390br, 390c, 390cr, 390fbl, 390tc, 390tl, 390tr, 391bl, 391br, 391c, 391cl, 391cr, 391fbl, 391fbr, 391tc, 391tl, 392, 393bl, 393br, 393c, 394bc, 394bl, 394ca, 394cb, 394clb, 394crb, 394tl, 394tr, 395bc, 395bl, 395cb, 395cla, 395cra, 395tc, 396, 397bl, 397br, 397cl, 397cra, 397cra, 398bc, 398cl, 398cla, 398cr, 398cra, 398tc, 398tl, 399bl, 399cl, 399clb, 399cra, 399crb, 399ftl, 399rl; Judith Miller / WH Peacock 237crb, 255br; Judith Miller / Wheels of Steel 233bl, 234cl, 234ftl, 235fbl; Judith Miller / Woolley and Wallis 2c, 16bc, 16br, 17bc, 19fcl, 19tc, 20br, 20cl, 20cr, 20tl, 21cl, 21fbl, 21tl, 22crb, 23bc, 23bl, 23br, 23c, 23cl, 23cr, 23tc, 23tl, 24bc, 24c, 24cl, 24ftl, 24tc, 24tl, 25bl, 25br, 25ca, 25cl, 25tl, 26br, 26cl, 26fbl, 26fbr, 26ftr, 26tl, 27bc, 27ca, 27cb, 27cla, 27clb, 27tc, 27tl, 33br, 34bc, 34c, 34tl, 34tr, 35bc, 35cb, 35cl, 35clb, 35tc, 37tc, 40tl, 40tr, 41tl, 42fbl, 43cl, 43tc, 45bc, 46bc, 46c, 46crb, 47fbr, 48c, 49bc, 49bl, 49cl, 49cc, 49tl, 50cr, 50tl, 51bl, 51tr, 52cr, 52tc, 56cb, 57c, 57cb, 57cr, 57tl, 58br, 58cb, 58cr, 58tc, 58tl, 58tr, 59ca, 59cl, 59tl, 69bl, 69br, 69c, 69tc, 70bc, 70tc, 70tl, 71bl,

71c, 71cr, 71tl, 76cb, 79br, 79tc, 79tl, 85bl, 86cr, 89bl, 163tl, 164tr, 165tc, 165tl, 176bl, 177cr, 178bc, 179cla, 181tl, 182tr, 183cl, 183tl, 262cb, 273bl, 275crb, 275tc, 277cra, 368bl, 368cl, 368cr, 368fbl, 371cl, 371fcl, 371ftl; Judith Miller / Linda Bee 295cra; **Fieldings Auctioneers:** 19tl, 45bl, 292cb; **Javan Liam / Harrogate:** 13cl; **Andy McConnell:** 139br; **Andy McConnell / Glass Etc:** 13cla, 93br, 98cb, 99br, 99cr, 114cb, 115tr, 129, 129bc, 131tc, 132cb, 133tc, 133tl, 133tr, 134cb, 135bc, 135fcl, 135tc, 139bl, 139c, 139cl, 139tc, 139tr; **Geoff Lawson / Andy McConnell:** 130cb, 131tl; **Kim Thrower / Andy McConnell:** 135cl; **Liz McAvoy / Andy McConnell:** 135bl; **William Shaw:** 12cla; **Woolley and Wallis:** 19bc, 19tr, 20tc, 21br, 21cr; **Dominic Winter:** 13clb, 185tc, 186bc, 186bl, 187bl, 187br, 189cl, 189cr, 189tc, 190cb, 191bc, 191bl, 191br, 191c, 191cl, 191cr, 191fcl, 191tc, 191tr, 192c, 193bc, 193bl, 193c, 193cr, 193tc, 193tl, 194bc, 194bl, 194br, 194c, 194cl, 194fbl, 194tr, 195bl, 195br, 195c, 195cb, 195cl, 195clb, 195tc, 195tl, 196cb, 197bc, 197c, 197cl, 197cr, 197tc, 197tl, 198bc, 198tc, 198tr, 199bc, 199bl, 199br, 200bc, 200bl, 200br, 200cl, 200cc, 200tc, 200tl, 200tr, 201bl, 201br, 201c, 201cl, 201cr, 201fcl, 201tc, 201tl, 201tr, 203br, 203cl, 205bc, 205bl, 205br, 205cl, 205cr, 205ftr, 206bl, 206br, 206cl, 206cr, 206fbl, 206fbr, 206tc, 206tl, 206tr, 207tc, 207tl, 207tr, 208c, 209bl, 209br, 209c, 209cl, 209cr, 209tc, 209tl, 210br, 210cl, 210cr, 210fcl, 210fcr, 210tc, 210tl, 210tr, 211bl, 211br, 211c, 211cl, 211cr, 211fbl, 211fbr, 211tc, 211tl, 213cr, 213fcl, 214c, 215cr, 215fcl, 216c, 217cr, 217tc, 217tl.

Jacket images: Front: Colin Baddiel (www.colinsantiquetoys.com): tl (model cars); **Linda Bee:** clb, fcrb; **Biblion** (www.biblio.co.uk): fcl; **Bidgoods** (www.bidgoods.co.uk): br (tea cups, jug), crb; **Andy McConnell / Glass Etc** (www.decanterman.com): bl, cl; **Carol Mead:** br (ship teapot), fbl, tl (silver plane); Set Pieces (www.setpieces.com): cr, fbr, fclb, fcr, ftl, ftr, tr. **Back: Wheels of Steel** (www.graysantiques.com): ca. **Spine: BBC Antiques Roadshow:** tc. **Front Flap:** Bidgoods: bc.

All other images © Dorling Kindersley
For further information
see: **www.dkimages.com**

Andy McConnell (Glass) did not contribute pp. 110–113.